Accession no.
D0231491

pd
10.01.0̄

Media Law for Journalists

2

Media Law for Journalists

With a Foreword by Sir Harold Evans

Ursula Smartt

LIBRARY

ACC. No. 36624657   DEPT. pd   3rd.

CLASS No. 343.9985MA

UNIVERSITY OF CHESTER

⑤ SAGE Publications

London ● Thousand Oaks ● New Delhi

© Ursula Smartt 2006

First published 2006

Apart from any fair dealing for the purposes of research
or private study, or criticism or review, as permitted
under the Copyright, Designs and Patents Act, 1988,
this publication may be reproduced, stored or transmitted in
any form, or by any means, only with the prior permission
in writing of the publishers or, in the case of reprographic
reproduction, in accordance with the terms of licences issued
by the Copyright Licensing Agency. Enquiries concerning
reproduction outside those terms should be sent to the
publishers.

SAGE Publications Ltd
1 Oliver's Yard
55 City Road
London EC1Y 1SP

SAGE Publications Inc.
2455 Teller Road
Thousand Oaks, California 91320

SAGE Publications India Pvt Ltd
B-42, Panchsheel Enclave
Post Box 4109
New Delhi 110 017

British Library Cataloguing in Publication data

A catalogue record for this book is available
from the British Library

ISBN-10 1-4129-0846-9   ISBN-13 10-978-1-4129-0846-7
ISBN-10 1-4129-0847-7 (pbk)   ISBN-13 10-978-1-4129-0847-4

Library of Congress Control Number available

Typeset by C&M Digitals (P) Ltd., Chennai, India
Printed on paper from sustainable resources
Printed and bound in Great Britain by The Alden Press, Oxford

CONTENTS

ACKNOWLEDGEMENTS

My grateful thanks go to a number of people in the media who encouraged me to write this book. It stemmed from my teaching on journalism courses at a number of higher education establishments. Grateful acknowledgement is made to the following, who assisted me with this project:

- Brian Pillans, Media Law Lecturer at Glasgow Caledonian University
- Christopher Jordan, Bench Legal Manager, Ealing Magistrates' Court, London
- Tom Thomson, former Bureau Chief of Reuters, who facilitated Scottish media lawyers and editorial contacts in the Scottish print media
- Winifred Thomson, for her invaluable help in explaining the Scottish Children's Hearing System, being one of the first of Glasgow's citizens to serve on the Children's Panel in 1968
- Peter Watson, Solicitor Advocate and Media Lawyer of Levy & McRae, Glasgow
- Charles McGhee, Editor of the *Glasgow Evening Times*
- Sir Harold Evans.

While every care has been taken to acknowledge sources and copyright, as well as establish permission to reproduce materials and codes of practice (with the PCC and Ofcom, for example), my publishers and I tender our apologies for any accidental infringement.

I would also like to thank my husband Mike Smartt, a BBC TV reporter and correspondent for 25 years, founder and Editor-in-chief of BBC News Interactive, for his help and advice.

FOREWORD

As a young reporter, before there was such a thing as a course for the training of journalists – or even (I guess) an Ursula Smartt – I was utterly baffled by all the vague warnings I got when I returned from courtrooms with juicy quotes in Pitman's shorthand. Nobody could quite explain what was wrong with the utterly shocking story I had written. Actually, only the skeleton of my report in a preliminary hearing about child prostitution made it into my weekly paper, but my mentor, a reporter nearing retirement, sprinkled a few allegeds into the report and sent it off to the *News of the World*. There it was subtly sanitised again.

Now, had Ursula Smartt's book been around, I reckon that even at the age of 16 I could have navigated the shoals and rapids myself. This is not a compliment to me. It is a compliment to her. She has organised this extensive tutorial with case studies, tips and analysis. Why did Naomi Campbell, walking in a public street, win damages for invasion of privacy and Gordon Kaye, pursued to a hospital bed, did not? Why should reporters and editors count to ten before rushing through the 'qualified privilege' loophole for defence of publication in the public interest created by *Reynolds v. Times Newspapers* [1999]? The answer is to read *Galloway v. Telegraph* [2004], where the then pro-Iraq Labour MP won $150,000 damages for a story in the *Daily Telegraph* accusing him of making money out of the UN oil for food programme. The High Court faulted the *Daily Telegraph* for relying on information that could not be regarded as 'inherently reliable'. Question to Ursula, the *Daily Telegraph*, High Court, Galloway and all: had the honorable participants possessed then Mr Paul Volcker's critical and well-documented United Nations Report on Mr Galloway's '18 million barrels of oil' in October 2005, would they have regarded the UN and Mr Volcker as inherently reliable and would Mr Galloway have been on good ground going back to court for another exoneration?

I had been inclined to think that the British press had been liberated from the most onerous restrictions since I dubbed it the half-free press in a mid-1970s Granada Guildhall lecture. The success of the *Sunday Times* in the thalidomide case at least removed some of the menacing vagueness from contempt of court and new horizons opened up with the subsequent incorporation of the *European Convention on Human Rights* into English law. However, reading the variety of cases discussed so well by Ursula Smartt reminded me again of Hilaire Belloc's injunction to 'tread softly because we are observed'. I certainly have no time at all for the gross intrusions of privacy and malicious gossip masquerading as news, but the mainstream press still seems unduly hampered in its essential role in comparison with the United States.

The author is particularly helpful on defamation, the commonest anxiety, but the curious thing is that, in my 14 years as Editor of The *Sunday Times* and one as editor of *The Times*, we had to defend very few libel cases. We won on justification for all except one, as I recall. A man with building ambitions wrecked a house designated as of historic and architectural merit and we said that he had 'vandalised' it. The court said a man could not vandalize his own property. It struck me then as judicial pedantry, but the vandal/owner reaped only derisory damages. I went before the judges many times, but most often because investigative reporting associated with insight ventured into seas nobody had sailed before.

The law of confidence, for instance, lay like a submerged reef across our path in the thalidomide case and our publication of Richard Crossman's Cabinet diaries. The Argyll case in 1967 was the first time confidence was extended from the protection of commercial property to private affairs. In that case, the Duke was prevented from publishing his account of the conduct of the Duchess and, in the Crossman case, the Attorney General built on Argyll to extend the law of confidence from the marriage bed to the conduct of a government. The Lord Chief Justice ruled that confidence did so apply – we and the book publishers won only because the ingenious Widgery declared we were publishing history.

The Crossman diary case did lead to an easing of the official rules prescribing when history might be written, but I still regard confidence as one of the more worrying aspects of English law. It had been settled law that a confidence might be broken to ventilate an 'iniquity' but, when the *Sunday Times* tried to publish Distillers' documents on the thalidomide tragedy, Mr Justice Talbot ruled that negligence in the manufacture of a devastating drug did not represent iniquity: 'There is no crime or fraud,' said the judge. 'In my view, negligence, even if it could be proved, could not be within the same class as to constitute an exception to the need to protect confidentiality.' Mrs Thatcher invoked confidence in the Spycatcher case and no doubt it will be deployed again some time.

I was very lucky in my editorships to have had wise counsel from a number of legal advisers (James Evans, Anthony Whittaker) and the barristers we engaged, as well as consistently robust backing from management. The lawyers were all ready to engage their minds with us to find good legal reasons for not suppressing a scandal and the management at the Westminster Press and Thomson never flinched.

Not every editor and reporter can count on such good fortune, but every one – not simply new entrants to our craft – can benefit from Ursula Smartt's lucid and frequently entertaining book. My hope is that, while enjoining prudence, it will also inspire resistance to limitations on free expression and free enquiry that is in the public interest.

Sir Harold Evans,
New York, December 2005

INTRODUCTION

Welcome to *Media Law for Journalists*, which provides an opportunity for those studying journalism or already working in the media to understand the English and Scottish legal systems.

The book is intended to provide the reader with two things: first, a detailed introduction to the subject matter and an explanation of what to expect when studying for a journalism qualification and, second, a comprehensive revision and reference guide to the main issues in contemporary legal journalism, with plenty of case studies and references to legal and regulatory sources.

Media Law for Journalists is intended first and foremost as a course textbook to supplement lectures in practical journalism and assist practitioners who are working in the UK from other jurisdictions. It should save you time when revising for exams or preparing assessed coursework. The 'Tips' [!] feature identifies key areas for study. Exam questions, additional reading advice and extensive case studies (such as PCC adjudications) provide guidelines on what examiners are looking for and practical hints as to what not to do when working in the journalistic field. The book should help you to organise your subject matter and extract the most important points from your lecture notes and other learning materials on your course.

How to use this book

This book provides you with a comprehensive guide to the commonly taught journalism curriculum in England, Wales and Scotland. It is based on the author's own practical experience of teaching law on journalism courses, in conjunction with practical guidelines and advice from a number of UK journalists, such as the former Editor-in-chief of BBC News Interactive, Mike Smartt, the former Reuters Bureau Chief Tom Thomson and a number of close journalist friends in the English and Scottish media.

The aim of *Media Law for Journalists* is to help you pass the necessary exams, but, as important, it should also keep you out of jail when court reporting or reporting on individuals or events. It should be used as a main course textbook and can assist course teachers with their lecture and seminar notes.

If you are a new undergraduate journalism or media student, you will, no doubt, have a compulsory law module as part of your course. All law core curriculum topic areas are covered and up to date at the time of going to print. That said, *Media Law for Journalists* is useful at every level of journalism study (including postgraduate) and covers professional examinations, such as those run by the National Council for the Training of Journalists (NCTJ). Core curriculum topics (such as human rights) are provided in each chapter so that you can drop in on themes and make connections to practical work situations.

You can use this book to give you a quick overview before starting your journalism course, or familiarise yourself with English and Scottish jurisdictions before beginning work on, say, an English or Scottish newspaper or magazine. The book can also be used for reference throughout your course and as a practical legal guide throughout your professional career. Each chapter contains within it the following features:

- an introduction to the topic – the key purposes and core areas of the law curriculum
- learning outcomes – what an examiner can expect from you
- 'Tip' boxes – summarising key information, handling the information in exams or serving as reminders of key legal issues in practical situations
- sample questions
- case law and case studies
- suggestions for further reading.

The chapters go into the legal core curriculum in great detail. They will help you to understand the workings of English and Scots law within a practical journalistic setting. What is most important for you as a journalist is to communicate effectively within the permitted legal setting.

Before you start your course or embark on your career in journalism, you should ensure that you have read the syllabus thoroughly and obtained an overall impression of the necessary legal aspects. This book will then help you place emphasis on those areas of law that you find difficult, by way of the 'Tip' feature, indicated by an exclamation mark and a box in the text. A good way to revise, is to: first attend to a topic that you *do* understand, which will leave you on a high note, then return to areas that cause you difficulty – this should be done on another day and the 'Tip' boxes will help you to avoid making unnecessary mistakes.

You can read this book in one of two ways:

- skim read (or speed read):

  - let your eyes skim the page (also called 'diagonal reading')
  - make a note of the 'Tip' text in the form of bullet points to memorise
  - look at the tables that summarise topic areas
  - use the appendices and index to locate information
  - notice the core curriculum topics that form the chapter headings

- slowly and in depth:
  - read each part, slowly and carefully
  - read case law and case studies, picking up on all the details
  - read recommended textbooks in addition to this book
  - read with an enquiring mind and make critical notes as you do so
  - take regular breaks during this kind of reading
  - tackle some of the recommended questions
  - make a note of all case and book references (including page and chapter numbers and headings in textbooks).

Read this book with a view to:

- gaining an in-depth understanding of English and Scots law relating to practical media and journalism studies (to be expanded on in your lectures, seminars, textbooks, further reading and any practical journalism experience)
- answering exam questions or preparing for an assignment
- helping you to concentrate and focus on practical journalism issues within a legal context
- helping you to think like a media law specialist (in the way an examiner, editor or publisher wants you to).

Common exam and revision questions

At the end of each chapter, you will be given some sample questions and these are there to help you revise and practise writing answers.

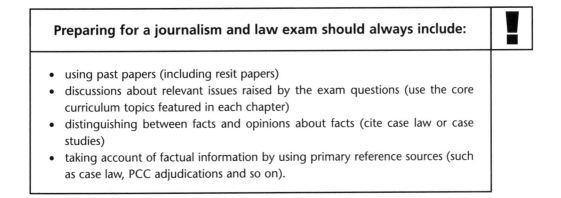

Preparing for a journalism and law exam should always include:

- using past papers (including resit papers)
- discussions about relevant issues raised by the exam questions (use the core curriculum topics featured in each chapter)
- distinguishing between facts and opinions about facts (cite case law or case studies)
- taking account of factual information by using primary reference sources (such as case law, PCC adjudications and so on).

Introducing the features

The key to success in your study of law on a journalism course is to learn how to think like a media law specialist. In short, think theoretically, analytically and like a lawyer. This book advises you on how to learn to speak and write using the correct journalists' language when studying or applying your skills. In other words, how to stay on the right side of the law when working as a journalist.

Tip!

The 'Tip' (signalled by the exclamation mark feature) helps you to structure and plan your exam answers. It also shows you how to write pieces that are within the law and report on legal cases going through the courts in a contemporaneous fashion. Each 'Tip' highlights some key information and offers advice about applying the law to the context of journalism. For example:

! **Which are the protected interests under Article 8 of the ECHR?**

- private life
- home
- family
- correspondence.

Learning outcomes

Your course will most likely present you with 'learning outcomes'. These are usually mentioned at the beginning of your course handbook. 'Learning outcomes' are elements of reflective practice that are set by your university or college in order to ensure successful assessment of student learning?

Make a careful list of all the particular learning outcomes for your course. No doubt you will be tested on these in your exam. They summarise what your examiners expect from you in your assessment and exam answers. Make sure they are relevant to each topic area (such as contempt of court).

Further reading

Each chapter concludes with a further reading section, which is designed to put the icing on the cake – that is, give you the chance to write a top-class, 'distinction'-type essay or piece of journalistic research. This feature gives you guidance on the main textbooks that you will be using on your course. These can be augmented via the bibliography and Internet sources listed in the appendices at the end of the book. Additionally, it can help those journalists who wish to advance their legal knowledge in a particular field.

The further reading sections are intended to show you how to appraise and analyse case law and advance your legal knowledge. Together with the case and statute law, selected bibliography, glossary of legal and parliamentary jargon and useful websites in the appendices, these sections provide you with the means to advance your legal knowledge and become truly excellent professionals.

Additional resources

The appendices include a Glossary of British parliamentary and legal jargon, and tables of cases and statutes which give you some topical legal information that might be useful to enhance your general legal knowledge and cite cases properly and correctly in the area of your journalistic legal study. The Bibliography and useful websites assist you with additional reading and up-to-date sources.

By the time you have read the appendices, you should be aware, and have a good knowledge of the various stages of the legal process. *Media Law for Journalists* has concentrated on the legal areas you are most likely to encounter as a journalist.

One word of warning: the study of law and its inherent disciplines, such as legal skills, research and ethical understanding, are unlike any other study you may have encountered up to now as a student or practitioner of journalism. Therefore, you may wish to use the legal database LEXIS/NEXIS (Butterworths) to find out more about case law and relevant statutes (Acts of Parliaments). This book will help you achieve this.

Thinking like a media law specialist

What does 'thinking like a media law specialist' mean? It means being able to understand what is going on in court and then communicating it effectively to the readers of your piece, who are almost certain to be non-specialists. You should be able to identify and interpret the legal language and separate it from everyday discourse and colloquialisms.

The chapters that follow provide you with the legal core curriculum required on most journalism courses. Chapter 1 introduces you to the English and European legal systems and major institutions. It is explained how access to the courts (civil and criminal) can be obtained and how court reporting is undertaken. Some examples of reporting are given from magistrates' and Crown courts – with a specific focus on reporting on juveniles, i.e. how to retain the anonymity of a young person under the age of 18 in English (court) reporting, and how more liberal reporting on juveniles over the age of 16 is permitted in the Scottish media, particularly those youngsters involved in criminal and family proceedings in Scots Law.

You will learn about the supremacy of European Union (EU) law over all 25 member states' (MS) laws and to distinguish EU from European human rights law. Apart from learning all about the English court structure, you will be made aware of the separate functions of the European Court of Justice and come to appreciate the complexities of the European Parliament, Commission and Council of Ministers, as well as the legislative functions. As English law is based on case law (common law), learning about at least some of the leading cases is essential.

Administration of justice in Britain is carried out in public – known as the 'open justice' principle. The journalist has a vital role in this. However, as Chapter 1 illustrates, a journalist needs to understand that this process is often far from straightforward. There are many rules and regulations that affect and often constrain the way court hearings can be reported. Failure to follow these can often land the representative of a media organisation in trouble and – in the most extreme cases – jail.

You will see that English and Scottish courts have their own power to regulate proceedings. There are express statutory obligations on magistrates' courts, for instance, to sit in open court unless there are express statutory provisions to the contrary, whether sitting in 'petty sessional' or 'occasional court-house' (s. 121 (4) *Magistrates' Courts Act 1980*). Particular provisions govern committal proceedings, requiring – unless there are statutory provisions to the contrary – that the examining justices sit in public.

There will be situations when names and addresses of defendants in criminal proceedings are withheld from the public and reporting restrictions may be imposed to prevent or postpone any publication of proceedings (see *R. v. Evesham Justices ex parte McDonagh and Another* [1988]). There is plenty of case law as well as statutory provision (*Contempt of Court Act 1981*, for example) to assist you with this. However, that said, it is important for you to realise that departure from the open justice principle is exceptional. Courts must justify their decisions to order reporting restrictions 'for the avoidance of the frustration of the administration of justice or the rendering of it impracticable'.

Generally, courts now tend to favour Art. 10 ECHR, which refers to the 'freedom of expression' and promotes the freedom of the press. If courts order reporting restrictions, say in an adult criminal trial, they must give adequate reasons for doing so (such as in terrorism trials for the protection of witnesses or in the interest of public security).

Chapter 2 centres on the important issue of human rights and fundamental freedoms enshrined in the *European Convention on Human Rights and Fundamental Freedoms* (the Convention). One of the biggest changes to the law in England has taken place comparatively recently with the incorporation of the Convention by way of the *Human Rights Act 1998*. Britain is unique in that it has no written constitution (unlike other democracies such as the USA, Spain, Germany, Greece and so on). The nearest we have come to enshrining fundamental human rights in UK legislation has been the *Human Rights Act 1998*. The 1998 Act came into force on 2 October 2000.

In the course of this chapter, you will become aware of the journalist's ever-increasing dilemma: 'freedom of expression' (as per Art.10 ECHR) versus an individual's right to privacy (Art. 8 ECHR). How a journalist's right to freedom of expression might well conflict with a person's right to privacy is highlighted by extensive case law (such as *Douglas v. Hello! Ltd* [2001]). Recent case law – such as Naomi Campbell's long-standing legal action against *The Mirror* – sets the precedent regarding individuals who are undergoing (in her case, drug) treatment and their protected right to privacy under Art. 8 of the Convention (see *Campbell v. Mirror Group Newspapers* [2004] UKHL 22). Whatever you might think privately, as a journalist you will have to think carefully when reporting the private lives of public figures, especially as gossip and speculation. It is for you to study this chapter carefully in the light of this debate.

You will therefore become very aware of Art. 8 ECHR ('right to privacy') and Art. 10 ECHR ('freedom of expression'). UK and European case law has shown that a newspaper's freedom to report anything about famous individuals is no longer unlimited. It is therefore important to note that ignoring the prevalence of human rights can be dangerous. An individual can now bring an action against a public authority (such as the police or a local council) on grounds of the Convention alone. In the famous case of *Douglas v. Hello!* [2001], the famous film star couple, Michael Douglas and his wife, Catherine Zeta-Jones, relied on Art. 8 in order to seek an injunction from the High

Court in November 2000 banning *Hello!* magazine from publishing unauthorised wedding photos because they had given exclusive rights to the rival *OK!* magazine.

The complexity of the situation is underlined by the fact that, under the *Human Rights Act 1998*, the role of the media has, on the one hand, been challenged under Art. 8 of the Convention regarding an individual's right to privacy, while, on the other hand, journalistic freedom of expression has been recognised under Art. 10 and in case law.

Chapter 3 explains the functions and complexities of the Press Complaints Commission (PCC) as well as the policy implications of a self-regulatory body. Furthermore, the role of the broadcasting regulator, Ofcom, is explained in this chapter. The PCC Code of Practice and the PCC case studies and adjudications will assist you with practical guidelines in your journalistic writing and future career.

Chapter 4 guides you through the legal obstacle course of 'contempt of court'. It raises important issues of what can and cannot be reported on in court, particularly in criminal proceedings – you will learn when court proceedings are 'active' and what you can and cannot report about a defendant. At the end of this chapter you will be able to recognise the common pitfalls for every court-reporting journalist under the 'strict liability' ruling.

Chapter 5 familiarises you with the strict reporting rules regarding juveniles, children and young persons under the age of 18 in English law, such as what can and cannot be reported during 'active' (youth) criminal court proceedings. Equally, you will discover what you may or may not write about a young person appearing in civil court proceedings, such as those held in a family court. English law in this respect is very protective (more so than Scots law – see Chapter 8). There are rare times when a young person, even when he or she has reached the age of 18, will be covered for life with an anonymity ruling by the High Court. Such life-long reporting bans were ordered in the case of Thomson and Venables, the two 10-year-old boys who were convicted of murder for the brutal killing of the toddler Jamie Bulger in 1993.

Chapter 6 focuses in some detail on the law of defamation. It is intended that this chapter informs you about the dangers of a slander or libel action that you might face concerning something you have written. It provides extensive case law in this area of legal study and it is intended that this chapter will helpfully result in lively debate during your tutorials or encourage good exam technique.

There are now statutory defences in 'libel' (that is, defamatory) actions and 'contempt', if a journalist can reasonably argue that he or she gave a fair and accurate report of court proceedings (such as under the *Contempt of Court Act 1981* or the *Defamation Act 1996*). Furthermore, journalists, editors and publishers have statutory rights to make representations against the imposition of restrictions on reporting or public access to proceedings.

Chapter 7 is a brief introduction to intellectual property (IP) legislation, with 'copyright' being an important topic in this area. Some knowledge of IP law will help you to protect your own original pieces of work. As this book is not intended for law students per se, this chapter does not go into great legal detail as IP is a difficult subject that is often left to postgraduate law study. By the end of the chapter, however, you should, be aware that copyright is vital to the protection of a journalists' or authors' work. You should certainly know by the end of it what 'passing off' means.

Chapter 8 is an introduction to the Scottish legal and courts system, which is very different from that of the English system. The main areas where Scots law differs from English law is in the reporting on children and young persons, and defamation.

This chapter also gives you detailed information on Scottish courts and the independence of the Scottish Parliament post the *Scotland Act 1998*. The Act brought about a fundamental constitutional change in that Scotland received its own and very distinctive Parliament (based in Edinburgh) and also incorporated the *Human Rights Act 1998* into Scots law (since 20 May 1999). How, in particular, Art. 10 of the Convention has impacted in the Scottish press is highlighted with some interesting case law examples. One such case, involving the *Human Rights Act 1998*, was that of Cox & Griffiths (1995), with the main protagonist being the then *Daily Record* editor, Peter Cox. This case is covered in detail.

As professional media lawyers (from the BBC, Reuters and Universal) have acted as consultants for this book, you will gain a realistic insight into the fast-moving world of newscasters, journalists and the stars. Finally, it is my aim to enthuse you about law in general and broaden your horizons in terms of policy decisions and the reality of media and broadcasting issues. If there is one thing that I would like to achieve with this book, it is that you become a fully rounded journalist who engages in and benefits from all the learning opportunities available to you on your course and during your career in journalism. I hope that this book will help you achieve that.

It is hoped that *Media Law for Journalists* motivates you and builds your confidence in studying this subject and ensures that, when writing about the law, you keep within it. Hopefully, this book will serve you well in your academic study and help you become an excellent journalist. I have made every effort to keep this book up to date, despite legislation – and particularly case law – changing all the time. You should additionally keep yourself up to date on new legal developments by using the recommended websites given at the end of the book.

Ursula Smartt
London, 2006

CHAPTER ONE

THE ENGLISH AND EUROPEAN LEGAL SYSTEMS

Key aim of this chapter:

> To enable you to understand the main principles of British parliamentary procedure, English and European law and the composition of all legal institutions.

Learning objectives

By the end of this chapter, you should be able to:

- demonstrate a sound knowledge and appreciation of the English and EU legal systems
- name English and EU sources of law
- give details of the English court structure
- understand and explain the supremacy of EU law
- clarify the supremacy and importance of EU institutions
- appreciate the difference between civil and criminal court procedures.

Chapter Contents

Introduction
The open justice principle
Sources of law
Court structure and key personnel
European Union law and institutions
Reporting restrictions and exclusion of the public

Introduction

This first chapter introduces you to the English and European Union (EU) legal systems so that you have a good grounding in basic legal principles and sources of law. The law in Wales is the same as that in England and so is referred to here as English law. However, the law in Scotland differs considerably in some respects from that in England and Wales and so it is dealt with separately in Chapter 8.

This chapter presents the basic rules regarding the UK Parliament, sources of law and the court structure (civil and criminal). The purpose of the media in court is to report the proceedings to the public, the majority of whom cannot be there in person but who have a right to be informed about what has taken place. It is, of course, the criminal cases that catch the greatest media attention. The only time the public can be excluded from court is where proceedings are held *in camera* – that is, closed to the public – but this is not necessarily the case for the press. One example of this is usually youth proceedings. Subsequent chapters cover when you are and are not allowed to report on such cases.

Since the incorporation of the *Human Rights Act 1998* into UK law, it has had a fundamental impact on all legislation (past and present) and you have to be aware of human rights issues (especially relating to Arts 8 and 10 ECHR) when reporting on the personal lives or court proceedings of individuals. This chapter introduces you to English, European and human rights legislation and the various courts and legal institutions involved.

It is important not to confuse human rights (Convention) legislation with European Union (EU) law, and neither must the European Court of Human Rights (ECHR) in Strasburg be confused with the European Court of Justice (ECJ) in Luxembourg. Human rights law and EU law are strictly separate and so are the courts. Suffice it to say, human rights should now be incorporated in every UK statute, and Convention rights may be invoked in all legal proceedings (negligence or breach of confidence in the civil courts or false imprisonment in the criminal courts, for example).

As a journalist, you should always seek to strike the right balance between the right to freedom of expression, the public's right to be informed (Art. 10 ECHR) and the protection of an individual's right to his or her privacy (Art. 8 ECHR). A sound understanding of these basic human rights principles is provided in this and all subsequent chapters. The main aim of this chapter is to promote greater understanding of the English justice system as a whole. You will learn to understand how the civil and criminal laws operate in practice by looking at the various agencies and key personnel involved in the civil and criminal processes, such as Her Majesty's Court Service (HMCS) and the Crown Prosecution Service (CPS). The criminal process is probably the most interesting to readers of the popular press. Next in line in the popularity stakes might be a defamation action (such as a libel case) in the High Court, followed by reporting of an industrial action in an employment tribunal (ET) or, in a coroners's court of a sudden and unexplained death.

The UK Parliament is made up of three parts:

- Crown
- House of Lords
- House of Commons.

Parliament is where new laws are debated and agreed and is referred to as the 'Legislature'. Parliament should not be confused with the government, although members of the government are also usually Members of Parliament (MPs). However, another responsibility of Parliament is to scrutinise what the government does. A 'Parliament' is the period of parliamentary time between one general election and another and each Parliament is made up of several parliamentary sessions.

Parliament is based on a two-chamber system. The House of Lords (HL) and the House of Commons sit separately and are constituted on different principles. However, the legislative process involves both houses. Under the provisions of the *House of Lords Act 1999*, 92 hereditary peers retained their seats as Lords of Parliament. In addition 75 peers were elected by their party groups – comprised of 42 Conservatives, 28 Cross-Benchers (no party allegiance), 3 Liberal Democrats and 2 Labour (these proportions being pro rata to the strength of the parties among the hereditary peers so that all have equal chance). These places are to be elected by the hereditary peers taking each party whip. The electoral system in each section was derived from multi-member first past the post. Where vacancies have arisen by the death of those elected, until November 2002, they have been filled by candidates who polled the highest number of votes and were not elected.

The UK Parliament
Parliament has three main functions, which are to: • examine proposals for new laws   • scrutinise government policy and administration   • debate the major issues of the day.

Hansard is the official report of the proceedings of Parliament. It is published daily when Parliament is sitting and records everything that is said and done in both the House of Commons and House of Lords, for which separate reports are issued. In the House of Commons, the *Hansard* reporters sit in a gallery above the Speaker and take down every word said in the chamber. In the Westminster Hall Chamber they sit next to the Chairman. The *Hansard* reporters in the HL sit below the Bar of the House, facing the Lord Chancellor.

The open justice principle

The open justice principle is clearly recognised by Parliament and the media have been given statutory rights to attend certain court proceedings from which the general public is excluded. In England, there is no rigid line of demarcation between civil and criminal courts as almost all the courts exercise both types of jurisdiction. The county courts are civil courts only and exercise exclusively one type of jurisdiction. It is obvious that full knowledge of the civil and criminal court structure is essential to a journalist working within the English media.

The open justice principle has been well established by case law, and the role of the press in reporting court cases has always been welcomed. Lord Halsbury (Lord Chancellor) L.C. referred to press reporting of proceedings in court as going beyond 'merely enlarging the area of the court, and communicating to all, that which all had the right to know' as being a positive duty to report proceedings and act as the 'watchdog' or the 'eyes and ears' of the general public and inform their readers and viewers about issues of public interest, including the administration of justice (*MacDougall v. Knight* [1889] AC 194, p. 200).

Lord Diplock explained in *A G v. Leveller Magazine Ltd* [1979] AC 440 that proceedings being held in open court meant not only that the press and public were to be admitted but also that nothing should be done to discourage the publication to a wider public of fair and accurate reporting of proceedings. Not only do defendants have to be identified but also justices and judges (*R. v. Felixstowe Justices, ex parte Leigh and Another* [1987] 1 All ER 551 QBD).

Sources of law

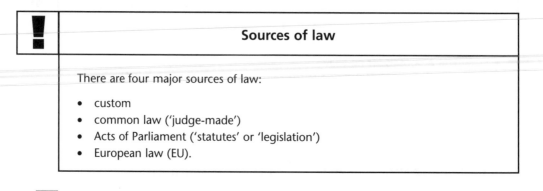

!	Sources of law
	There are four major sources of law: • custom • common law ('judge-made') • Acts of Parliament ('statutes' or 'legislation') • European law (EU).

Custom

A party to a legal dispute is alleging that they have the right to do something by virtue of custom. There are two types of custom – national and local. There are very few examples of national custom.

Common law

This goes back to 1066 when William the Conqueror of Normandy invaded England. Judges at that time would hear and decide cases according to local custom. A process then evolved whereby the best legal practice would be recorded, which was the beginnings of the development known as 'common to all' or common law. Common law (also known as 'judge-made law') is an important source of law today alongside statutory provision, and is known as the 'common law tradition'. Continental European law has a codified system (examples are the French or German Civil Code or Criminal Code).

Around the twelfth century, we see the origins of the 'doctrine of precedent'. This was where a number of scholars began to record the decisions of the courts. Hereafter, judges (justices) began to rely on these reported cases to assist them in making decisions when they were faced with other similar cases.

How to cite case names

Each case taken to court receives a case name:

- **Criminal cases**: *R. v.* [versus] *Smith,* (The '*R.*' stands for the Latin *rex,* king, or *regina,* queen). You say it as 'The Crown against Smith', which means the State is prosecuting the defendant for a criminal offence.
- **Civil cases**: *Smith v. Jones,* which you say as 'Smith and Jones'. Here, the individual (the claimant) brings an action against another individual (the defendant).

Today, common law complements statutes (acts of Parliament). For example, s. 1 *Sexual Offences Act 2003*, defines rape as:

(1) A person (A) commits an offence if:

    (a) he intentionally penetrates the vagina, anus or mouth of another person (B) with his penis;

     (b)   B does not consent to the penetration; and

     (c)   A does not reasonably believe that B consents.

  (2)   Whether a belief is reasonable is to be determined having regard to all the circumstances, including any steps A has taken to ascertain whether B consents.

In the case of *R. v. R.* (Rape: marital exemption) [1991] 4 All ER 481, the judges had to look to the old common law for assistance in defining what was unlawful as here the question was about rape within marriage. Since the ruling in *R. v. R.*, rape is now possible as a criminal offence within marriage and has become common law. It is presumed that the common law will apply unless an Act of Parliament specifically abolishes it or renders it redundant. The offence of rape carries a maximum life prison sentence.

Acts of Parliament (legislation)

Legislation goes through a number of stages before it becomes law (Act of Parliament or statute). All legislation starts with a Bill that is put before Parliament and can start in either the House of Commons or the House of Lords. Once a bill has completed its proper stages in one of the houses, the process is repeated in the other. After this, any amendments from the second house are considered by the first. When both houses agree on a Bill, then it may be presented to the Queen for Royal Assent. On those occasions when no agreement between houses can be reached, there are instruments by which generally the will of the fully elected House of Commons will eventually prevail.

!

How does a Bill become an Act of Parliament?

Bills go through the following stages in each house:

- first reading
- second reading
- committee stage
- report stage
- third reading.

Much of criminal law is now statutory (such as *Offences Against the Person Act 1861, Theft Acts 1968* and *1978; Road Traffic Act 1988; Misuse of Drugs Act 1971* and so on), but there is still plenty of case (common) law in, for example, murder and manslaughter offences. Civil law deals with disputes in contract, negligence, nuisance, defamation, and so on, and is largely statutory in tort law (*Sale of Goods Act 1979,* for example), but case law is still plentiful, particularly in defamation cases (see Chapter 6).

There are about 2000 cases each year recorded in law reports. The oldest reports date back some 700 years, the most recent ones (dating back at least 50 years) are now recorded on the legal database called LEXIS/NEXIS (Butterworths), on the Internet.

Law reports

- *Appeal Cases* (AC) Decisions from the Court of Appeal (CA), House of Lords (HL) and Privy Council.
- *Chancery Division* Decisions of the Chancery Division of the High Court and their appeals to the CA.
- *Family Division* Decisions of the Family Division of the High Court and their appeals to the CA.
- *Queen's Bench* Decisions of the Queen's Bench Division (QBD) of the High Court and their appeals to the CA.

When you look up legal cases, either in hard copy or online, they are cited as follows:

Hill v. Chief Constable of West Yorkshire [1988] 2 WLR 1049.

This means that the case was recorded in 1988 and is to be found in Volume 2 of the *Weekly Law Report* on page 1049.

The Hill case concerned a private (civil or tortious) action brought by Mrs Hill, the mother of one of the victims killed by Peter Sutcliffe (the 'Yorkshire Ripper'), in Leeds in 1979. Mrs Hill sued the West Yorkshire Police, arguing that they had been negligent in failing to catch the killer earlier and so prevent her daughter's murder (teenager Jacqueline Hill). In a tort action of this kind, there has to be so-called 'claimant's relationship of proximity' in order to prove negligence. It was held that there was no relationship of proximity between the police and the claimant's daughter because there was no reason for the police to believe that Jacqueline was in special danger from Sutcliffe. She was simply in the same general danger as any female member of the public in the area where the murders had been committed.

!	Case references in law reports

- **All ER** *All England Law Reports*
- **AC** Appeal Cases
- **Ch D** Chancery Division
- **Cr. App. R.** *Criminal Appeal Reports*
- **Fam.** Family Division
- **KB** King's Bench
- **QBD** Queen's Bench Division
- **WLR** *Weekly Law Reports*

Secondary legislation

This is also known as 'delegated legislation' or 'subordinate legislation' and is legislation made by ministers under powers granted to them in Acts of Parliament. The powers themselves are called statutory instruments (SI) and have the full force of law. This avoids the need for an Act of Parliament to be passed every time a detail needs to be updated or added to. About 3000 SIs are issued each year and are just as much a part of the law as the parent Act of Parliament. An example is the Statutory Instrument 2005 No. 40: *The Licensing Act 2003 (Transitional provisions) Order 2005*, which gives supplementary guidelines to local authorities and magistrates' courts under the *Licensing Act 2003* (transferring licensing powers from magistrates' committees to local authorities).

The House of Lords (HL) established procedures in 1992 whereby all bills with delegating powers are now examined before they begin their passage through the House. The HL Delegated Powers Scrutiny Committee keeps the extent to which legislative powers are delegated by Parliament to government ministers under constant review. There is an informal understanding in the Lords that, when the Committee has approved provisions in a bill for delegated powers, the form of those powers should not normally be the subject of debate during the bill's subsequent passage. The House of Commons has no equivalent committee.

One of the fundamental principles of constitutional law is the separation of powers – that is, executive (government and its servants, such as civil servants, police and so on), legislative (Parliament) and judicial (the courts and their justices). The eighteenth-century French philosopher Montesquieu believed that England was at the time a most excellent example of applied practice of its separation of powers. Arguably, this cannot be seen as completely true nowadays. To understand this, you need to know about the supremacy of Parliament. This is another fundamental constitutional principle, also known as 'parliamentary sovereignty'. Simply put, any British Parliament can make or unmake laws. This is highly unusual among Western democratic societies and could be seen as inter-ference from the State in legislation and the basic human rights of citizens.

However, since the incorporation of the Convention into UK law by means of the *Human Rights Act 1998* in 2000, parliamentary sovereignty has no doubt been eroded. Furthermore, EU law is now supreme to the UK and indeed all other 25 member states (MS) of the European Union, with the European Court of Justice (ECJ) being superior to the House of Lords in most cases (but not criminal). The Scottish Parliament (*Scotland Act 1998*) can make 'local' laws that affect Scotland (including those concerning health, education, criminal justice, trade and indus-try and so on; see Chapter 8). There has long been a heated debate in Parliament about whether or not the UK should have a written constitution, similar to its Continental European partners, but the strong arguments protecting cultural her-itage and legal flexibility in a multicultural society have so far prevailed.

Court structure and key personnel

Some courts are 'superior courts' and others are 'inferior courts'. Superior courts – the House of Lords (HL), Court of Appeal (CA), High Court and Crown Court – have unlimited jurisdiction and deal with the more important and difficult cases. These courts are known as 'superior courts of record'.

The county courts and coroners' courts are 'inferior courts of record'. Magistrates' courts are not courts of record.

A superior court of record has power to punish all forms of contempt of court while an inferior court of record can generally only punish contempt committed in the face of the court.

The House of Lords is the highest court in the UK, though the European Court of Justice (ECJ) is the Supreme Court for all European member states in European Community legislation matters. Judicial decisions of the HL can be overruled only by statute or a refusal of the House to follow them in later cases (see below).

Presiding over the HL is the Lord Chancellor, who sits on the 'woolsack' – a symbol of prosperity and wealth. He is appointed by the prime minister and is a member of the Cabinet (that is, it is a political appointment). He heads a depart-ment that is responsible, among other matters, for the administration of the courts (Department of Constitutional Affairs). He speaks for the government during debates and is entitled to vote like any other lord, but he does not hold a casting vote. The Lord Chancellor also presides over the HL in its capacity as a court and is entitled to sit on appellate committees. He also appoints judges.

The Court of Appeal (CA) is composed of the Lord Chancellor (L.C.) (Lord Falconer, Baron Falconer of Thoroton – all appointments as at June 2006), Master of the Rolls (M.R.) (Sir Anthony Clarke), the Lord Chief Justice (L.C.J.) (Lord

Phillips of Worth Matravers), the President of the Queen's Bench Division (QBD) (Sir Igor Judge), the President of the Family Division (Sir Mark Potter), the Vice-President of the Court of Appeal (Civil Division) (Lord Justice Brooke) and other Lords and Ladies Justices of Appeal (in order of seniority) e.g. Lord Justice Rose, Lord Justice Auld, Lady Justice Arden, Lady Justice Smith etc. From 3 April 2006 the role of the Lord Chancellor (L.C.) changed with the *Constitutional Reform Act* 2005. The Lord Chief Justice (L.C.J.) became head of the judiciary and the Judicial Appointments Commission is now responsible for selecting and making recommendations for judicial offices. The L.C. continues to be the government minister responsible for the judiciary and the courts system, but he is no longer a judge or head of the judiciary. The L.C.J. is now the the head of the judiciary. Now the L.C. must secure the agreement of the L.C.J. before he can make decisions about many areas of responsibility that affect or involve the judiciary.

The Lord Chief Justice is referred to by his title and name, followed by initials indicating his office, e.g. Lord Phillips C.J. (not Phillips L.C.J.). Other judicial peers in the Supreme Court are referred to similarly, e.g. Sir Anthony Clarke M.R.

Below follows a list and tables of how justices should be addressed orally and when writing to or about them.

Judges and the Bar

There are four heads of divisions:

- Lord Chief Justice (L.C.J.)
- Master of the Rolls (M.R.)
- President of the Family Division (P)
- Vice-chancellor (V.C.).

These are privy counsellors. They should be addressed by their judicial titles, prefixed by 'The Right Honourable'. For example:

Address (in correspondence)	Dear ...
The Right Honourable The Lord Chief Justice of England and Wales	Lord Chief Justice/Chief Justice
The Right Honourable The Master of the Rolls	Master of the Rolls
The Right Honourable The President of the Family Division	President

The Right Honourable The Vice-chancellor	Vice-chancellor
Retired Head of Division	Title in private capacity

Court of Appeal (CA)

Judges who sit in the Court of Appeal (Lords Justices of Appeal) are privy counsellors. They are known officially as Lords Justices. They should be addressed as follows:

Gender	Address in correspondence	Dear ...	Orally in court
Male	The Right Honourable Lord Justice Doe	Lord Justice	Lord Justice Doe or My Lord
Appointed but not sworn in	The Honourable Lord Justice Doe	Lord Justice	N/A
Retired	The Right Honourable Sir John Doe	Lord Justice or Judge	N/A
Female Officially	The Right Honourable Lord Justice Doe	Lord Justice	Lady Justice Doe or My Lady
Informally	The Right Honourable Lady Justice Doe	Lady Justice	N/A
Appointed but not sworn in	The Honourable Lord/Lady Justice Doe	Lord/Lady Justice	N/A
Retired	The Right Honourable Dame Mary Doe	Lady Justice/Judge	

High Court

Members of the High Court are not usually privy counsellors. Their official designation is as follows:

Gender	Office/position	Address (in correspondence)	Dear ...
Male	High Court judge and a privy counsellor	The Right Honourable Mr Justice Doe	Judge
	As above but retired	The Right Honourable Sir John Doe	Judge
	High Court judge but not a privy counsellor	The Honourable Mr Justice Doe	Judge
	As above but retired	Sir John Doe	Judge
Female	High Court judge and a privy counsellor	The Right Honourable Mrs Justice Doe (whether married or single)	Judge
	As above but retired	The Right Honourable Dame Mary Doe	Judge
	High Court judge but not a privy counsellor	The Honourable Mrs Justice Doe	Judge
	As above but retired	Dame Mary Doe	Judge

Please note that:

- forenames are not inserted unless there are two judges with the same or similar surname, in which case the junior judge of the two uses his or her forename and surname
- High Court judges are normally knighted as Knights Bachelor or appointed as Dame Commander of the Order of the British Empire as soon as possible after their appointment and should be addressed accordingly in their private capacities
- a High Court judge, or a more senior member of the judiciary, is never given the letters QC after his or her name, even if a Queen's Counsel when at the bar.

The Bar

Address (in correspondence)	Dear ...
Members of the Bar	Usual titles in their private capacities
Queen's Counsel (or, when the sovereign is a king)	John Doe Esq., QC John Doe Esq., KC
QC/KC when appointed to senior judiciary	Never use QC or KC

Most precedent cases (the ones you read in law books) will have been decided either by the HL or the CA (Criminal or Civil Divisions). Inferior courts (such as county or magistrates' courts) have limited jurisdiction and hear the less important or less difficult cases. Inferior courts are subject to the supervisory (prerogative) jurisdiction of the High Court. The employment appeal tribunal is also not part of the Supreme Court of Record, despite the fact that High Court judges sit on it and appeals from its decisions go to the Court of Appeal. In July 2003, Lord Falconer of Thoroton, Secretary of State for Constitutional Affairs and Lord Chancellor, proposed the possible introduction of a Supreme Court for the United Kingdom in a paper called 'Constitutional Reform'. This would essentially change the role of the House of Lords and its judicial business. Broadly speaking, the House of Lords currently chooses its own cases, in that nearly all appeals require the permission of the court below (rarely granted) or of the House (the majority of cases) before an appeal may be lodged. The government's proposals were at the time to abolish the jurisdiction of the House of Lords within the UK's judicial system. The functions currently performed by the Appellate Committee would be vested instead in a new Supreme Court, quite separate from Parliament. On 14 December 2004, Lord Falconer announced the preferred new site for such a Supreme Court, namely the Middlesex Guildhall, making the present Palace of Westminster 'entirely inappropriate'. Middlesex Guildhall is currently used as a Crown Court. After discussions with the law lords in August 2003 it was agreed the new Supreme Court needed to be at least 3500 square metres with sufficient space for both the 12 law lords and the Judicial Committee of the Privy Council currently based in Downing Street. Discussions as to the nature and location of a new Supreme Court have been ongoing.

Civil courts exist in order to resolve disputes between private citizens or between a citizen and a State authority, such as the police or a local authority. These disputes may involve such matters as breach of contract or wrongful exercise of power by some public authority in terms of judicial review (such as *R. v. Secretary of State for the Home Department, ex parte Venables*; *R. v. Secretary of State for the Home Department, ex parte Thompson* [1998] AC 407). In such cases, one party is seeking to obtain from the court some private remedy against the other.

County courts

There are about 240 county courts sitting locally every weekday (*County Courts Act 1984*). There are about 529 circuit judges and about 334 district judges on the 'circuit'. Circuit judges are appointed by the Queen on the recommendation of the Lord Chancellor. The statutory qualification is a 10-year Crown Court or 10 year county court qualification. Recorders may sit in both the Crown Court and the county courts. Most Recorders start by sitting in the Crown Court although after about two years they might be authorised to sit in the county courts after a period of training. Their jurisdiction is broadly similar to that of a Circuit judge but they will generally handle the less complex or serious matters coming before the court. The jurisdiction of county courts is limited:

- by a financial criterion – civil actions are to be commenced in a county court unless the value of the action is £50,000 or more, including claims for damages and personal injuries, with any actions over £50,000 being tried in the High Court
- by geographical criteria – the plaintiff is not allowed to pick and choose the forum
- in terms of its power to grant remedies – it cannot grant the prerogative remedies, such as 'mandamus', 'prohibition' or 'certiorari'. These are High Court writs meaning 'specific performance' or 'specific action', i.e. mandatory, prohibiting and quashing orders respectively, under s. 29 *Supreme Court Act 1981*.

The following tables show the written and oral form of judicial address for county court judges.

Circuit judges

Office/position	Address (in correspondence)	Dear...
Male	His Honour Judge Doe (QC if appropriate)	Judge
Also a peer	His Honour Judge The Lord Doe	Judge
Also a knight	His Honour Judge Sir John Doe	Judge
Retired	His Honour John Doe	Judge
Female	Her Honour Judge Doe (QC if appropriate)	Judge
Also a peeress	Her Honour Judge The Lady Doe	Judge
Also a dame	Her Honour Judge Dame Joan Doe DBE	Judge
Retired	Her Honour Mary Doe	Judge

Please note, forenames are not inserted unless there are two judges with the same or similar surname, in which case the junior judge of the two uses his or her forename and surname.

District judges

Address (in correspondence)	Dear ...	Orally
District Judge Doe	Judge	Sir or Madam
Senior District Judge, Principal Registry of the Family Division	Judge	Sir or Madam

District judges are assigned on appointment to a particular circuit and may sit at any of the county courts or District Registries of the High Court in that circuit (as well as magistrates' courts).

Crown Courts

Criminal litigation in England is adversarial (as opposed to the continental term inquisitorial). The terms 'adversarial' (also known as 'accusatorial') and 'inquisitorial' reflect particular historical developments rather than the practices of modern legal systems. In broad terms, adversarial justice refers to the (English) common law system of conducting proceedings in which parties have the primary responsibility for defining the issues in dispute and for investigating and advancing the dispute (as opposed to say in France and Germany where these functions are carried out by a judge). An adversarial criminal justice system offers a 'party prosecution' of a dispute under common law. This means that the parties (e.g. the Crown Prosecutor and defence lawyer) each present the facts to the court. 'Inquisitorial' refers to civil code systems (like France or Germany) in which the inquisitorial judge has such primary responsibility.

Criminal courts exist in order to hear and determine accusations against persons that they have broken the criminal law. The highest court for most serious crimes is the Crown Court. Most accusations are made by a Crown Prosecutor representing the state (Crown Prosecution Service – CPS). There are, however, other prosecuting agencies such as the HM Revenue and Customs, the Post Office or the Department of Social Security (DSS). On a finding of guilt, the criminal courts have power to inflict punishment; this is either in form of a fine, a Community Sentence or imprisonment.

A Crown Court sits in 78 locations in England and Wales and deals with the more serious criminal cases transferred from magistrates' courts, such as:

- murder
- rape
- robbery.

A Crown Court also hears appeals against decisions made in the magistrates' courts and deals with cases sent from magistrates' courts for sentence. Crown Court trials are heard by a jury of 12 people and a judge. Most juries are selected by computer from the electoral register each year to try crimes in Crown Courts, but also in some coroners' inquests and some civil cases (such as defamation actions in the High Court).

Crown Courts hear all 'indictable offences' (such as murder or rape). No matter how serious the charge, the defendant has to appear first before a magistrates' court, where he or she confirms name and address and the legal adviser (formerly 'clerk to the justices') reads out the charge. Magistrates can then commit the defendant to the Crown Court.

What are indictable offences?
<ul><li>serious offences on statute, such as grievous bodily harm with intent (GBH), s. 18 *Offences against the Person Act 1861* [OAPA], and robbery, s. 8 *Theft Act 1968*)</li><li>serious sexual offences, such as rape, *Sexual Offences Act 2003*</li><li>serious common-law offences, such as homicide – murder/manslaughter</li><li>any offence punishable by long or life imprisonment.</li></ul>

Magistrates' courts

Magistrates' courts (MC) are inferior courts and not ones of record, as mentioned earlier. Apart from carrying out the criminal justice function for youth (youth courts) and adult criminal matters, it also has civil functions in family, licensing, betting and gaming matters (licensing functions ceased by the end of 2005 – alcohol licensing matters now being handled by local authorities).

There are currently about 30,000 'ordinary' members of the public acting as lay magistrates who are unremunerated justices of the peace (JP) in the local criminal courts. They deal with about 95 per cent of all criminal matters at first instance. Their powers have been extended under the *Criminal Justice Act 2003* and will soon extend from imprisoning a person for 6 months to 12 months for a single criminal offence. Magistrates deal with summary and most triable-either-way offences.

Magistrates deal with two categories of crime !▪

- summary offences (less serious ones, such as driving offences and harassment)
- triable-either-way offences (more serious ones, such as theft and assault).

Apart from magistrates, there are about 130 district judges (DJs) who operate mostly in London and greater metropolitan areas. DJs have at least seven years' experience as barristers or solicitors and two years' experience as deputy district judges. They sit alone and deal with more complicated or sensitive cases, which can include those arising from extradition and fugitive orders or serious fraud.

What are summary offences? !▪

- less serious offences (s. 40 CJA 1988)
- adults (over 18) are tried 'summarily' (i.e. by magistrates – schedule 1. *Interpretation Act 1978*)
- most summary offences are statutory (i.e. written in the form of an Act of Parliament).

The most interesting, yet tricky, category of crimes are triable-either-way offences. If the accused is charged with an 'either-way' offence, the prosecution must provide the bench with advice as to where the case should be heard – 'the CPS advises that this case can be heard in the magistrate' court', for example.

What are triable-either-way offences? !▪

- offences that can be tried 'either way' – either at a magistrates' or a Crown Court
- the defendant (when over 18) chooses whether he or she wants to be tried summarily (magistrates') or on indictment (Crown Court with judge and jury
- those prescribed as 'either-way' offences in the statutes, such as 'criminal damage' in s. 1 *Criminal Damage Act 1971*, 'making off without payment' in s. 3 *Theft Act 1978* and 'assault occasioning actual bodily harm' (ABH) in s. 47 OAPA.

District judges (Magistrates' courts)

The *Access to Justice Act 1999* came into force in January 2000, and amalgamated the provincial and metropolitan stipendiary benches to form one unified court service throughout England and Wales under the auspices of the Department of Constitutional Affairs (DCA). On 1 April 2005, Her Majesty's Courts Service (HMCS) brought together the Magistrates' courts Service and Court Service (Crown Court and all other civil courts) into one single organisation. HMCS is now an executive agency of the DCA and carries out the administration and support for the Court of Appeal, the High Court, the Crown Court, the Magistrates' courts, the County courts and the Probate Service. Stipendiary magistrates were renamed district judges.

Address (in correspondence)	Dear ...	Orally
Senior District Judge (Chief Magistrate)	Judge	Sir or Madam
Deputy Senior District Judge (Magistrates' Courts)	Judge	Sir or Madam
District Judge (Magistrates' Courts) Doe	Judge	Sir or Madam

Please note that it is incorrect to omit the part of the title in brackets. The Senior District Judge (Chief Magistrate) and Deputy Senior District Judge (Magistrates' courts) should not be addressed by their own names, so you cannot say or write 'Senior District Judge (Chief Magistrate) Doe' or 'Deputy Senior District Judge (Magistrates' courts) Doe'.

Magistrates

Address (in correspondence)	Dear ...
Justice of the Peace (JP)	John Doe Esq., JP

The Court Structure of Her Majesty's Courts Service (HMCS)

Her Majesty's Courts Service carries out the administrative and support for the Court of Appeal, the High Court, the Crown Court, the magistrates' courts, the county courts and the Probate Service.

House of Lords*
Appeals from the Court of Appeal and in exceptional circumstances from the High Court (also Scotland and Northern Ireland)

Court of Appeal
Criminal Division
Appeals from the Crown Court
Civil Division
Appeals from the High Court, tribunals and certain cases from county courts

---

High Court
Queen's Bench Division
Contract and tort, etc.
Commercial Court
Admiralty Court
Administrative Court
Supervisory and appellate jurisdiction overseeing the legality of decisions and actions of inferior courts, tribunals, local authorities, Ministers of the Crown and other public bodies and officials

---

Family Division
Divisional Court
Appeals from the magistrates' courts

Chancery Division
Equity and trusts, contentious probate, tax partnerships, bankruptcy and Companies Court, Patents Court
Divisional Court
Appeals from the county courts on bankruptcy and land

Crown Court
Trials of indictable offences, appeals from magistrates' courts, cases for sentence

---

County Courts
Majority of civil litigation subject to nature of the claim

Magistrates' Courts
Trials of summary offences, committals to the Crown Court, family proceedings courts and youth courts

---

The Tribunals Service*
Hears appeals from decisions on: immigration, social security, child support, pensions, tax and lands
(* not administered by HMCS)

Source: http://www.hmcourts-service.gov.uk/aboutus/structure/index.htm

Court of Appeal

The jurisdiction of the Court of Appeal (CA), Criminal Division, is to hear appeals in criminal cases from those convicted in the Crown Court. Such an appeal is against the conviction and/or sentence, but can only be made with leave from the CA or if the trial judge certifies that the case is fit for appeal. The CA also hears cases referred to it by the Attorney General (AG) and the Criminal Cases Review Commission (CCRC). Three judges normally hear appeals, without a jury. In the case of an appeal against a sentence, only two judges can hear the case.

The jurisdiction of the CA, Civil Division, is mainly to hear appeals in civil cases from all three divisions of the High Court and from county courts. This type of appeal is normally heard by three judges. If, in the interest of economy, only two judges hear a case and they are divided in their opinion, the case must be reargued before an uneven number of judges, no fewer than three, before any appeal can be taken to the HL.

The CA can sit anywhere in England (though it usually sits in London) and the hearing is not a retrial. Each judge delivers his or her own separate judgment after carefully reading all the documents in the case and hearing counsel's arguments. In civil cases, dissenting judgments are recorded, but not in criminal cases.

High Court

The High Court of Justice – to give it its full title – is principally a civil court. It is comprised of three divisions:

- Queen's Bench Division (QBD)
- Chancery Division
- Family Division.

Judges of the High Court often sit in London, but there are also High Courts in Birmingham, Bristol, Caernarfon, Cardiff, Carlisle, Chelmsford, Chester, Exeter, Leeds, Lewes, Lincoln, Liverpool, Manchester, Middlesborough, Newcastle, Norwich, Nottingham, Oxford, Preston, Sheffield, Stafford, Swansea, Truro, Warwick and Winchester.

It is comprised of the Lord Chancellor (President of the Chancery Division), but he or she never sits, the Lord Chief Justice, who presides over the Queen's Bench Division, the President, who presides over the Family Division, the Vice-chancellor, who is Vice-president of the Chancery Division, the Senior Presiding Judge and a number of ordinary High Court judges, who are at times referred to as 'puisne' (that is, lesser or assistant) judges. The maximum number is 98.

To qualify for appointment as a puisne judge of the High Court, a person must either have a ten-year High Court qualification (s. 71 *Courts and Legal Services Act 1990*) or have been a circuit judge for at least two years. Puisne judges are appointed by the sovereign on the advice of the Lord Chancellor, who assigns him or her to a particular division dependent on the volume of business before the court.

The Queen's Bench Division (QBD)   The Queen's Bench Division of the High Court is comprised of the Lord Chief Justice, assisted by a number of puisne judges.

The QBD's judicial strength reflects both the volume of business in the division and the fact that QBD judges spend a certain amount of time away from London on circuit in the provinces trying High Court civil actions and, as judges of the Crown Court, in criminal cases.

The QBD acts mainly as a civil court where a single judge tries such cases as breach of contract and actions in tort at first instance. Most actions are either settled or abandoned – only about 1 per cent result in a trial. A person who has been dealt with by the magistrates or who has appealed unsuccessfully to the Crown Court may also appeal on a point of law to the QBD. This procedure is also available to the prosecution. The magistrates or the Crown Court will be asked by the appellant to state their findings on fact and the questions of law that arose.

The Chancery Division   The Chancery Division of the High Court is presided over by the Lord Chancellor, assisted by a number of puisne judges.

It is purely a civil court, largely concerned with the administration of equity. It deals with the sale, exchange or partition of land, land charges, redemption or foreclosure of mortgages, execution of trusts, administration of the estates of the deceased, bankruptcy, dissolution of partnerships, contentious probate business and interpretation of wills, the appointment of a guardian in a minor's case, and company law, at first instance. Additionally, the Chancery Division has some appellate jurisdiction in taxation or insolvency, land registration and patents.

The Family Division   The Family Division of the High Court acts in all matrimonial matters, the maintenance of minors and any other proceedings with minors (*Children Act 1989*), adoption, applications for consent to the marriage of a minor, and child abduction a nd custody (*Child Abduction and Custody Act 1985*).

The divisional court of the Family Division deals with appeals in family matters, such as financial provision orders. It is presided over by the President (until 2004 it was Dame Elizabeth Butler-Sloss).

The Attorney General (AG)

The Attorney General is a barrister (usually a QC) and almost invariably has a seat in the House of Commons. As a member of government, his principal function is to give advice on points of law and represent the Crown in important cases, both criminal and civil. He or she can initiate civil proceedings on behalf of the public, such as to prevent a public nuisance, and certain other proceedings. Prosecutions under the Official Secrets Act can only be begun with his consent. He is regarded as leader of the English bar, but does not have a private practice while in office.

The AG's office is most important in journalistic challenges. You will read a number of cited cases that start '*AG v.*' such as (*AG v. Guardian Newspapers Ltd* [1987], known as the 'Spycatcher case').

The Director of Public Prosecutions (DPP)

The Director of Public Prosecutions is a barrister or solicitor appointed by the Home Secretary who acts under the supervision of the AG. The AG's duties include initiating and conducting certain criminal cases, especially those of importance and complexity. Certain other prosecutions can only be begun with his or her permission and he or she may give advice to police forces on possible prosecutions. The DPP acts for the Crown in criminal appeals to the CA and the HL and is also responsible for the Crown Prosecution Service (CPS).

European Union law and institutions

The European Union (EU) represents 25 member states (MS). The basic principles that underpin the EU are laid down in its first treaty, the *Treaty of Rome 1957*:

- freedom of movement of goods and services
- freedom of movement of capital
- freedom of movement of workers (and their families).

This important treaty, signed in 1957, established the European Economic Community (EEC) in 1958. Some described the EC treaty as the first written constitution of the EU and its institutions. The treaty set the agenda for the development of a common market (the EEC), with two fundamental freedoms:

- freedom of movement of workers (Art. 39 EC)[2]
- freedom of movement of goods (Arts 23–26 EC).

> ## Founder countries of the EEC – the EU – and its treaty !
>
> - France, West Germany, Italy, Belgium, The Netherlands, Luxembourg
> - *Treaty of Rome*, March 1957.

The *Treaty of Rome 1957* is the basis for all future treaties. Its main aims are to promote:

- harmonious economic activity throughout the community while respecting the environment
- sustainable and non-inflationary economic growth
- convergence of economic performance – economic monetary union – (EMU)
- high level of employment and social protection
- good standards of living and quality of life
- solidarity and peace among member states (MS).

With the *Treaty on the European Union 1992* (TEU), also known as the 'Maastricht Treaty', the word 'Economic' was dropped from the title 'European Economic Community' (EEC) to signify a change of emphasis in its activities, but uncertainty remained about the correct designations of the various institutions.

The TEU introduced a three-pillar structure in 1993: the EC (Economic Community), ECSC (European Coal and Steel Community) and Euratom, acting together under the first pillar, were known collectively as the EC. The TEU brought about major changes in the way the community operates and many regard it as marking the point when the member states moved away from seeking economic union and towards openly seeking political and social union. Although there was considerable opposition in some countries, particularly the UK, the treaty was eventually adopted. It broadens the scope of community power, extending it into areas of foreign policy, home affairs and monetary union. There now exists a consolidated version of the TEU of 2002, which consolidates Protocols annexed to the Treaty on European Union, to the Treaty establishing the European Community (EC), and to the Treaty establishing the European Atomic Energy Community (EAEC). The 2002 Treaty also includes the enlargement of the EU, accessing the ten new countries. The *Treaty of Nice 2001* amended the TEU and created the protocol for the enlargement of the EU from 2004–2009. The Treaty for the Constitution of Europe was proposed on 16 December 2004; France and The Netherlands voted in referenda during 2005 and both countries rejected the Constitution with overwhelming 'no' responses.

!

The founding treaties are:

- Treaty on the European Union 1992 (TEU)
- Treaty establishing the European Economic Community 1957 (EEC)
- Treaty establishing the European Atomic Energy Community (EURATOM) 1957
- Treaty establishing the European Coal and Steel Community (ECSC) 1957.

!

Their consolidated versions are:

- Treaty establishing the European Community (Consolidated Version 1997)
- Treaty on European Union (Consolidated Version 1997)
- Treaty establishing the European Community (Consolidated Version 1992).

!

Other countries that have joined, and hope to join, the EU

- 1972: UK, Republic of Ireland, Denmark
- 1981: Norway, Greece
- 1986: Spain, Portugal
- 1990: Former East Germany (German Democratic Republic)
- 2004: Cyprus, Czech Republic, Estonia, Hungary, Latvia, Lithuania, Malta, Poland, Slovenia, Slovakia
- Proposed entry 2007: Bulgaria, Romania
- Possibly Turkey from 2012.

In January 2001, 11 MS joined the common currency – the euro – in a move towards economic monetary union, as enshrined in Art. 2 EC of the *Treaty of Rome 1957.*

It can be said that, since those early days of the EEC, we have moved closer to a European Federation, though we have by no means reached a 'United States of Europe'. This became only too clear, when France and the Netherlands voted against the proposed European Treaty (the Constitution) in 2005.

EU sources of law

The EU treaties (such as the *Treaty of Rome 1957*) are primary sources of legislation and supreme to all laws of each of the 25 MS. It can be said that EU treaties largely deal with customs duties, non-discrimination of workers, competition law and state monopolies. What EU law is not (yet) is a body of criminal law – *corpus juris*. So EU law has, essentially, a commercial and employment law character. EU treaties are *not* to be confused with the *European Convention on Human Rights and Fundamental Freedoms* [ECHR] (The Convention).

Some important EU treaties
• *Treaty of Rome 1957*, also known as the 'EC Treaty' • *Single European Act 1986* (SEA) • *Treaty on European Union 1992* (TEA), also known as the 'Maastricht Treaty' • *Amsterdam Treaty 1997*, which renumbered all the treaties' articles • *Treaty of Nice 2000*, which approved the accession of ten further MS • *Athens Treaty 2003,* which involved ten new MS signing accession to the EU.

Then there are secondary sources of law, and their meaning is enshrined in Art. 249 EC. These are:

- regulations
- directives
- decisions.

Regulations

'A Regulation shall have general application. It shall be binding in its entirety and directly applicable to all Member States.' (Art. 249 EC)

Regulations are the most important sources of secondary legislation in that they are of general application and take effect in all MS without the need for further implementation at a national level – that is, they are directly applicable. Regulations are effectively 'black letter' law.

!	**What are EU regulations?**

- legislation that is similar to Acts of Parliament
- they have binding legal force – 'black letter law'
- they are binding on all MS, with immediate effect and being generally applied in, for example, all MS, companies and individuals
- they are directly applicable – that is, implementing legislation is unnecessary for the regulations to become law in MS.

One example is *Council Regulation (EEC) No. 1612/68* of the Council of 15 October 1968 on 'Freedom of movement for workers within the Community'. This gives Community workers the right to travel freely and without a work permit between MS and to seek work in another MS.

Another example is *Council Regulation (EEC) No. 3677/90* of 13 December 1990 on 'Laying down measures to be taken to discourage the diversion of certain substances to the illicit manufacture of narcotic drugs and psychotropic substances'.

Directives

> A Directive shall be binding, as to the result to be achieved, upon each Member State to whom it is addressed, but shall leave to the national authorities the choice of form and methods. (Art. 249 EC (Consolidated Version 1992))

Directives specify a legal objective or obligation addressed to a specific MS. It is then up to the individual MS to decide how best to achieve that objective. In the UK, this takes the form of an Act of Parliament. The Council always specifies a time limit within which the MS has to implement the directive (normally between one and three years). An example is *Directive 2004/38/EC* (of the European Parliament and the Council of 29 April 2004) 'On the right of citizens of the Union and their family members to move and reside freely within the territory of the Member States', which amends *Council Regulation (EEC) No 1612/68* and repeals *Directives 64/221/EEC*. This allows for families of workers of MS to travel and reside with the EU worker – the family members do not necessarily have to be from the EU.

What are Council directives?	!

- laws that are binding only on MS to which they are addressed
- only the result of a directive is binding
- require MS to implement directives – that is a MS must pass implementing legislation such as an Act of Parliament in the UK, usually within one to three years of their implementation.

Decisions

> A Decision shall be binding in its entirety upon those to whom it is addressed. (Art. 249 EC (Consolidated Version 1992))

Decisions are administrative acts that are binding on an individual (such as a company or MS) to whom they are addressed. The Commission will issue a decision when they have concluded that an undertaking has been breached (such as regarding competition policy).

One example is *Council Decision No. 813/86/ECSC* of 14 March 1986 on 'Protection against imports which are the subject of dumping between the Community of Ten and the new Member States or between the new Member States during the period throughout which the transitional measures laid down by the Act of Accession of Spain and Portugal apply'.

What are decisions?	!

- binding in their entirety
- only binding on those to whom addressed, such as MS, companies, individuals
- no need to implement legislation.

Recommendations and opinions

> Recommendations and opinions shall have no binding force.

One such example is *Council Recommendation of 22 December 1995* on 'Harmonizing means of combating illegal immigration and illegal employment and improving the relevant means of control'.

European institutions

The EC Treaty also established the five major institutions of the Community.

!	**The institutions of the EU**
	• Commission • Council of Ministers (or Council of the EU) • Parliament • European Court of Justice (ECJ) and Court of First Instance • Court of Auditors.

The Commission   The Commission is the most powerful of the EU's institutions and exists to administer the Community on a day-to-day basis. It is supposed to be independent of national governments. The Commission remains the most controversial institution of the EU, as its politicians are unelected, such as Peter Mandelson from the UK, Margot Wallström from Sweden, Günther Verheugen from Germany and Viviane Reding from France.

Its job is to represent and uphold the interests of the EU as a whole. It drafts proposals for new European laws, which it presents to the European Parliament and the Council. It is also the EU's executive – that is, it is responsible for implementing the decisions of Parliament and the Council, which means that it manages the day-to-day business of the European Union, implementing its policies, running its programmes and spending its funds.

Like the Parliament and Council, the European Commission was set up in the 1950s under the EU's founding treaties. The Commission attends all the sessions of Parliament, where it must clarify and justify its policies. It also replies regularly to written and oral questions posed by MEPs.

There is at present one commissioner from each EU country. If and when Bulgaria and Romania join the European Union, it will have 27 MS. At that point, the Council – by a unanimous decision – will fix the maximum number of commissioners. There must be fewer than 27 of them and their nationality will be determined by a system of rotation that is absolutely fair to all countries.

Currently, a new Commission is appointed every five years, within six months of the elections to the European Parliament. The present Commission's term of office runs until 31 October 2009. Its President is José Manuel Barroso, from Portugal.

The Commission and its main functions (Brussels or Luxembourg)

!

- To propose legislation to Parliament and the Council
- To manage and implement EU policies and the budget
- To enforce European law (jointly with the ECJ)
- To represent the EU in international matters, such as negotiating agreements between the EU and other countries.

The Council of Ministers   The Council is the EU's main decision-making body. Like the European Parliament, the Council was set up by the founding treaties in the 1950s. It represents the interests of the MS. Council meetings are attended by one minister from each of the national governments of the MS. It depends on the agenda and the subjects set, as to which minister attends. The Council also has wider responsibility for general policy issues, so its meetings are attended by whichever minister or state secretary each government chooses.

Each minister is empowered to commit his or her government to a decision – that is, the minister's signature is the signature of the whole government and each minister in the Council is answerable to his or her national Parliament and to the citizens that Parliament represents. This ensures the democratic legitimacy of the Council's decisions. Altogether there are nine different Council configurations, which are:

- General Affairs and External Relations
- Economic and Financial Affairs (ECOFIN)
- Justice and Home Affairs (JHA)
- Employment, Social Policy, Health and Consumer Affairs
- Competitiveness
- Transport, Telecommunications and Energy
- Agriculture and Fisheries
- Environment
- Education, Youth and Culture.

The Council sets the political agenda and the presidency rotates among the MS every six months. A summit is then held, when heads of state (governments) meet to decide on future policy and strategy and set the agenda for the next six months, such as the Copenhagen Summit, December 2002, with ten heads of MS. Britain held the EU presidency during the second half of 2005, with Tony Blair being the presiding head of state from 1 July–31 December 2005.

!	**The European council and its responsibilities (Brussels)**

- *legislative*: to pass European laws (jointly with the EP)
- *economic policy*: to coordinate main economic policies of MS
- *foreign policy and home affairs*: to conclude international agreements between the EU and other countries or international organisations
- *budgetary*: to approve the EU's budget (jointly with the EP)
- *security and common foreign policy*: to develop the EU's Common Foreign and Security Policy (CFSP) (guidelines for which are set by the Council of Europe)
- *justice and home affairs*: to coordinate cooperation between the national courts and police forces in criminal matters.

The European Parliament (EP)   The European Parliament has, perhaps confusingly, three places of work:

- Brussels in Belgium
- Luxembourg
- Strasburg in France.

Luxembourg is home to the administrative offices – the 'General Secretariat'. Meetings of the whole Parliament – known as 'plenary sessions' – take place in Brussels, although one week every month the Parliament sits in Strasburg. Committee meetings are also held in Brussels.

The EP is directly elected by the citizens of the European Union (EU) to represent their interests (more than 455 million people). Elections are held every five years and every EU citizen who is registered as a voter is entitled to vote. The fact that the EP is directly elected by the citizens helps to guarantee the democratic legitimacy of European law. The present EP, elected in June 2004, has 732 members from all 25 EU countries. Fewer than one third of them (222) are women.

| **The main functions of the European Parliament** **(Brussels, Luxembourg, Strasburg)** | **!** |

- *legislative*: passing European laws, jointly with the Council in many policy areas
- *supervisory*: EP has democratic supervision over other EU Institutions (esp. the Commission); has the power to approve/reject the nomination of Commissioners; has the right to censure the Commission as a whole
- *budgetary*: the power of the purse (shared with the Council) over the EU budget and can influence EU spending. Can adopt or reject a budget in its entirety.

Members of the European Parliament (MEPs) do not sit in national blocks, but in seven Europe-wide political groups. Between them, they represent all views on European integration, from the strongly pro-federalist to the openly Eurosceptic.

Political groups in the EP (as at 2 June 2005)

European People's Party (Christian Democrats) and European Democrats	EPP-ED	268
Socialist Group	PES	201
Alliance of Liberals and Democrats for Europe	ALDE	88
Greens/European Free Alliance	Greens/EFA	42
European United Left – Nordic Green Left	GUE/NGL	41
Independence/Democracy	IND/DEM	36
Union for Europe of the Nations	UEN	27
Non-attached	NI	29
Total		**732**

Number of seats per MS (as at 2 June 2005)

Belgium	24	Lithuania	13
Czech Republic	24	Luxembourg	6
Denmark	14	Hungary	24
Germany	99	Malta	5
Estonia	6	Netherlands	27
Greece	24	Austria	18
Spain	54	Poland	54
France	78	Portugal	24
Ireland	13	Slovenia	7
Italy	78	Slovakia	14
Cyprus	6	Finland	14
Latvia	9	Sweden	19
		United Kingdom	78
Total			**732**

Source: http://europa.eu.int/institutions/parliament/index_en.htm

The *Treaty of Rome 1957* gave the EP only a consultative role – more or less all the legislative power going to the Commission and the Council of Ministers. Subsequent treaties have extended the EP's influence to some extent, however, so it can now amend and adopt legislation so that the Parliament and Council share the power of decision-making in a large number of areas. So, for example, the EP approves the EU budget every year. The monitoring of expenditure is the responsibility of the Parliamentary Committee on Budgetary Control, which makes sure money is spent on what was agreed on and tries to prevent fraud. The EP exercises overall political supervision of the way the EU's policies are conducted.

The weakness of the EP – particularly in its lack of legislative decision-making – has attracted much criticism. This might be one of the reasons for the fact that few people vote in EU parliamentary elections and most cannot name their MEP. More crucial than this however, is that the Community and the EP still suffer from a democratic deficit – that is, the MEPs who are directly elected by the citizens of Europe actually do not have any real power in shaping the future of Europe or the European Constitution.

The European Court of Justice (ECJ) (also known as the Court of Justice of the European Communities) and Court of First Instance (CFI) The ECJ was established to ensure that in the 'interpretation and application of this Treaty the law is observed' (Art. 220 EC). The ECJ is not like the English court structure or legal hierarchy and has no appeal system, so the judgments of the ECJ are binding on all MS.

The ECJ – located in Luxembourg (with a few Advocates-General working in Strasburg) – can sit in plenary sessions, but, increasingly, due to the heavy workload, forms into chambers of three or five judges. Cases brought by an MS or Community institution must be heard in a plenary session.

The Court has 15 judges who represent the MS, all of whom are required to possess qualifications required for appointment to the highest judicial offices in their respective countries. They are appointed for a term of six years and can be reappointed.

They are assisted by six Advocates-General, who must be similarly qualified. What is important to remember is that the ECJ does *not* decide or rule on a particular case that is transferred either from a court of an MS or an individual of that MS. Judgments are given in the language of the case and are subsequently translated into all languages of the MS.

To ease the enormous caseload before it annually (there are extensive waiting times of up to five years), the ECJ was enhanced and supported from 1989 onwards by the Court of First Instance (CFI). The CFI's main duty is to sift cases and, whenever possible, return cases to national courts so that they make their own decisions.

The jurisdiction of the CFI is severely restricted, as it cannot hear cases of political or constitutional importance or any action brought by an MS or Community institution. The CFI cannot issue preliminary rulings. The CFI's caseload largely consists of the more complicated and technical disputes in relation to trade quotas, but it also handles all the employment matters that arise within the Commission itself.

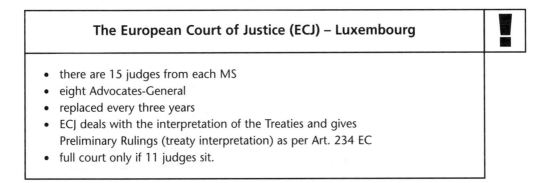

The European Court of Justice (ECJ) – Luxembourg

- there are 15 judges from each MS
- eight Advocates-General
- replaced every three years
- ECJ deals with the interpretation of the Treaties and gives Preliminary Rulings (treaty interpretation) as per Art. 234 EC
- full court only if 11 judges sit.

The Court of First Instance (CFI) – Luxembourg

- forms part of the ECJ
- consists of 15 judges
- members of CFI may be called upon to perform the task of an Advocate-General
- CFI chamber sits in a court of three to five judges; one single judge may sit in chambers
- decides on first proceedings and sifts applications from MS.

Since 2003, Advocates-General are required to give an opinion on a case only if the ECJ considers that this particular case raises a *new* point of law. Judgments of the ECJ are decided by a majority and pronounced at a public hearing. Unlike in English courts, dissenting opinions are *not* expressed. Decisions are published on the day of delivery (for example, in the House of Lords).

Judges of the ECJ

Office/Position	Address (in correspondence)	Dear...
Judge of the Court of Justice of the European Communities	The Honourable Mr Peter Doe Judge of the Court of Justice of the European Communities	Judge
Advocate-General to the Court of Justice of the European Communities	The Honourable Mr Peter Doe Advocate-General	Advocate-General
Member of the Court of First Instance of the European Communities	Peter Doe, Esq. Judge of the Court of First Instance of the European Communities	Judge

The Court of Auditors   The Court of Auditors was set up in 1975 and is based in Luxembourg. The Court's job is to check that EU funds (from MS taxpayers) are properly collected and spent legally and economically. Its aim is to ensure that the taxpayers get maximum value for their money and it has the right to audit any person or organisation handling EU funds.

The Court has one member from each MS, appointed by the Council for a renewable term of six years. The members elect one of their number as president for a renewable term of three years. Hubert Weber, from Austria, was elected President in January 2005. The Court's role has been enhanced since some scandalous 'misappropriations' by certain commissioners during the mid to late 1990s.

The Court of Auditors has no legal powers of its own. If the auditors discover fraud or irregularities, they inform the European Anti-fraud Office (OLAF). The Maastricht Treaty of 1992 created some new Community institutions – the Court of Auditors and the European Central Bank (ECB) in Frankfurt.

Reporting restrictions and exclusion of the public

Though you are now familiar with the 'open justice principle', there will be times in which a court will have to consider departing from the general 'open justice' principle. Common-law powers and statutory restrictions enable the court in certain circumstances to exclude the public (in camera). This does not necessarily mean that the media will be completely excluded. You might, on special application to the court (via the editor-in-chief), be able to attend, but may not necessarily report current court proceedings. You need to find out via the court's legal adviser (formerly 'the clerk to the justices') whether or not temporary or permanent reporting restrictions have been imposed in a particular case (such as a terrorism trial). There are occasions when statute automatically restricts reporting of court proceedings – most commonly in youth justice proceedings where strict reporting restrictions and anonymity orders apply to children under the age of 18 (s. 39 *Children and Young Persons Act 1933;* see also Chapter 5). Remember, this is not necessarily the case in Scotland where you can report on children over the age of 16 (see Chapter 8).

When you are reporting on a case in, say, a magistrates' court, the open justice principle applies to all adults (those over 18) – that is, everyone has the right to know who the defendant is, where he or she is from and what the charge is. You may report these details (name, address, charge) in full on an adult, unless he or she (through his or her lawyer) has applied for an anonymity order. The defendant may ask for his or her address to be withheld. It will be the magistrates who will grant such an anonymity order, though they rarely do this because it is felt that the public has the right to know.

Reporting restrictions – what can you report?

- name of the court
- name of the judge
- names, ages, home addresses and occupations of the defendant
- names of certain witnesses (check with legal adviser)
- offence(s) the defendant is charged with
- names of counsel and solicitors in proceedings
- date and place to which proceedings are adjourned
- bail arrangements
- whether or not legal aid has been granted (the *Access to Justice Act 1999* abolished the term 'legal aid' and replaced this with 'Community Legal Services'. However, 'legal aid' is still used colloquially in the court today.)

When can a defendant's particulars be withheld? Under common law, magistrates have the power to order that a name or other matter be withheld from the public and the press. This departs from the general rule of open justice. Lord Diplock stated in *AG v. Leveller Magazine Ltd*:

LIBRARY, UNIVERSITY OF GLAMORGAN

> Since the purpose of the general rule is to serve the ends of justice, it may be necessary to depart from it where the nature or circumstances of the particular proceeding are such that the application of the general rule in its entirety would frustrate or render impractical the administration of justice ... only to the extent and no more than the extent that the court reasonably believes it to be necessary in order to serve the ends of justice. (*AG v. Leveller Magazine Ltd* [1979] 1 All ER 745)

Magistrates also have statutory power to make directions prohibiting the publication of a name or other matter in connection with the proceedings. Sections 4 and 11 of the *Contempt of Court Act 1981* gives the court the power to prohibit the publication of a name or other matter in connection with the proceedings as appears necessary to the court for the purpose for which it was withheld. This means, there are circumstances in which the court of its own volition or on the application of one of the parties may seek a restriction of the matter that may be published under Sections 4 and 11. For instance, this can be a defendant's full address (in charges of paedophilia). However, the general rule is in favour of open justice, which means that all matters in open court must be fully and freely reported.

In the Judicial Review case of *R. v. Tower Bridge Magistrates' Court, ex parte Osborne* [1987], Mrs Osborne's solicitor sought an anonymity order from Tower Bridge Magistrates' Court. She was charged with theft and appeared for committal for trial. Her solicitor sought to ensure that her address was not published to avoid its disclosure to her husband, who had been severely harassing her.

In another Judicial Review case, *R. v. Evesham Justices, ex parte McDonagh and Another* [1988], the magistrates were not as sympathetic as in Mrs Osborne's case above. On 21 January, 1987, the defendant, Mr Philip Norman Hocking, a divorced sheep farmer and former Member of Parliament, appeared at Evesham Magistrates' Court and was convicted, fined and ordered to pay costs for using a Land-Rover without an MOT certificate. Mr Hocking asked, via his solicitor, for his address not to be revealed in open court as his ex-wife had sought revenge by damaging his car and throwing his possessions from the home window. While the magistrates had allowed Mr Hocking to provide details of his address on a piece of paper, rather than stating his current address in open court, the journalist for the *Evesham Journal* applied for a declaration from the High Court that she ought to be able to publish his full address. This was granted.

The ruling of the Divisional Court of the High Court in the *Evesham Justices* case might be helpful to you if you find yourself in a similar situation:

1   Cases where it is necessary for the identity or address of a defendant to be protected from publicity are rare.
2   Justices should not be motivated by sympathy, or simply protect the comfort and feelings of a defendant (see: s. 11 *Contempt of Court Act 1981*).

3   An anonymity order should only be made when the administration of justice would otherwise be frustrated or rendered impracticable.

Criminal courts also have the power to postpone the publication of reporting on court proceedings or any part of the proceedings (s. 4(1) *Contempt of Court Act 1981*) for the following reasons:

1   It must be necessary for avoiding a substantial risk of prejudice to the administration of justice in the proceedings, or in any other proceedings which are pending or imminent.
2   It must be for such period as the court thinks necessary for that purpose.

In a case from Northern Ireland, *R. v. Newtownabbey Magistrates' Court, ex parte Belfast Telegraph Newspapers Ltd* [1997], a possible attack on the defendant by ill-intentioned people was not regarded as a reason for making an order, as what had to be protected was 'the public interest in the administration of justice rather than the welfare of those who were parties to proceedings conducted in the course of that administration'. The defendant in this case was charged with indecent assault, but no details are given in the law report of what the fears for his safety actually were.

If any of the defendants in a criminal court object to their full (or partial) details being mentioned by the media, the court has to be satisfied that it is in the interests of justice to grant them a full or partial anonymity. Above all, the open justice principle must prevail, that anything said in court must be public and can be reported.

Reporting restrictions – if ordered – apply until the trial of *all* defendants in the case has concluded. However, the restrictions can be lifted in whole or in part provided that the court is satisfied, after hearing the representations of all the accused where any of them object, that it is in the interests of justice to do so (ss. 41 and 42 *Criminal Procedure and Investigations Act 1996*).

What can you report in serious fraud trials?	❗

- name of defendant
- name and address of a business, office or registered company
- relevant business information (that which the accused was involved in)
- defendant's own account
- name and address of any firm in which the defendant was a partner (other companies of which the defendant was a director or partner, for example).

When you are reporting in court, you can only report what was said in court (contemporaneous reporting). If you are unsure, a transcript of court proceedings can be obtained from the larger Crown Court offices. However, it takes time to get hold of these and your deadline may have passed by the time the transcript becomes available. If you do write a contemporaneous report of legal proceedings held in public, and you report in good faith fairly and accurately, you cannot be held guilty of contempt of court under the strict liability rule (s. 4(1) *Contempt of Court Act 1981;* see also Chapter 4). As a representative of the media, you should always be given the opportunity to make representations to assist the court considering making an order, as the press is best able to represent the public interest. If it is a notorious case and there is a lot of media representation in court, it is best to elect one person to represent the press.

It is common practice of the Press Association to keep on file any such orders for reference purposes. You can obtain the precise terms of such anonymity orders when you are preparing a court report article. This will usually include:

- name(s) or other matters that must be withheld as ordered by the court
- press should be given the opportunity to make representations
- a court order should state its precise scope, the time at which it will cease to be in effect and the specific purpose for making the order
- copies of the order should be kept, displayed and handed out to the press.

Reporting on sexual offences

Where a person has been charged with a sexual offence, he or she may apply to the court for certain reporting restrictions (such as the withholding of his or her full address). You need to take special care because the law gives automatic anonymity and reporting restrictions to victims of sexual attacks (*Sexual Offences (Amendment) Act 1992*; sch. 2 *Youth Justice and Criminal Evidence Act 1999*). Indeed, the *Sexual Offences (Amendment) Act 1992* imposes a lifetime ban on reporting the identity of the alleged victim once an allegation has been made that an offence has been committed. This protection continues after someone has been charged.

As such reporting restrictions are mandatory, no court order is required, even in the case of a child victim, and you as a journalist need to know this. The trial judge in such proceedings has the discretion to lift or relax any reporting restrictions in place if the court feels that such restriction or banning orders might impose unreasonable restriction on the freedom of the press – that is, it should always be in the public interest to report even the most heinous crimes. The (alleged) victim can even apply (in writing) to the court to have reporting restrictions lifted.

Sexual offences	**!**

Reporting restrictions apply to the following six categories of sexual offences:

- rape
- attempted rape
- aiding, abetting, counselling or procuring rape
- incitement to rape
- conspiracy to rape
- burglary with intent to rape.

Once an allegation of rape has been made, the victim's name, address, workplace, school or other educational establishment or picture must not be published in his or her lifetime if it is likely to identify him or her as a victim of the offence. The alleged rapist is not identified either, because this might lead people to suspect who the victim might be (jigsaw identification).

Civil and other courts

Inquests

An inquest is 'inquisitorial' in its procedures. Inquests are set up in order to examine unexplained deaths, such as death in custody, suicide or accidental death.

An inquest is usually chaired by a coroner who questions witnesses. He or she might choose for a jury to be present in this civil procedure. The jury may return a verdict of murder, manslaughter or infanticide (killing of an infant under 12 months by the mother).

The jury may be composed of at least 7 but no more than 11 people. Under the *Coroners Act 1988*, a jury must be summoned when there is reason to suspect that death occurred in circumstances the continuance or possible recurrence of which is prejudicial to the health or safety of the public.

A jury is not compulsory for a road accident inquest.

The office of coroner is one of the most ancient in English law. The coroners' courts, though regarded as inferior courts of record, have jurisdiction to punish contempt committed in their face (*R. v. West Yorkshire Coroner, ex parte Smith* [1982] 3 All ER 1098; see also *R. v. West Yorkshire Coroner, ex parte Smith* [No. 2] [1985] 1 All ER 100 DC).

A coroner must be a barrister, solicitor or doctor of at least five years' standing. They inquire into violent, unnatural or sudden deaths or those that take place in some forms of custody. If the death was due to natural causes (established during a post-mortem), a coroner may dispense with the inquest.

Due to its 'inquisitorial' nature, the inquest's process is for the coroner to choose and question each witness for the inquiry. He or she can allow or prevent questions being put by others. *The Coroners' Rules 1984* regulate the proceedings.

The *Coroners' Rules 1984* forbid a rider to the jury's verdict, which appears to determine liability in civil law or in criminal law. It has become the convention to report that a coroner's jury *returns* a verdict and that a coroner sitting without a jury *records* a verdict.

Fair, accurate and contemporaneous reports of inquest proceedings held in public are protected by absolute privilege – that is, there is a complete bar on any defamation action. Rule 17 of the *Coroners' Rules 1984* says that every inquest should be held in public, except when any inquest or part of an inquest may harm national security. The QBD's Divisional Court held in 1998 that an inquest remained public even when a member of a police armed response unit was allowed to give evidence behind a screen (*R. v. Newcastle upon Tyne Coroner, ex parte A.* QBD 19 December 1997 (Crown Office list, unreported), *The Times*, 19 January, 1998).

Rule 37 states that a coroner can take documentary rather than oral evidence from any witness where such evidence is unlikely to be disputed. This rule provides that the coroner must announce publicly at the inquest the name of the person giving documentary evidence and directly read aloud such evidence. However, there are exceptions, and a coroner who is so minded can lawfully prevent the press and public from learning the contents of some documentary evidence. It has been the custom of coroners, for instance, not to read out suicide notes and psychiatric reports.

When reporting inquests, it is the convention to report that a coroner is sitting with or without a jury and the type of verdict he or she has returned – accidental death, death by misadventure or suicide, for example. Fair, accurate and contemporaneous reporting is crucial following the event.

!	Inquests
	The purpose of an inquest is to establish: • who the deceased was • how, when and where he or she died • the particulars that need to be registered.

A jury at Leeds Crown Court in the Harold Shipman inquest, for instance, returned a verdict of suicide on 22 April 2005 after a ten-day hearing at Leeds Crown Court. Shipman was found hanged in his cell in Wakefield Prison on 13 January 2004, a day before his 58th birthday. He had been convicted in 2000 for murdering 15 patients, but is thought to have killed a further 235.

Tribunals

Tribunals are bodies other than the normal courts that are held when there is an adjudication or a dispute. There are about 78 different types of tribunals and they are becoming increasingly important as the ordinary courts do not have the specialist knowledge or expertise required as the law develops in different areas. Parliament now considers tribunals to be cheaper, quicker and less formal than court proceedings.

Currently, over 2000 tribunals deal with a wide variety of matters, including the National Health Service, transport, taxation and employment. The commonest types of tribunals today are:

- employment tribunals
- rent tribunals
- rent assessment committees
- valuation tribunals
- social security appeals tribunals (SSATs)
- medical appeal tribunals
- disability appeal tribunals
- attendance allowance boards
- pension appeal tribunals
- family health committees
- National Health Service tribunals
- mental health review tribunals
- General Medical Council
- solicitors' disciplinary tribunals
- Bar Council.

This is how tribunal chairmen should be addressed in writing or when presiding (orally):

Tribunal chairmen

Address (in correspondence)	Dear ...
Tribunal Chairman	Normal title in his or her private capacity

Employment tribunals (previously known as industrial tribunals) provide a large number of good stories relating to such matters as complaints of unfair dismissal, sexual or racial discrimination at work, exclusions from a trade union, disputes over contracts of employment, redundancy payments, matters of health and safety at work and claims of equal pay. These tribunals sit at 24 permanent centres in England in hired accommodation. About 50 tribunals sit each working day.

Local or public inquiries

Local inquiries are ordered by a minister and are comparable to administrative tribunals. Some Acts of Parliament provide that a public inquiry must be held and objections heard before a minister makes a decision affecting the rights of individuals or public authorities. Examples would be the compulsory redevelopment of land for council housing or the building of a new prison.

An inquiry is conducted by an inspector on behalf of the minister who ordered it. By the *Planning Inquiries (Attendance of the Public) Act 1982*, evidence at planning inquiries held under the *Town and Country Planning Act 1971* must be given in public. Proceedings are as informal as during a tribunal.

Court reporting and human rights

Arts 6 and 10 ECHR have extended the open justice principle and require all courts to comply with the rights to fair and public hearings, public pronouncement of judgments and the right to receive and impart information, subject to strictly limited exceptions. Art. 6 ECHR ('right to a fair trial') allows all courts to be open to the public. Though case law in the Strasburg European Court of Human Rights (ECHR) has mainly concerned civil cases, general principles applicable to criminal proceedings have also been discussed.

The courts have made it clear that they will usually uphold the journalist's right to 'freedom of expression' (Art. 10 ECHR). They would not normally grant anonymity to a defendant to spare his or her feelings or to help them avoid unnecessary publicity. Reported cases do not make it clear in what circumstances it is appropriate to make an anonymity order, as most cases have been concerned either with the circumstances in which it is inappropriate to make an order or, if an order is appropriate, courts have felt constrained from explaining why.

The general ECHR ruling is that everyone is entitled to a fair and public hearing within a reasonable time limit by an independent and impartial tribunal established by law. Judgments must be pronounced publicly, but the press and public may be excluded from all or part of the trial in the interest of morals, public order or national security in a democratic society, or where the interests of juveniles or the protection of the private lives of the parties so require, or to the extent strictly necessary in the opinion of the court in special circumstances where publicity would prejudice the interests of justice.

The ECHR has made it clear by case law that the guarantee of a fair trial (Art. 6) is one of the fundamental principles of any democratic society within the meaning of the Convention and proceedings being conducted in open contributes to this by:

- protecting the litigant against the administration of justice in secret with no public scrutiny
- being one of the means whereby confidence in the courts, superior and inferior, can be maintained
- rendering the administration of justice 'visible and transparent'.

Art. 6 was challenged in relation to court reporting of proceedings in *Diennet v. France* [1996] 21 EHRR 554. This case concerned a general medical practitioner who was the subject of disciplinary proceedings before the French Medical Association during the 1980s on the grounds that he was undertaking medical 'consultations by correspondence' with a view to making prescriptions for a slimming course. He was found guilty and disqualified from practising medicine for three years. He argued that the proceedings were a breach of Art. 6 as they were not held in public. The French government argued that the proceedings would include references to medically confidential material of patients of the applicant and, therefore, there was good reason to exclude the public from the disciplinary hearing. The ECHR held that this rule is not absolute and that there was no good reason to exclude the public in this case, stating that 'hearings are to be held in public is a fundamental rule of the Convention'.

Since the *Human Rights Act 1998* came into force in 2000, the media has been particularly concerned about accurate identification of those involved in court proceedings. Announcement in open court of names and addresses enables the precise identification vital to distinguish a defendant (in both criminal and civil proceedings) from someone in the locality who bears the same name, and so avoids inadvertent defamation.

Does reporting on and identification of peoples' particulars in court proceedings conflict with their human rights? Not really. The Judicial Studies Board in line with Department of Constitutional Affairs' guidelines has stated that under Art. 10 ECHR, the public has a right to know and there should be general freedom of expression as regards reporting on adult proceedings in the courts (particularly in criminal proceedings). If a defendant makes an anonymity application, the prosecutor in the case should consider making an application that – in the interests of justice – the case must be fully reported on within the guidelines of the 1981 Act. However, the prosecutor may seek to protect the identity of a (CPS) witness under s. 11 *Contempt of Court Act* (e.g. a blackmail vitim), or in order to protect a forthcoming prosecution involving the same defendant or prosecution witness, where it is considered that publicity of the first trial is likely to prejudice the proceedings which are pending. Such applications should remain the exception and the prosecution should not act in a way which may be construed as unduly interfering with the public's right to information. Any undue interference would be in breach of Art. 10 of the European Convention on Human Rights which guarantees the right to receive and impart information.

The 1981 Act defines a publication as any 'speech, writing, broadcast, cable programme or other communication in whatever form, which is addressed to the public at large or any section of the public'. However, to be held as causing a serious risk of substantial prejudice and possibly contravening any human rights, the publication in question must be judged in relation to mode of trial, date of trial, place of trial and the content of the publication itself.

As we have learnt, a trial is at its most vulnerable when conducted before a jury. Judges and court officials should be above any bias or media hype. In many recent test cases, the courts have assumed that people's memory fades over time, and so does prejudice. Physical proximity and location (of the newspaper or local news report) is important too; for example, material published in the *Hull Daily Mail* is unlikely to affect proceedings in Surrey. Any publication that demonstrates 'fair and accurate' reporting in the spirit of the 1981 Act, as long as reporting is contemporaneous with all legal proceedings, will not be held in contempt under s. 4 CCA. However, any (background) reporting that comments on the defendant's earlier character or criminal record (e.g. that he had escaped from prison) will be held in contempt and will also contravene his right to privacy under Art. 8 ECHR.

As you have learnt, magistrates' courts have the option to exclude the public, but not bona fide representatives of newspapers, broadcasters and news agencies during the testimony of witnesses aged under 18 in any proceedings relating to an offence against, or conduct contrary to, decency and morality (s. 39 *Children and Young Persons Act 1933*). If a magistrates' court does have the power to sit in camera (such as for a youth court or family proceedings), it can employ less restrictive derogations from open justice that will still protect the administration of justice.

Bear in mind that s. 47 of the *Children and Young Persons Act 1933* permits the press – but not the public – to attend youth court proceedings. Remember, that everyone is presumed innocent until proven guilty, so your reporting must be fair and impartial at all times and must not interfere with the course of justice in any way, as this would be 'prejudicial'.

It is at the discretion of the court to admit the public or not, and it has been encouraged to use its powers to admit the public by the Home Office and the Department of Constitutional Affairs (DCA). However, each court also has the discretion to *exclude* the public, but not, in all circumstances, bona fide representatives of newspapers, broadcasters and news agencies.

QUESTIONS

1 Explain the term 'common law' and cite some examples drawn from criminal and civil law.

2 Explain how an Act of Parliament comes into existence.

3 What is meant by 'delegated legislation' (also known as 'secondary legislation' or 'statutory instrument')? Give examples of different types and explain them. What are the advantages and disadvantages of using delegated legislation?

4 What is the procedure when a defendant pleads not guilty at a magistrates' court?

5 What are the principal functions of a County court?

6 What were the main objectives of the EC Treaty (*Treaty of Rome 1957*)?

7 What are the principal institutions of the EU?

8 Explain the differences between a Regulation, a Directive and a Decision.

9 Explain how the European Union has changed since the EC Treaty.

FURTHER READING

Deards, E., and Hargreaves, S. (2004) *European Union Law*. Oxford: OUP.

Elliott, C., and Quinn, F. (2005) *English Legal System*, 6th edn. London: Longman/ Pearson.

Slapper, G., and Kelly, D. (2004) *The English Legal System*, 7th edn. London: Cavendish.

Weatherill, S. (2004) *EU Law: Cases and materials*, 6th edn. Oxford: OUP.

Notes

1 On 11 June 2003, Prime Minister Tony Blair announced a ministerial reshuffle; and, further, that the post of Lord Chancellor (the Lord Irvine of Lairg) was to be abolished and that a new Department of Constitutional Affairs (DCA) under Lord Falconer was to replace the present Lord Chancellor's Department (LCD). The DCA was to incorporate the Wales and Scotland Offices. This announcement came completely unexpectedly. See 'Constitutional Reform: Reforming the Office of the Lord Chancellor', House of Commons Standard Note SN/PC/2105; also ref. SN/CP 13/03. Since then, parliamentary debates have been ongoing as to whether or not a US-style top-level 'Supreme Court' should replace the House of Lords, a proposed voiced by Lords Donaldson, Bingham, Steyn and Phillips (see 'Proposals for a Supreme Court for the United Kingdom' SN/HA/2701).

2 The *Treaty of Amsterdam 1997* (TOA) renumbered all the treaties' articles. Citations and quotations in this book use the new article numbering system, except in references to pre-1997 case law, which use the old numbering system.

CHAPTER TWO

PRIVACY AND HUMAN RIGHTS

Key aim of this chapter:

> To help you understand the main principles of human rights legislation and their relevance within a professional context.

Learning objectives

By the time you reach the end of this chapter and have completed the reading and a period of reflection, you should be able to:

- understand the meaning of 'privacy' and 'confidentiality' in English law
- demonstrate a sound knowledge and appreciation of the principles of human rights, as enshrined in the European Convention (the 'Convention')
- link the Convention to the *Human Rights Act 1998*
- understand the significance of the European Court of Human Rights in relation to UK courts
- recognise the most important human rights articles (ECHR) and place these in a journalistic context
- link human rights issues to case law and problem-solving exercises
- recognise the practical implications and journalistic dilemmas in privacy issues
- understand the limitations of the public interest test
- apply the *Freedom of Information Act 2000* in practical situations.

Chapter contents

Introduction

Privacy and human rights are now fundamental to journalistic practice. Though an individual's right to privacy has long been enshrined in various other legal systems, it is important to note that, in English law, there is, as yet, no such right.

In France – famed for its strict privacy laws – the tort of privacy was first recognised as far back as 1858 ('Declaration of the Rights of Man')[1] and was added to the Civil Code in 1970.[2] The United States has the 'Bill of Rights' and the 'liberty' clause of the 14th amendment, granting individuals anonymity rights in terms of 'intimacy' and 'solitude'.[3] Art. 10 of the German constitution enshrines privacy in the words, 'letters, post, and telecommunications shall be inviolable' and, in 1983, the Federal Constitutional Court, in a case against a government census law, formally acknowledged an individual's 'right of informational self-determination', which is limited by the 'predominant public interest'.[4] This landmark court decision derived the 'right of informational self-determination' directly from Art. 2 of the German constitution, which declares protective personal rights (*Persönlichkeitsrechte*). Furthermore, the world's first data protection law was passed in the German Land of Hessen in 1970.[5] Sweden's constitution provides for the protection of an individual's right to privacy and so does s. 2 of the *Instrument of Government Act 1974*.[6] At the same time, freedom of the press is protected by the *Freedom of the Press Act 1949*.[7]

In the UK, however, those in a 'public situation', such as walking in the street, have no specific rights to privacy. In recent years, however, several court cases have been won by private individuals who saw their faces splashed across newspaper front pages. For this reason, some cautious editors have even begun to blur the features of those in crowd scenes. In July 2002, newsreader Anna Ford was angered when first the Press Complaints Commission (PCC) and then the High

Court refused to agree that paparazzo pictures taken of her on holiday breached her privacy. Ford and her then boyfriend were snapped rubbing suntan lotion on each other on a beach. No matter how secluded, it was ruled that a publicly accessible beach in Majorca in August was not a place where she could reasonably have expected privacy.

Showing an individual in a false light is largely remedied in English law by the tort of defamation and, therein, 'malicious falsehood' (see Chapter 6). Most remedies, however, rest in the common (case) law tradition – and under the *Defamation Act 1996* in the form of 'making of amends' – that is, damages and apologies. Scotland, with its separate legal system (see Chapter 8), has a general right to privacy by virtue of the principle of *actio injuriarum*, providing a remedy for 'injuries to honour'.[8]

British privacy law has advanced with Art. 8 ECHR. For instance, J. K. Rowling obtained a successful injunction to protect the confidentiality of her then latest book, *Harry Potter and the Half-blood Prince*, in June 2005. It was to be published on 16 July 2005, but attempts were made by two men to sell stolen copies of the book to journalists prior to that date. David Hooper, a media lawyer at Reynolds Porter Chamberlain, obtained a wide ranging 'John Doe' injunction, inter alia, invoking Art. 8 ECHR.[9]

A 'John Doe' injunction is shorthand for the fact that such a court order binds the world at large – namely, any unnamed and presently unknown people who wrongfully come into possession of original material, such as the new Harry Potter book, and seek to disclose its contents to the public at large. Any disclosure of the original work's contents before 16 July 2005 in the case of the new Harry Potter book would have been unlawful. The 'John Doe' order meant that those who set out to destroy the reading public's legitimate sense of anticipation, privacy and excitement (usually for money) were likely to have been in contempt of court.

Why the British media appears to be so obsessed with the personal lives of others – particularly celebrities – is an important cultural discussion. Journalists ought to bear in mind that, to date, the right to privacy in public places is not absolute. This was demonstrated amply when Prince Harry tried to (over) exercise his right to privacy when on holiday with his friend Chelsy Davy in December 2004. Like Anna Ford in her case mentioned above, the royal Prince was sunning himself with his girlfriend on a public beach. Prince Harry, irritated by the presence of the media and paparazzi, particularly in the shape of a *News of the World* reporter and photographer, contacted the local Mozambique authorities, demanding that the photographer be removed not only from the beach but also from the island. The photographer was escorted off the island by armed military personnel. In London, Clarence House Press Office contacted the PCC with regards to violation of Clause 3 of the PCC Code of Practice. Eventually, no formal complaint was made and you can conclude that not even a prince's right to privacy is automatically guaranteed when in a public place.

In this chapter, you will find a number of cases where judicial decisions have been made regarding an individual's right to privacy when featured in the media. It is worth noting that the courts often make reference to the PCC's Code of Practice (for example Clause 3 'Privacy'), such as in Michael Douglas's or Naomi Campbell's cases. However, why should judges have the power to make 'editorial' decisions by restricting freedom of expression (Art. 10 ECHR) in the name of privacy (Art. 8 ECHR)? In a series of high-profile cases, judges seem to have developed a right to privacy in relation to free speech, particularly trying to restrain the media.

In *Gary Flitcroft v. The People* [2003], despite the above trend, the paper won the case. Here, the learned justices took the opportunity to advance and comment on the law of privacy and the protection of confidence. Lord Chief Justice Woolf stated:

> Where the protection of privacy is justified … an action for breach of confidence will now, where this is appropriate, provide the necessary protection.

In this chapter, we look at some important judgments in this respect – the most important ruling being that of the HL in Naomi Campbell's case in 2004 regarding individuals who are undergoing (in her case, drug) treatment.[10] Whatever sympathies journalists may have for public figures whose private lives are made the subject of national gossip, speculation and news stories in the media, many argue that allowing judges to decide what can be published erodes everyone's right to free speech. It is for you to study this chapter carefully in the light of this debate.

Apart from the right to privacy and the influence of the *Human Rights Act 1998* on journalistic practice, this chapter also introduces you to the importance of the *Freedom of Information Act 2000* (FOI), which came into force in 2005. We examine whether or not the FOI has made a difference to journalistic freedom to investigate public authorities and governmental practices, such as the government's decision to wage war on Iraq in March 2003.

So, can journalists now see *all* of the prime minister's correspondence? Has the FOI changed the way journalists can now access all information in order to support their stories? After all, freedom of information legislation helped the *Washington Post* report fully on US Defence Secretary Donald Rumsfeld's relationship with Saddam Hussein in the 1980s. It led to the *Irish Times* revealing the spiralling costs of a proposed new national stadium in Ireland, resulting in the plan being abandoned. It also enabled a Swedish newspaper to expose how top army officers were regularly breaking the rules for using official vehicles for private journeys.

There will be times when the FOI may lead you to scoops; other times it may only lead you to more background information for a particular investigative piece. If British journalists had had a freedom of information statute earlier, who knows how much better informed they would have been about topics such as the outbreak of foot and mouth disease, Gulf War syndrome, the hospital 'superbug' MRSA or even visas for Filipino nannies? Perhaps we will find out in due course, if journalists decide to revisit some of these stories that they had found difficult to obtain information about at the time.

Privacy and confidentiality

Although there is no fully developed or coherent substantive law protecting personal privacy in Britain, some veil of secrecy may be drawn over domestic intimacy by the doctrine of breach of confidence, such as the Duke of Argyll's account of his stormy marriage with the Duchess in *Argyll v. Argyll and Others* [1967].[11] In the case, the court held that the publication of confidential information relating to letters about the claimant's private life and personal affairs could be restrained on the ground that communications between husband and wife were capable of being confidential information, the disclosure of which by one party to the marriage could be restrained by an injunction. The *Argyll v. Argyll* decision was applied to cover correspondence relating to the Prince of Wales, Prince Charles, and his bride-to-be, Lady Diana Spencer. The Prince obtained an ex parte injunction against the publication of tape recordings purported to be of conversations with 'Lady Di'.

The decision in the Prince Albert case (*Albert v. Strange* [1849][12]) is still regarded as the decisive authority on breach of confidence. The case concerned an action to restrain the unauthorised publication of etchings drawn by Queen Victoria and Prince Albert and of a catalogue of their work. The defendant, a workman at the printing shop, had obtained the etchings from the printers, to whom they had been given in confidence for the purpose of a private publication at Windsor Castle. Knight Bruce V.C. (Vice-Chancellor) stated:

> Addressing the attention specifically to the particular instance before the Court, we cannot but see that the etchings executed by the plaintiff and his Consort for their private use, the produce of their labour, and belonging to themselves, they were entitled to retain in a state of privacy to withhold from publication ... I think, therefore, not only that the defendant here is unlawfully invading the plaintiff's right, but also that the invasion is of such a kind and affects such property as to entitle the plaintiff to the preventive remedy of an injunction.

The court injuncted both the catalogue and the exhibition.

Today, the media are generally thought to be justified in publishing information in breach of confidence if the public interest in doing so outweighs the public interest in preserving the confidence. This defence originates from the narrow rule that the courts applied in *Gartside v. Outram* [1856].[13] This was applied by Mr Justice Scott in *Cork v. McVicar* [1984] *Times*, 31 October (unreported) where John [the Hat] McVicar had agreed to write a book with Cork, a former policeman, about corruption in the Metropolitan Police Force. Cork never approved the manuscript, but the *Daily Express* published his allegations of corruption. Mr Justice Scott agreed that the publication could not be restrained because the matter (of police corruption) had to be properly in the public interest.[14]

The concept of privacy is not limited to isolated individuals, also includes the general 'zone' of the family. This in turn includes the home, correspondence with others (such as letters), telephone conversations and a person's well-being. In the absence of a right to privacy in English law (in the form of a statutory or constitutional principle), there is a general concern as to limited availability of legal remedies in English law for the invasion of someone's privacy. In *Malone v United Kingdom* [1984],[15] the ECHR held that the United Kingdom had breached Art. 8 ECHR regarding the interception of telephone communication and the release of metering records (information about telephone numbers dialled and the duration of conversations, but not the contents) to the police. The breach was because the interference with the right to privacy had not been authorised by law, though the court did not inquire further into whether or not the interference was justified. In the earlier case of 1979,[16] Megarry V.C. held that the conversation could not be said to be confidential information:

> It seems to me that a person who utters confidential information must accept the risk of any unknown overhearing, that is inherent in the circumstances of communication ... when this is applied to telephone conversation, it appears to me that the speaker is taking such risks of being overheard as are inherent in the system.

There are numerous examples of invasion of privacy in the British press, often the most private and embarrassing facts of famous TV, film or football stars being revealed. The British press loves to delve into the private lives of politicians, too. Such was the case in 1992 when a Scottish paper revealed that Mr Paddy Ashdown, then Leader of the Liberal Party, had had an extramarital affair some years earlier. The information had been stolen from the office of the politician's solicitor. Though an interdict (a Scottish injunction) was sought to stop the Scottish press from revealing Mr Ashdown's secrets, this was not successful.

It can be said that English ('interlocutory' or interim) injunctions tend, at least initially, be more successful than Scottish ones. In 1993, the then Conservative Secretary of State for the National Heritage Department, David Mellor, became the centre of the media's focus when it was revealed that he was having an extramarital affair with the actress Antonia de Sancha. The press had obtained the information by recording the minister's telephone conversations. Interestingly, this was not held to be a contravention of the *Interception and Communications Act 1985*, as the recording was made on a different telephone extension from the subscriber's telephone. The 1985 Act had, in fact, been written as a result of the *Malone* judgment, s. 1 of the Act establishing a statutory offence for the interception of communication.[17]

The issue of what can be in the 'public domain' was further discussed in the 1997 Barrymore case. Famous TV show host Michael Barrymore was granted an injunction to prevent the *Sun* from publishing articles based on an interview with Barrymore's former lover.[18] In the court, Jacob J considered the disclosures to the media by one partner in a homosexual relationship of details of that relationship to be in breach of confidence. Jacob J. (Chief Justice) said:

> When people kiss and later one of them tells, the second person is almost certainly breaking a confidential relationship, although this might not be the case if they merely indicate that there had been a relationship and do not go into detail. In this case the article went into detail about the relationship and crossed the line into arguable breach of confidence.

Based on the Argyll judgment on 'domestic intimacy', this principle was extended to cohabiting couples in Barrymore's case. This represented an important milestone in the development of the law of breach of confidence, which now includes the protection of 'partners' (as opposed to only married couples). It gave Michael Barrymore a protection in law. The story could therefore be injuncted – that is, his former lover could be restrained from selling his 'kiss and tell' story to the press.

One area, that has always been protected, concerning which the High Court may order an injunction against publication, is the disclosure of confidential information and 'official secrets'. An injunction is an equitable remedy in civil law and, until the Spycatcher case in the 1980s, an injunction was primarily used to restrain publication of confidential material by the media relating to political interest and information. During the 1986–88 Spycatcher actions, the AG sought injunctions against the *Guardian*, the *Observer* and the *Sunday Times* newspapers in order to prohibit the publication of extracts from Peter Wright's book, *Spycatcher*, on the grounds of safeguarding public security and the fact that Wright had signed the *Official Secrets Act 1911*.[19]

Wright had formerly been a senior officer of MI5, Britain's internal security service. At the time of the case, he had retired to Australia and was about to publish his memoirs with publishers in New South Wales. The AG's injunction was so worded that it would prevent *any* publication – including in Australia – in spite of the fact that the book had already been on sale in the USA, with individual copies being available that could be imported from there into the UK. Their Lordships' initial granting of the injunction in the Spycatcher case caused a furore. Lord Scarman (a former Lord of Appeal in Ordinary) wrote of his disappointment that the HL had placed emphasis on private rights and obligations at the expense of

> the more fundamental law providing the right of the public to access to information already in the public domain and the public right of free speech, of which the freedom of the press is an important constituent. *The Times*, 3 August 1987

Further letters to the newspapers accused the law lords of 'dangerous judicial arrogance'. Some clearly saw the Spycatcher case as the government's attempt (via the AG) to 'gag' or muzzle the press.

Subsequent actions in the Spycatcher case (*AG v. Guardian Newspapers Ltd* (No. 2) [1990][20] saw another attempt by the AG to prevent publication of the book and serialisation in the newspapers of secret service information acquired by Peter Wright. Issues around privacy and government confidentiality arose during heated debates in both the houses of Parliament during the final interlocutory stages, when Lord Goff of Chieveley so eloquently said:

> In the vast majority of cases, in particular those concerned with trade secrets, the duty of confidence will arise from a transaction or relationship between the parties – often a contract, in which event the duty may arise by reason of either an express or an implied term of that contract. It is in such cases as these that the expression 'confider' and 'confidant' are perhaps most aptly employed.

Eventually, the injunction was lifted, the HL giving reasons that included the fact that the book was already in the public domain because it had been published in other countries (Australia) and reference to the earlier Crossman diaries case, saying that such information can not be injuncted forever.[21]

In an important decision by the ECHR in 1991,[22] it decided that, although the granting of the original Spycatcher interlocutory injunctions against The *Guardian* (and other British newspapers) before the date of publication of the book in the USA in July 1987 was justified, the continuation of those injunctions by the HL beyond that date was not 'necessary in a democratic society' and, accordingly, constituted a violation of Art. 10 ECHR ('freedom of expression').

On 19 November 2005, Clarence House announced that Prince Charles was suing the *Mail on Sunday* for printing extracts from his diary which he had written on a recent visit to China. The action, should it come to court, is for infringement of the Prince's copyright and breach of confidentiality. The editor of the

Mail on Sunday was faced with the dilemma when the 'brown envelope' landed on his desk containing photocopies of the diary, whether to print this piece of dynamite or not. In the diary extracts, the Prince had made derogatory remarks about the Chinese Communist leadership during the British handover of Hong Kong. He described the Chinese leaders as 'appalling old waxworks'; he had also railed against Tony Blair and his coterie of advisers.

Could the piece that ensued be protected by the doctrine of duty of confidentiality owed by a servant to his employer or by copyright? Copyright only protects against reproduction of a substantial proportion of the original document; it does not extend to disclosure of the information contained in it (see Chapter 7). In any case, there would be statutory defences available to the editor and journalist that deal with 'fair dealing' for the reporting of current or news events. The courts might regard the Prince's diaries as 'private' and no doubt the person or servant who passed the information on to the *Mail* will have done so for a financial inducement. There might even be an offence under the *Prevention of Corruption Act 1906*. But does the information carry the necessary quality of confidentiality as recognised by the courts? Or should the information be of public interest? A spokesman for the Prince stated that there were no plans to take similar action against other newspapers, including the *Guardian*, which reprinted the diary extracts.

The Human Rights Act 1998 and the European Convention

Arguably, there is still no right to privacy in English law, though, with the Naomi Campbell ruling by the HL in 2004, privacy has advanced in common law. Even so, it has to be said that, until fairly recently, English law did not recognise a common law right to privacy at all. This changed with the incorporation of the European Convention into UK law by means of the *Human Rights Act 1998* (HRA). The first test case was that of *Douglas v. Hello!* in 2001.[23]

Until the coming into force of the HRA in October 2000, press freedom prevailed over the individual's right to privacy and the media were often at liberty to reveal 'all' about, say, a famous footballer's private affairs or a politician's 'cash for questions'. With the incorporation of the *European Convention on Human Rights and Fundamental Freedoms 1950* ('the Convention') into UK law on 2 October 2000 by means of the *Human Rights Act 1998*, however, fundamental human rights were incorporated into UK domestic legislation. In the course of your career in journalism, you must be aware of the HRA and its significant impact on all walks of life, particularly regarding Art. 8 ECHR ('right to privacy') and Art. 10 ECHR ('freedom of expression').

The contents of the 1998 Act are based on the European Convention, which was signed by all Council of Europe member states, including, Britain, on 4 November 1950 in Rome and came into force on 3 September 1953. The scope of the Convention was extended by the First Protocol and has formed an addendum since 1952.[24] The primary objective of the Convention was to avoid the sorts of atrocities and abuses of human rights witnessed in Europe during World War II. Though some of the European Council members were British and the Convention was, to a large extent, drafted by British lawyers, the Convention was never incorporated into UK domestic legislation.[25] Most Council of Europe MS incorporated the Convention by adopting the 'monist' approach – that is, any international treaty becomes effective in national law on ratification without any further legislation. However, the 'dualist' approach – used in the UK, the Commonwealth and Scandinavian countries – sees national law and international law as separate areas, So, for an international treaty such as the Convention to become effective in domestic law, a national statute to that effect has to be adopted. It was only in 1998 that the British government ('New' Labour had won the General Election in 1997) incorporated the Convention into UK law by means of the Human Rights Bill 1997. This then became the *Human Rights Act 1998*.

Why did it take so long for the UK to adopt the Convention, with its catalogue of basic human rights, into its domestic legislation? It is generally felt that politicians' deep-rooted mistrust of the judiciary and the fact that incorporation of the Convention would mean 'letting Europe in by the back door' had held several governments back since the 1960s. Ardent anti-Europeans at the time feared that the ECHR in Strasburg would be too liberal, too woolly and too ill-defined, and so undermine UK legislation. This argument was partly advanced by UK judges, who felt that they would in future be unable to build up a body of case law on the Convention, which was so fundamental to the British legal system and its constitutional tradition. It was McGarry VC's view in *Malone v. Metropolitan Police Commissioner* [1974] that English courts should not be deterred from developing 'new rights'. He stated that this was already possible by making 'analogies with the existing rules, together with the requirements of justice and common sense'.[26] Britain being one of the few countries without a written constitution, there was the argument that the *Bill of Rights 1688* was sufficient.

By 1997, some 40 MS of the Council of Europe had incorporated the Convention into their domestic legislation, but not Britain and Ireland. This meant that UK and Irish individuals could not invoke the Convention before their national courts or tribunals, so individuals had to resolve legislative ambiguity in relation to human rights issues in line with the Convention via petitions to the Strasburg court.[27] Due to campaigns by a number of pressure groups in 1996–97 (such as 'Charter 88'), Jack Straw MP, the then Shadow Home Secretary, and Paul Boateng MP, then Shadow Minister for the Lord Chancellor's

Department, urged incorporation of the Convention into UK law to give greater protection to liberty:

> For over 50 years British people have been subjected to the European Convention of Human Rights – a convention signed, ratified and supported by successive United Kingdom governments, including the present Conservative administration. Yet, because the Convention has never been incorporated into UK law British people are not able to have those rights protected by British courts ... We aim to change the relationship between the state and citizen, and to redress the dilution of individual rights by an over-centralising government that has taken place over the past two decades ... the new Act will improve awareness of human rights issues throughout our society.[28]

After Labour won the General Election in 1997, the government's White Paper, 'Rights brought home: the Human Rights Bill', was presented to Parliament in October of that year, incorporating the best part of the Convention into UK law. The then Lord Chancellor, Lord Irvine of Lairg, stressed that the legal and political significance of the incorporation of the Convention and the implementation of the *Human Rights Act 1998* should not be underestimated as this represented a 'shift to a rights-based system of positive entitlements, away from the traditional view of liberty as the "negative right" to do whatever is not prohibited'.[29] Now firmly part of UK law, the Convention guarantees and reinforces fundamental human rights of individuals.

Just an aside at this point. The ECHR was set up in Strasburg by the Council of Europe MS in 1959 to deal with alleged violations of the 1950 Convention. Since 1 November 1998, it has sat as a full-time court, composed of a number of judges equal to that of the MS that are party to the Convention. The ECHR examines the admissibility and merits of applications submitted to it. It sits in chambers of 7 judges or, in exceptional cases, as a Grand Chamber of 17 judges. In 2004, the ECHR completed 21,100 cases, delivering 20,348 decisions and 739 judgments.[30]

Since the Convention's incorporation into UK legislation, the British judiciary has been expected to be bold in applying the Convention strictly as new case law has continued to be gathered. Such an approach has received the support of the HL. In the words of Lord Hope in the judicial review case of *R. v. Director of Public Prosecutions, ex parte (1) Sofiane Kebeline (2) Ferine Boukemiche (3) Sofiane Souidi* [1999]:

> In this area difficult choices may have to be made by the executive or the legislature between the rights of the individual and the needs of society. In some circumstances it will be appropriate for the courts to recognise that there is an

area of judgment within which the judiciary will defer, on democratic grounds, to the considered opinion of the elected body or person whose act or decision is said to be incompatible with the Convention.[31]

The HRA 1998 marks a significant change in British constitutional life and requires the courts to not only protect the Convention rights but also make 'declarations of incompatibility' wherever domestic law (such as an Act of Parliament) is judicially seen to conflict with European Convention rights. Some of the Convention rights are only 'substantive', which means that they are not necessarily 'absolute' in English law, and, in certain situations, British courts may derogate from the Convention under Art. 15 ECHR. Such a derogation may be needed in 'times of emergency', such as war situations.[32]

!

Substantive rights and freedoms of the Convention

- Art. 1: Obligation to respect human rights
- Art. 2: Guarantees the 'right to life'
- Art. 3: 'Prohibition of torture and inhuman or degrading treatment or punishment'
- Art. 4: 'Prohibition of slavery and forced labour'
- Art. 5: 'Right to liberty and security'
- Art. 6: 'Right to a fair trial'
- Art. 7: 'No punishment without law' – that is, prohibition as a result of retrospective penal legislation
- Art. 8: 'Right to respect for private and family life' – right to privacy
- Art. 9: 'Freedom of thought, conscience and religion'
- Art. 10: 'Freedom of expression'
- Art. 11: 'Freedom of assembly and association' – such as the right to join a trade union
- Art. 12: 'Right to marry' – this provides that men and women of marriageable age have the right to marry and to found a family according to national laws
- Art. 14: 'Prohibition of discrimination'.

Section 12 HRA provides that special regard is to be given to the right of 'freedom of expression' wherever the issue arises in relation to the public interest test in disclosure of material that has journalistic, literary or artistic merit[33] (see *Imutran v. Uncaged Campaigns Ltd*, etc. [2001]).[34]

Art. 8 ECHR: Protection of privacy and family life

Art. 8 of the Convention is one of the most open-ended regarding substantive rights, covering a growing number of issues and extending to protect a range of interests that do not fit into other Convention categories. This is partly because neither the Commission nor the ECHR attempted any comprehensive definition of Art. 8 interests, adapting them to meet changing times. Here is the full text:

Art. 8 ECHR

(1) Everyone has the right to respect for his private and family life, his home and his correspondence.

(2) There shall be no interference by a public authority with the exercise of this right, except such as is in accordance with the law and is necessary in a democratic society in the interests of national security, public safety or the economic well-being of the country, for the prevention of disorder or crime, for the protection of health or morals, or for the protection of the rights and freedoms of others.

Art. 8 ECHR contains both 'negative' and 'positive' obligations. This means that the state is under a negative obligation – to not interfere with privacy rights – but ECHR case law has extended Art. 8 to impose a positive duty to take measures to prevent private parties from interfering with these rights.[35]

Which interests are protected under Art. 8?

- private life
- home
- family
- correspondence.

It can be said that most British cases to date have been brought under Art. 8 (1) ECHR, 'right to respect for private life', including incidental claims to respect for home, family or correspondence. The best-known cases involved the famous film stars Michael Douglas and Catherine Zeta-Jones versus *Hello!* magazine [2001 HL] and supermodel Naomi Campbell's case against the *Mirror* Group [2004 HL]. Please be aware that the HL's ruling in Campbell's case is not straightforward and sits awkwardly alongside Art. 10 ECHR, challenging the right to freedom of expression – that is, press freedom.

In *Campbell v. MGN Ltd* [2004],[36] supermodel Naomi Campbell won a privacy action in the HL against the *Mirror* newspaper, which had made public her battle against drug addiction. In the earlier action in the CA, Justice Sir Michael Morland ruled that Ms Campbell's damages were awarded merely for breach of confidentiality and of the Data Protection Act, but the HL granted Campbell the full right to privacy. As Lord Carswell said (p. 165):

> It seems to me that the publication of the details of the appellant's [Ms Campbell's] course of treatment at NA [Narcotics Anonymous] and of the photographs taken surreptitiously in the street of her emerging from a meeting went significantly beyond the publication of the fact that she was receiving therapy or that she was engaged in a course of therapy with NA. It revealed where the treatment was taking place and the text went into the frequency of her treatment. In this way it intruded into what had some of the characteristics of medical treatment and it tended to deter her from continuing the treatment which was in her interest and also to inhibit other persons attending the course from staying with it, when they might be concerned that their participation might become public knowledge.
>
> This in my view went beyond disclosure which was, in the words of the Court of Appeal, 'peripheral to' the publication of the information that the appellant was a drug addict who was receiving treatment and was capable of constituting breach of confidence. One cannot disregard the fact that photographs are a powerful prop to a written article and a much valued part of newspaper reporting, especially in the tabloid or popular press (hence the enthusiasm of paparazzi to obtain pictures of celebrities for publication in the newspapers). I think that the Court of Appeal dismissed them too readily as adding little to the reports already published and that they were not justified in rejecting the judge's conclusions on this.

Examined more closely, this case is far from trivial. As Baroness Hale of Richmond said in *Campbell v. MGN Ltd* (p. 144):

> What is the nature of the private life, respect for which is in issue here? The information revealed by the article was information relating to Miss Campbell's health, both physical and mental. Drug abuse can be seriously damaging to physical health; indeed it is sometimes life-threatening.

So, just how private can our personal lives be now since the Campbell case ruling? You need to see the Campbell ruling as setting a precedent regarding the right to privacy of an individual (under Art. 8) who is undergoing treatment.

Art. 10 ECHR: Freedom of expression

What is the journalist to make, then, of the conflict between Art. 8 and 10 ECHR? In order to understand and argue your case for 'freedom of expression' more fully, you need to learn a little more about Art. 10. It provides that:

Art. 10 ECHR

(1) everyone has the right to freedom of expression. This right shall include freedom to hold opinions and to receive and impart information and ideas without interference by public authority and regardless of frontiers. This Article shall not prevent States from requiring the licensing of broadcasting, television or cinema enterprises.

(2) The exercise of these freedoms, since it carries with it duties and responsibilities, may be subject to such formalities, conditions, restrictions or penalties as are prescribed by law and are necessary in a democratic society, in the interests of national security, territorial integrity or public safety, for the prevention of disorder or crime, for the protection of health or morals, for the protection of the reputation or rights of others, for preventing the disclosure of information received in confidence, or for maintaining the authority and impartiality of the judiciary.

Although Art. 10 guarantees the right to 'receive information', it does not require the State to provide access to information that is not already available (*Leander v. Sweden* [1987]).[37] This has changed with the *Freedom of Information Act 2000*, but with exceptions and exemptions (see below).

To understand how the conflict between Art. 8 and 10 has been debated in the courts, we need to examine the case of *Douglas v. Hello! Ltd.* [2001].[38] The background to the case was that paparazzi wedding photos had appeared in *Hello!* magazine in December 2000, days before the official shots were published in the rival *OK!* magazine, with which Michael Douglas and Catherine Zeta-Jones had an exclusive contract. The couple's deal to publish exclusive photographs in *OK!* magazine meant that the wedding was a 'trade secret' and they had a right to expect that it would remain secret until they released the pictures in a way they controlled.

A *Hello!* photographer – Rupert Thorpe – had surreptitiously taken photos at the couple's wedding at the Plaza Hotel in New York. The couple then sought an injunction via the High Court to stop issue 639 of *Hello!* being published. Counsel for the film stars argued that the illicit photos in *Hello!* breached their right to privacy under Art. 8 (1) ECHR. The injunction was granted, restraining *Hello!* from publishing and distributing issue 639. *Hello!* appealed and the CA set the injunction aside, acknowledging that the magazine would suffer financial loss by having to pull a large number of magazines off the newsagents' shelves, as issue 639 had already been distributed. The couple cross-appealed, which resulted in the HL ruling that 'freedom of expression' ought to prevail in this case over the individuals' right to privacy under Art. 8 ECHR.

The reason the Douglas case was so important was that this was the first time British judges had had to apply the Convention in English law. Until the CA's decision in the Douglas case, it was generally accepted that the legal duty of confidence (as discussed above) was limited to that which derived from:

- express or implied contractual terms
- the special nature of the relationship between the parties in general, where equity requires exchanges of information to be treated confidentially where:
  - the particular relationship cannot function effectively without it
  - in all the circumstances, the public interest in protecting the relationship clearly outweighs any countervailing public interest/s, such as freedom of information and expression.

The Douglas case returned to court in February 2003. In the Chancery Division of the High Court, Michael Douglas and Catherine Zeta-Jones sued *Hello!* for £1.75m and breach of confidence. Together with the publishers of *OK!* magazine, the famous couple maintained that the rival magazine *Hello!* had deliberately set out to 'spoil' (harm) *OK!*'s business by encouraging paparazzi to take pictures of the wedding. The then nine-months pregnant, Oscar-winner Zeta-Jones (33) told the court that she was left feeling 'devastated' and 'violated' when she discovered 'unflattering' paparazzi pictures had been taken during her wedding.

The judge said that there was no doubt the couple had suffered real distress and that the *Chicago* film star had cried when she learned of the unauthorised photographs. Mr Justice Lindsay also said that *Hello!* had not acted 'in good faith'. During the hearing, *Hello!* owner Eduardo Sanchez Junco defended himself and the magazine by stating that the couple had been more concerned with making money than protecting their privacy.

Mr Justice Lindsay ruled that the couple's commercial confidence had been breached at the point when *Hello!* infringed the couple's exclusive £1m deal with *OK!*. However, the judge did not grant the couple the right to privacy under Art. 8 ECHR. Mr Justice Lindsay referred to the 'trump card' quotation by Lord Justice Hoffmann in the 2001 CA action, that 'freedom of speech always wins', thus confirming Art. 10 ECHR. When the court case was over, *Hello!*'s Publishing Director,

Sally Cartwright, said that 9 of the 13 charges against the magazine had been dismissed and that *Hello!* had been cleared of any intent to damage the couple. The ruling was seen as a landmark test for the right to freedom of expression, and journalists were relieved that it did not establish a new law of privacy at that time.

The battle was not over. *Hello!* cross-appealed, and secured a significant legal victory (against *OK!*) in the House of Lords on 18 May 2005: confidentiality did not extend to *OK!*. *Hello!*'s appeal succeeded on the basis that while they had breached the Douglases' confidentiality, the House of Lords ruled that confidentiality did not extend to *OK!* and therefore *OK!* would not be entitled to recover the losses it suffered from the breach. The fact that *OK!* magazine had lost out on sales and had to rush out its print run did not mean *Hello!* deserved punishment for having got there first. The judgment ruled: 'For these reasons we conclude that the judge was wrong to hold that *OK!* was in a position to invoke against *Hello!* any right to commercial confidence in relation to the details of the wedding or photographic images portraying these' (the *Guardian*, 19 May 2005).

What is most important for journalists in the Douglas actions is that all respective courts – the CA in 2001 and the Chancery Division in – 2003 – rejected the couple's claim that the wedding photos intruded on their privacy. At this point, the courts favoured a journalist's right to free speech, which, in their words, must never be curtailed.

How, then, is the Internet regulated in terms of a person's right to privacy? The question is pertinent to an incident in March 2003. At the time, an unnamed English footballer was the centre of 'love rat' allegations. Subsequently, the captain of Premier League side Blackburn Rovers Gary Flitcroft was 'outed' on a BBC site called Celebdaq, an online celebrity trading game. It had all started when the *News of the World* hooked up with a former girlfriend of the footballer in question. The paper intended publishing 'intimate' letters and 'personal' pictures of their time together.

In *Gary Flitcroft v. The People* [2003], the footballer's lawyers asked the High Court for an injunction preventing publication of the story. Meanwhile, the *Mail on Sunday* was about to expose him as a 'love cheat'. However, a contributor to a message board on the BBC website revealed the footballer's identity.

The CA in the Flitcroft case finally decided that the 'freedom of expression' under Art. 10 ECHR was a matter for editors to decide. Lord Chief Justice Woolf said in his ruling:

> Once it is accepted that the freedom of the press should prevail, then the form of reporting in the press is not a matter for the courts, but for the Press Complaints Commission and the customers of the newspaper concerned.

Freedom of Information Act 2000

The Human Rights Act (HRA) already grants a right to 'receive' information, but the demand for a right to know is a demand for something much more, emphasising not just receiving the knowledge but gaining access to it. This may now be in place with the *Freedom of Information Act 2000* (FOI), which came into force on 1 January 2005.

The Act gives the public new rights of access to information held by public authorities.[39] This now means that anybody may request information from a public authority that has functions in England, Wales and Northern Ireland.

It was understood that the FOI would give British journalists the sort of tool of which colleagues in other countries – such as Sweden or France[40] – have made extensive use of for years. Since the FOI came into force, the media is said to have been one of the most enthusiastic users of it, gaining access to previously unobtainable government information. How much is revealed still depends on the attitude of the authorities as there are many exemptions that the government can invoke to prevent disclosure. Therefore, a journalist does not have unlimited access to *any* information. The rights conferred to individuals under the Act are subject to 'procedural' and 'substantive limitations' and there are 42 of these.

!	**What are a journalist's rights under the FOI?**

- to be told whether or not the public authority holds the information requested
- if so, to have that information communicated to them
- a public authority's duty is to provide reasonable advice and assistance to applicants seeking information
- a public authority's duty is to provide an open and public 'publication scheme' – that is, information approved by the FOI Commissioner is kept online or in a recorded in a paper format.

The question journalists have asked from the moment the FOI came into force was, whether the traditional British tendency to official secrecy would change. Some of the leading papers, such as the *Independent*,[41] and BBC News Online tested this belief thoroughly during the first six months of 2005. BBC News Online revealed that, for instance, 'Britain's 10 oldest state secrets were disclosed by the Home Office' in February 2005 in advance of the Act. These had previously remained secret under the 'Lord Chancellor's Instrument', a legal device that keeps files closed for a century. On one occasion, BBC News Online's Martin Rosenbaum accessed the Prime Minister's office. He reported:

> The friendly staff were welcoming to me and Michael Crick, the reporter I was with, and gave us a large pile of Mr Blair's correspondence with other world leaders, which we sat down and read. But we weren't in Downing Street – we were in Stockholm in the office of the Swedish Prime Minister, Goran Persson.[42]

Sweden has long had freedom of information legislation. The world's first freedom of information act was the Riksdag's (Swedish Parliament) *Freedom of the Press Act of 1766*. The Act required that official documents should 'upon request immediately be made available to anyone making a request' at no charge. The Swedish *Freedom of the Press Act* is now part of the Constitution and provides that 'every Swedish citizen shall have free access to official documents'.[43]

According to Martin Rosenbaum on BBC's News Online, the Swedish government appeared quite happy to make available the sorts of documents that Britain prefers to keep secret. Rosenbaum then tried the same approach with the British Prime Minister's office:

> But when we asked Downing Street for copies of Tony Blair's letters to [Sweden's Prime Minister] Goran Persson, we were told they could not release them as it might 'damage our international relations'.[44]

The British so-called '30-year rule' has disappeared, and, with the FOI, journalists are now able to make a request for information at any time rather than waiting for 30 years until valuable 'official secrets' are permitted into the public domain. By February 2005, various government departments had released over 50,000 files that were less than 30 years old. These included Cabinet minutes, papers and files from the Prime Minister's office and the Foreign and Commonwealth Office from 1974, which included momentous years in British and world history.

Media interest rightly concentrates on access to contemporary information, but some subjects are of historical and media research interest. Examples include whether or not the BBC comedy 'Porridge' could be filmed inside a prison, Metropolitan Police information on the escape from Durham Prison of John McVicar and Ministry of Defence records about the Cold War and the service of the Prince of Wales in the Royal Navy.

What types of information can you obtain using the 'public interest' test? It is for government officials to decide and the ultimate decision lies with the Freedom of Information Commissioner. He or she may conclude, for instance, that the information you requested is exempt because of the risk of 'prejudicing international relations' and therefore should be kept an 'official secret'.

What are the exemptions under the FOI?
• matters of national security (ss. 23 and 24)   • defence (s. 26)   • international relations (s. 27)   • relations within the United Kingdom (s. 28)   • the economy (s. 29)   • investigations and proceedings conducted by public authorities (s. 30)   • law enforcement (s. 31)   • court records (s. 32)   • audit functions (s. 33)   • parliamentary privilege (s. 34)   • formulation of government policy (s. 35)   • prejudice to effective conduct of public affairs (s. 36)   • communications with Her Majesty or other members of the royal household (s. 37)   • health and safety (s. 38)   • environmental information (s. 39)   • personal information (s. 40)   • information provided in confidence (s. 41)   • legal professional privilege (s. 42)   • commercial interests (s. 43).

The FOI covers some 100,000 public bodies, including local councils, police forces, primary schools and GP surgeries. The Act grants general rights of access in relation to recorded information held by public authorities. Where access is denied, the public authority has a duty to give a reason.

You will have to expect time delays if you are involved in getting requests dealt with under the FOI, which will make your job as a daily news reporter difficult. However, the Act should be invaluable for longer-term investigations and research. Under the Act, you are able to write to the National Archives to request information and its staff must respond within 30 working days. The same procedures apply to records held by other government departments and public authorities – you may write to them to request information and they should send a reply within 20 days.

At the start of 2005, government departments had received about 40 requests about the process leading up to the Iraq War in 2003. On 25 January 2005, ministers announced that the full text of the AG's advice to the government on the legality of the war would not be made public under the FOI. Ministers said that this type of information was protected by legal professional privilege. The Lord Chancellor, Lord Falconer of Thoronton QC, said in January: 'It must be right to maintain confidentiality between lawyer and client – whether it is a solicitor and someone buying a house, a barrister and someone appearing in court or, as in this case, the Attorney General and the government.' Richard Thomas, the Information Commissioner, received a large number of complaints regarding the withholding of this information from the media. In March 2003, the 'independent watchdog' then decided to release some of the sensitive advice and government secrets 'in the public interest'.

Following the FOI Commissioner's releasing the information, Channel 4 News revealed that a senior Foreign Office lawyer – Elizabeth Wilmshurst – had resigned from the AG's office over the Iraq conflict. Ms Wilmshurst's letter to the AG in March 2003 had suggested that the AG, Lord Goldsmith QC, originally believed a new UN resolution was needed to make the war legal. It was then reported that the AG had written another letter to Tony Blair on 7 March 2003, saying that the war might be illegal and it was safer to get a new UN resolution. On 17 March, however, the AG said the invasion was legal under a previous UN resolution, with no new agreement needed. Ms Wilmshurst had quit two days before the war because she believed the invasion to be a 'crime of aggression'.

The FOI Commissioner, Richard Thomas, said on Radio 4's 'Today' programme (25 March 2005) that he had received a number of complaints from individuals and newspapers after ministers refused applications under the new Act to publish the legal advice relating to the war on Iraq. 'We will be going through a process of examining those complaints', he said. Mr Thomas added that, so far, he had received about eight complaints about the government's decision (to withhold war-on-Iraq information), but he would not be drawn on the timing of his investigations. He added: 'We have recently signed a memorandum of understanding with Lord Falconer [the Lord Chancellor] on behalf of all government departments. It sets out the basis for cooperation in the interests of efficiency between my office and government departments … The departments will provide my office with all relevant information, including everything that has been withheld or redacted, and we undertake to keep it appropriately secure and not to release it to third parties.'

Finally, free speech cannot be defended on the basis of a right to know. Journalists often defend their coverage of private lives on this basis – a way of stressing that people should know about issues that may be in the public interest. The 'public interest' test is a useful journalistic standard. It is recognition of the fact that journalists make editorial judgments about what counts as newsworthy and what we think is important for people to know and why. The concept exists now in the PCC's Codes as well as human rights legislation. However, even though speech about private matters should not be censored, it's not true that anyone has a 'right' to know about somebody's private life. Although some information is rightly considered to be 'in the public interest', other material may not be published merely because it interests the public.

Selected case studies and tasks

You are asked to find (via LEXIS/NEXIS), read in detail and analyse the following case by providing the following information requested of you.

Case Study No. 1

AG v. Jonathan Cape Ltd (Sub nom 'Crossman Diaries' case) [1976] 1 QB 752[45]

1 Describe the facts in the Crossman Diaries case.
2 Who was Richard Crossman? Do some political background research.
3 What, according to Lord Widgery, are the 'three elements' normally required for a case of breach of confidence to succeed? You are asked to refer back to the Prince Albert case [1849].
4 What was the outcome of the Crossman Diaries case?
5 What were the reasons given by Lord Widgery C.J. on the application for an injunction?
6 What, in your own words, is meant by 'Cabinet confidentiality'?

Case Study No. 2

Douglas v. Hello! Ltd [2001] 2 All ER 289.

1 Describe the facts in *Douglas v. Hello! Ltd*.
2 State the legal principles in relation to the *Human Rights Act 1998* (HRA) and the European Convention (ECHR) that make this case so important.
3 Why was the *Douglas v. Hello! Ltd* case so important?

QUESTIONS

1 (a) Describe the facts in the *Spycatcher* case (*AG v. Guardian Newspapers Ltd* (No. 2) [1990] 1 AC).
(b) Explain what was meant in this case by a 'special relationship' between the Crown and those who work in its service.
(c) What eventually happened to Peter Wright's publication?

Note:
Answer the essay-type questions below by using discursive argument and back each argument using statutory and case law.

2 Free speech cannot be defended on the basis of a right to know. Is it a journalist's absolute right to cover the private lives of famous people on this basis?

3 Why should the law protect individuals' privacy at all costs? Discuss with reference to leading cases, in which the rich and famous complained about media invasions of their privacy.

4 Has the *European Convention on Human Rights* (1950) lost its original purpose, which was that privacy meant freedom from interference by the state? Is it now not a legal tool for British judges to mean that anybody can be protected under the right to privacy? Discuss.

5 What is the current legal ruling relating to the equitable doctrine of parliamentary confidentiality and how does this fit in with the *Freedom of Information Act 2000*? Refer to case law.

6 Having studied developing common law, which, in your opinion, prevails: the right to privacy or the right to free speech in our democracy? Discuss.

7 How is a journalist to know who will be upset in an age when an increasing number of people voluntarily decide to tell all about their emotional lives? Discuss with reference to legislation and case law.

FURTHER READING

Barendt, E. (1989) 'Spycatcher and freedom of speech', *Public Law*, 204.

Bindman, G. (1989) 'Spycatcher: judging the judges', *New Law Journal*, 139, 94.

Bryan, M. W. (1976) 'The Crossman diaries: developments in the law of breach of confidence', *The Law Quarterly Review*, 92, 180.

Howard, A. (ed.) (1979) *Diaries of a Cabinet Minister: Richard Howard Stafford Crossman, 1964–'70*. London: Hamish Hamilton.

Lee, S. (1987) 'Spycatcher', *The Law Quarterly Review*, 103, 506.

Leigh, I. (1992) 'Spycatcher in Strasbourg', *Public Law*, 200.

Lowe, N. V., and Willmore, C. J. (1985) 'Secrets, media and the law', *The Modern Law Review*, 48, 592.

Markesinis, B. (1999) 'Privacy, freedom of expression, and the horizontal effect of the Human Rights Bill: lessons from Germany', *The Law Quarterly Review*, 115.

Moreham, N. (2001) *'Douglas and Others v. Hello! Ltd* – the protection of privacy in English private law', *The Modern Law Review*, 64, 767.

Nicol, A., Millar, G., and Sharland, A. (2001) *Media Law and Human Rights*. London: Blackstone.

Turnbull, M. (1989) 'Spycatcher', *The Law Quarterly Review* 105, 382.

Williams, D. G. T. (1976) 'The Crossman diaries', *The Cambridge Law Journal*, 1.

Wilson, W. (1990) 'Privacy, confidence and press freedom: a study in judicial activism', *The Modern Law Review*, 53, 43.

Wright, P. (1987) *Spycatcher: The candid autobiography of a secret intelligence officer*. Australia: William Heinemann and Viking Press.

Notes

1 The 'Rachel' affair: judgment of 16 June 1858, Trib. pr. inst. de la Seine, 1858 D.P. III 62. See Jeanne M. Hauch, (1994) 'Protecting Private Facts in France', p. 68.

2 Code Civile, Article 9, Statute No. 70–643 of 17 July 1970. The right of privacy is not explicitly included in the French Constitution of 1958, but the Constitutional Court ruled in 1994 that the right of privacy was implicit in the Constitution (Décision 94–352 du Conseil Constitutionnel du 18 Janvier 1995).

3 The 'right of privacy' has evolved to protect the freedom of individuals to choose whether or not to perform certain acts or subject themselves to certain experiences. This personal autonomy has grown into a 'liberty', protected by the due process clause of the 14th amendment. However, this liberty is narrowly defined and generally only protects the privacy of family, marriage, motherhood, procreation and childrearing. Further extensions of this 'right of privacy' have been attempted under the 1st, 4th and 5th amendments to the US constitution, but a general right to personal autonomy has yet to take hold beyond limited circumstances.

4 Bundesverfassungsgericht (BverfGE) 65,1.

5 Federal Act on Data Protection, 27 January 1977 (Bundesgesetzblatt, Part I, No. 7, 1 February 1977), as amended in 1990.

6 Regeringsformen, SFS 1974: 152.

7 Tryckfrihetsförordningen, SFS 1949: 105.

8 See: Kilbrandon, 'The Law of Privacy in Scotland' (1971) 2 Cambrian LR 35.

9 'Lawyer of the week', *The Times*, 21 June 2005, p. 7.

10 *Campbell (Appellant) v. MGN Limited (Respondents)* [2004] UKHL 22.

11 [1967] Ch. 302; [1965] 1 All ER 611.

12 [1849] 64 ER 293.

13 [1856] 26 LJ Ch. 113.

14 *The Times*, 31 October 1995.

15 [1984] 7 EHRR 14.

16 The matter concerned the earlier case of *Malone v. Metropolitan Police Commissioner* [1979] 1 Ch. 344.

17 In order for a civil action to be brought, the party to the intercepted conversation must identify himself and such identification may also be inevitable in any criminal proceedings. S. 2 of the Act establishes the exception, essentially giving legislative approval to the old system of ministerial warrants for interception of telecommunications or postal communications, with a quasi-judicial system of review in the form of a tribunal added via s. 7. Therefore, this gives the State the right to intercept telephone conversations in the interests of national security and the purpose of detecting or preventing serious crime (s. 2(2) (a) and (b)).

18 *Barrymore v. Newsgroup Newspapers Ltd* [1997] FSR 600.

19 *AG v. Guardian Newspapers Ltd* [1987] 3 All ER 316.

20 [1990] 1 AC 109; [1988] 3 WLR 776; [1988] 3 All ER 545; [1989] 2 FRR 181.

21 *AG v. Jonathan Cape Ltd* (sub nom Crossman Diaries case) [1976] 1 QB 752.

22 *Sunday Times v. UK* [No.2] [1992] 14 EHRR 229, ECHR.

23 *Douglas v. Hello! Ltd* [2001] 1 All ER 289, CA.

24 This includes the peaceful enjoyment of one's possessions (Art. 1), the right to education; the right of parents to ensure education of their children in conformity with their own religious and philosophical convictions is upheld (Art. 2); the right to take part in free elections (Art. 3).

25 The Council of Europe is the continent's oldest political organisation, founded in 1949. It groups together 46 countries, including 21 countries from Central and Eastern Europe (including Russia) and has granted observer status to 5 more countries (the Holy See, the United States, Canada, Japan and Mexico). It is distinct from the 25 Member States (MS) of the European Union (EU), but no country has ever joined the Union without first belonging to the Council of Europe. Its headquarters is in Strasburg. The Council was set up to defend human rights, parliamentary democracy and the rule of law, to develop continent-wide agreements to standardise member countries' social and legal practices and to promote awareness of a European identity based on shared values and cutting across different cultures. Since 1989, its main role is as human rights watchdog for Europe's post-communist democracies (e.g. the Baltic States).

26 *Malone v. Metropolitan Police Commissioner* [1974] Ch. 344. This case was concerned with the police 'bugging' the plaintiff's telephone. It was held that no right to privacy was recognised by English law and none could be imported by way of reference to Art. 8 of the Convention.

27 *R. v. Morrissey* and *R. v. Staines* [1997] TLR 231.

28 See J., Straw, and Boateng, P. (1997) 'Bringing Rights Home: Labour's Plans to Incorporate the European Convention on Human Rights into United Kingdom Law', Consultation Paper [1997] EHRLR, p. 74.

29 See Lord Irvine of Lairg, The Tom Sargant Memorial Lecture, 16 December 1997: 'The Development of Human Rights in Britain under an Incorporated Convention on Human Rights' (The Lord Chancellor's Department, 1997). Also, 'Lord Irvine of Lairg L.C. at the proposal of the Act and its place in the British constitution', *Hansard*, HL, 3 November 1997, col., 1227–38.

30 Solemn hearing of the European Court of Human Rights on the occasion of the opening of the judicial year Friday, 21 January 2005. Speech by Mr Luzius Wildhaber, President of the European Court of Human Rights.

31 [1999] 3 WLR 175.

32 In addition to the substantive articles of the Convention, there exists a series of protocols on matters ranging from the right to peaceful enjoyment of possessions (First Protocol, Art. 1 – as in *Stretch v. UK* [2003]), education (First Protocol, Art. 2), the holding of regular free elections (First Protocol, Art. 3), freedom of movement (Fourth Protocol), abolition of the death penalty (Sixth Protocol), appeals in criminal cases and sexual equality (Seventh Protocol), procedural matters under the Convention (Ninth Protocol) and minority rights (Tenth Protocol). The UK is not a party to the Fourth, Sixth or Seventh Protocols.

33 The test in s.12(3) HRA 1998, which applied on an application to restrain prior publication, was whether or not the applicant had established a real prospect of success at trial, rather than that success was more likely than not.

34 [2001] EMLR 563; *Imutran Ltd v. (1) Uncaged Campaigns Ltd (2) Daniel Louis Lyons* (11 January 2001) [2001] EMLR 21; [2001] EMLR 563; [2001] IPD 24031; [2001] HRLR 31; [2002] FSR 20. Ch.D (Sir Andrew Morritt VC): The claimants were entitled to continued injunctions restricting publication of covertly obtained information about treatment of laboratory animals for s. 12 in application.

35 *Y. v. The Netherlands* [1985] 8 EHRR 235.

36 *Campbell (Appellant) v. MGN Ltd (Respondents)* [2004] UKHL 22.

37 [1987] 9 EHRR 433.

38 [2001] 2 All ER 289.

39 The term 'public authority' is defined in the Act and includes all public bodies and government departments in the UK. The BBC, Channel 4 and S4C are the only broadcasters covered by the Act.

40 Two laws in France provide for a right to access government records: (1) Loi no. 78–753 du 17 juillet 1978 de la liberté d'accès au documents administratifs, and (2) Loi no. 79–587 du juillet 1979 relative à la motivation des actes administratifs et à l'amélioration des relations entre l'administration et le public.

41 'You may ask questions – but the Government still has the freedom not to answer them', editorial, the *Independent*, 2 February 2005.

42 http://news.bbc.co.uk/1/hi/magazine/4134811.stm

43 Decisions by public authorities to deny access to official documents may be appealed against in general administrative courts and, ultimately, in the Supreme Administrative Court. The Parliamentary Ombudsman has some oversight functions regarding freedom of information.

44 http://news.bbc.co.uk/1/hi/magazine/4134811.stm

45 See also *AG v. Guardian Newspapers Ltd* [Contempt] [1999] *The Independent*, 30 July 1999, QBD; *AG v. Guardian Newspapers Ltd* (No.1): *Guardian/Observer – Spycatcher case* [1987]; 1 WLR 1248.s

CHAPTER THREE

SELF-REGULATORY BODIES

Key aim of this chapter:

> To enable you to understand the main principles followed by regulatory bodies for the UK print press and communications industries.

Learning objectives

By the end of this chapter you should be able to demonstrate:

- a sound understanding of the roles of the PCC and Ofcom
- a good knowledge and appreciation of the role of the PCC and procedures it follows
- a thorough understanding and appreciation of what is meant by 'voluntary regulation'
- that you understand and appreciate the responsibilities of editors, authors, publishers and distributors of the print media regarding privacy issues
- a sound knowledge of the PCC Code of Practice
- a sound knowledge and appreciation of the role and procedures of Ofcom
- that you appreciate the separate functions of Ofcom
- that you are familiar with some PCC adjudications in problem-solving exercises.

Chapter Contents

Introduction

In this chapter, we look at the two main self-regulatory bodies – namely the Press Complaints Commission (PCC) and the Office of Communications (Ofcom). For someone who wishes to complain about a particular TV or radio broadcast or feels aggrieved by a newspaper article, these bodies are an alternative to going to court.

A major part of this chapter is taken up with PCC adjudications. You will be asked specific questions relating to the various case studies at the end of this chapter, so you should spend some time reading the adjudications carefully before venturing into giving your essay-style answers.

The chapter closes with explanations of the statutory corporation Ofcom, which deals with television, radio, telecommunications and wireless communications services and reports annually to Parliament.

What are the merits of voluntary regulatory bodies?

One major advantage is speed, as these bodies – the PCC or the media watchdog Ofcom – tend to deal with complaints from members of the public much faster than is possible via court procedures, such as a libel action. The PCC's ability to hand out 'informal' advice and publish decisions and commentaries regularly makes it dynamic, too. More than 90 per cent of complaints to the PCC come from ordinary people and only a handful are received from celebrities.

The PCC Code of Practice explicitly states that 'it is the responsibility of editors to cooperate with the PCC as swiftly as possible in the resolution of complaints. In the case of *Mr Darrell Desbrow v. The Scotsman* (see Case Study 3, later in this chapter), the newspaper had taken four months to reply to a straightforward complaint from Mr Desbrow. Therefore, the PCC concluded that the newspaper had not fulfilled its responsibility and this clearly breached the Code of Practice, so adjudicated in favour of the complainant.

The PCC's generally speedy decisions mean that roughly 72 per cent of complaints are resolved in 43 days and about 84 per cent within 64 days. In 2004, the Commission investigated 218 new complaints about privacy intrusion. Altogether, the the PCC received 3618 complaints in 2004 (compared with 3649 in 2003). The vast majority of complaints are resolved 'informally' – that is, they are immediately referred to the editor of the particular newspaper or magazine being complained about and usually resolved satisfactorily or withdrawn.[1]

There are, of course, many who see the PCC as purely self-regulatory and toothless, having no real powers. The Commission's membership is composed of mainly journalists and editors, though it claims that 10 out of the 16 members are independent of the industry – the rest being drawn from newspapers and magazines throughout the UK. It is particularly in the area of privacy that some have found the PCC to be rather spineless.

In July 2002, the BBC newsreader Anna Ford was angered when the PCC refused to agree that paparazzi pictures taken of her on holiday breached her privacy. Anna Ford and her then boyfriend were photographed with long lenses as they were rubbing suntan lotion on each other. She was not satisfied with the PCC's adjudication and turned to the High Court in a libel action. However, the High Court ruled that Majorca in August was not a place where she could reasonably have expected privacy and so rejected her claim.

This might show that, when there is an alleged breach of a PCC Code, an adjudication by the PCC may seem a poor remedy. In short, the PCC cannot stop breaches that are threatened and it cannot grant compensation either. If an individual (like Anna Ford) feels that her PCC adjudication has not been sufficient to protect her right to privacy, she may ask the courts to intervene in order to gain full respect for private life (Art. 8 ECHR).

Section 12 *Human Rights Act 1998* provides legal remedy in such cases, by either an injunction or damages. However, s. 12 equally emphasises the importance of freedom of expression (Art. 10 ECHR). Where there is a tension between Arts. 8 and 10 ECHR, judges have to balance the need to protect privacy with the need to allow freedom of expression. This was made clear in the *Douglas v Hello!* case [2001].

The PCC came under fire in the House of Commons during debates in Parliament in March 2003. Its powers were described as 'limited' and its decisions branded as being beyond scrutiny. Leading the attack was the barrister Michael Tugendhat QC, who had represented Michael Douglas and Catherine Zeta-Jones as well as *OK!* magazine in their challenge to *Hello!* magazine during November and December 2000. An eminent barrister, he had called on the government to introduce new powers to stop damaging stories getting into papers in the first place. Giving evidence to a Commons inquiry into privacy and media intrusion, Michael Tugendhat QC had complained that there were no real sanctions against newspapers that breached privacy. He told the Committee: 'While the PCC has done a pretty good job over the last few years, ultimately it's limited.' He concluded: 'The problem with the PCC is that, unlike broadcasting which is licensed, the press is not. Broadcasting licences can be taken away. In the case of the press there's no sanction.'[2]

Arguably, there is no need for any new legislation at this stage. This still leaves us with the question: Why is the British media, and therefore the general public, so interested in the private lives of celebrities?

Relevant statutory legislation

In this chapter (and the legislation quoted in this book generally), journalists may need to be aware of the following Acts of Parliament, European directives and regulations. Please note that certain enactments may not extend to Scotland, Northern Ireland and the Channel Islands, where different legislation may apply.

- *Charities Act 1992*
- *Children and Young Persons Acts 1933* and *1963*
- *Children Act 1989*
- *Communications Act 2003*
- *Contempt of Court Act 1981*
- *Copyright, Designs and Patents Act 1988*
- *Council of Europe Convention on Transfrontier Television*
- *Criminal Justice and Public Order Act 1994*
- *Criminal Justice Act 2003*
- *Criminal Laws Acts (NI) 1967* and *1977*
- *Data Protection Act 1998*
- *Defamation Act 1996*
- *Directive on Transfrontier Television 1989 89/552/EEC*
- *European Union Amsterdam Treaty 1997*, Art. 13
- *Human Rights Act 1998*
- *Hypnotism Act 1952*
- *Lotteries and Amusements Act 1976*
- *Magistrates' Courts Act 1980*
- *Obscene Publications Act 1959*
- *Official Secrets Acts 1911* and *1989*
- *Political Parties, Elections and Referendum Act 2000*
- *Protection from Harassment Act 1997*
- *Public Interest Disclosure Act 1998*
- *Public Order Act 1986* and *Criminal Justice and Public Order Act 1994*

- *Race Relations Act 1976*
- *Representation of the People Act 1983*
- *Sex Discrimination Act 1975*
- *Terrorism Act UK 2000*
- *Wireless Telegraphy Act 1964*
- *Youth Justice and Criminal Evidence Act 1999.*

The Press Complaints Commission (PCC)

The PCC was set up in 1991, replacing the Press Council, to provide a quick, accessible and economic route for members of the public to complain about their representation in newspapers. On 10 January 1994, the Privacy Commissioner Professor Robert Pinker was appointed, with special powers to investigate complaints about privacy under the PCC Code of Practice.

The PCC deals with complaints from members of the public about editorial content in newspapers, periodicals and magazines. The PCC is therefore the voluntary (but not necessarily independent) regulator for the 'print media' in the publishing industry. It takes the view that some legal restrictions on the press are necessary (such as concerning court reporting) and thinks that imposing new laws would be a retrograde step. The central aim of the PCC's work is to resolve disputes amicably between a newspaper or magazine and the person complaining, without the individual having to go to court to, for example, undertake a defamatory action or go through proceedings concerning human rights issues.

It remains debatable whether or not the PCC is totally independent, being 'peopled' as it is by journalists and principal newspaper editors from the UK. However, one of the main aims of the PCC is to ensure that the public interest is being upheld.

The public interest !

- detecting or exposing crime or a serious misdemeanour
- protecting public health and safety
- preventing the public from being misled by some statement or action of an individual or organisation
- where public interest is invoked, the PCC will require a full explanation by the editor, who will need to demonstrate how the public interest was served
- in cases involving children, editors must demonstrate an exceptional public interest to override the normally paramount interests of the child.

Today, the PCC (referred to hereafter as the 'Commission') has more than 400 members from the print press. The Commission's 16 members are drawn from the ranks of editors and senior executives on regional and national newspapers. The Chairman in 2005 was Sir Christopher Meyer, Britain's former ambassador to the USA.

The Commission deals with approximately 3000 complaints per year, about 90 per cent of cases being resolved successfully where the finding is that the Code of Practice may have been breached. Of the remainder, where a dispute continues, the Commission reaches a final decision about whether the Code has been breached or not. Sometimes, as you will see from the example of the Beckhams' case below (Case Study 2), the Commission decides not to act at all.

The PCC's Board

✓ 16 members, including the chairman and lay members.
✓ Editors of regional and national newspapers, chosen by an independent appointments committee.
✓ Financed by the Press Standards Board of Finance (from registration fees from the newspaper and magazine publishing industry).

The PCC Code of Practice: general principles for print journalism

What is the Code of Practice? The Code of Practice is wide-ranging, with 17 clauses, plus guidelines on the 'public interest' test covering four main aspects: accuracy, privacy, methods of news gathering and vulnerable members of society. It sets out firm guidelines and general principles for publishers, authors, journalists and distributors. The Code of Practice provides the Commission with a framework within which it can address complaints from members of the public. It is expected that all members of the press adhere to the duty to maintain the highest professional and ethical standards and abide by the Code. The PCC Code is designed to set the benchmark for those standards.

The Code is to protect the rights of the individual and uphold the public's right to know. The Commission expects journalists to abide fully by the essential workings of this agreed Code and that it be honoured not only in the letter but also in the full spirit. The Code should not be interpreted so narrowly as to compromise its commitment to respect the rights of the individual, nor so broadly that it prevents publication in the public interest. The Commission thus expects editors to be fully familiar with the Code and administer and abide by it responsibly. Should there be a challenge to editors and authors under the Code by an individual, they are expected to cooperate fully and swiftly with the Commission to assist the resolution of such complaints. Any publication that is criticised by the Commission under one of the clauses must print any adjudication in full and with due prominence.

The Commission does not have legal powers of cross-examination or subpoena and should take a flexible and commonsensical approach to trying to resolve complaints. It has consistently underlined, for instance, that if the accuracy of an article is challenged, editors cannot rely on Clause 15 of the Code – which relates to the protection of confidential sources – as a 'trump card' to justify the publication of material.

Who drafts the PCC code of practice? !

- representatives of the print industry via the Code Committee
- code Committee, comprised of editors from the print press
- members of the Code Committee appointed by the Appointments Commission
- nominations from five UK publishers' associations.

The Code is changed periodically (most recently in 2005 – see Appendix 2). Changes take account of public and parliamentary opinion as well as reports, concerns from readers and adjudications from the PCC. Changing practices and technology within the industry are also taken into account. The following list shows the main areas of practice within the Code.

The PCC Code of Practice

- *Accuracy* A reference to inaccurate, misleading or distorted pictures is included to deal with the potential problems of picture manipulation.
- *Right to reply* Every complainant must be given the right to respond to an allegation. Equally, the same right exists for an editor of a newspaper or journal, so both sides can respond.

- *Privacy* Everyone is entitled to respect for his or her private life. There is a new stipulation regarding the taking of pictures 'in private places' ('where there is reasonable expectation of privacy' – Clause 3 definition of 1998).
- *Harassment* Pictures taken as a result of 'persistent public pursuit' are banned. There are new requirements for editors to not publish material from freelance sources that do not meet the standards of the Code. One of the chief concerns at the time of Princess Diana's death was about the role of the paparazzi and the manner in which some photographs were sought. To address this concern, the provision on Harassment was added (Clause 4); this includes a ban on information or pictures obtained through 'persistent pursuit'.
- *Grief and shock* The Code includes a reference to stories published at times of grief or shock regarding the methods used for news gathering. Here, journalists must use sensitivity at all times. Approaches must be made with sympathy and discretion and publication must be handled sensitively, especially at inquests or inquiries.
- *Children* There is the stipulation that children should be able to complete their time at school free from unnecessary intrusion. Protection is now available to all 'pupils', not just those under 16. There is a ban on payments to minors, except when it is in the interests of the child. Protection is given to the children of those in the public eye.
- *Children in sex cases* Children under the age of 16 who are involved in sexual cases, as witnesses, victims or defendants, must not be identified. Please note that this goes against child identification legislation such as the *Contempt of Court Act 1981* or s. 39 of the *Children and Young Persons Act 1933*, where there is to be no identification under the age of 18 of youngsters involved in 'active' court proceedings.
- *Clandestine listening devices* These must not be used, for example to intercept telephone conversations.
- *Hospitals* Journalists must identify themselves to responsible executives and obtain permission before entering non-public areas.
- *Victims of sexual assault or rape* Under no circumstances must these victims be identified.
- *Discrimination* Journalists must take great care to avoid prejudicial or pejorative (uncomplimentary) references to a person's race, colour, religion, sex or sexual orientation, physical or mental illness or disability, *unless* the facts are directly relevant to the story.

Full details of the Code of Practice can be found in Appendix 2.

While it is not possible to discuss every clause of the PCC's Code of Practice here, some areas worth noting are covered next.

Accuracy

In dealing with complaints about accuracy (Clause 1), there are the rare occasions when the Commission is not in a position to make a finding – perhaps because of a conflict or lack of evidence (see Case Study 2 below: *David and Victoria Beckham v. Sunday Mirror* [2003]). In the Beckhams' case, the newspaper was obliged either to provide on-the-record corroborative evidence or, in the absence of such evidence, offer the complainant an opportunity to reply. The editor of the *Sunday Mirror* complied on both counts. However, if such an offer is rejected, it can be difficult for the Commission to make a finding concerning the accuracy of the original article where no corroborative material exists to support the information from confidential sources and establish whether or not the story is true. In such circumstances, it may also not be possible for the Commission to judge whether any proposed offer is a proportionate remedy or not because the Commission cannot be certain if the material under complaint is inaccurate or not. Therefore, in the Beckhams' case, the Commission decided on a 'No finding' result – that is, the PCC declined to proceed with the matter.

Let us look at an example of a complaint that was upheld. In the PCC Report No. 34 (1996), the Queen's Press Secretary, Charles Anson, complained about *Business Age*. The magazine had reported that the Queen's personal wealth approximated £2.2bn in its article on 'The Rich 500'. Anson complained, under Clauses 1 (accuracy) and 3 (privacy), that the report was inaccurate, misleading and delved into the Queen's private affairs. Furthermore, that the Queen had not been given a right to reply (Clause 2). The Commission adjudicated that the 'article presented speculation as established fact, the magazine failed adequately to check its facts and it made a number of errors which were not properly addressed'. The complaint was upheld under all clauses.

The accuracy test	!
• Clause 1 – accuracy • newspapers and periodicals must take care to publish accurately • they must not mislead or distort material • they must report fairly, without being partisan.	

Privacy

Clause 3 of the Code, about privacy, was enhanced by Art. 8 ECHR, as incorporated into UK legislation by the *Human Rights Act 1998*. As with the aforementioned, this is an area where journalists are likely to be challenged as they have to balance their journalistic rights of freedom of expression (Art. 10 ECHR) with those where the law protects an individual's right to privacy and respect for family life, especially since the HL ruling in Naomi Campbell's case.[3] After Ms Campbell had already been awarded some damages in the CA against *The Mirror* newspaper for breach of confidentiality and the *Data Protection Act* because the paper had made her battle against drug addiction public, the supermodel eventually won her privacy case in the HL against *The Mirror* newspaper to secure her privacy under Art. 8 ECHR.

Naomi Campbell v. Mirror Group [2004] HL

Facts: In January 2001, *The Mirror* obtained information that Miss Campbell had acknoswledged her drug dependency by going regularly to meetings of Narcotics Anonymous (NA) for help in ridding herself of the addiction. On 1 February 2001, *The Mirror* newspaper carried as its first story on its front page a prominent article headed, 'Naomi: I am a drug addict'. The photographs of her attending the NA meeting were taken by a freelance photographer specifically employed by the newspaper to do the job; he had taken the photographs covertly, while concealed some distance away inside a parked car. The article was supported on one side by a picture of Miss Campbell as a glamorous model, on the other side by a slightly indistinct picture of a smiling, relaxed Miss Campbell, dressed in baseball cap and jeans, over the caption, 'Therapy: Naomi outside meeting'. The Lord Nicholls of Birkenhead, para. 2.

By a narrow margin of 3:2 in the HL, Ms Campbell eventually won her case. The HL held that the tabloid had overstepped the mark by publishing the times and nature of her treatment. Furthermore, the covert photography was ruled by the HL as a severe intrusion into the model's privacy, particularly as she was still undergoing treatment. Thus, this intrusion amounted to a contravention of Art. 8 (Privacy). Campbell's eventual victory in the HL set a precedent for UK privacy law and it would seem that the law of confidentiality amounts to the same thing. Privacy can now come with a hefty price tag.

In relation to the PCC Code of Practice, it can safely be said that most complaints to date involve privacy issues under Clause 3 (i):

everyone is entitled to respect for his or her private and family life, home, health and correspondence. A publication will be expected to justify intrusions into any individual's private life without consent.

Long-lens photography has long been an issue – particularly with famous people in private places, such as hospitals or private clinics. In the 1995 Earl

Spencer hearing, the Commission ruled that *any* photography in private places without the victim's or complainant's consent is unacceptable. The Earl's complaint was against the *News of the World* (PCC Report No. 29 of 1995) and its headline story of 2 April, which read, 'Di's sister in booze and bulimia clinic ... royal exclusive', and the subheading, 'Earl Spencer's ailing wife has secret therapy'. The paper reported 'Victoria Spencer, 29, suffering from bulimia ... is also believed to have a drink problem.' Earl Spencer filed a number of complaints in relation to the intrusion into the privacy of his wife, namely under Clauses 3 (Privacy), 9 (Hospitals) and 4 (Harassment). All complaints were upheld. The Commission noted that the breach of the codes was compounded by the publication of a photograph of the countess in the private grounds of the clinic.

In October 2002, the Sunday newspaper *The People* was reprimanded by the Commission for publishing pictures taken with a long-lens camera of former *Coronation Street* actress Julie Goodyear sitting in her back garden. As the Code states categorically, long-lens photography used to take pictures in private places is outlawed.

The People decided to publish the pictures, even though the Editor, Neil Wallis – on the Commission's Board at the time – was fully aware of the Code. Goodyear, famous for playing barmaid Bet Lynch in the soap, complained about the pictures, saying that she clearly had an expectation of privacy in her own garden. However, Wallis argued that the garden was not hidden by trees or bushes and claimed that it was possible to see Goodyear from public places bordering her property. In its defence, *The People* enclosed copies of contracts showing that it had previously paid Goodyear for features and stories about her home. She could not now legitimately complain that her privacy had been invaded when in the past she had been willing to use similar photographs for her own purposes, Wallis argued. The Commission upheld the actress's complaint, saying that, as a long-lens camera had been necessary to take the pictures:

> It was unlikely passers-by – even if they could have seen figures in the garden – would have been able to identify the complainant ... It was clear that the complainant had a reasonable expectation of privacy where she was sitting.

The Commission conceded that, in previous adjudications, it had ruled that people could limit their rights to privacy by selling information or pictures of their private lives. However, it stressed that this did not mean they lost all rights to protection under the Code: 'In this case, the editor made the wrong decision', stated the Commission.

| ! | Privacy |

- Clause 3 – Privacy
- enhanced by Art. 8 ECHR – the right to privacy and respect for family life
- everyone is entitled to respect for his or her privacy – family life, home, health, private correspondence
- most complaints to the PCC relate to Clause 3
- 'private places' are 'public or private property where there is a reasonable expectation of privacy'
- the use of long-lens photography is strictly forbidden
- regarding cases involving children, editors must demonstrate that there is an exceptional public interest to be served in order to override the normally paramount interests of the child.

PCC adjudications: selected case studies

The following have been taken from the Commission's website with kind permission from the PCC. Study each case and adjudication carefully before you answer, in an essay style, the questions that follow. Compare each complaint with the PCC Code and note on what grounds the complainant has based his or her argument – Clause 3 – privacy – for example.

CASE STUDY

Case Study 1: *Miss Elizabeth Noble v. News of the World* [2003]

Clauses noted: 1, 3 and 11

Complaint

Miss Elizabeth Noble of Tyne and Wear complained to the Commission that an article published in the *News of the World* on 2 November 2003 headlined, 'With all thy worldly goods I me endow' was inaccurate and intrusive, in breach of Clauses 1 (Accuracy) and 3 (Privacy) of the Code of Practice. She also complained that the journalist responsible for the piece had sought to obtain information by means of misrepresentation, in breach of Clause 11 (Misrepresentation) of the Code.

Facts of the adjudication

The article reported that a man had admitted in court to defrauding several women, including the complainant, to whom he had been engaged. The complainant said that the article attributed comments to her that she had not made and had published her photograph without permission. Moreover, she said that she had deliberately not responded to requests for information from the freelance reporter responsible for the article, who had also misled her by presenting himself as a freelance working for magazines.

The newspaper said that the comments and the photograph had been made available for use by the complainant through her friend – a fellow victim of the conman. It provided a statement from the freelance reporter in which he said that he had not approached the complainant under false pretences. He also claimed that the complainant had been considering selling her story to a magazine prior to the *News of the World* piece appearing.

The complainant said that she only decided to sell her story to a magazine after seeing the misleading piece in the *News of the World*. She had not provided her 'friend' with the comments attributed to her and had only sent her fellow victim a photograph in order that she might see what she looked like – it was contained in a private e-mail and was certainly not for publication.

The newspaper argued that the story had already received coverage in a local newspaper and was, therefore, in the public domain. However, in the absence of further evidence, it offered to write directly to the complainant to apologise for the distress caused by the article and the lengthy nature of the investigation.

Decision

The complaint was upheld

Reasons

The Commission acknowledged the newspaper's claim that it had accepted material for the story from a freelance journalist in good faith. Nevertheless, the preamble to the Code of Practice makes clear that editors and publishers must ensure that the Code is observed rigorously not only by their staff but also by anyone who contributes to their publications.

In this instance, the Commission noted that, after three months of investigation, no evidence had been provided to show that the complainant had made the comments attributed to her. Consequently, while acknowledging the newspaper's offer to apologise for the distress caused by the story and the time taken to investigate the matter, the Commission could come to no other view than that the article was inaccurate and in breach of Clause 1 of the Code.

With regard to the complaint under Clause 3, the Commission noted that the photograph of the complainant had been made available to the freelance journalist by a fellow victim of the conman at the centre of the article, but there was no evidence that the complainant had intended the contents of her e-mail to be published. Indeed, it had been sent three months before the article appeared. Publishing material without consent that had been sent in a private e-mail – in the absence of any public interest for doing so – was deemed a breach of Clause 3 of the Code, which entitles individuals to respect for their correspondence.

Turning to the complaint under Clause 11, the Commission noted that the journalist had described himself to the complainant as 'a true life feature writer for the women's weekly magazines and … not a journalist'. After receiving an e-mail from the complainant in which she expressed concern about the *News of the World* article, he said, 'Yes I saw that article. That's why I steer clear of the papers and just work for magazines.' It was clear to the Commission that the freelance had sought to obtain information by misrepresenting the precise nature of his work. His deception had continued even after the article had been published in the newspaper and there seemed to be no public interest defence for his behaviour. The result was a breach of Clause 11.

This case prompted the Commission to remind editors that they must take care to ensure that material submitted by freelance journalists for publication has been obtained in accordance with the Code.

Relevant precedents

Shipman v. Daily Mirror 7/9/2001 [Report 56 PCC]. Mrs Primrose Shipman complained through Messrs Pannone and Partners of Manchester that material contained in an article headlined 'Shipman wife begs him: tell me truth' published in the *Mirror* on 9 July 2001 was obtained in breach of Clause 11 (Misrepresentation) and was intrusive in breach of Clause 3 (Privacy) of the Code of Practice. The Commission upheld the complaint under Clause 3 but did not censure the newspaper. It made no finding under Clause 11.

Railtrack plc v. The Independent 29/1/2001 [Report 57 PCC]. Mr Kevin Groves, Acting Head of Media, Railtrack plc, complained to the PCC that information for an article headlined 'What am I bid for a front-page story?' published in the *Independent* on 29 January 2002, was obtained in breach of Clause 11 (Misrepresentation) and that the subsequent article was inaccurate in breach of Clause 1 (Accuracy) of the Code of Practice. The complaint was upheld.

Case Study 2: *David and Victoria Beckham v. Sunday Mirror* [2003]

Clauses noted: 1 and 15

Complaint

David and Victoria Beckham complained to the Commission through their solicitors that an article in the *Sunday Mirror* dated 16 November 2003 headlined 'All over' contained a large number of inaccuracies in breach of Clause 1 (Accuracy) of the Code.

Facts of the adjudication

The complaint arose as a result of an article about the marriage of David and Victoria Beckham. It was headlined 'World Exclusive' and 'All over' and covered almost the entire front page and the whole of pages 2–5 inside. The five pages had subheadlines in large letters, such as, 'Posh in threat to end the marriage. She tells Becks to quit Spain or else', 'Romance in ruins' and 'She's so mad'. The article purported to describe the marital difficulties of the couple in considerable detail and suggested that their marriage was on the brink of breakdown.

The solicitors complained that the allegations of marital breakdown in the article were false. They alleged that there were 16 different inaccurate statements in the article and asked for an urgent adjudication on the complaint in order to prevent the general public from being misled about the state of the couple's marriage. They said that the enormous amount of space given by the *Sunday Mirror* to the matter had led to the allegations being repeated by other newspapers and magazines, copies of which they enclosed. They also made submissions about the role of the Commission and the significance of evidence given by its chairman to a Commons Committee, which, they said, would require the newspaper to publish any apology or adverse adjudication on the front page with due prominence.

In subsequent correspondence, the solicitors referred to the Beckhams' denials of the allegations. They also enclosed the transcript of a television interview with Victoria Beckham in which she further denied the claims. They maintained that the substance of the article had come to the attention of millions of people and that only a front-page retraction would provide an adequate remedy.

The editor of the newspaper replied, saying that she was extremely concerned to read of the Beckhams' reaction to the article. She reserved her position about any response to the detail of the complaint, but said she was keen to resolve the matter and would be happy to publish a retraction and an apology with due prominence in a positive article about the Beckhams. This would be placed on an early news page, perhaps page 4 or 6, and would include statements to the effect that the marriage was not in trouble, that there was no ultimatum from Victoria or talk of a trial separation and that there had been no argument about the children's schools or where they should live.

When this offer was rejected, she dealt with the 16 substantive complaints. She pointed out that the complaints fell into three separate categories: first, that Victoria Beckham had threatened to end the marriage unless David Beckham returned to London; second, that there had been a row over the children's schooling; and, third, that there had been a row over Victoria's relationship with a named person. She said that the *Sunday Mirror* article was based on both information that was already in the public domain that had not attracted any formal complaint from the Beckhams and new information that came from sources that had been reliable in the past. Under Clause 15 of the Code, the newspaper was entitled to withhold the names of its informants. The newspaper had no reason to doubt the truth of the information supplied, but it was prepared to accept the Beckhams' denials in order to reach an amicable settlement.

The editor also enclosed a number of recent, lengthy newspaper articles that had made similar allegations to those of the *Sunday Mirror* but had not resulted in complaints to the

Commission. Some of these articles went back as far as September 2003, some two months before the *Sunday Mirror* article appeared, and were based on the separate inquiries of the newspapers concerned. She said it was important for the Commission to take this context into account and argued that the offer that she had made was in proportion to it.

The solicitors again rejected the offer, but indicated that their clients would be interested in seeing the sort of article that the newspaper was prepared to write. The newspaper responded by providing a draft apology to be published on page 2 under the heading 'David and Victoria Beckham'. The complainants rejected this offer and submitted their own wording for an apology, which they insisted should appear on the front page along with their photographs.

Decision

No finding. The Commission declined to proceed with the matter.

Reasons

Turning to the details of this complaint, it is important to understand that this complaint was made only under Clause 1 of the Code (Accuracy). No complaint was made in relation to Clause 3 of the Code (Privacy). The Commission was confined to making a decision about whether or not any of the 16 items could be shown to be inaccurate. In considering whether or not it could make a finding in this case, the Commission took a number of factors into account.

The Commission noted that the 16 individual complaints fell into two distinct groups. In the first, there were those items that were of a factual nature, relating to statements the Beckhams were alleged to have made to each other. In the second, there were those complaints about the conclusions that the newspaper had drawn from the alleged facts it had published about the marriage.

Regarding the first group, the Commission noted that the newspaper had, as it was entitled, relied on unnamed sources who could not be produced as witnesses. However, it had also provided evidence that stories about the Beckhams' marriage had been circulating for at least two months before they complained to the Commission. Indeed, similar stories, apparently based on different sources from those of the *Sunday Mirror*, were still being published after the date of the article under complaint. Despite this, the Commission has received no formal complaint about any of these other articles. As to the second group of complaints, the Commission took the view that the newspaper was reasonably entitled to draw its own conclusions from the information that it had received and which it believed to be reliable. This was in line with Commission policy in other cases.

Given the fact that the newspaper could not provide corroborative evidence to support its claims, it was right for it to provide an opportunity to the complainants to dispute the allegations. The newspaper offered either a positive story on an early news page – which would amount to an apology and retraction of the claims – or a statement of the Beckhams' position and apology on page 2 of the newspaper. The newspaper believed that its offer, in all the circumstances, was proportionate. The complainants, through their solicitors, took the view that they were at least entitled to an extensive front-page apology.

The Commission regretted that it was not possible to reconcile the two positions and negotiate an amicable resolution to this complaint. However, neither was it possible for the Commission to make a finding regarding the facts of the matter. The newspaper had two confidential sources for its claims – and had also pointed to allegations that had appeared elsewhere – while the complainants had simply denied the claims, although they also had the means to do so publicly on television and in other newspapers. With the evidence before it, the Commission was not in a position to decide whether the references to the state of the Beckhams' marriage at that time were accurate or not. It followed that it could not therefore reasonably come to a conclusion about whether or not the newspaper's offer was a proportionate remedy to the complaint. In this very unusual situation, the Commission reluctantly came to the view that there was no satisfactory way of proceeding with the complaint and that it should cease to deal with it. However, although the Commission could not come to a decision under the Code, it expected the newspaper to stand by its final offer to publish a statement on page 2 of the newspaper. To do so would be within the spirit of conciliation that self-regulation encourages.

Case Study 3: *Mr Darrell Desbrow v. The Scotsman* [2003]

Clause noted: 1

Complaint

Mr Darrell Desbrow of Kirkcudbrightshire complained to the Commission that an article headlined 'Most visitors feel ripped-off' published in the *Scotsman* on 10 September 2003 was inaccurate in breach of Clause 1 (Accuracy) of the Code. The article was a feature on tourism in Scotland and focused on the perception that the country did not offer value for money. The complainant contended that the comparative table of holiday prices that accompanied the text of the article had confused the exchange rates of sterling to euros and sterling to dollars. The complainant wrote to the newspaper directly three times, but did not receive acknowledgement of his correspondence.

The editor of the *Scotsman* failed to respond to three letters from the Commission Eventually, the newspaper's editor wrote to the complainant. Mr Desbrow, apologising for being so tardy in his overall response. The newspaper offered to publish a correction in its 'Corrections and clarifications' column and change its system for responding to readers who make complaints. The complainant argued that these offers were rendered inadequate by the four months it had taken for the paper to respond substantively to the complaint.

CASE STUDY

Decision

The complaint was upheld.

Reasons

The Commission considered that the newspaper's offer to publish a correction with regard to the inaccuracy and apologise directly to the complainant would generally have represented an appropriate form of remedial action. It also welcomed the newspaper's proposal to change its system for responding to readers' concerns. However, the Commission regretted the length of time taken for the newspaper to respond substantively to the complaint. The Code of Practice explicitly states that 'it is the responsibility of editors to cooperate with the PCC as swiftly as possible in the resolution of complaints'. In taking four months to reply to a straightforward complaint, the newspaper had not fulfilled its responsibility and the result was a breach of the Code. The Commission urged the newspaper to change its procedures for dealing with complaints as soon as possible so that a similar situation would not arise in future. 10/9/2003 (Report 65 PCC).

Relevant precedent

De Silva/Wijeyesinghe v. The Sunday Times Report 56. Mr Neville de Silva of Harrow and Mr Bodipala Wijeyesinghe of Carshalton complained separately that a number of articles published in the *Sunday Times* in April and July 2001 on the subject of the civil war in Sri Lanka were inaccurate and that no opportunity to reply had been given in breach of Clauses 1 (Accuracy) and 2 (Opportunity to reply). The complaints were upheld.

Case Study 4: *Ms Michelle Ryan v. Star magazine* [2004]

Clause noted: 3

Complaint

Ms Michelle Ryan of London complained to the Commission through A. & J. Management that an article published in *Star* magazine on 12 July 2004 headlined, 'Neighbourhood Celebwatch' intruded into her private life, in breach of Clause 3 (Privacy) of the Code.

The article described in general terms the area in which the complainant lived and provided a number of photographs of places where she allegedly spent time, including her home, her gym and a number of local shops. While her home address was not specified, the complainant suggested that the information provided in the article – particularly in relation to the gym – was sufficient to compromise her security by enabling people to trace her whereabouts.

CASE STUDY

The magazine did not accept that it had breached the Code, but offered to resolve the complaint in any case by writing to the complainant to apologise for any offence or distress caused by the piece. In addition, it said that it would take more care in the future in relation to any use of photographs of Ms Ryan and any accompanying copy. The complainant's agent did not consider the magazine's offered remedy to the complaint to be sufficient and suggested that the magazine should publish an apology.

Decision

The complaint was not upheld.

Reasons

The Commission has previously censured publications that identify the precise locations of the homes of high-profile individuals, mindful of the particular security problems that can arise as a result. In this case, however, while the Commission could understand why the complainant was uncomfortable with the published article and pictures, it concluded that they did not breach the Code for three principal reasons. First, the Commission was not persuaded that the magazine had provided sufficient information for people who were unfamiliar with the complainant to cause a nuisance to her – for instance, by turning up at her home. Second, the photographs of buildings and shops in her neighbourhood – taken in public places – did not include the complainant herself. She had not therefore been followed or endured any physical intrusion by journalists or photographers as she went about her daily business. Third, there was no actual evidence that the article had led to any security problems for the complainant. Having said that, there is a particular need for vigilance in this area and the Commission therefore welcomed the magazine's attempts to resolve the matter and, especially, its undertaking to take more care when dealing with such features in future.

Relevant rulings

Dynamite v. Islington Gazette Report 63. The singer Ms Dynamite complained to the Commission through her record company Polydor that an article and accompanying photograph headlined 'Chart star's dream house is right next door to mum' published in the *Islington Gazette* on 26 March 2003 intruded into her privacy in breach of Clause 3 (Privacy) of the Code of Practice. The complaint was upheld.

A well known entertainer v. Mail on Sunday Report 51. A well-known entertainer complained that an article and accompanying photographs published in the *Mail on Sunday* on 16 July 2000 intruded into her privacy and that of her child in breach of Clause 3 (Privacy) and Clause 6 (Children) of the Code of Practice. The complaint was *not* upheld.

Case Study 5: *Ms Kimberly Fortier v. Sunday Mirror* [2004]

Clauses noted: 3 and 4

Complaint

Ms Kimberly Fortier complained to the Commission through the Simkins Partnership that an article published in the *Sunday Mirror* on 29 August 2004 headlined, 'Blunkett lover: It's all over' included a photograph that had been taken in a manner that breached Clause 4 (ii) (Harassment) of the Code of Practice. She also complained that publication of the image intruded into her privacy in breach of Clause 3 (Privacy) of the Code and breached Clause 4 (iii) (Harassment) because the photograph constituted 'non-compliant material'.

The complainant was the subject of considerable press attention when it was alleged that she had been having an affair with the then Home Secretary. The first story about the alleged relationship appeared on 15 August 2004, although it did not name the complainant. The following day, the complainant was identified in another newspaper and her solicitors contacted the Commission, alleging that she was being harassed. In line with its normal procedures, the Commission communicated these concerns to the relevant newspapers, at which point the situation eased and Ms Fortier did not pursue any formal complaints. Her solicitors also wrote directly to several editors – including that of the *Daily Mirror* – on 16 August, requiring 'the activities comprising harassment, persistent pursuit, and the questioning, telephoning, pursuing or photographing of our client to cease'.

On 26 August, the complainant was approached while out walking with her son in Los Angeles and was photographed. Although her representatives warned several national newspaper editors that to publish any resulting picture would be to publish 'non-compliant material' in breach of Clause 4 (iii) (Harassment) of the Code, a picture of the complainant appeared in the *Sunday Mirror* on 29 August. Her solicitors submitted a formal complaint to the Commission, arguing that in light of their previous requests for harassment of their client to cease, the taking of the photograph was in breach of Clause 4 (ii) of the Code and its publication in breach of Clause 4 (iii), which requires editors to take care not to use material that is obtained in breach of the Code. Moreover, they argued that the photographer's approach on 26 August constituted harassment in its own right, given that the complainant had told him at the time that she did not want her photograph taken. Having stated that the complainant was on a public street when she was approached, her solicitors later said that she had in fact entered the grounds of a library when she was photographed and had not therefore been pictured in the street. However, they argued that the location was not in fact relevant because the complaint related to harassment, which can occur anywhere. In addition, they said that publication of the image intruded into their client's privacy, in breach of Clause 3 of the Code. Ms Fortier was not, said her solicitors, a public figure and both the newspaper and the freelance photographer were aware that she did not wish to be photographed.

The newspaper argued that the complainant was, in fact, a public figure, by virtue of her work in the media industry and her numerous appearances on radio and in newspapers and magazines. In addition, it had been alleged without challenge that she had – as a married woman with children – conducted an affair with the then Home Secretary. The newspaper contended that she had therefore put herself at the centre of a story, publication of which was legitimately in the public interest.

While the complainant's solicitors had told several newspapers (including the *Daily Mirror*, which was also part of the MGN group) not to engage in intimidation, harassment and persistent pursuit and to cease questioning, telephoning, pursuing and photographing her, the newspaper maintained it had done none of those things. Its legal adviser suggested that it would be 'a ludicrous situation if any person who was in the news as a result of their own actions could successfully demand that they should not be photographed in public'. On this occasion, Ms Fortier had been photographed by a freelance journalist while walking along a road – a place where she could not have had a reasonable expectation of privacy. Regarding that encounter, the journalist had approached her once, having taken her photograph. The paper accepted that she had not given her consent to be photographed, but this did not mean that the complainant had been harassed because there had been, as both sides agreed, only one approach.

The complainant's solicitors maintained that their client was not a public figure, but simply someone whose job carried with it the inevitable consequence of being to some extent in the public eye. She had no official, governmental, regulatory, legal or administrative function of any kind and therefore had an entitlement to privacy. Publication of the specific picture accompanying the article was not in the public interest and was wholly unnecessary.

Decision

The complaint was rejected.

Reasons

Noting that no complaint had been lodged about the more general coverage of the complainant's alleged affair with the then Home Secretary, the Commission's central task in this case was to decide whether or not the taking and publication of the particular photograph under contention was in breach of the Code and, if it was, whether or not there was justification in terms of public interest for that breach.

Clause 4 (Harassment) requires journalists not to engage in 'intimidation, harassment or persistent pursuit' and there was no evidence that those responsible for taking the picture in question had behaved in this way. Similarly, there did not appear to have been questioning or telephoning of the complainant in a way that would infringe the requirements of the Code. While the complainant had apparently been distressed by the approach, something that the Commission regretted, it did not appear that the photographer had 'persisted' in taking her photograph after having been asked to desist. The photographer had asked the complainant if she wished to pose for a picture and she had indicated that she did not. At some point – either before he spoke to her or afterwards – he took a photograph. Neither account of the incident led the Commission to conclude that there had been a breach of the Code. However, the matter under Clause 4 did not end there because the Commission had to consider the further argument that the request of 16 August to journalists and photographers to desist from approaching the complainant was still relevant on 26 August. The solicitors had contended that this was the case and that any approach made after the 16 August would therefore breach the Code.

The Commission found this argument difficult to accept. It was certainly not disputed that the newspaper was aware of the complainant's earlier request and also aware of her request – made after the photograph was taken – that any resulting image not be published. However, the purpose of Clause 4 is to protect individuals and provide relief from physical intrusion by journalists and photographers, whether they are on their own or in a group. The Commission responds quickly and flexibly to any complaints under Clause 4 because it recognises the immediacy of any problem and is well placed to organise the disbanding of press packs by passing on messages to desist.

The Commission does not consider it appropriate – or within the meaning of Clause 4 – to assume that a request for journalists and photographers to desist from approaching a complainant lasts in perpetuity. It would be artificial not to recognise that circumstances change. The Commission judges each case on its merits and, on this occasion, it noted that the approach had taken place ten days after the request to desist, during which time there had been demonstrable developments in the story. Indeed, the article that accompanied the photograph had reported the news that the complainant had contacted the then Home Secretary in order to bring an end to their alleged relationship. In these circumstances, the Commission found no breach of the Code in the photographer's approach to the complainant, which took place in public and without any physical intimidation. It followed that there was also no breach of Clause 4 (iii) regarding the use of non-compliant material.

Ms Fortier also complained under Clause 3, arguing that publication of the photograph intruded into her private life. The complainant's solicitors had at no stage argued that she was in a place where she had a reasonable expectation of privacy when she was photographed. The Commission does not generally consider that the publication of photographs of people in public places breaches the Code. In this case – in circumstances where there had been no harassment – the Commission did not consider that there was any particular reason to divert from this general principle. Exceptions might be made if there were particular security concerns, for instance, or in rare circumstances when a photograph reveals something about an individual's health that is not in the public interest.

The Commission noted that the newspaper and the complainant's solicitors had disagreed about whether or not the complainant was a public figure. Whether or not this was the case, it had been alleged publicly that she was having a relationship with a senior politician. Her identity had been established in the public domain without complaint. There was a general public debate about the life of a senior politician with whom the complainant was allegedly involved. No complaints had been received from the politician or from the complainant about the content of the numerous articles about their alleged relationship. The Commission could not agree that, in this context, the publication of a photograph – which contributed to the public debate and was taken in accordance with the Code at a time when the story was developing – was intrusive. For all these reasons, the complaint was rejected.

Case Study 6: *A married couple v. Daily Mail* [2004]

Clause noted: 1

Complaint

A married couple from Cheshire complained to the Commission that an article headlined, 'She was the 12-year-old British girl who ran away with a US Marine she met on the Internet. But what was the REAL story behind their "romance" … and how much are her family to blame?' published in the *Daily Mail* on 26 February 2004 contained inaccuracies in breach of Clause 1 (Accuracy) of the Code of Practice.

The parents of the 12-year-old girl abducted by Toby Studabaker, a United States Marine, complained that the article, which blamed them for the circumstances that led to the incident, was inaccurate and misleading on several counts.

The complaints could be separated into three distinct categories. The first concerned the emotional state of the victim in the aftermath of events. The complainants said that the description of their daughter as 'cooped up indoors', 'tearful' and 'isolated' was inaccurate. Equally, the girl did not remain convinced that she was 'deeply in love' with Studabaker, she did not blame her parents for 'interfering' with her life, nor did she still have plans for reconciliation with her abductor. Furthermore, it was not the case that the complainants' daughter had insisted that nothing sexual happened and had refused to give any details of what had occurred.

The second group of complaints related to descriptions of the complainants and their relationship with their daughter by unnamed sources. They stated that references to the family as 'dysfunctional', 'tense' and 'not particularly well-equipped for dealing with pubescent girls' – and to the mother specifically as 'domineering', 'controlling' and 'prone to odd behaviour' – were untrue. In addition, inferences drawn from these descriptions – such as that the complainants' daughters found it difficult to develop their own personalities – were distorted.

The final category of complaints related to the complainants' other daughter. The article alleged that she had 'left the family home as soon as she turned 16' and had become pregnant before her 16th birthday. The complainants said that she was 16 when she became pregnant and left home when she was nearer to 17. The complainants argued that the newspaper had relied on unsubstantiated opinion in writing the article and did not accept that the newspaper should be allowed to use confidential sources in such a serious matter. They considered that a public apology was required.

The newspaper regretted that the article had upset the complainants. The sources for the article – which included a close family member, a neighbour and the mother of one of the victim's schoolfriends – could not be revealed owing to the sensitive subject matter. Regarding the description of the family as 'dysfunctional', the newspaper said that this term was used on more than one occasion by people who knew them well and were close to the police inquiry. Similarly, the sections referring to relationships within the family came from those directly involved in the investigation. The newspaper argued that the fact that the victim was often on her computer for up to 11 hours a day – which was mentioned in open court and not disputed – suggested a degree of dysfunctionality within the family. The article comprised freely held opinions based on facts that were established in the public domain. The newspaper said that the police – as well as the close family member – insisted that the victim continued to be unable to accept what had happened. One police officer had remarked that she had to be treated as a 'hostile witness', owing to her reluctance to implicate Studabaker. This was mentioned in court. Furthermore, this point was already fully in the public domain as it had been included in a previous article on the matter in a separate newspaper.

Finally, the newspaper considered that the reference to the complainants' other daughter leaving home at 16 was not a fundamental mistake or a significant inaccuracy in the context of the article as a whole. The fact that their daughter did not stay at home once she was legally able to move elsewhere illustrated a degree of unease within the family environment. Nonetheless, the newspaper was prepared to annotate its records so that the complainants' concerns would be taken into account in any future references to the case. It was, in addition, ready to consider any reasonable course to help to resolve the matter, including publishing an anonymous letter from the complainants in response to the article.

Decision

Following an offer of remedial action from the newspaper, no further action was required.

Reasons

First, the Commission made clear that it could well understand that the complainants found the contents of the article distasteful. Nonetheless, it emphasised that it could only come to a decision under the terms of the Code. Clause 1 (Accuracy) permits the publication of opinion – even from anonymous sources – provided that it is clearly distinguished as such. The Commission noted that the article contained a number of anonymous personal opinions about the complainants and their family – views with which the complainants clearly disagreed. The Commission found, however, that they had been presented as opinion in accordance with the Code, not as fact. Moreover, it noted that some of the claims to which the complainants had objected had already been established in the public domain both by virtue of being revealed in court and in a sister newspaper article, regarding which no previous complaint had been made.

However, there were some instances where the complainants objected to the underlying accuracy of the claims and the newspaper relied solely on anonymous sources, either directly or when summarising their views. Clause 14 (Confidential sources) of the Code imposes an obligation on newspapers to protect anonymous sources of information. Nonetheless, it is the Commission's normal practice when considering complaints about the accuracy of claims made by such sources to examine whether or not there is any material to corroborate the claims and, if not, to ask the newspaper to afford the complainant an opportunity to reply. This general approach is designed to prevent newspapers from using Clause 14 as a trump card to defend any allegation of inaccuracy.

As noted above, the newspaper had shown that some of the details under dispute had been established elsewhere in the public domain and the Commission was satisfied that there was no breach of the Code on those points. Turning to the outstanding matters, it was clear to the Commission that the newspaper was constrained in offering any remedial action by the legal requirements preventing any on-the-record response from the complainants. In these circumstances, the Commission considered that the newspaper's dual offer to annotate its records with the complainants' concerns and publish an anonymous letter from them putting their point of view was a proportionate and suitable remedy to the complaint. No further action was required.

Relevant precedents

Mr Paul McKenna v. Daily Mirror, 18/10/2003 (Report 65 PCC). Mr Paul McKenna complained to the Commission through his solicitors that an article published in the *Daily Mirror* on 18 October 2003 headlined 'It's a load of doc and bull' was inaccurate in breach of Clause 1 (Accuracy) of the Code of Practice. The complaint was rejected.

David and Victoria Beckham v. Sunday Mirror, 16/11/2003 (Report 65 PCC). David and Victoria Beckham complained to the Commission through their solicitors that an article in the *Sunday Mirror* of 16 November 2003, headlined 'All over' contained a large number of inaccuracies in breach of Clause 1 (Accuracy) of the Code. The complaint arose out of an article about the marriage of David and Victoria Beckham. It was headlined 'World Exclusive' and 'All over', and covered almost the entire front page and the whole of pages 2–5 inside with sub-headlines such as, 'Posh in threat to end the marriage. She tells Becks to quit Spain or else', 'Romance in ruins' and 'She's so mad'. The article purported to describe the marital difficulties of the couple in considerable detail and suggested that the marriage was on the brink of breakdown. Decision: No finding.

EMI Records Limited v. News of the World, 6/1/2003 (Report 65 PCC). EMI Records Ltd complained to the Commission through solicitors that an article in the RAV column headlined 'Kylie to sign for £35M' published in the *News of the World* on 1st June 2003 was based on inaccurate material – which had not then been corrected promptly – in breach of Clause 1 (Accuracy) of the Code. The article reported that the pop star Kylie Minogue was on the verge of signing a recording contract worth £35 million. According to the complainant no such deal had ever been discussed or contemplated between Ms Minogue and her record company. In fact, her current contract (which the complainant said was also inaccurately described) was not due for renewal for some time. During the course of the PCC investigation, the solicitors provided signed statements by their client's Business Affairs Director and from Ms Minogue's managers which said that no £35 million deal, or anything like it, had ever been contemplated or taken place. In light of remedial action offered by the newspaper, there were no further issues to pursue under the Code. An adjudication was sent to the parties on 9 December

2003 but has been amended following representations made to the Commission by the complainant's solicitors. Decision: no further action.

The Rt Hon Charles Clarke MP v. The Times (Report 58 PCC). The Rt Hon Charles Clarke MP complained to the Commission that an article headlined 'Blair ally leads push against Speaker', published in *The Times* on 9 February 2002, contained inaccurate material in breach of Clause 1 (Accuracy) of the Code of Practice. Following an offer of remedial action by the editor to make the complainant's position clear, no further action was required.

The role of Ofcom

Ofcom – the Office of Communications – has been the UK's regulator for the communications industry since 2003, when it took over responsibility for regulating almost all of the UK's communications industry, with one exception – the BBC, which is still currently regulated by its governors.

Ofcom inherited the duties of the five former regulators it replaced: the Broadcasting Standards Commission, the Independent Television Commission, Oftel, the Radio Authority and the Radiocommunications Agency. Ofcom is an independent regulatory body that, in addition, fulfils duties enacted in the provisions laid down in the *Communications Act 2003*.

The newly revised Ofcom Code for TV and Radio (2005) came into force on 25 July 2005 and condenses the six codes inherited from Ofcom's predecessors into a framework of clear rules and principles.[4] As well as setting standards to protect those under the age of 18, the Code allows broadcasters as much freedom of expression, in line with Art. 10 ECHR, as is consistent with the law (s. 12 HRA 1998), as well as the flexibility to differentiate between services and enable their audiences to make informed choices. Art. 10, together with Art. 8, ECHR, regarding the right to respect for a person's private and family life, home and correspondence, have been the focal point of the revision of the Ofcom Code.[5]

Ofcom's Code of Practice (2005)[6]

- *Freedom of expression* Broadcasters may transmit challenging material, provided it is editorially justified and the audience given appropriate information.
- *Commercial references* Deregulation of sponsorship and commercial references.
- *Protection of those under 18* Protection of children by means of PIN mechanisms for premium subscription film services and hard-core pornography.
- *Promotion of cultural diversity* Duty to foster plurality and informed citizenship.
- *Support innovators and creators* Driven by fair competition between all providers.[7]

Ofcom has far-reaching responsibilities for television, radio, telecommunications and wireless communication services. It covers both content and infrastructure in the communications sector. The *Communications Act 2003* provides that Ofcom is subject to inspection by the National Audit Office and accountable to the Public Accounts Committee regarding propriety and value for money.

Ofcom's executive and Board provide its strategic direction. Ofcom is the main statutory instrument of regulation with a fundamental role in the effective implementation of the *Communications Act 2003*. Ofcom has a Board with a non-executive chairman and both executive and non-executive members. Ofcom does not have a director-general with sole decision-making responsibility, a Board consisting of entirely part-time members or a body of commissioners.

The executive runs the organisation and answers to the Board, while the work of both the Board and executive are informed by contributions from a number of advisory bodies. The Board is chaired by Lord Currie of Marylebone (2006). There are eight additional members, including the Chief Executive of Ofcom and two members from the executive. Ofcom's Board members meet formally every month. Ofcom is structured so that the main decision-making body of Ofcom is its Board. There are also several committees and advisory bodies with delegated powers.[8]

Regulating the digital age

One of Ofcom's main challenges has been dealing with communications industries in the digital age. During late 2004, Ofcom investigated digital radio and the perceived benefits it would offer both broadcasters and listeners – greater choice, enhanced services, such as onscreen programme information, ease of use and reduced audio interference. In December 2004, Ofcom was seeking views (via its website) on a number of potential options for digital radio, including:

- allocating three more blocks of spectrum in VHF Band III to complete the coverage of DAB local digital radio throughout the UK
- proposing to raise the current 20 per cent limit on the use of DAB digital radio multiplexes for non-programme-related data, such as multimedia downloads – this would require approval from the Secretary of State for Culture, Media and Sport
- replacing specific requirements for audio bit rates for DAB digital radio services with a system of coregulation to define audio quality standards that meet audience expectations.

Under s. 355 of the *Communications Act 2003*, Ofcom is required to carry out a review of any local radio licence that undergoes a change of control in order to ensure that the character of the service, quality and range of programming and amount of local content are not prejudiced as a result of the change of control. One example was the proposed merger of Capital Radio and the GWR Group plc. Ofcom's report of 22 December 2004 determined that 30 GWR local analogue radio licences would undergo a change of control as a result of the merger.

- *GWR Bristol and Bath FM* Separate weekday breakfast services are currently provided for each of the Bristol and Bath areas. Provision is written into the licence to ensure continued provision of these separate services.
- *MFM/Buzz Wrexham and Chester FM licence* A separate weekday breakfast service for the Wirral is currently provided and this provision is written into the licence to ensure that this separate service is continued.
- Ofcom has concluded that none of the statutory ownership rules would be breached by the merger.
- Specifically, Ofcom concluded that the specific ownership rules designed to protect plurality in relation to local analogue radio licences, local digital multiplex licences and local digital sound programme service licences would not be breached if the merger were to go ahead as currently envisaged.[9]

Ofcom is also now the UK's telecommunications regulator and, in January 2005, the government's Trade and Industry Select Committee (TISC) was asked to scrutinise the body's strategic review of the industry to assess the regulator's approach to promoting the right framework for a competitive broadband market. In particular, the TISC focused on the UK's broadband market, including 'local loop unbundling' (LLU) and the functional separation of BT.

In November 2004, Ofcom had rejected calls to break up BT.[10] It called instead for the telecommunications industry ('Telco') to make 'substantive behavioural and organisational changes' and provide equal access to its wholesale product range. Ofcom had noted in its 2004 report that breaking up BT would be tricky, needing an 'Enterprise Act' market investigation as well as some form of referral to the Competition Commission. Ofcom's report concluded that, if equal access failed and BT would not change sufficiently, then splitting the Telco would be appropriate as a 'last resort'.

Ofcom's penalties

One of Ofcom's roles is to set penalty guidelines under s. 392 of the *Communications Act 2003* when a member of the communications industry has contravened the Code or parts of it, particularly in relation to competition with other providers.[11] Ofcom will then determine an appropriate and proportionate penalty. In addition, Ofcom must have regard to any representations made to them by the regulated body in breach. Accordingly, Ofcom, in setting the level of penalty, will consider all relevant circumstances.

Ofcom's penalties

In general, Ofcom is likely to consider the following factors first when determining the starting figure of any penalty:

- the seriousness of the contravention
- any precedents set by previous cases
- the need to ensure that the threat of penalties will act as a sufficient incentive to comply.

Ofcom's punishment criteria

Certain specific criteria may be relevant when adjusting the starting figure of any penalty, depending on the type of contravention. This may include, but would not necessarily be limited to:

- what gain was made by the regulated body in breach – financial or otherwise
- what degree of harm was caused
- what the increased cost incurred by consumers was
- the size and turnover of the regulated body
- to what extent a contravention was caused by a third party
- what the duration of the contravention was
- whether or not a similar penalty regarding the same conduct had already been imposed.

QUESTIONS

1(a) In Case Study 1 (*Miss Elizabeth Noble v. News of the World*), why, in your opinion, was the complainant's case upheld? State with clear reference to the Code and give reasons.

1(b) What is the warning issued to editors regarding the Code that resulted from this November 2003 case?

2 Why, in your opinion, did the Commission decline to proceed with the Beckhams' matter in Case Study 2 (*David and Victoria Beckham v. Sunday Mirror*)? Give detailed reasons to back up your argument.

3 In Case Study 3, what, in your opinion, was the main reason for adjudicating in favour of Mr Desbrow versus the *Scotsman*?

4 In Case Study 4, having said that there is a particular need for vigilance in this area of intrusion into a celebrity's private life, why, in your opinion, did the Commission not uphold the complaint of Ms Ryan under Clause 3?

5 In the then high-profile case involving Ms Fortier (Publisher of *The Spectator* magazine) and the then Home Secretary Mr David Blunkett (Case Study 5), the complainant particularly raised the 'harassment' issue under Clause 4. This requires that journalists not to engage in 'intimidation, harassment or persistent pursuit'. Why, in your opinion, was Ms Fortier's complaint not upheld by the Commission in spite of her being very distressed indeed and pregnant at the time?

6 In Case Study 6, what was it that particularly aggrieved the parents regarding their 12-year-old daughter and the newspaper's coverage of events?

7 Describe what is meant by the 'public interest' test and how this might be applied by Ofcom. Give examples related to the communications industry.

8 In March 2003, there was a proposal before Parliament to grant the media 'watchdog' Ofcom more power over editorial content in the communications industry (such as over the BBC). How, in your opinion, does this submission fit with the industry's self-regulation, as already seen in the PCC? Discuss.

FURTHER READING

PCC, 'Editors' Code of Practice 2005, available from PressBoF, 48 Palmerston Place, Edinburgh EH12 5DE. E-mail: editorscode@fsmail.net

Shannon, R. (2001) *A Press Free and Responsible: Self-regulation and the Press Complaints Commission, 1991–2001*. London: John Murray.

Notes

1 For a full report on the PCC in 2004, visit: www.pcc.org.uk/2004/index.html

2 See also report by Ciar Byrne, 'PCC under fire at Commons inquiry', the *Guardian*, 25 February 2003.

3 *Campbell (Appellant) v. MGN Limited (Respondents)* [2004] UKHL 22.

4 The 2005 Code also gives effect to a number of requirements relating to television in EC Directive 89/552/EEC, as amended by EC Directive 97/36/EC ('The Television Without Frontiers Directive').

5 Others – Art. 9 ECHR (the right to freedom of thought, conscience and religion), Art. 14 ECHR (the right to enjoyment of human rights without discrimination on grounds such as sex, race and religion) – are given in Appendix 3 of the Code.

6 On 10 June 2005, Ofcom published its new Broadcasting Code for TV and Radio. Section 319 of the *Communications Act 2003* and s. 107 of the *Broadcasting Act 1996* require Ofcom to draw up a code for TV and radio covering standards in programmes, sponsorship, fairness and privacy.

7 For a full version of the Ofcom Broadcasting Code 2005, visit: www.ofcom.org.uk/tv/ifi/codes/bcode/#content

8 These include the Consumer Panel, Content Board, Nations and Regions Advisory Committees and Older Persons and Disabled Persons Advisory Committee.

9 'Radio – Preparing for the Future' (report of 15 December 2004). The review was undertaken as result of a requirement under s. 67 of the *Broadcasting Act 1996* for Ofcom to report to the Secretary of State on the progress and future prospects of digital radio. Additionally, s. 314 of the *Communications Act 2003* requires Ofcom to produce guidance on the inclusion of local material and local production in analogue commercial radio.

10 See Ofcom's phase two report, 'Strategic Review of Telecommunications' (November 2004).

11 Parliament agreed that, from 1 November 2004, complaints about advertising on television and radio would be dealt with by the Advertising Standards Authority (ASA) rather than Ofcom. The ASA's main obligation is to ensure that *all* advertising, wherever it appears, meets the high standards laid down in the advertising codes (for the latest ASA adjudications see: http//www.asa.org.uk/asa/adjudications). Ofcom can revoke a licence of an authority which has contravened the ASA code (see the case of the teleshopping channel 'Auctionworld Ltd' 17/11/2004).

CHAPTER FOUR

CONTEMPT OF COURT

Key aim of this chapter:

> To enable you to understand the main principles and implications of contempt of court.

Learning objectives

By the end of the chapter you should be able to demonstrate:

- a sound knowledge and appreciation of the complexities and principles of contempt of court in civil and criminal proceedings
- a thorough knowledge of the *Contempt of Court Act 1981* (CCA)
- an understanding of the meaning of 'strict liability' and its implications for proceedings against newspaper publishers, editors and journalists
- an understanding of the meaning of 'substantial risk' as applied by the courts in leading case law
- an awareness and understanding of the meaning of 'active' and 'inactive' court proceedings and the practical implications for journalists
- an awareness of and ability to apply common and statutory legislation in relation to 'contempt' proceedings
- an understanding of the interrelationships and conflicts between the CCA and the HRA (especially Arts 8 and 10 ECHR)
- that you recognise the role of editorial policy in the decision-making process
- that you can express reasoned and critical arguments in the problem-solving case study exercises.

Chapter Contents

Introduction

The question of contempt – together with that of defamation (see Chapter 6) – is one of the most important for any journalist. In this chapter, you will be alerted to the dangers and pitfalls of contempt and what reporting on 'active' court proceedings means. Do not forget, however, the basic principle of 'open justice'. In general, court proceedings must be held in open court, press and public have the right to attend, evidence is communicated publicly and nothing is done to discourage the publication to the wider public of fair and accurate reporting of those proceedings.

Contempt (as established in common law authority by the famous Thalidomide case)[1] means prejudicing court proceedings. This is particularly important in criminal proceedings where the greatest risk for a court reporter lies in the publication of material that might sway a juror's mind and thereby prejudice a fair trial for the accused.

A journalist can be held in contempt by publishing anything that interferes with the course of justice (in a civil or criminal court case) once proceedings are regarded as 'active' – the meaning of which will be explained in the light of the *Contempt of Court Act 1981* (CCA). Punishment can be a severe fine or, at worst, two years' imprisonment for an editor. Imprisonment is rare, however, and last recorded in *R. v. Bolam, ex parte Haigh* [1949][2] (a judicial review case), where the *Daily Mirror* published sensational suggestions that a man arrested for one particularly 'foul' murder was not only guilty but guilty of other murders, too. The newspaper's editor was imprisoned for three months.

That the courts set very high fines today for contempt was demonstrated in *AG v. Express Newspapers* [2004][3] where the Divisional Court (DC) of the High Court ordered the publishers of the *Daily Star* to pay a fine of £60,000 for contempt under s. 2(2) CCA, for publishing the names of two footballers accused of gang-raping a teenage girl in a London Hotel on 10 October 2003. The publication happened in spite of the fact that the police and the prosecution had issued warnings to newspaper editors not to publish as the investigations were of a very sensitive nature and the victim had, up to that point, not known the identity of the alleged assailants, who were later acquitted.

For a long time, courts relied on case law, but, as time went on, this was held insufficient and, for this reason, the CCA was enacted. The Act limits a journalist's or editor's freedom by means of the operation of the 'strict liability' rule. This provides that a person can be guilty of contempt by publication, regardless of intent, in 'active' court proceedings. How this might interact or even conflict with the *Human Rights Act 1998* is discussed later in this chapter. As journalists, it is necessary understand that the principle enshrined in Art. 10 ECHR ('freedom of expression') is not absolute. Statutory restrictions have been imposed by the CCA so that magistrates and judges have the power to exercise discretion in the interests of justice, to make reporting restriction (or complete banning) orders. The aim is that, properly used, the CCA can ensure the continuing application of the principle of open justice.

You will be expected to have regard for and be able to discuss the impact of the *Human Rights Act 1998* (HRA) and leading Convention rights under Arts 8 and 10 in relation to privacy, contempt and the media. How the courts have actually used the CCA and the rules on 'strict liability' and 'substantial risk' of prejudice will be shown in case law as it has developed since the Act of 1981 came into force. You need bear in mind, however, balancing the administration of justice and the need for openness in the courts to allow the media to inform the public remains an area of controversy.

Definitions of contempt of court in common law

Any journalist can fall foul of the law of contempt of court in a number of ways. The main function of the law of contempt is to preserve the integrity of the legal process in order to provide a fair trial. In criminal proceedings particularly, extraneous information (such as background material on a defendant) might sway a juror's mind one way or the other. A reporter or editor may also be in contempt by republishing anything that interferes with the course of justice generally. Great dangers lie in reporting a retrial after a jury's 'hung verdict'.

Nowadays, judges might order a complete reporting ban under the CCA after a jury fails to agree or the prosecution fails unexpectedly for some reason. One such example was the trial of former SAS soldier Andrew Wragg, accused of murdering his terminally ill son. The jury was dismissed at Lewes Crown Court on 3 May 2005 as it failed to reach a verdict. The 11-day trial at Lewes Crown Court heard how Wragg had admitted smothering his 10-year-old wheelchair-bound son Jacob, claiming it was a mercy killing because the boy suffered from 'abnormality of mind' due to Hunter Syndrome. Jacob died on 24 July 2004.[4] After deliberating for more than 11 hours, the jury could not reach a verdict. Mrs Justice Anne Rafferty ordered a retrial for November 2005 and a total reporting ban on any background information until the conclusion of the case. There was indeed no media coverage until the outcome of the retrial. On 12 December 2005, Andrew Wragg (38), from Worthing, West Sussex, was found not guilty of murdering his son Jacob, but admitted manslaughter on grounds of diminished responsibility. He was given a two-year suspended prison sentence at Lewes Crown Court. Summing up, Mrs Justice Anne Rafferty told Mr Wragg: 'I have no doubt she [Mrs Mary Wragg, Jacob's mother] was complicit. Had I concluded otherwise I should have formed a harsher view of you' (BBC News Online, 12 December 2005).

Legal rules – either in common or statutory law – are there to preserve the integrity of the legal process and safeguard the dignity of the court. If an editor is found to be in breach of a court order – violating reporting restrictions in rape or juvenile cases, for example – this can be deemed contempt. The leading case in this area is the so-called Thalidomide case (*AG v. Times Newspapers* [1974]),[5] in which the then Editor of the *Sunday Times*, Harold Evans (later Sir Harold, knighted for services to journalism in 2004), started a crusade against the UK drugs company Distillers for distributing the drug Thalidomide.

Between 1955 and 1957, the chemical compound α-Phthalimidoglutarimide was developed by Chemie Grünenthal GmbH in the German town of Stolberg. The new substance, named Thalidomide, became the active agent of the calming and sleep-inducing drug Contergan, which was introduced on to the market on 1 October 1957 in West Germany. Thalidomide (Contergan) became infamous in the early 1960s in the context of one of the biggest drug disasters of recent history as a result of the drug being prescribed to combat symptoms associated with morning sickness in pregnant women. When taken during the first trimester of pregnancy, Thalidomide prevented the proper growth of the foetus, resulting in horrific birth defects, such as severe deformations of the vertebral column and the extremities. There followed epidemic malformations (including those of internal organs) wherever the drug was sold in Europe, Asia, Australia, America and Africa. Though the first child afflicted by Thalidomide damage to the ears was born on 25 December 1956, it took about four and a half years before Australian gynaecologist Dr McBride, of Sydney, suspected that Thalidomide was the cause of the limb and bowel malformations in three children he had seen at Crown Street Women's Hospital.

The first prosecution of Chemie Grünenthal was actioned in 1961 and, on 27 May 1968, seven members of Chemie Grünenthal stood trial at Aachen court. The case was that they had put on sale a drug that caused an unacceptable degree of bodily harm without having tested it properly and they had failed to react to information on side-effects in due time, instead trying to suppress information.

The court had its final session on 18 December 1970. There followed an out-of-court settlement with an agreed 100 million Deutschmarks being paid to the malformed children. By 28 September 1973 the German Ministry of Health had set up detailed instructions for granting compensation in cases of Thalidomide (Contergan) damage, including a point scale for fixing the sum depending on the degree of damage.

The English Thalidomide HL law report gives us detailed background to the case (*AG v. Times Newspapers* [1974]), which was that Distillers had marketed Thalidomide in the UK from 1957 until 1961. The drug was taken off the market in 1961, which was when the German law suit started. From 1961 to 1968, some 70 actions were brought against Distillers in the English courts by malformed children and/or their parents, and all – except for two parents – settled out of court at that time.

Hugo Young reported in the *Guardian* of 20 February 1968 that each of the 62 'thalidomide babies' whose parents had sued the company Distillers at first had been offered 'substantial damages' by the company. Young commented: 'The Distillers Company (Bio-chemicals) Ltd. is to pay to each child 40 per cent of the total damages to which it would have been entitled had their actions been tried and been wholly successful.' Mr Desmond Ackner QC, on behalf of the parents and children, told Mr Justice Hinchcliffe, presiding: 'Under the terms of settlement the damages payable to the infants will be very substantial. If the actions had continued, the plaintiffs could have failed to recover a penny piece.' As part of the settlement, all allegations of negligence against the company had to be withdrawn. Mr Michael Kerr QC for Distillers said that the withdrawal of the negligence allegations was important because of the reputations of doctors and scientists who had assessed thalidomide on the company's behalf and who had always maintained 'that these tragic events' were not foreseeable in the then state of knowledge.

The formulations of each of the 62 cases and the disclosure of the relevant papers involved some 300,000 documents. This was the first time in a British court that a child had claimed damages for injuries suffered before birth. The problem of fact was that the plaintiffs had to establish that the defendants (Distillers) were in breach of their duty of care to the unborn infant plaintiffs, assuming that such a duty existed. The cases settled at the time were those involving malformation to the foetus; there were cases remaining where the drug was alleged to have caused peripheral neuritis, and these claims still had to be litigated. Mr Justice Hinchcliffe concluded at this time: 'In my judgment the plaintiffs are well advised to accept the offer of the defendants.' By June 1971 there were still some 389 outstanding law suits in the High Court.

The first article in the *Sunday Times* on 24 September 1972 criticised Distillers for not offering parents of Thalidomide-affected children more generous compensation. The paper suggested that Distillers had not taken proper care before putting Thalidomide on the market and was being extremely miserly with its settlements. It referred to poor trust fund settlements to the parents over only ten years and noted high pre-tax profits of the company. Six more articles of this kind were planned.

On 12 October 1972, Distillers asked the Attorney General (AG) to injunct any further publications, claiming contempt of court, because (civil) court proceedings were still active. On 20 October – after an appeal from the *Sunday Times* – the Queen's Bench Division of the High Court lifted the injunction on the grounds that the newspaper editor believed all the facts to be true and the matter was in the public interest. On 17 November the AG cross-appealed and a further injunction was granted. This was followed by a heated debate in Parliament on 29 November, where the 'freedom of the press' was argued in line with public interest notification and it was suggested that the public had a right to know about the Thalidomide atrocities regarding hundreds of malformed children.

On 16 February 1973, the CA discharged the second injunction, allowing *The Times* to continue publication. On 1 March, the AG's appeal to the HL was eventually successful, in that a permanent injunction (to the UK print press) was granted.

It was at this point that Lord Reid set the precedent for contempt of court in common law. His main points of law were that the courts were still determining outstanding claims of Thalidomide affected-children and parents, which meant that any article on the matter (even well-constructed background material) could interfere with the course of justice – that is, outstanding negligence claims in the High Court. The HL viewed the first article in the *Sunday Times* in 1972 as putting immense moral pressure on Distillers, its shareholders and the wider public and this had amounted to contempt of court. The HL finally granted the injunction with the famous words that now signify contempt before the *Contempt of Court Act 1981* came in to force:

> There has long been and there still is in this country a strong and generally held feeling that trial by newspaper is wrong and should be prevented ... What I think is regarded as most objectionable is that a newspaper or television programme should seek to persuade the pubic, by discussing the issues and evidence in a case before the court, where civil or criminal, that one side is right and the other wrong.

There are circumstances in which statute automatically restricts the provision of certain details in reports of court proceedings, such as in youth justice cases under the *Children and Young Persons Act 1933*. In other circumstances, common law powers and statutory restrictions enable the court to exclude the public and the media and impose temporary or permanent restrictions on the media's reports of court proceedings by making a court order. In all such circumstances, courts are encouraged to exercise discretion in hearing media representations when considering imposing an order or lifting one already in force. Such discretion should be exercised in addition to any formal rights that the media might have for appeal or review. This is designed to ensure that problems are resolved quickly.

The law provides particular protection to contemporaneous reports of court proceedings and has recognised the 'perishable' nature of news. Courts have acknowledged the importance of hearing and resolving issues relating to reporting as soon as possible (in *Reynolds v. Times Newspapers Ltd* [2001]). If the necessary balance between the general principle of open justice and properly competing interests is to be achieved, a clear understanding of the legal basis for the imposition of restrictions is necessary by magistrates, court staff and the media.

What does this mean in practical terms for journalists when reporting court proceedings? Daily court listings of cases to be heard are available in each court house and can be obtained from the legal managers (court clerks). Additionally, you can obtain a register of decisions in magistrates' courts either online from the Court Service. Provisional court listings are now available to the media on request. Such lists will usually contain each defendant's name, age, address and, where known, his or her profession and the alleged offence. You may wish to get in touch with court staff to check the progress of cases and, when court reporting, you must ensure the accuracy of names and charges or other matters (visit: www.hmcourts-service.gov.uk). The Home Office and the Data Protection Commissioner (DPC) have stressed that lists, the provision of registers and other information by counts does not contravene the *Data Protection Act 1998*.

What is the duty of editors? They should ensure that – once they have received the court register – there are no relevant legal restraints on publication (that is, reporting restrictions) in relation to any of the defendants. Editors must ensure that when (especially junior) reporters cover a court case, they act responsibly in court (adhere to all forms of 'contempt' and court etiquette according to the CCA) and cover each case accurately and contemporaneously, so that fair and truthful articles are published about all the cases in court.

Contempt of Court Act 1981 (CCA)

By the late 1970s it became clear, that common (case) law would no longer suffice and 'contempt' had to be set in statute. For this reason, as well as covering courtroom etiquette and behaviour, the *Contempt of Court Act 1981* (CCA) came into being (covering England, Wales and Scotland). Its primary purpose is to preserve the integrity of the legal process, particularly in criminal trials, but it also covers civil proceedings, including family court proceedings (such as adoption or care orders in magistrates' courts or child anonymity orders in family courts).

Though the danger of contempt is greatest for a court reporter when covering criminal cases, the *Sunday Times* Thalidomide ruling showed that there can be certain dangers when covering high-profile civil cases. For as soon as a writ has been issued, silence must prevail in the press. Even writing about an 'imminent' case about to be tried, a newspaper editor and/or reporter may get into trouble, the emphasis being on the protection of victims (e.g. in medical negligence cases). Editors such as (Sir) Harold Evans argued that the *Contempt of Court Act 1981* in this respect was too vague, and that the vagueness of the 'imminence' doctrine in civil law be abolished.

Contempt of Court Act 1981 (CCA)   !

Its principal aims and objectives are:

- to preserve the integrity of the legal process
- to give the accused a fair trial
- to avoid extraneous information which night swaying a juror's (or magistrate's) mind.

A superior court of record (such as HL, High Court or Crown Court) has the power to punish all forms of contempt, while an inferior court of record (such as a magistrates' court) can generally only punish contempt committed in the face of the court (s. 12 CCA). Magistrates do not have the power to punish contempt of court by publication, but they can jail for a month or impose a fine of up to £2500 on anyone insulting them, the witnesses, lawyers or officers of the court. Courts martial (military) are not courts of record and do not, therefore, possess any inherent power to punish for contempt of court. The Queen's Bench Divisional Court may, however, punish contempts on their behalf (this also applies to coroners' courts and other inquests – see below).[6]

The following are some general guidelines for members of the public attending court proceedings (including those in Scotland). As journalists, you should abide by these too, if you ignore them, you could be found guilty of contempt, leading to a fine or a period of imprisonment, jeopardising your career.

> **!**
>
> ## How to avoid contempt of court for members of the public
>
> - be quiet when seated in the public gallery
> - be polite and courteous to court personnel, such as the judge, sheriff, stipendiary magistrate, JP, ushers and so on
> - remove your hat
> - do not attend if you are under the influence of drink or drugs
> - there is no smoking, eating or drinking allowed in court
> - no audio or video recording or photography is allowed, including using mobile phones
> - either turn mobile phones off or set to silent
> - no dogs are allowed, other than guide dogs
> - no children under 14 are allowed other than 'babes in arms', or if they are giving evidence.

What about taking photographs in the courtroom? Does this amount to criminal contempt 'in the face of the court' contra s. 41 *Criminal Justice Act, 1925*, in addition to the CCA? As we have seen above, there are a number of things that you need to avoid doing if you do not want to be held in contempt of court. The common factor is that they all involve an affront to the dignity of the court and the process of the administration of justice.

In the case of *R. v. D. (Vincent)* [2004],[7] the CA was required to consider an appeal against a 12-month prison sentence under s. 41 of the 1925 Act, that had been imposed by the trial judge at Liverpool Crown Court on the defendant's brother who was taking photos with his mobile phone in court.

The facts of the *R. v. D. (Vincent)* case show the seriousness of this matter and it also the first case where a modern device – in this case a mobile phone – was used and challenged under a very old statute. The brother of the appellant was on trial for various offences relating to Class A drugs. Due to the seriousness of the charges, the defendant was classed as a 'Category A' prisoner, so tight security had to be enforced throughout the trial, such as having special security guards, searching the public in the public gallery and an elaborate witness protection scheme. After the judge had seized the appellant's mobile phone, it was revealed that the appellant had taken three photos: one of the court canteen, one from the public gallery towards the witness box and the third of the appellant's brother (the defendant) in the secure dock. This also showed the figure of a prison officer.

The trial judge charged the appellant with a summary offence contra s. 41(1) *Criminal Justice Act 1925*, which reads:

No person shall –

> a) take or attempt to take in any court any photograph, or with a view to publication make or attempt to make in any court any portrait or sketch, of any person, being a Judge of the court or a juror or a witness in or a party to any proceedings before the court, whether civil or criminal

This means that the trial judge decided to deal with the appellant's conduct not under the *Contempt of Court Act 1981*, but as a criminal contempt under the 1925 Act.

The CA with Lords Woolf LCJ, Aikens and Fulford had to consider whether the appellant's sentence (12 months) was either wrong in principle or manifestly excessive. Lord Aikens noted that this was the first case of criminal contempt that involved a 'third-generation mobile phone' device. He then concentrated on the main reason that had led the trial judge and, ultimately, the CA to their judgment namely that the intimidation of juries and witnesses a growing concern to the criminal justice system:

> Intimidation of juries and witnesses is a growing problem generally in criminal cases. Recently there have even been physical attacks on prosecuting counsel in a case. A person could use photographs of members of the jury or a witness or advocates or even a judge in order to try to intimidate them or to take other reprisals. Witnesses who are only seen on a screen or who are meant to be known only by an initial could possibly be identified. The anonymity of dock officers or policemen who are involved in a case could be compromised if a photograph is taken and is used to identify them.

> (para. 15)

The CA upheld the prison sentence and dismissed the appellant's appeal on the grounds that taking illegal photographs in court 'has the potential to gravely prejudice the administration of criminal justice'. There were also concerns about the ease with which photos could now be passed on to third parties by electronic means and so could easily fall into the wrong hands. Though the appellant had pleaded guilty to having committed a criminal contempt, their Lordships in the CA did not accept this as a sufficiently mitigating factor. The appellant had argued that he had taken the photos in a 'spirit of fun' – explaining that the third photo of the appellant's brother in the dock was to be sent to his own daughter on her 18th birthday as a text message greeting from her uncle, who had not seen her for some time since he was on remand awaiting trial. Their Lordships further stated that this was a 'chilling development', as taking photos during such a lengthy, costly and complicated trial had seriously jeopardised court time and the process of justice.

The *R. v. D. (Vincent)* case shows that the courts have the power not only under the CCA 1981 but also under s. 41 of the *Criminal Justice Act 1925* to impose criminal punishment for taking photos in the courtroom with modern devices and advanced technology.

To show that *all* types of courts and tribunals are covered by the 1981 Act, here is an example from a coroner's court. In 1985, six police officers obtained an injunction to restrain London Weekend Television from broadcasting a filmed reconstruction of events surrounding the arrest and subsequent death in police custody of a Hell's Angel.

The injunction was granted on the ground that the broadcast would amount to 'an inquest' and, in fact, an actual inquest was due to be resumed. In rejecting the TV company's appeal against the injunction, the CA held that proceedings become active for contempt purposes as soon as a coroner has opened the inquest. Contempts of coroners' courts, such as prejudicial comment in the press, can only be punished by the Queen's Bench Division (QBD) of the High Court.

What is strict liability?

Most importantly for journalists, the CCA 1981 created the strict liability rule under ss. 1–3, 5 and 7 of the Act where there is 'substantial risk' of prejudice to forthcoming legal proceedings ('substantial risk' is explained below). S.1 of the 1981 Act provides that a person (author, journalist, editor or publisher) can be guilty of 'contempt by publication', regardless of intent.

Contempt of Court Act 1981 (CCA)

s. 1 'In this Act "strict liability rule" means the rule of law whereby conduct may be treated as a contempt of court as tending to interfere with the course of justice in particular legal proceedings regardless of intent to do so.'

s. 2 (1) The strict liability rule applies only in relation to publications. For this purpose, 'publication' includes speech, writing, a broadcast or other communication, in whatever form, that is addressed to the public at large or any section of the public.

s. 2 (2) The strict liability rule applies only to a publication that creates a substantial risk that the course of justice in the proceedings in question will be seriously impeded or prejudiced.

s. 2 (3) The strict liability rule applies to a publication only if the proceedings in question are active within the meaning of this section at the time of the publication.

In *AG v. Mirror Group Newspapers (MGN) Ltd* [1997][8] – also known as the Gillian Taylforth case – Lord Justice Schiemann set out the principles for the application of the strict liability rule. He said that each case must be decided on its own merits and the court would test matters as they were at the time of publication. The court would not convict someone of contempt unless it was sure that the publication in question had created some substantial risk that the course of justice would not simply be impeded or prejudiced but seriously so.

The case of *AG v. MGN* concerned an article in the *Daily Mail* of 13 May 1995 in which the columnist Lynda Lee-Potter had commented on the 'stormy relationship' between Gillian Taylforth (then of the TV soap *EastEnders* and more recently of the *Footballer's Wives* TV series) and Geoffrey Knights. Similar articles in five other national newspapers referred, inter alia, to a previous conviction of Mr Knights relating to assault and wounding offences during April and May 1995.

Some articles had also included large photos accompanied by banner head-lines. Mr Knights was about to stand trial at Harrow Crown Court on serious assault and wounding charges relating to a cab driver (contra s. 18 *Offences Against the Person Act 1861*). If he was found guilty, this could attract a life sentence. Some of the newspaper reports carried this story. At the trial on 3 October 1995, Judge Sanders stayed (halted) the proceedings against Knights on the grounds that the said newspaper articles and their pretrial coverage could seriously impede the accused's chances of a fair trial. The AG brought contempt proceedings against all the national newspapers.

However, on appeal, the QBD refused to hold five national newspapers in contempt of court. The QBD dismissed all contempt charges on the grounds that none of the articles complained of had, in their view, created any greater risk of serious prejudice than that which had already been created by earlier publicity. Giving reasons, Lord Justice Schiemann referred to the previous CA ruling in *AG v. Guardian Newspapers Ltd* (No 2) [1990],[9] stating that, 'The court will not convict of contempt unless it is sure that the publication has created (a) substantial risk of serious effect on the course of justice', meaning that the publication(s) in question must seriously impede or prejudice the administration of justice. Later, the Lord Chancellor commented that the law of contempt ought to be changed.

Strict liability	!
<ul><li>a journalist, editor or publisher is guilty of contempt regardless of intent, when court proceedings are 'active'</li><li>to be in contempt, the publication must create 'substantial risk' of serious prejudice to court proceedings.</li></ul>	

What is substantial risk?

In assessing 'strict liability', the courts look at whether or not the publication has created 'substantial risk'. This means whether or not it is likely that an article or a photograph will come to the attention of, say, a potential juror in a forthcoming criminal trial. The test applied is whether or not the publication is likely to impact on an 'ordinary' reader who could be a notional juror at the time of the trial.

The greatest dangers for any journalist or newspaper editor lie in creating prejudice and, thus, being in contempt of court once the jury has started to try a case. Fair and accurate reporting of a case at that stage is crucial. Even information that has previously been in the public domain is not exempt from this. At the onset of the *Contempt of Court Act 1981*, the *Guardian* was fined £5000 for contempt because, during a trial, it recalled that two of the accused had previously escaped from custody.

Civil trials are not free from the danger of contempt either, as we saw with the Thalidomide case. In that case, the HL regarded the first article by Harold Evans in the *Sunday Times* in 1972 to be in potential contempt because it put moral pressure on the drugs company Distillers, its shareholders and the wider public, as the parents of the malformed children were suing the drugs company for damages in the High Court over a long period of time.

More recently, however, courts have taken the view that a jury when properly instructed by a judge is capable of looking at the evidence fairly. Judges in famous trials will now tell the jury at the outset to disregard what they have read or heard in the press, such as the extensive press coverage before the Soham trial at the Old Bailey from October to December 2003, when Ian Huntley stood trial and was found guilty of the murder of the two 10-year-old girls Jessica Chapman and Holly Wells.

In *AG v. Guardian Newspapers Ltd* (No. 3) [1992],[10] the *Guardian* published an article criticising judges for their propensity to impose reporting restrictions during major fraud trials. The article, written by a city editor, mentioned a trial of six defendants at Manchester Crown Court, during which reporting restrictions had been imposed because one of them faced a pending trial on the Isle of Man. The CA ruled that the publication of a statement that a defendant was awaiting trial in criminal proceedings did not necessarily create a substantial risk that the course of justice would be 'seriously impeded'. The AG's application was dismissed on the grounds that there was no substantial risk – that is, no contempt.

What is 'substantial risk'?

- a publication must create serious prejudice
- it depends on a number of factors, such as the type of court/hearing/proceedings – there is greater risk in criminal courts, for example – and in courts with juries, such as Crown Court or the High Court in cases of libel
- there must be a practical risk, not just a theoretical one.

What does the word 'publication' mean in conjunction with 'substantial risk'? This was considered in *AG v. ITN and Others* [1995].[11] Here, the court went further than before in its consideration of the meaning of 'publication' in the print media, extending it to also mean broadcasts. Following the arrest of two Irishmen on suspicion of murdering a police officer, an early evening ITN news bulletin reported that one of the suspects (namely Magee) was a convicted IRA terrorist and had escaped from prison. The news item showed a poor-quality photograph of him. The following morning, the story was covered in the early editions of three national newspapers and one Northern England regional paper (*The Northern Echo*). They referred to the IRA fugitive as a suspect in the murder of the policeman. Later editions of the newspapers and further news bulletins by ITN did not report on the matter – probably when the risk of contempt had been fully understood.

The murder trial took place some nine months later in London, where the defendant's lawyer argued that proceedings should be stayed as the newspapers and ITN had created, through their early reports, a substantial risk of prejudicing the jury in this case. Application was made via the AG, but the CA dismissed the application. Giving reasons, Leggatt LJ said that frequent reporting on IRA 'outrages' at that time lessened the reporting on individual IRA terrorists and suspects. He said that the 'leakage' in the *Northern Echo* had been negligible and the story had only been carried in the early editions of the nationals. Furthermore, the effect of the early ITN news bulletin was also negligible. Between the coverage and the actual trial, enough time had elapsed (nine months), 'that the odds against the potential juror reading any of the publications is multiplied by the long odds against a reader remembering it, [and] the risk of prejudice is, in my judgment, remote'.

!	**Publication**
	'Publication', is any: • writing • speech • broadcast • 'other' communication, such as the Internet • picture image addressed to any section of the public.

In *R. v. (Rosemary) West* [1996],[12] the CA dismissed an appeal by Rosemary West against her convictions for murder. One of her grounds of appeal was that adverse press coverage about her and her husband Fred meant that she could no longer receive a fair trial (the 'Cromwell Road House of Horrors'). The Lord Chief Justice, Lord Taylor, rejected this argument. He said that to hold such a view would be simply ludicrous – that is, if allegations of murder were sufficiently horrendous as to shock the nation, the accused could not be tried at all and that would be absurd. He continued, 'moreover, provided the judge effectively warns the jury to act only on the evidence given in court, there is no reason to believe that they would do otherwise.' The CA adopted a robust attitude and dismissed the appeal by Rosemary West against her convictions for murder.

When Tracey Andrews, who was jailed for life for murdering her fiancé after claiming he had been the victim of a road rage attack, appealed in 1998 against her conviction because of pretrial publicity, the CA rejected the appeal. Lord Justice Roche said the reporting was not one-sided, nor had there been 'a blaze' of adverse publicity. The court did not consider that the jury at the trial could have been prevented from reaching a proper verdict by reporting in the media on the issues about which it had to decide.[13]

!	**What actions are the riskiest in terms of being guilty of contempt?**
	• criticising a decision to prosecute, such as criticising the CPS or prosecution witness • anticipating the course of a trial, such as predicting the outcome, giving odds on the jury's verdict and so on • referring to a person's previous convictions, such as a defendant's 'bad character' (or antecedents, also known as previous conviction).

Below are some tasks. You will be asked to look up some cases that prove this point.

TASKS

Look up the following cases and give reasons for the defendant/s being found guilty of contempt:

- *R. v. Kray* [1969] 53 Cr. App. Rep. 412 – the Kray twins' second murder charge
- *R. v. Evening Standard ex parte AG* [1976], *The Times*, 3 November 1976 – Peter Hain, 'ID Parade'
- *AG v. (Ian) Hislop* [1991] 1 QB 514 – Editor of *Private Eye* concerning Sonia Sutcliffe – the Yorkshire Ripper's wife.
- *AG v. Morgan* [1998] EMLR 294 – Piers Morgan, Editor of *News of the World*, regarding an undercover reporter and a forgery trial.

Have a look at the following case, which involved the popular BBC TV news quiz *Have I Got News for You* at a time when the programme was chaired by Angus Deayton. Ian Hislop, Editor of *Private Eye*, and the actor and comedian Paul Merton were team captains during the programme that was broadcast on 29 April 1994 between 10 and 10.30 p.m. The programme, screened on BBC 2 at the time, had over a million viewers and was repeated the following evening (*AG v. BBC and Hat Trick Productions Ltd* [1997]).[14] The matters complained of surrounded the upcoming fraud trial of the Maxwell brothers, Kevin and Ian, sons of the deceased newspaper tycoon Robert Maxwell; the trial was to begin on 31 October 1994. The brothers were charged with two counts of conspiracy on indictment to defraud the trustees and beneficiaries of the Mirror Group Pension Fund, which had been established by the late Robert Maxwell, who was named as co-conspirator in the forthcoming trial.

During the programme, Paul Merton and his team members were playing the 'odd one out' round where one of the four photos shown to his team was of pensioners. Merton's team explained that this picture symbolised the pensioners 'allegedly' defrauded by Robert Maxwell and his sons. Some banter then ensued between Merton, Hislop and Deayton, where numerous references were made to the assumed 'guilt' of the Maxwell brothers and their father. The court held that the programme makers, Hat Trick Productions, were guilty of serious contempt and of taking 'serious' risks, considering that the fraud trial was pending. Reasons given by the court were that the comments made during this particular part of the programme were 'irrelevant' and 'rude' and, though the programme was known to have a humorous content, the comments made were obviously relevant to a forthcoming criminal trial. The team had quite clearly implied that the Maxwells were guilty of fraudulent conduct. Due to the fact that the programme had a substantial national audience (and that the programme was repeated), plus the fact that the comments were reiterated throughout the programme as a running joke, meant that this amounted to a serious breach of the CCA – contempt of court. Both respondents (the BBC and Hat Trick Productions) were fined £10,000 each.

!	Guilty of contempt
	• if a publication creates a 'substantial risk' of serious prejudice or an impediment to particular court proceedings it will be guilty of contempt • special care must be taken when proceedings are active • don't take a tape recorder, dictaphone, camera or other recording equipment into court • strict liability offences mean you can be guilty of contempt regardless of intent!

When are proceedings 'active' and 'inactive'?

We have learnt, that s. 2 CCA 1981 limits a journalist's (editor's or publisher's) action in certain ways by means of strict liability – that is, they can be found guilty of contempt by publication, regardless of intent, where there is a substantial risk of serious prejudice or impediment to proceedings and where court proceedings are active.

What, though, does 'active' actually mean? Active court proceedings are often referred to as 'sub judice' under s. 2 CCA 1981.

!	Active (*sub judice*) proceedings in criminal cases
	These occur when: • a person has been arrested (known at this stage as a 'suspect') • a warrant for his or her arrest has been issued • there are bail conditions, including police bail • a summons has been issued • a person has been charged (with a criminal offence).

Inactive criminal proceedings

These occur when:

- a suspect is released without charge (watch out for bail conditions, though)
- no arrest is made within 12 months of a warrant being issued
- a case is discontinued or discharged
- the court orders the charge to 'rest' on file
- a charge or summons is withdrawn
- the end of the period of inquiry, which is 12 months from the date of warrant, an arrest has passed and the accused has been released without charge
- person, arrested with out warrant, is released without charge
- a defendant is acquitted or sentenced
- a defendant has pleaded guilty
- a defendant is found to be 'unfit' for trial or 'unfit to plead' ('insane' under the *Mental Health Act 1983*).

The most substantial risk for any journalist is when reporting on active criminal court proceedings at a magistrates' or Crown Court. However, you should still watch out when reporting on certain civil proceedings, such as in the High Court.

Active civil proceedings

These occur when:

- arrangements for hearings are made – the 'setting down for trial'
- a date is set for the hearing
- the hearing begins.

Inactive civil proceedings

These occur when:

- a case is disposed of
- a case is discontinued
- a case is withdrawn.

A party to any (civil or criminal) proceedings may ask the High Court for an interlocutory injunction before the trial, which means asking the court for reporting restrictions or a complete reporting ban until the trial is over. If there are reporting restrictions, journalists can find this information out from either the AG's office (if he has sent special instructions to court officials) or, in the lower courts, via the courts' legal advisers. There is also a useful website for the Court Service (www.hmcourts-service.gov.uk).

! | **It is a journalist's duty to**

- take all measures to check when proceedings become active
- use extreme caution at all times when reporting criminal cases
- check his/her sources carefully
- make exact notes in court (shorthand!) or buy the court transcript.

It in doubt, don't write, report or broadcast it! Even if a verdict has been passed, the journalist is still not out of danger, since the defendant/s may not have been sentenced. Daily reports of court cases can be written as long as they are contemporaneous. A carefully constructed background article can be protected by the defence of discussion.

Defences

Strict liability offences can often be committed without journalists intending to prejudice legal proceedings. This is especially true for new and inexperienced journalists who can often commit contempt accidentally by, for example, publishing a suspect's previous convictions without realising that he or she is currently facing criminal charges. This sort of offence stands in sharp contrast to what the courts call 'deliberate contempt', which occurs rarely, but, when it does, involves a publisher of a newspaper deliberately trying to influence legal proceedings, or putting unfair pressure on witnesses (for example, by paying them – 'cheque book journalism') or making 'scurrilous' (scandalous) attacks on the judiciary. To avoid contempt you must also not report on jury deliberations, which is an offence under s. 8 CCA. Finally, there is the offence of 'disobedience' in court or to an order of court, which is when the presiding judge (or magistrate(s)) has ordered reporting restrictions or a complete reporting ban and this is ignored – for example, if a journalist writes a background article about a rape victim (maximum fine to editor/publisher is £2000 under s. 63(3)(a) CJA 1991 and £5000 under the *Magistrates Court Act 1980*).

What happens if a judge (or the AG) finds that there has been contempt or serious prejudice committed by your publication? The commonest practice is that the judge can stay (halt) the court proceedings if he or she thinks that there has been too much adverse publicity regarding the case. Under the strict liability rule of the 1981 Act, there is no need to prove that *actual* prejudice took place – that is, it is not necessary to find a juror who read the said article – provided the risk is 'substantial'.

However, you will have read above that courts have taken the view more recently that juries, when properly instructed by the judge, are quite capable of looking at the evidence fairly evenly and, though they may have read some articles about a famous case in the press, they can disregard what they have read or heard in the media. This is often referred to as the 'reasonable man or person' (on the Clapham Omnibus) test. Usually, therefore, a carefully constructed background article can be protected by the defence of discussion in 'good faith' s. 5 CCA).

What are your general defences if you are held in contempt? A publisher, editor or author (journalist) can make use of s.1, s. 3(1) CCA 1981:

> s. 3(1) A person is not guilty of contempt of court under the strict liability rule as the publisher of any matter to which that rule applies if at the time of publication (having taken all reasonable care) he does not know and has no reason to suspect that relevant proceedings are active.
> (2) A person is not guilty of contempt of court under the strict liability rule as the distributor of a publication containing any such matter if at the time of distribution (having taken all reasonable care) he does not know that it contains such matter and has no reason to suspect that it is likely to do so.
> (3) The burden of proof of any fact tending to establish a defence afforded by this section to any person lies upon that person.

Additionally, there is s. 5 of the Act, which provides you with a rather liberal interpretation in order to encourage public debate and criticism on matters of 'public interest' and importance:

> A publication made as or as part of a discussion in good faith of public affairs or other matters of general public interest is not to be treated as contempt of court under the strict liability rule if the risk of impediment or prejudice is merely incidental to the discussion.

In *AG v. English* [1982][15] (known as the Dr Arthur case) the AG accused the then Editor of the *Daily Mail* of prejudicing the trial of a doctor charged with allowing a Down syndrome baby to die. The article concerned the wider debate surrounding euthanasia and the 'mercy killing' of a premature baby born with

Down syndrome and a severely malformed intestine, where the mother had rejected the baby at birth. The *Daily Mail* had published an article by Malcolm Muggeridge, a pro-life supporter, who was very strongly against euthanasia. The article demonstrated his 'outrage' at what was said to be the 'common practice' of allowing malformed children to die. The HL allowed the Editor's and author's defence on 'public interest' test grounds (s. 5 CCA 1981).

Where, then, are the greatest risks to journalists when reporting news or current affairs? The short answer is that *anything* that generally interferes with the course or administration of justice (including republication) or *anything* that interrupts trial proceedings may potentially be in contempt of court.

Reporting on juries

We have learned that, in common law (see the Thalidomide case earlier), it is contempt of court to publish *any* material that interferes with the course of justice as a continuing, active process in civil or criminal proceedings. Reporting on juries in the UK is also strictly limited, so do not be misled by reported jury proceedings in the United States (such as the Michael Jackson trial in Santa Maria, California, during the early part of 2005). The law in this country is different and is covered by s. 8 CCA 1981 and the *Criminal Justice Act 1925*. No research is allowed into juries – for example, into the reasons for their verdicts.

Under s. 8 CCA 1981, it is deemed contempt of court to seek or disclose information about statements made, opinions expressed, arguments advanced or votes cast by members of a jury in the course of its deliberations. Therefore, you cannot even do a background piece and will be found guilty of contempt if you publish interviews with jurors by disclosing details of their discussion in the retirement room. Any reporting of what transpires among the jury from the time it is asked to withdraw to when it returns its verdict is likely to be a contempt of court. Any such report may well defeat the whole purpose of the jury withdrawing (that is, keeping the secrets of the jury room in the interests of justice). There must be no photos or court drawings of jurors in order to protect them from potential harassment, intimidation, embarrassment or reprisal. In some major trials, the jury is often accommodated in a secret location. The HL held in 1994 that this prohibition applies not just to the jurors themselves but also to anyone who publishes the information they receive. What is permissible, however, is to publish a juror's view at the end of a trial, provided you do not refer to statements made, opinions expressed, arguments advanced or votes cast in the course of the jury's deliberations in the case.

Such a thing happend in the Jubilee Line fraud case, which was dramatically abandoned in March 2005 when one of the jurors talked about the 21-month trial during a BBC Radio 4 interview. She told the *Today* programme that having to attend the trial over such a long period of time had wrecked the jurors' lives because of the stress and the difficulty of surviving on the poor expenses rates provided by the court services. The trial was estimated to have cost £60m and the Lord Chancellor, Lord Falconer of Thoronton, told the press that having juries in complicated fraud trials was an idea that would most likely be scrapped in the near future.[16]

Does the *Human Rights Act 1998* conflict with the CCA?

Possibly. Some have viewed the *Human Rights Act 1998* (HRA) as a menace to the traditional common law system and would not agree with the then Home Secretary, Jack Straw (1997), who argued that the incorporation of the *European Convention on Human Rights* (ECHR) into English law would become like America's Bill of Rights. As we saw in Chapter 2, there have been a few legal challenges in privacy law, such as the case brought by Naomi Campbell, the supermodel, against the *Mirror* newspaper, that upset the apple cart and brought about a need for change in the way newspapers invaded a person's privacy.[17]

Every new bill that now passes through Parliament is scrutinised by the Joint Committee on Human Rights to see whether or not it is compatible with the ECHR. This means that primary and secondary legislation must be read in a way that is compatible with Convention rights (Ch. 43 (3)(1) HRA). Section 12 HRA must be read in conjunction with important legislation relating to Art. 10 ECHR ('freedom of expression') – s. 12 (4) HRA possibly being the most important of the two. Section. 12 (1) HRA is usually invoked when individuals ask the courts for an injunction. This was used in the first legal challenge by Naomi Campbell.[18]

s. 12 HRA – relating to 'freedom of expression' – and Art. 10 ECHR

- This section applies if a court is considering whether or not to grant any relief, which, if granted, might affect the exercising of the Convention right to freedom of expression.
- If the person against whom the application for relief is made (the respondent) is neither present nor represented, no such relief is to be granted unless the court is satisfied that:

    - the applicant has taken all practicable steps to notify the respondent
    - there are compelling reasons for not notifying the respondent.

- No such relief is to be granted so as to restrain publication before trial unless the court is satisfied that the applicant is likely to establish that publication should not be allowed.
- The court must have particular regard to the importance of the Convention right to freedom of expression and, where the proceedings relate to material that the respondent claims, or which appears to the court, to be journalistic, literary or artistic material (or to conduct connected with such material), to:

  - the extent to which:

    (a) the material has, or is about to, become available to the public
    (b) it is, or would be, in the public interest for the material to be published

  - any relevant privacy code.

Whether the HRA conflicts with the existing CCA or not is not very clear. So far, case law is still developing and teaches us different outcomes each year. Certainly, the courts must interpret legislation strictly in line with the HRA 1998, so that media freedom is not restricted, as enshrined in Art. 10 ECHR ('freedom of expression'). What, though, about the strict liability rule of the CCA 1981 and common law tradition as set out by Lord Reid in the *Sunday Times* Thalidomide case of 1974? Is this not incompatible with Art. 10?

So far, the CCA 1981 has been held compatible with the HRA, in that Art. 6 ECHR provides the power to punish for contempt ('right to fair trial'). Furthermore, it was held that regulators such as Ofcom and the PCC must comply with HRA (see s. 12(4) HRA 1998). For instance, the new Ofcom Code 2005 was drafted in the light of the HRA 1998 – in particular, the right to freedom of expression, as expressed in Art. 10 of the Convention, which encompasses the audience's right to receive creative material, information and ideas without interference, but subject to restrictions prescribed by law and necessary in a democratic society (see Chapter 3).

In summary, the role of the media is now well recognised in case law in relation to the European Convention – and the *Human Rights Act 1998*.

But the Director of Liberty, Shami Chakrabarti, invoked the Human Rights Act in connection with the failed 21 July 2005 London bomb attacks, when she wrote to the Attorney General, Lord Goldsmith, demanding that he warn the press to tone down its reporting on the possible suspects and future trials in prejudicing any future juries. The 'red tops' had provided headlines such as 'Got the Bastards' (*Sun*) and 'Brave police catch ALL the suicide bombers' (*Daily Express*). Chakrabarti had argued that such headlines were jeopardising the suspects' right to a fair trial, and that the newspapers' freedom of expression should be curtailed.

In response to this, Andrew Neil commented in the *Guardian* on 8 August 2005 that 'in this more democratic age it is surely time to start treating jurors as adults equipped to sift through the evidence ... We still labour under the Contempt of Court Act 1981, which says newspapers and broadcasters can be prosecuted if they "create a substantial risk that the course of public justice will be seriously impeded or prejudiced" ... British judges are sensitive about their courts being treated with contempt and have implemented a strict interpretation of the law which, in effect, gags the media from saying anything about a case once arrests have been made – even though there is precious little evidence to show that juries have ever been "contaminated" by press coverage.' Neil called on Lord Goldsmith to employ more liberal guidelines so that there would not need to be a news and comment blackout once anybody has been arrested and charged.

QUESTIONS

Answer the questions below in essay style, using discursive argument. Back up each of your arguments with statutory and case law.

1 The public interest test is a useful journalistic tool and may be a form of defence. In recognition of this fact and in line with the PCC Code of Practice, can a journalist or an editor make an editorial judgement and go ahead with printing a story that he or she regards as 'newsworthy'? Discuss your reasons.

2 Free speech is too important a democratic right to be undermined by law. Why should journalists not report on emotional damage and distress displayed in court? Should the courts be able to justify censorship? Discuss.

Notes

1 *AG v. Times Newspapers* [1974] AC 273 HL.
2 [1949] 93 SJ 220.
3 [2004] All ER (D) 394; 25 November 2004.
4 Hunter Syndrome is a hereditary disease in which the breakdown of a mucopolysaccharide (a chemical that is widely distributed in the body outside of cells) is defective. This chemical builds up and causes a characteristic facial appearance, abnormal function of multiple organs and, in severe cases, early death.

5 [1974] AC 273.

6 See *R. v. Davies* [1906] 1 KB 32.

7 [2004] EWCA Crim 1271.

8 [1997] 1 All ER 456.

9 [1990] 1 AC 109 (sub nom 'Spycatcher' case).

10 [1992] 1 WLR 874.

11 [1995] 2 All ER 370.

12 [1996] 2 Cr. App R 374, CA.

13 *The Daily Telegraph*, 15 October 1998.

14 [1997] EMLR 76.

15 [1982] 2 All ER 903.

16 *The Times*, 21 June 2005, p. 2. Also, BBC TV/ online news, report by Margaret Gilmore: 'Six men have walked free after a fraud case costing £60m and lasting 21 months collapsed at London's Old Bailey. They were accused of conspiring to corrupt officials on a London tube line extension.'

17 *Campbell v. Mirror Group Newspapers Ltd* (sub nom *Campbell v. MGN Ltd*) [2004] UKHL 22

18 *Campbell v. Mirror Group Newspapers Ltd* [2002] EMLR 30, QBD.

CHAPTER FIVE

JUVENILES AND THE LAW

Key aim of this chapter:

To enable you to understand the main issues that arise when reporting on juveniles – that is, young people under the age of 18. These are issues concerning criminal and civil youth legislation and court procedures.

Learning objectives

By the end of this chapter you should be able to:

- show a sound knowledge of youth justice legislation for criminal and civil court proceedings
- appreciate policy changes in youth justice legislation in relation to reporting on children and young people
- express reasoned and critical arguments clearly and in appropriate journalistic contexts in relation to case studies
- show an awareness and understanding of the need for different legislation for youths and adults.

Chapter Contents

Introduction

There will be occasions when the open justice principle and the right of the media to report are restricted in order to ensure fair trials for and the protection of those who are vulnerable, such as children. The media's recognition of this is reflected in its own codes of practice (such as the PCC's Codes). There is extensive youth justice legislation that supports and encourages responsible reporting, to the extent of urging restraint even when the law – in more recent times – allows publication in certain circumstances.

At common law, the court can exclude the public in youth justice, family court and county court proceedings (known as 'in camera' proceedings). There is statutory legislation that offers protection in the *Contempt of Court Act 1981* (CCA), the *Children and Young Persons Act 1933*, the *Children Act 1989* and the *Youth Justice and Criminal Evidence Act 1999*. That said, it does not mean that representatives from the media can be completely excluded. Journalists are allowed to be present at most proceedings involving youths, but they may not necessarily be allowed to report on them. It is for the presiding judge or magistrate to decide. If the court has the power to sit in camera, it can employ less restrictive derogations (deviations) from open justice, which would protect the administration of justice. In youth justice proceedings, this will usually involve reporting restrictions or enabling information to be withheld in open court.

Finally, the issue of life-long injunctions is discussed. The leading case is that of Jamie Bulger's killers – the then 10-year-olds Robert Thompson and Jon Venables who, in 1993, were found guilty at Preston Crown Court of the murder of 18-month-old Jamie Bulger. In *Venables and Another v. News Group Newspapers Ltd and Others* [2001], the Family Court Division of the High Court was asked to decide whether or not there could be a life-long reporting ban and anonymity order on the two convicted boys, who had, by then, turned 18. At issue here was whether or not the media could be further restricted by way of a life-long injunction from reporting anything on the two convicted killers once the boys had turned 18 and had been released from youth custody.

When such injunctions are sought (and there had only been one previously, in the case of Mary Bell, which is referred to later in this chapter), the courts have to consider whether or not constraining the freedom of the press is necessary. The family court in the Venables and Thompson case decided that there was a 'pressing social need' for a permanent reporting restriction. This was supported by convincing and concrete evidence that the life-long ban was necessary to save the boys from genuine threats to their lives.

Children, juveniles and the law

In the case of children and young people (those under the age of 18), different considerations apply when a young person is, for instance, charged with a criminal offence from those that would appy to an adult. The most important statute for you to note initially is the *Children and Young Persons Act 1933*. The general rule to remember is given under s. 39 of the 1933 Act:

> There shall be no publication (of name, school, address, workplace, photo) of a young person, either as a defendant or a witness, if he is under the age of 18.

Normally, if a child or young person (under 18) has committed a criminal offence, he or she will be tried summarily by magistrates in a youth court. In more serious (indictable) cases, such as rape, a youth will usually be tried in the (adult) Crown Court (see below). If a child or young person (aged 10 and above) is charged with murder (or manslaughter), he or she will not be tried summarily, but will be committed for trial to the Crown Court, charged with murder (homicide). If the young person is aged 14 or over and the offence is serious and may lead to a long period of imprisonment, he or she will also be committed to the Crown Court. Additionally, if the juvenile or young person is charged in conjunction with an adult offender (aged over 18), a magistrates' court may consider it necessary in the interests of justice to commit them both for trial to the Crown Court.

Youth courts (for children aged 10 or over, but under 14, or young people aged 14 or over, but under 18) will normally try children and young people. They are part of magistrates' courts and usually operate in camera (with the public excluded). There should be three justices of the peace (JPs) sitting and one of them *must* be a woman.

The procedure is different from that of an adult magistrates' court, avoiding both a criminal environment and excessive publicity. The appearance of the court must be informal and not intimidating to the youth. Present may be solicitors for each party (for example for the infant, the father, the mother, social services and so on) and representatives from social services, the school or the church will usually also be there.

!	**Personnel in a youth court**

The people allowed in to a youth court are:

- the justices
- court officers
- the parties
- their legal representatives
- witnesses
- other authorised people (these can include the media).

Reporting on juveniles in court cases: practical issues

Considerable changes were made in terms of naming (and shaming) juveniles, particularly in the criminal courts, with the *Youth Justice and Criminal Evidence Act 1999*. It came into force in relation to criminal proceedings in magistrates' and Crown Courts on 7 October 2004.

The purpose of the trial of a young person is to determine guilt and decide the appropriate sentence if the young defendant pleads guilty or is convicted. The purpose of the (juvenile) trial process under the 1999 Act is that the young defendant should not be exposed to intimidation, humiliation or distress. A Practice Direction from the Lord Chancellor (2000) stated that:

> all possible steps should be taken to assist the young defendant to understand and participate in the proceedings. The ordinary trial process should, so far as necessary, be adapted to meet those ends.[1]

The overriding principle is still that enshrined in s. 44 of the *Children and Young Persons Act 1933:* the welfare of the young defendant must be of the utmost priority.

The starting point for you, if you are reporting on a criminal trial of a juvenile under the age of 18, is s. 39 of the *Children and Young Persons Act 1933*. When a juvenile appears in a youth court as a defendant or witness, there is an automatic reporting ban, so names, addresses or the mention of anything or anybody that could lead to the identification of the youth are not allowed to be reported.

There is, of course, very often the danger of 'jigsaw identification'. This can happen when an adult in a case is named and, as a result, the identification of a child in the same case could be inferred or deduced. Perhaps fellow pupils of the child's school are identified and, together with other information reported during the proceedings, the child's identity can be worked out. Thus:

---

s. 39 *Children and Young Persons Act 1933*   !

- no report of the proceedings shall reveal the name, address or school or include any particulars likely to lead to the identification of any child or young person concerned in the proceedings as being the person by or against or in respect of whom the proceedings are taken, or as being a witness
- no picture shall be published of any child or young person so concerned
- the words 'conviction' and 'sentence' must not be used in connection with children and young people.

Courts have sometimes attempted to make orders banning the identification of dead children, even though the names of the deceased children have already been published in reports of the death or of an inquest. Courts have also attempted to make orders in cases involving child battery or sexual abuse within families that the name of the adult defendant should not be published. Newspapers have frequently persuaded courts against imposing or renewing orders to prevent identification of young babies who have been victims of violence. It is difficult to see that a child of such tender years would suffer any ill effects from being named.

What you *cannot* report concerning a youth   !

- name
- address
- school, youth club, work, training place and so on
- photo (not even if it is pixelated)
- names of people (such as parents) in conjunction with the youth or child.

In certain circumstances, a reporting ban may be lifted by a presiding trial judge under s. 39 of the 1933 Act (now in parts substituted by the *Criminal Justice and Public Order Act 1994*), so certain aspects may be reported on. This was the case at the end of the Jamie Bulger murder trial in November 1993. On the first day of the hearing of the Thompson and Venables trial, 1 November 1993, at Preston Crown Court, Mr Justice Morland had imposed reporting restrictions under s. 39 of the 1933 Act to restrain media publicity throughout the trial. At the conclusion of the trial, after their convictions but before sentence, the judge lifted the reporting restrictions (as a result of an application by News Group

Newspapers), so that the public might be informed of the names and backgrounds of the two defendants. Morland J said in his judgment in open court:

> It is necessary for me to balance the public interest in lifting reporting restrictions and the interests of the defendants. I lifted the reporting restrictions as set out in my order of 24 November. I did this because the public interest overrode the interest of the defendants following the murder, and I considered that the background in respect of the two boys' family, lifestyle, education and the possible effect of violent videos, on the defendants' behaviour ought to be brought out into the open because there was a need for an informed public debate on crimes committed by young children. However, public interest also demands that they have a good opportunity of rehabilitation. They must have an opportunity to be brought up in the units in a way so as to facilitate their rehabilitation.

Though the judge granted comprehensive injunctions restricting full publication of further information about the two boys, with no limit of time (under s. 39 of the 1933 Act), the media launched a full onslaught on the boy killers and their families. Also, in spite of the fact that further injunctions were granted at a judicial review hearing by Lord Justice Pill (Divisional Court, 19 April 1996), restraining the publication of any further information, the press kept running stories about the boys and their families while the boys were in secure youth (custody) accommodation until 2001.

The 1999 Act gives the courts the power to exclude all but one of the press (often a representative of the Press Association) when hearing witnesses in these cases or when there are reasonable grounds for believing that the presence of people other than the accused may intimidate witnesses. This is particularly relevant in sexual cases. The Act makes it an offence to report before the end of the trial any 'special measures order' made to protect a vulnerable or intimidated witness or any prohibition on the accused person's cross-examination of a witness. The reporting ban on juveniles and young people takes effect from the time a criminal investigation begins.

Reporting example

Usually, your reporting on a young person involved in criminal proceedings should read like this:

> A 16-year-old boy has been charged with the murder of a father of three, stabbed to death outside his home. The teenager was arrested on Sunday by police investigating the death of Benjamin Durao, 35, in Brixton last

month, Scotland Yard said. Two boys aged 14 and 16 and a man, 24, were previously arrested and bailed in connection with the inquiry. The 16-year-old, who cannot be named for legal reasons, is due to appear at Balham Youth Court on Tuesday. A 14-year-old has been charged with making threats to kill and blackmail. Angolan national Mr Durao was attacked in the Myatts Field Estate in Brixton, South London, on 17 December [2004]. He had chased a group of boys who returned to his home after damaging his front door hours earlier. He later died in a South London hospital.

BBC News Online, 10 January 2005

In 1990, Lord Justice Watkins said in the Divisional Court that the mere fact that the person before the court was a child or young person would normally be good reason for imposing reporting restrictions (under s. 39 of the *Children and Young Persons Act 1933*). However, several judges did not accept this view. When two boys aged 15 and 16 were accused at the Old Bailey of taking part in a gang rape, Judge Nina Lowry said:

> I do not think it right or in the public interest that the identity of the two perpetrators of this crime should be cloaked in anonymity. The matter should be out in the open in the community where they live.

Lord Justice Watkins' view was also rejected in 1992 in the CA case of *R. v. Lee* [1993][2] when Lord Justice Lloyd said:

> For our part we would not wish to see the court's discretion fettered so strictly. There is nothing in s. 39 about rare or exceptional cases. There must be a good reason for making an order under s. 39.

In its judgment, the court gave its approval to the refusal of Judge Michael Coombe at the Old Bailey the previous month to continue a s. 39 order in relation to a 14-year-old boy who took part in a robbery while on bail on a rape charge. Judge Coombe had said he could see no harm to the boy and there would be a powerful deterrent effect on his contemporaries if his name and photograph were published. The public interest in knowing the identity of the boy therefore outweighed any harm to the boy himself. The detailed facts of the case are set out below.

R. v. Lee [1993] 2 All ER 170, CA (Criminal Division)[3]

In 1991, the defendant, a 14-year-old boy, was convicted of raping a 14-year-old girl. At the start of his trial in the Crown Court, the judge made an order under s. 39 *Children and Young Persons Act 1933* prohibiting the publication of any particulars leading to the identification of the defendant. The boy was subsequently sentenced to two years and ten months' imprisonment.

On 4 June 1992, the defendant was convicted of further offences committed while on bail for rape. Once again, at the start of that trial, an order was made under s. 39 preventing his identification. However, when the defendant was sentenced on 25 June that year, the judge lifted the anonymity order under s. 39 and reports identifying the defendant appeared in national newspapers that evening and the following morning.

Later that day the defendant applied to the Crown Court judge for the reimposition of the reporting restriction. However, the judge refused to reverse his decision, although he imposed a temporary restriction while the defendant made an application to the CA for an order under s. 39 prohibiting the publication of his offence particulars, which would – he argued – lead to his identification by means of jigsaw identification (see also p. 253).

At the hearing of that application to the CA, the question arose as to whether or not the CA had jurisdiction to impose such an order in relation to proceedings in the court below – the Crown Court. The defendant argued that s. 39 enabled a court to make an order in relation to 'any proceedings', which meant the whole course of the proceedings from the start of the case (at the magistrates' court) to the Crown Court, until the conclusion of the proceedings in the CA. Lee (the appellant) further argued that, as the proceedings were continuous and indivisible, the CA had jurisdiction under s. 39 to make an order restricting publication of the proceedings including the Crown Court.

The CA held that it could make an order under s. 39 in relation to *any* criminal court proceedings before it, once criminal proceedings had commenced, and that there was nothing in s. 39 to state otherwise. It followed that if the defendant wanted to challenge any proceedings in any court, he would have to do so under judicial review.

Since the Lee case, it has been possible for the courts to lift any reporting restrictions on a juvenile if the court and presiding justices feel that the case and the criminal offence lie within the public interest.

Now, under the *Crime (Sentences) Act 1997,* a youth court has some power to waive the automatic ban on the identification of juveniles. For example, a court can allow a *convicted* juvenile to be named when magistrates believe that it would be in the public interest to do so. Also, a youth court (or the Home Secretary) has the power to lift the restrictions on identifying any juvenile concerned in the proceedings to avoid injustice to him or her.

Since the Act came into force, a number of newspapers have made successful applications to youth courts and reporting restrictions were lifted. A Home Office circular (1998) stated that the lifting of such reporting restrictions on youths would be particularly appropriate where either the offending was persistent or serious or had an impact on a number of people, or alerting others to the offenders' behaviour would help prevent further offending.

The lifting of reporting restrictions is usually because it is in the public interest, but the family of an offender, or the offender him- or herself, must not be under the threat of harassment or serious harm from others as a result. One such example is that of Stefan Gilmore – the youngest ever disqualified driver (then aged 10). When Lewes Crown Court sentenced the 12-year-old in January 2005 to an 18-month Detention and Training Order (DTO) – after already at 10 being the youngest subject of an Anti-Social Behaviour Order (ASBO) – Judge Anthony Niblett decided to lift the reporting ban on the boy 'in the public interest'.[4]

Children charged with murder

When children are convicted of murder, they are given special 'life sentence' dispensation under the *Children and Young Persons Act 1933*. Parliament has laid down under s. 53(1) of the 1933 Act that a child shall not be sentenced to life imprisonment, but, in lieu, shall be sentenced to be detained during 'Her Majesty's Pleasure' (HMP). Thus, HMP imposed on a young person is not the same as a mandatory life sentence imposed on an adult murderer, as an order of detention involves merely an authority to detain the young prisoner indefinitely. This means that the Home Secretary has to decide from time to time, taking into account the punitive as well as the rehabilitative elements, whether or not detention of the young person is (still) justified. Life imprisonment, on the other hand, involves an order of custody for life, which means that the Home Secretary has to consider whether or not and when release is justified via the Parole Board. Furthermore, the 1933 Act requires that, when dealing with children, a court is bound to take into account the welfare of the child.

'Her Majesty's Pleasure' was the sentence imposed on two 11-year-old boys – Robert Thompson and Jon Venables – on 24 November 1993, at Preston Crown Court, after they were found guilty of the heinous murder of 18-month-old Jamie Bulger (the boys were both 10 years old at the time of the killing in February 1993).

The presiding trial judge had ordered eight years as an HMP tariff. After their sentence, the Lord Chief Justice advised the Home Secretary (then Michael Howard, Conservative) that the tariff period should be increased to ten years. However, following a public petition containing some 278,300 signatures, a campaign organised by a popular newspaper demanding that the applicants should remain in detention for (natural) life – the Home Secretary, exercising his discretion under s. 35 of the *Criminal Justice Act 1991*, decided that the penal element in the sentences should be increased to 15 years. In reaching that decision, the Home Secretary stated that he had had regard to the public concern about the case, as evidenced by the petitions and other correspondence he had received. His decision was also in accordance with a policy statement dated 27 July 1993 in which he stated that young offenders sentenced to detention during Her Majesty's Pleasure should, like adults on whom mandatory life sentences are imposed, serve an identified penal element in their sentence before their release is considered.

The boys then applied for a judicial review to quash the Home Secretary's decision (*R. v. Secretary of State for the Home Department, ex parte Venables and R. v. Secretary of State for the Home Department, ex parte Thompson* [1998] AC 407, HL).[5] The Divisional Court held that the Home Secretary's continuing duty to keep the detention of a young offender during HMP under continuous review was inconsistent with the concept of an identified penal element in the sentence to be served. The court accordingly quashed the Home Secretary's decision. The Home Secretary appealed to the CA, which accepted his argument that he was entitled to set a tariff but dismissed his appeal on the grounds, inter alia, that he had wrongly taken into account the public petition and media campaign in setting the tariff and therefore there had been procedural unfairness in reaching the decision. The Home Secretary appealed to the HL. The applicants cross-appealed against the CA's decision that the Home Secretary was entitled to impose the tariff (by 1998, there was a new Labour government in power and Jack Straw was the new Home Secretary).

The boys then took their case to the European Court of Human Rights (ECHR) (*V. v. UK* [1999]).[6] The ECHR held it unlawful (ultra vires) for the Home Secretary to have adopted a policy that, even in exceptional circumstances, treated as irrelevant the progress and development of a child who was detained during Her Majesty's Pleasure pursuant to s. 53(1) of the 1933 Act.

At the ECHR hearing, the boys relied on various rights under the *European Convention for the Protection of Human Rights and Fundamental Freedoms 1950* (the Convention), including the prohibition of torture or inhuman or degrading treatment (Art. 3) and right to a fair trial (Art. 6). The ECHR ruled that the two boys had received an unfair trial and that the (adult) court proceedings, as well as the subsequent sentencing, had seriously breached the children's right to a fair trial – that is, that the UK courts had violated Arts 3 and 6 of the Convention. The ECHR found that the Home Secretary had ignored the duty of care, relevant to a young (life sentence, that is, HMP) prisoner, and had simply applied 'adult' rules for life prisoners. In short, the children's progress and future development had been ignored when sentencing the two boys.

Reporting on children in a Crown Court

Some young defendants accused of committing serious (indictable) crimes may be very young and immature when standing trial in a Crown Court (the minimum age is 10) – as happened with Jamie Bulger's killers, Thompson and Venables. If the child or young person appears in a Crown Court, there is no automatic ban on identifying him or her in a report on the proceedings – usually the court still applies a s. 39 reporting ban (under the *Children and Young Persons Act 1933*).[7] Journalists must check this, though, before any reporting is undertaken, especially if they miss the beginning of the proceedings when such an order may be made.

The extended powers under the *Youth Justice and Criminal Evidence Act 1999* authorise the judge to lift reporting restrictions on a youth (a young person under the age of 18) in order for him or her to be identified by the press if a restriction has previously been imposed. The judge must give reasons for the lifting of the anonymity order – if he or she thinks that identification of the young defendant would be in the public interest, (by 'naming and shaming' the boy and/or his parents, for example).

> The words 'conviction' and 'sentence' must not be used in connection with children and young people. **!**

If a young defendant is 'indicted' jointly with an adult defendant, the court should consider at the plea and directions hearing (PDH) whether or not the young defendant should be tried on his own. The judge decides this in the interest of justice as well as the welfare of the young person. The judge may, at this stage, give a s. 39 (anonymity) order, or a direction under s. 45 of the *Youth Justice and Criminal Evidence Act 1999*, which may lift reporting restrictions, in full or in part.

Juvenile trials (especially if the young defendant is tried on his or her own) will usually be in a 'court-friendly' atmosphere – that is all participants (if at all possible) will sit at the same level in the courtroom. A young defendant should normally, if he or she wishes, be free to sit with family members or others in a like relationship and in a place that permits easy, informal communication with his or her legal representatives and others with whom he or she wants or needs to communicate. The presiding judge will explain the course of the proceedings to the young defendant in terms that he or she can understand. The judge would normally remind those representing a young defendant of their continuing duty to explain each step of the trial to him or her and should ensure, so far as practicable, that the trial is conducted in language that the young defendant can understand. A youth trial in a Crown Court will be granted more frequent breaks, taking full account of a young defendant's inability to concentrate for long periods. Robes and wigs are not normally worn and 'jailors' (court or custody security officers) normally do not wear uniform either.

Facilities for reporting the trial – subject to any directions given under s. 39 of the 1933 Act or s. 45 of the 1999 Act – must be provided, but the court may restrict the number of those attending in the courtroom to report the trial to such number as is judged practicable and desirable. In ruling on any challenged claim (by the media) to attend the courtroom for the purpose of reporting the trial, the court must be mindful of the public's general right to be informed (the public interest test). Where access to the courtroom by reporters is restricted (such as in trials of vulnerable witnesses, or defendants in cases with sexual connotations), arrangements will normally be made for the proceedings to be relayed (either by audio and/or visual means) to another room in the same court complex to which the media have free access.

Part II of the 1999 Act protects a large number of vulnerable witnesses and their identification while they are under 18, or even during their lifetime. The aim was to allow a greater number of vulnerable witnesses to give evidence in criminal proceedings and improve the quality of the evidence they give. Solicitors and barristers practising in youth (and Crown) courts are now quite familiar with the use of video-recorded evidence when child witnesses are involved (either as the defendant or prosecution witnesses). There is only one notable exception – if the child defendant is a witness in his or her own trial. Section 16 of the 1999 Act renders all witnesses under 17 at the time of the hearing eligible for assistance by way of special measures – video-recorded evidence. Section 21 states that a child witness is in need of special protection if the case involves giving evidence in connection with allegations of kidnapping, false imprisonment, cruelty, sexual crime, assault and injury or threat of injury to anyone.

Schedule 2 of the 1999 Act relates to reporting restrictions for victims of sexual offences.[8] The 1999 Act also defines 'publication' as including written reports of speeches, television broadcasts and any other type of communication (including the Internet) addressed to the public. Additionally, s. 25 of the *Youth Justice and Criminal Evidence Act 1999* permits the court to exclude people of *any* description from the court during the giving of evidence by a child or vulnerable adult witness in cases relating to a sexual offence or where there are grounds for believing that the witness has been or may be intimidated.

Reporting on incest and sexual offence cases

- the adult may be identified (see PCC code clause 7ii)
- the term incest should not be used
- the offence should be described as 'serious offences against young children' or similar appropriate wording
- the child should not be identified
- take care that nothing in the report implies a relationship between the accused and the child.

Reporting on children in family courts

Section 69 of the *Magistrates' Courts Act 1980* (MCA) permits the media and press agencies to attend family proceedings, with the exception of adoption proceedings, from which the public is otherwise excluded (in camera). The punishments available to the courts (for contravening any publication orders) are different from those in an 'adult' magistrates' court. If a journalist breaches a s. 39 court order, he or she will be held in contempt of court. If ss. 39 and/or 49 of the 1933 Act are breached, the maximum fine that can currently be imposed on a journalist (editor and/or publisher) can be up to £5000.

Youth and family court rules have been made under s. 144 of the MCA 1980, which enable private (in camera) sittings in certain circumstances in proceedings where the court might exercise its powers under the *Children Act 1989* and the *Family Proceedings Courts (Children Act 1989) Rules 1991*. With the exception of adoption proceedings, the court has the discretion to allow other people – including those with no direct connection with the case – to attend family proceedings hearings.

The *Children Act 1989* largely covers family court proceedings and rationalises the law on caring for, bringing up and protecting children generally. The 1989 Act covers both the civil (county courts, family courts in magistrates' courts and the Family Division of the High Court) and the criminal courts (youth courts as part of magistrates' courts and the Crown Court). Reporting on *any* family proceedings in magistrates' courts is controlled by the complicated restrictions in the 1989 Act, as well as s. 71 of the *Magistrates' Court Act 1980*. Essentially, these state that no report of family proceedings in a magistrates' court shall be published, other than the following.

> ## ❗ What can you publish on children appearing in family courts?
>
> - the names, addresses and occupations of the parties and witnesses
> - the grounds of the application and a concise statement of the charges, defences and countercharges in support of which evidence has been given
> - the submissions on any point of law arising in the proceedings and the decision of the court on the submissions
> - the decision of the court and any observations made by the court in giving it.

The punishments available to courts in criminal proceedings dealing with those under the age of 18 are different from those imposed on adults.[9] In the case of a child (aged 10–13), there is a maximum permitted fine of £250. A young person (aged 13 and over, but under 18) can be fined a maximum of £1000. These maximum permitted fines may be raised by the Home Secretary. A child or young person – depending on various age restrictions – may be made the subject of an absolute or conditional discharge, referral order, parental bind-over, parenting order, child safety order, reparation order, action plan order, supervision order, compensation order or attendance centre order. The minimum age for sentencing to imprisonment is 21 (in a youth court). Those aged between 18 and 20 go to a Young Offenders Institution (YOI). No criminal proceedings at all can be brought against a child under the age of 10.

Life-long reporting bans and human rights issues

We have learnt that the public can be excluded from youth justice proceedings, but only very rarely is the press totally excluded. It was not envisaged with the *Youth Justice and Criminal Evidence Act 1999* that the press should routinely be excluded alongside the rest of the public, even in exceptional cases (such as children involved in incest or sex offence cases as vulnerable witnesses). Even if the media is to be excluded, one nominated representative must be permitted to remain in cases involving 'special measures' (such as live video links). This was granted in *R. v. Camberwell Green Youth Court, ex parte D. and Others*,[10] where it was held that the granting of live-link special measures did not involve breaches of Arts 6 or 14 ECHR.

We now turn to the issue of life-long reporting bans by means of High Court injunctions. The issue was first raised in the case of Mary Bell. In 1968 in

Newcastle upon Tyne, 10-year-old Mary was convicted of the murder of two little boys aged 3 and 4, by strangulation.[11] As in the later Thompson and Venables criminal court proceedings, Mary Bell was 11 when she stood trial in an adult Crown Court. She was convicted of murder on two counts by reason of diminished responsibility. She was sentenced to detention for life under Her Majesty's Pleasure (s. 53(1) of the *Children and Young Persons Act 1933*). At trial, her name was released to the public.

1968: Mary Bell found guilty of double killing

An 11-year-old girl has been sentenced to life in detention after being found guilty at Newcastle Assizes of the manslaughter of two small boys. Mary Bell is said to have strangled the boys, aged four and three, 'solely for the pleasure and excitement of killing'. The jury heard Mary, also known as May, was suffering from diminished responsibility at the time and therefore found her not guilty of murder. Her accomplice, known only as Norma, aged 13, who had been jointly charged with Mary, was acquitted. As the verdict was read out, Mary broke down and wept. Mr Justice Cusack described her as dangerous and said there was a 'very grave risk to other children if she is not closely watched'. Mary's mother and grandmother, who were sitting behind her on the benches, also wept when the verdict was announced

('On this day' BBC news archive online,
17 December 1968 – visit: http://news.bbc.co.uk/onthisday
and enter 17 December in searchline)

After her conviction, Mary spent 12 years in Red Bank Approved School near Newton-le-Willows, Lancashire. She was released on licence in 1980 and was provided (at her request) with a new identity. There then followed a number of applications to the courts for an anonymity order on behalf of 'Mary Bell', now known as *Re.: X*. There followed three periods when X's identity and whereabouts were either discovered or at risk of discovery.

The first was after she formed a settled relationship with a man and she subsequently gave birth to Y on 25 May 1984. Y was made a ward of court five days later on the application of the local authority in the area where they lived and X and the father were given joint care and control with a supervision order to the local authority. In July 1984, the *News of the World* became aware of the birth of Y, and 'Mary Bell' (*Re.: X*) was granted an injunction, prohibiting the identification of Mary's, her daughter's and the child's father's identities. Mr Justice Balcombe granted the injunction in line with the wardship proceedings prohibiting identification of X and of Y (Re: *X. C. C., v. A.* [1985]).[12] This total anonymity ban and reporting restriction were to continue until the daughter's (Y's) 18th birthday.

The second period was in 1988 when there were two events. The identities of X and Y were revealed in the village in which they then lived. Parents at the school attended by Y drew up a petition to exclude Y from school and there was a demonstration against her at the school. She was 4 years old at the time. The relationship between X and the little girl's father had already failed in early 1988, 'Mary Bell' (X) having formed a relationship with B and left her first partner, taking Y with her. She and B remained together. Later, in 1988, Y's father sought to obtain financial advantage by selling an untrue story about X, which was published in October 1988. An injunction was obtained against him in November 1988. The family had to move again and X established another new identity.

The third period was in 1998, after the publication of Gita Sereny's book, *Cries Unheard*, which set out the life of 'Mary Bell' (with X's – Mary's – collaboration). Mary was to be paid a substantial sum of money after the publication of Sereny's book. The Home Secretary at the time, Jack Straw, was aware of the proposed publication, which evoked considerable press publicity, and tried to oppose payment to Mary Bell, now in her forties. Prime Minister Tony Blair even attacked the payment as being 'inherently repugnant'. The AG tried, without success, to find a legal way to stop the payment to Mary Bell, and Jack Straw attacked his own officials for failing to prevent the book being published. In an unprecedented move, Straw condemned the payment to Bell in an open letter to the mothers of the murdered boys published in the *Sun* newspaper. He stated, that, by cooperating with the book, Bell had forfeited her right to anonymity.

Straw's letter was an open invitation to the media for the injunction to be broken. X's (Mary Bell's) whereabouts were discovered and she and her family had to move in a hurry at the instance of the local police on the grounds of public safety and the safety of the family. Within hours, dozens of reporters surrounded Bell's house, forcing her and her daughter (Y) to flee. It was in this traumatic manner that Bell's daughter learned of her mother's past. On this occasion, they were able to return home after two weeks. There were other incidents, both initiated by the press and members of the public. In total, X and Y had to be relocated under compulsion on five separate occasions, prompted by press intrusion and harassment.

Media interest in Mary Bell and her daughter has not ceased and there have been numerous press articles about her. In December 2002, her acquitted co-accused, Norma, made a statement to the press and an article was published by the *Sun* on 15 December 2002. As a result, the Newcastle *Evening Chronicle* led with the headline on Friday, 11 April 2003: 'Time to unmask Mary Bell'. There followed a two-page article with the subheading 'Still haunted', in which some members of the family of one of the two children killed expressed the wish that Mary Bell should be named and shamed.

It was at this point that Mary (X), her daughter (Y) and Mary's partner (B) applied for a life-long injunction *contra mundum* ('against the world') to the Family Court Division of the High Court on 17 April 2002. The claimants sought an injunction to prevent the disclosure of their identities, addresses and other information that might identify them (*X. (a woman formerly known as Mary Bell) and Another v. O'Brien and Others* [2003]).[13] The defendants were Y's father and two newspaper publishers.

The claimants (X and Y) argued, inter alia, that there was a serious risk that their rights under Art. 8 ECHR would be breached if the injunctions were not granted. There were, they said, exceptional circumstances in the case – the young age at which the offences were committed, the length of time elapsed since the offences were committed, the need to support rehabilitation, the adverse affect of publicity on rehabilitation and the first claimant's (Mary Bell's) mental state. With regard to the second claimant (her daughter), it was argued that her situation was so inextricably linked with that of the first claimant that it was not possible to treat them separately. Dame Elizabeth Butler-Sloss said:

> It is clear that, at least from time to time, Mary Bell remains the subject of press and other media interest and, I presume, remains of interest to the reading public. She has none the less been able to live a largely settled life in the community despite a number of changes of identity and moves. She has now lived in the community for 23 years. She and B have created a family life and brought up Y who has developed into a charming and well-balanced girl according to the evidence provided to me. Y intends for the foreseeable future to continue to live with her mother and B. X and her daughter seek the opportunity for each of them to continue to enjoy the protection from press and public intrusion into their lives by the grant of the injunctions they now seek from this court ...
>
> The evidence before me, which I accept, from the police, the probation service, social services, a previous probation officer who has remained very close to X, and from her member of Parliament is that, if their identity and whereabouts are disclosed, X and Y are at considerable risk of press intrusion and harassment, public stigma and ostracism. X is, according to the medical evidence to which I refer later, a vulnerable personality with mental health problems and the prospect of such intrusion has already had an adverse effect upon her mental and physical health. The absence of the protection of an injunction will have a serious effect upon her health and well-being. In the absence of injunctions the press, other parts of the media and members of the public would have the right to track down X and Y and report who they are and where they live ... Exceptionally I shall therefore grant injunctions *contra mundum* to protect the anonymity of X and of Y.

In May 2003, the High Court's Family Division granted Mary, her daughter and her partner life-long anonymity under the *Human Rights Act 1998*, on the grounds that they were entitled to a private and family life.

When individuals ask the courts for reporting bans or even life-long injunctions, the court has to apply s.12 of the *Human Rights Act 1998*, which now requires that the courts balance the possible interference with a claimant's Art. 8 rights to privacy against the journalists' right to freedom of expression found in Art. 10 of the Convention. This came under discussion when Jamie Bulger's killers, Thompson and Venables, were about to be released from youth custody in 2001 (after they had turned 18). Lord Chief Justice Woolf had made the decision in November 2000 to release the boys from youth custody. He made tariff recommendations that rendered it likely that their parole board would make a decision in 2001 about the boys' reintegration into the community. This meant that the young men would be released from their secure youth unit on 'licence' rather than be transferred to adult prison. The Prison Service reported that the boys had been sufficiently 'rehabilitated' in their respective secure units and a possible transfer to an adult prison would move the two 18-year-olds to 'a school of crime'.

In *Venables and Another v. News Group Newspapers Ltd and Others* [2001],[14] the two claimants sought injunctions against three newspaper groups that would restrict publication, for life, of their identities and whereabouts. The claimants argued to the President of the Family Court Division, Dame Elizabeth Butler-Sloss, that there was a real likelihood that the press intended to publish details of their present and future whereabouts and descriptions of their appearances, and the publication of such details would endanger their lives in view of threats that had been made against them. The newspapers contended that the court had no jurisdiction to grant such injunctions in relation to adults.

In response, the claimants contended that such a jurisdiction could be found in the law of confidence, taking into account the implementation of the *Human Rights Act 1998*. They relied primarily on the 'right to life', Art. 2 ECHR, the prohibition against torture or inhuman or degrading treatment, under Art. 3 ECHR, and Art. 8, 'right to privacy'. The newspapers relied on s. 12(4) *Human Rights Act 1998*, which required the court to have particular regard to the right to 'freedom of expression' under Art. 10 of the Convention.

The Family Court President, Dame Elizabeth Butler-Sloss, ruled that this presented an 'exceptional' case. She imposed life-long reporting restrictions on the press in relation to Thompson and Venables to protect the confidentiality of any information on them. The reasons given were that *any* information on the boys would probably lead to serious physical injury or to the death of either of the young men. She stated that there was a legitimate aim to protect the young men from serious and possibly irreparable harm. Dame Butler-Sloss also stressed that there was no way to protect them than by seeking relief from the court.

Dame Butler-Sloss referred, inter alia, to the existing law of confidence and stated that it covered identification information, which the claimants had sought to have protected. She relied on the speech given by Lord Goff of Chieveley in *AG v. Guardian Newspapers Ltd* (No. 2) [1990] – the *Spycatcher* case,[15] – stating that, since an equitable duty of confidence arose from an obligation of conscience, it must be material to consider whether or not a reasonable person would recognise public disclosure as not being 'just in all the circumstances'. She ruled, as per Spycatcher, that there did not need to be a formal relationship between the parties. She ruled that the right to life (Art. 2) was an unqualified right and failure to provide protection would be incompatible with the Convention. There had been enough evidence before the court that the boys' future lives would be in substantial danger. One of the statements before the court included a report from the manager of the secure unit where Thompson was placed and reports from the supervising probation officers of both Venables and Thompson. The secure unit had fought hard to keep the media away in order for the boys not be bullied or victimised by other inmates. The units had also been working hard at that time towards the reintegration of the claimants into the community.

The solicitor for Venables – Mr Dickinson, who had acted for the boy since 1994 – made four statements, which included information about what he described as relentless inquiries from the media about his client over the years. These inquiries had been from all over the world. He referred to a number of breaches of the existing injunctions. He said that, since 1993, there had been a sustained and high level of media interest in the case and the claimants that showed no signs of diminishing. It was his firm belief that, on his release and for many years thereafter, Venables was at risk of death or serious physical harm. Venables' father, in a statement, referred to the intense media pressure to which his family had been subject at an earlier stage. As a result of this pressure, the family had had to move on several occasions, his younger children were made wards of court and injunctions were granted for their benefit to restrain publicity.

The following newspaper cuttings were made available to the court.

- The *Sun*, 27 January 1994 – An uncle of the victim said: '... if the judge's recommendation is followed, then the streets won't be safe in eight years' time'.
- The *Sun*, 1 February 1994 – Following the newspaper's campaign, an article set out that 80,000 telephone calls had been made to the television channel to say Bulger's killers must rot in jail. A coupon was attached to the article to be sent by readers to the Home Secretary expressing support for the view that the claimants should stay in prison for life.

- The *Sun*, 26 May 1994 – The mother of the victim said: 'They aren't safe to walk the streets. We must not give them the chance to do it again.'
- *Sunday Mirror*, 31 October 1999 –In an article entitled 'Society must be protected from this pair of monsters', Denise Bulger said:

> I will do everything in my power to keep them caged and I hope that Jack Straw will back me up. If they ever do get out I have sworn to go looking for them. When I find them they will wish they were dead. I will make sure they know what it is to really suffer … wherever they go, mothers like me will be after their blood.

For these reasons, Dame Elizabeth granted a life-long injunction, which has restricted press freedom for life *contra mundum* in respect of the two killers of Jamie Bulger. Though she regretted that she had to curtail 'free speech' under Art. 10 ECHR, she stated that the evidence before the court had established that sections of the press would support, and might even initiate, efforts to find the young men after their release and expose their identities and addresses. If Thompson's and Venables' new identities were discovered, neither of them would have any chance of a normal life and there was a real and strong possibility that their lives would be at risk. In these exceptional circumstances, Dame Butler-Sloss ruled, it was necessary to place the right of confidence above the right of the media to publish freely information about the claimants. Accordingly, injunctions were granted against the whole world, protecting, inter alia, any information leading to the identity or future whereabouts of the claimants.

QUESTIONS

Answer the following questions using short sentences.

1 What age group of juvenile offenders is dealt with in a youth court?

2 Define what is meant in law by:

a) a child
b) a young person.

3 When can a youngster aged 16 be named in criminal court proceedings? Cite the relevant legislation.

4 Does a family court or youth court hearing in camera mean that you, as a reporter, cannot attend the hearing at all?

5 What does the *Children Act 1989* stipulate about the naming of children involved in family proceedings?

6 What might be the dangers in publishing interviews with (named) parents who complain that their children have been removed from them without just cause?

7 What are the differences in reporting terms as per s. 39 *Children and Young Persons Act 1933* and s. 45(5) *Youth Justice and Criminal Evidence Act 1999*?

8 Discuss the reasons given by Dame Elizabeth Butler-Sloss for her decision in *Venables and Another v. News Group Newspapers Ltd and Others* [2001].

9 What would happen if an ISP published information on the identity and whereabouts of 'Thompson' or 'Venables' in the US state of Alabama? Discuss with reference to case law and equitable remedies.

10 Do you agree with the High Court ruling (2005) to grant Maxine Carr (then 27) a life-long injunction to protect her identity? Carr was the former girlfriend of Ian Huntley, convicted of the murder of 10-year-old schoolgirls Holly Wells and Jessica Chapman in December 2003. Carr was convicted at the same time of perverting the course of justice.

FURTHER READING

Muncie, John (2004) *Youth and Crime*, 2nd edn. London: Sage.

Notes

1 See Practice Direction by the Lord Chief Justice of England and Wales (Woolf LCJ): Trial of Children and Young Persons in the Crown Court of 16 February 2000.
2 *R. v. Lee* [1993] 1 WLR 103, CA.
3 See also [1993] 1 WLR 103, 96 Cr. App. Rep. 188, 157 JP 533, [1993] Crim. LR 65.
4 See full report 'Locked up at last, Britain's youngest thug aged just 12', the *Daily Express*, 17 January 2005, p. 8.
5 See also [1997] 3 All ER 97, [1997] 3 WLR 23, [1997] 2 FLR 471, [1997] Family Law 786.
6 [1999] 30 EHRR 121, ECt HR.
7 In addition to the automatic reporting restrictions of the 1933 Act (s. 48(b) and (d)), the 1999 Act amends some of the reporting restrictions and grants judges the power to lift reporting

restrictions, if they see fit. This is in addition to reporting restriction under s. 4(2) of the *Contempt of Court Act 1981*.

8 All restrictions on reporting matters relating to the identity of complainants in sexual offences are contained in the *Sexual Offences (Amendment) Act 1992* and the *Sexual Offences Act 2003*.

9 Largely covered by the *Children and Young Persons Act 1933*, but also by the *Crime and Disorder Act 1998*, such as Anti-Social Behaviour Orders (ASBOs).

10 Unreported, QBD Administrative Court, 3 February 2003.

11 The story is eloquently told by Gita Sereny in her moving account *Cries Unheard: The story of Mary Bell* (1998), where the author describes the investigations and court proceedings and subsequent development of the girl. The author, a journalist, followed this case for 30 years. This book is based on months of in-depth interviews with the adult 40-year-old Mary Bell. The case caused a major uproar in England at the time. Another girl, Norma Bell (no relation), aged 13, was tried with Mary but acquitted. Mary Bell was tried as an adult, found guilty of double murder and sentenced to 'life' imprisonment under Her Majesty's Pleasure. The child was demonised across the country by the English press as the 'bad seed' who was 'inherently evil'.

12 [1985] 1 All ER 53, [1984] 1 WLR 1422.

13 [2003] EWHC 1101 (QB), [2003] EMLR 37; [2003] 2 FCR 686; [2003] ACD 61, QBD.

14 [2001] 1 All ER 908, Family Division; [2001] 2 WLR 1038, [2001] 1 FLR 791, [2002] 1 FCR 333, [2001] Family Law 430.

15 [1990] 1 AC 109 at 281.

CHAPTER SIX

DEFAMATION

Key aim of this chapter:

To help you understand the main principles of the tort of defamation.

Learning objectives

By the end of the chapter you should be able to:

- demonstrate a sound knowledge and appreciation of the principles of the tort of defamation (libel and slander)
- be familiar with some of the leading cases in common law in order to express reasoned and critical arguments in appropriate and related journalistic contexts.

Chapter Contents

Introduction
Defamation and its dangers
Libel or slander?
Juries or no juries?
Innuendo
Malicious reporting

Introduction

As journalists, you will soon become aware of the concepts of 'libel', 'slander' and 'defamation'. The threat of an action for defamation is one of the most inhibiting factors you will face and something that you should be aware of constantly. Simply put, a defamatory statement is one that injures a person's reputation.

As a journalist, you must be aware of the jurisdictions in which you are working. Modern libel and slander laws are implemented in many, but not all, Commonwealth nations, the United States and Republic of Ireland. They have descended from English defamation law (part of tort law). Today, all may distinguish 'libel' or 'slander' as different legal concepts. Most early legal systems in the areas affected can relate today's laws back to verbal injuries, which were largely treated as criminal or quasi-criminal offences – the essence of the injury lying not in pecuniary loss, which may be compensated by damages, but in the personal insult that must be atoned for, so a vindictive penalty took the place of personal revenge. As we will see, some English common law cases in this area of law are rather dated. It was not until the *Defamation Act 1996* that some of the defences changed and actions could be settled between the parties out of court. The Act is discussed in detail at the end of this chapter (see also Appendix 3).

Individuals concerned that their privacy is being invaded often seek protection of their rights. If this cannot be done by means of the PCC (see Chapter 3), they may wish to go to court in order to sue a publisher or editor (or both) of a newspaper in the tort of defamation. In order to lessen the risk of defamation, media organisations often employ solicitors on staff or retainer. They are frequently called on to 'clear' a potentially defamatory article or programme for publication or broadcasting purposes. Technology is adding to the risks as many potentially defamatory articles go unnoticed because the people concerned miss the news item on radio or television or fail to read the paper in which it is published. However, news websites, where material is often archived and can be searched, leave themselves open to retrospective action (who has not put their own name into Google?)

Defamation and its dangers

The early history of the English law of defamation is somewhat obscure. Civil actions for damages seem to have been reasonably frequent as far back as the reign of Edward I (1272–1307). There was no distinction drawn between words written and spoken. When no pecuniary penalty was involved, cases fell within the old jurisdiction of the ecclesiastical courts. It is uncertain whether or not any generally applicable criminal process was in use.

The crime of *scandalum magnum* – spreading false reports about the magnates of the realm – was established by statutes, but the first fully reported case in which libel is said to be generally punishable at common law was one tried in the Star Chamber in the reign of James I. The law and terminology of the time are largely taken directly from Roman sources, with libels treated as a breach of the peace. From that time onwards, we find both the criminal and civil remedies in full operation. In admiralty law, a libel was the equivalent of a civil lawsuit. The plaintiff was referred to as the 'libellant'.

Defamation

The most generally accepted definition of a defamatory statement is that given by Professor Winfield:

> Defamation is the publication of a statement which tends to lower a person in the estimation of right-thinking members of society generally or which tends to make them shun or avoid that person.

In English law, a defamatory statement is libellous if it is in permanent form, such as writing or pictures or even a waxwork figure, as per *Monson v. Tussauds Ltd* [1894],[1] where Lopes LJ stated:

> Libels are generally in writing or printing, but this is not necessary; the defamatory matter may be conveyed in some other permanent form. For instance, a statue, a caricature, an effigy, chalk-marks on a wall, songs or pictures may constitute a libel.

692

! Defamatory statements

A statement is defamatory if it:

- **exposes** a person to hatred, ridicule or contempt
- **causes** him to be shunned or avoided
- **lowers** him in the estimation of right-thinking members of society
- **disparages** him in his office, profession or trade.

The jury decides whether a person has been libelled or not.

! Who is responsible?

- commercial publishers
- authors
- journalists
- newspaper and magazine/journal editors
- TV editors and producers
- internet editors, such as those at BBC News Online, FT, Reuters
- all other newspaper sources online.

Films can also be subject to libel actions. This was held in the case of *Youssoupoff v. Metro-Goldwyn-Mayer (MGM) Pictures Ltd* [1934],[2] where the CA found it necessary to show not only that the communication is permanent but also that it is visible. This principle can now be applied to all forms of moving images – TV, video, DVD and so on. Lord Atkin broadened the definition further in *Sim v. Stretch* [1936]:[3]

> The conventional phrase exposing the plaintiff to 'hatred, ridicule or contempt' is probably too narrow ... I do not intend to ask your Lordships to lay down a formal definition, but after collating the opinion of many authorities I propose in the present case the test: would the words tend to lower the plaintiff in the estimation of right-thinking members of society generally?

What is 'publication'?

The communication of:

- words
- pictures – film, TV, DVD and so on
- visual images – photographs, waxworks, digital imaging and so on
- gestures
- the Internet.

A statement can include an implication. A large photograph of, say, the Prime Minister, Tony Blair, with the headline 'Corrupt politicians' might be held to be an allegation that Tony Blair was personally corrupt.

Of increasing significance in almost all jurisdictions is the tort (delict) of 'misrepresentation', involving the making of a statement that is untrue if not defamatory. Thus, if a surveyor states that a house is free from the risk of flooding, he or she has not defamed anyone, but may still be liable if someone purchases the house relying on this statement.

What is an imputation?

Defamatory imputation is a form of words that tends to:

- lower the claimant in the estimation of right-thinking members of society generally
- expose him or her to hatred, contempt or ridicule
- cause him or her to be shunned or avoided.

An imputation:

- may be defamatory even when it is true
- is not necessarily defamatory when it is untrue.

!	What does the plaintiff have to prove?

In order to win a libel action, the plaintiff must prove that:

* the statement is defamatory
* words must be shown to have a defamatory meaning
* the defendant's statement refers to the plaintiff (reasonable person must think so)
* the statement has been published.

Plaintiff does not have to prove that:

* the statement is false (defendant has to prove this)
* there was any intention to discredit him or her
* any damage was done to plaintiff's reputation.

Either party in a defamation action has the right to claim trial by jury, but, since the *Defamation Act 1996*, parties are encouraged to make an 'offer of amends' and settle out of court early (see below). Up until very recently (before the 'McLibel' ruling of the ECHR),[4] cynics would say that it is only the rich and famous who can afford libel actions in the defamation (High) court. This kind of tort does not attract legal aid status – that is, legal aid is not generally available to bringers or defenders of defamation actions. Indeed, libel cases have been notoriously expensive. Some actions in defamation have bankrupted plaintiffs, such as the disgraced historian David Irving, who denied the Holocaust. Irving lost his 2002 libel action against Deborah Lipstadt, an American academic, who said in her 1994 book that he had misinterpreted historical evidence to minimise Hitler's culpability in the Holocaust. Mr Justice Gray ruled that Irving was 'an active Holocaust denier, anti-Semitic and racist', who had 'distorted historical data to suit his own ideological agenda'. In his final verdict he stated that:

> The answer to that question requires me to decide whether the failure on the part of the Defendants to prove the truth of those charges materially injures the reputation of Irving, in view of the fact that the other defamatory charges made against him have been proved to be justified. The charges which I have found to be substantially true include the charges that Irving has for his own ideological reasons persistently and deliberately misrepresented

and manipulated historical evidence; that for the same reasons he has portrayed Hitler in an unwarrantedly favourable light, principally in relation to his attitude towards and responsibility for the treatment of the Jews; that he is an active Holocaust denier; that he is anti-Semitic and racist and that he associates with right-wing extremists who promote neo-Nazism. In my judgment the charges against Irving which have been proved to be true are of sufficient gravity for it be clear that the failure to prove the truth of the matters set out in paragraph 13.165 above does not have any material effect on Irving's reputation.[5]

However, the ECHR, in its latest (2005) ruling on the 'McLibel' case, as it's come to be called, held that in the case of the anti-McDonald's campaigners Helen Steel and David Morris those had been a violation of Art. 6 (1) ECHR ('right to a fair hearing') and Art. 10 ECHR ('freedom of expression'). The crux of this was that the couple ought to have received legal aid during their three-year trial. On the day of the judgment, 15 February 2005, the *Daily Mail* commented that the floodgates would now open for 'anyone to say what they like about the commercial world, be sued and let taxpayers meet the costs'. A cartoon in the *Daily Telegraph* showed a McDonald's employee handing a man his meal, saying, 'Would you like legal aid with that?'

To be successful in a libel action, the words complained of must be interpreted in their context and the plaintiff is not allowed to select passages that are prima facie libellous if the passage taken as a whole is not defamatory (such as mere newspaper headlines). This was held in the *Neighbours* case, *Charleston v. NGN Ltd* [1995]. Today, actions for any published statements that defame a named or identifiable individual or individuals in a manner that causes them loss in their trade or profession or causes a reasonable person to think worse of them are brought in the High Court.

There is a right to trial by jury in claims for libel and slander under s. 69 of the *Supreme Court Act 1969*, subject to certain exceptions, such as in prolonged cases where lengthy examination of documentation takes place.[6]

It can be said that English defamation (tort) law has been severely criticised in the past decades. This is, first, because it still largely rests on the common law tradition and, second, because it can no longer be afforded by the 'common man'. Currently, as the law stands, there is no legal aid available, though this may change in the light of the 'McLibel' ruling of the ECHR in February 2005. Even more recently, important changes have been brought about, first, by the *Defamation Act 1996* and, thereafter, by the *Human Rights Act 1998*, which have impacted greatly on a journalist's right to free speech (Art. 10 ECHR).[7]

<table>
<tr><td>!</td><td>What Defamation is</td></tr>
</table>

- an attack on someone's reputation
- it need not impute moral turpitude.

Under defamation law, a defendant has a complete defence of justification if the words in question are shown to be substantially true (see below).

Reference must be to the plaintiff

What happens, if a journalist unintentionally refers to a fictitious name that he or she has made up and it turns out there is such a person 'out there'? The question should be, did the journalist or author intend to refer to an unnamed individual or was the individual unintentionally defamed? What if the defendant uses a fictional name and a real person claims to have been defamed? The following case of *Hulton v. Jones,* dating back to the early twentieth century is still the leading case in this area.

CASE STUDY

Hulton(E) & Co. v. Jones [1910] AC 20

In 1909, the *Sunday Chronicle* published a light-hearted sketch about a certain 'Artemus Jones' and the tendency of 'sober' Englishmen, once abroad, to lead a 'gay' life (in the original meaning of the word). The sketch read: 'Whist! There's Artemus Jones with a woman who is not his wife, who must be, you know – the other thing … Whist!'

The seemingly fictional character was described as a churchwarden from Peckham. A real Artemus Jones – a barrister practising on the Welsh circuit – sued for libel, claiming that some of his friends thought that the article referred to him. The claimant was awarded substantial damages. The HL upheld the claim and the defendants were held liable, although they had not intended to defame the plaintiff. The HL ruled that intention in this case was immaterial – what mattered was whether or not reasonable readers would think that the words used applied to the claimant.

Libel or slander?

There are two forms of defamation in English law: libel and slander. In the course of your career, you will mostly be concerned with libel – that is, defamation in permanent form (unless you work in radio). Slander is defamation in a transient form, such as the spoken word. Broadly speaking, you can follow these principles: a defamation communicated in writing is termed 'libel', while one made via the spoken word is termed 'slander'.

Some jurisdictions have a separate tort, or delict, of 'verbal injury' or 'convicium' (such as in Scots law) involving the making of a statement, even if truthful, designed to injure the claimant out of malice. Some also have a separate tort, or delict, of 'invasion of privacy', in which the making of a true statement may give rise to liability. However, neither of these comes under the general heading of 'defamation'.

The underlying distinction is between permanent and transient communications. The *Defamation Act 1952* and the *Theatres Act 1968* regarded all defamatory communications, including spoken statements (radio and TV broadcasts,[8] performances and plays) as 'libel'. Both acts, libel and slander, share a common legal history, although they may be treated differently in some legal systems.

For either libel or slander to be actionable, it must be 'communicated to a third party' – that is, some person other than the claimant. Libel is actionable per se and is a crime (though not serious enough to institute criminal proceedings with imprisonment) as well as a tort. Slander requires proof of special damage – damage that is quantifiable in monetary terms. This was illustrated in the Victoria Beckham case. The action against Victoria Beckham, wife of the famous footballer David Beckham, was brought by the shopowners Tim and Glynis McManus and their son Anthony. Mrs Beckham had suggested, on entering the shop, GT's Recollections, in the Bluewater Shopping Centre in Kent in March 2001, that an autograph of her husband's displayed in the shop was not genuine. In the High Court, the plaintiffs' solicitor stated how unfortunate reports of Posh Spice's visit had appeared in local and national newspapers, which had not only upset the McManus family but also affected their business. 'The McManuses had obtained the autographed photograph of David Beckham from someone they believed to be a reputable dealer and they firmly believed, as they always had, that the autograph of Mr Beckham was genuine', 'said Mr Skrein, the plaintiffs' solicitor, who further stated that 'the claimants had no choice but to institute these proceedings for slander. They were determined to vindicate their reputations.'

Mrs Beckham's counsel, Justin Rushbrooke, told the High Court's Mr Justice Gray that she apologised for the 'hurt and damage' she had caused the defendants: 'Mrs Beckham happily accepts that the McManuses are honest and reputable traders and seek to obtain their memorabilia from respected sources.' Victoria Beckham was not in court for the resolution of the case. In addition to an apology, Mrs Beckham agreed to pay the claimants' legal costs and give the shop official merchandise signed by her husband. The claimants' solicitor, Michael Skrein, concluded: 'The good-natured approach which has enabled settlement to be reached is underscored by the fact that Mrs Beckham will be providing the McManuses with a set of official merchandise which her husband has signed.'[9]

!	Libel or slander?
	• libel concerns the written word or printed form • slander concerns the spoken word.

Juries or no juries?

Defamation actions in the High Court can (but do not necessarily have to) be heard by 'libel' juries. However, these (civil) juries have been known to make unrealistically high awards of what has been described as 'Mickey mouse money' for damages in the past, damages that far exceeded the sums that would be awarded in cases of, say, serious personal injury. This was particularly evident in 1987 when the Conservative politician Jeffrey Archer won libel damages of £500,000 for allegations that he had had sex with a prostitute. It was later established that Archer had lied in court and he served time in prison for this offence. Then there was the Yorkshire Ripper's wife, Sonia Sutcliffe (see below), who took out a libel action against *Private Eye* and was awarded £600,000. Other examples follow.

CASE STUDY

Sutcliffe v. Pressdram Ltd [1991] 1 QB 153

On 23 January 1987, the plaintiff, Sonia Szurma Sutcliffe, issued a writ against the defendants, Pressdram Ltd, for libel in relation to two articles appearing in *Private Eye* on 30 January 1981 and 11 February 1983 (and further material published on 3 and 17 February 1989 being critical of the plaintiff), in which the defendants asserted that the plaintiff had made a deal worth £250,000 with the *Daily Mail* for her story as the wife of the Yorkshire Ripper, Peter Sutcliffe, who, in 1981, had been convicted of the murder and assault of a number of women.

The plaintiff asserted that, in their 'natural and ordinary meaning', the words meant and were understood to mean that, finding herself married to a killer, she had agreed to sell her story to a newspaper for that sum. In a counter-claim the defendants denied on 11 May 1987 that, in their natural and ordinary meaning, the words complained of bore, were understood to bear or were capable of bearing the meaning alleged by the plaintiff or any defamatory meaning, claiming justification.

On 24 May 1989, the jury found in favour of the plaintiff regarding both articles and awarded her the sum of £600,000. Though the defendants asked for a retrial to adduce new evidence, the CA dismissed this and the libel damages remained.

Rantzen v. Mirror Group Newspapers (1986) Ltd [1994] QB 670, CA[10]

The plaintiff – a successful television presenter and the founder and chairman of the ChildLine charity for sexually abused children – brought a libel action against the defendants regarding four articles published in *The People* newspaper on 3 February 1991. She claimed they bore the meanings (a) that the plaintiff had protected a teacher who had helped her to expose sexual abuse at a boys' school by keeping secret the fact that he was himself an abuser, thereby abandoning all her moral standards and, in particular, her publicly professed concern for abused children; (b) that the plaintiff (in spite of her position as founder of ChildLine), had taken no action regarding what she knew, thus putting at risk the children at the school where the alleged abuser was still teaching; (c) that the plaintiff's public statements and activities on behalf of sexually abused children, given her misconduct and culpable omissions, were insincere and hypocritical; and (d) that the plaintiff had untruthfully told the Editor of *The People* that publication of the story would hamper police inquiries into the matter, whereas the reason was to avoid publication of the facts of her misconduct and culpable omissions. The defendants pleaded 'justification' and 'fair comment'.

The jury found in favour of Rantzen and awarded her damages of £250,000. The defendants appealed, seeking a reduction of the damages in accordance with s. 8 *Courts and Legal Services Act 1990* and Art. 10 ECHR.

The CA concluded that the jury award of £250,000 was 'excessive and unreasonable' and that 'the jury must have applied the wrong measure of damages'. The CA concluded that this kind of damages award was wholly disproportionate to the damage done to the plaintiff's reputation – that is, Esther Rantzen was still able to continue her successful career. The CA referred to the previous authority in *Sutcliffe v. Pressdram Ltd*,[11] where it was recommended that juries ought to pay attention to the purchasing power of the award they are minded to make and of the income it would produce. The jury in the Sutcliffe case was reminded of the cost of buying a motorcar or a holiday or a house. The CA also made reference to Art. 10 ECHR and that a journalist's right to free expression should not be curtailed. At that time, though, the European Convention had not been incorporated into UK legislation, so it only remained persuasive.

At the time of Sutcliffe and Rantzen judges in defamation actions were still constrained by legal authority (the *Courts and Legal Services Act 1990*) from steering the jury towards any particular level of award. In the Rantzen case, the newspaper publishers (MGN) had appealed against the jury's award, contending that it was wholly disproportionate to the damage done to the plaintiff's reputation. The CA concluded that it would not be right to allow reference to be made to awards by juries in previous cases, but it took the view that awards made by the CA stood on a different footing.

As the body of (common) defamation law has developed over time, judges have become more 'liberated' in the manner of their direction of libel juries, as they remind them, when awarding damages, of conventional levels of awards and general damages paid for pain and suffering and loss of amenity in personal injury cases. The Rantzen and Elton John (below) cases now stand as precedent authorities given to judges in order to direct juries on the size of 'exemplary damages'. It was in the Elton John case, some three years later, that the CA went a step further in giving guidance to future libel juries regarding their awards for damages. Here, juries were, inter alia, referred to as 'sheep lost on an unfenced common, with no shepherd'.

CASE STUDY

John v. Mirror Group Newspapers [1997] CA, QB 586[12]

The plaintiff, the well-known musician and entertainer Elton Hercules John – began an action against the defendant publishers of the *Sunday Mirror* newspaper, claiming compensatory damages for defamation in an article appearing in the newspaper on 27 December 1992. The article – located on an inside page and prominently advertised on the front page, which also bore a photograph of the plaintiff – claimed that the plaintiff had a bizarre diet, with the headlines, 'World exclusive' and 'Elton's "diet of death"'. The 'Exclusive from Tony Brenna in Los Angeles and Paul Scott in London' on pp. 4 and 5 of the paper read:

> Rock superstar Elton John is hooked on a bizarre new diet which doctors have warned could kill him. Millionaire Elton's weight has plummeted since he started eating food then spitting it out without swallowing. The star, who suffered from the eating disorder bulimia, has told friends in America: 'I am on the "don't swallow and get thin diet", and I can tell you it works. I have got the best of both worlds. I get the flavour without becoming a blimp.'

The libel judge ruled that there was sufficient evidence to place before the jury on the issue of exemplary damages. The jury found in John's favour, awarding him £75,000 in compensatory damages and £275,000 in exemplary damages.

The newspaper publishers appealed about the size of the damages award and the CA allowed the appeal (in part) regarding the damages and how assessing the amount of an award of damages could be brought to the jury's attention.

The CA reaffirmed the fundamental soundness of the traditional approach in *Sutcliffe v. Pressdram Ltd* [1991] and *Rantzen* [1994] and ruled that the judge's guidelines to the jury in this case had been sufficient. The CA commented that, as the article did not attack the plaintiff's personal integrity or damage his reputation as an artist, the jury's award had been 'excessive' and the sum of £25,000 should be substituted. The court further stated that it was clearly undesirable for higher compensation to be given for loss of reputation than for many cases of severe mental or physical injury, citing typical awards for victims suffering personal injury and inviting juries to compare the damage a libel plaintiff suffered. They pointed out that, for instance, a paraplegic is awarded a maximum of £125,000 compensation for the injury, while a lost arm is worth £45,000 and a lost eye £20,000. The CA even went so far as to suggest that there should be a £125,000 limit on defamation awards. John's appeal was allowed in part.

Since the Sonia Sutcliffe, Elton John and Esther Rantzen cases, courts have been given increased power to substitute the juries' damages awards with lower sums. Libel juries can now be directed at a defamation trial that damages awarded must be realistic and not excessive under s. 8 of the *Courts and Legal Services Act 1990.*[13] We have seen in the Esther Rantzen and Elton John cases that the CA's ability to fix an appropriate level of award is now an important weapon against excessive awards given by libel juries. The advice for the control of juries outlined in both these cases ensures that the modern law will not be subjected to the same criticism. Today, trial without a jury is possible and will be decided on by the presiding judge if it is regarded as more expedient and less costly (as in *Irving v. Lipstadt* [1996]).

The law is often highly technical, with complicated rules of evidence and demarcation between the different functions of judge and jury and frequently quite arbitrary applications can seriously blur a case. It is now possible to apply under the Rules of the *Supreme Court Act* (Order 82 and Rule 3A), on a preliminary application, for a judge to fix, before trial, the permissible meanings of the allegedly defamatory words, so as ascertain the degree of injury to the plaintiff's reputation and evaluate any defences raised.

Innuendo

An innuendo is a remark or question with oblique, typically disparaging meaning. The intention is usually to insult or accuse someone in such a way, that one's words, taken literally, are innocent. It is often referred to as 'double entendre'. When the plaintiff complains about an innuendo, he claims that the words have hidden meaning, and is only defamatory in circumstances to persons 'in the know'. Innuendo is often used in sitcoms or comedy sketches. The plaintiff must show that the context turns the apparently innocent statement into a defamatory one; and the statement remains non-defamatory, until he proves that it is not. The plaintiff must then plead according to the meaning that he attributes to the words used, and must prove the existence of facts to support that the innuendo complained of did, in fact, have hidden meaning. The leading case is very old and leads back to the 1930s. In *Tolley v. Fry* [1931] the HL defined innuendo. The following quotation from its judgment in the case is still cited today in defamation actions when the 'right-thinking' members of society test is applied:

> To write or say of a man something that will disparage him in the eyes of a particular section of the community but will not affect his reputation in the eyes of the average right-thinking man is not actionable within the law of defamation.

Greer LJ, *Tolley v. Fry*, 479

CASE STUDY

Tolley v. Fry (J. S.) & Sons Ltd [1931] 1 KB 467; [1931] AC 333

Mr Tolley, the plaintiff, was a well-known amateur golfer. Without his consent, the defendants produced an advertisement using the plaintiff as a caricature with a caddie, each of them with a packet of Fry's chocolate protruding from their pockets. The caricature was accompanied by doggerel verse that used Mr Tolley's name and extolled the virtues of the chocolate – the implication being that Fry's chocolate was as good as Tolley's golfing ability.

The plaintiff sued for libel, claiming that the innuendo was he had accepted money for the advertisement and thereby lost his amateur status.

The judge at the trial ruled that the advertisement *was* capable of being defamatory and, on appeal, the HL upheld this ruling.

The Tolley and Fry case is usually cited in similar actions, such as *Kaye v. Robertson* [1991]. It is also used in the 'privacy interest' test, which protects a person's private interest in addition to a person's reputation.

CASE STUDY

Berkoff v. Burchill [1996] 4 All ER 1008

Julie Burchill, a well-known journalist and columnist, had twice made throwaway remarks about Stephen Berkoff, an actor and film director, in film reviews in The *Sunday Times*. At first she said that 'film directors, from Hitchcock to Berkoff, are notoriously hideous-looking people', then second, in a review of Mary Shelley's *Frankenstein*, she wrote:

the creature is … rejected in disgust when it comes out scarred and primeval. It's a very new look for the Creature – no bolts in the neck or flat-top hairdo – and I think it works: it's a lot like Stephen Berkoff, only marginally better-looking.

Berkoff sued in libel.

The CA had to consider the implication and innuendo of the meaning 'hideously ugly' and whether or not these words were capable of being defamatory. Furthermore, the CA had to decide whether or not the words would cause Mr Berkoff to be 'shunned and avoided' and whether or not they would result in 'ridicule'.

Neill LJ argued that the words *would* make him an object of ridicule as the articles gave the impression that 'he was not merely physically unattractive in appearance but actually repulsive'. Neill LJ stated that:

Words may be defamatory, even though they neither impute disgraceful conduct to the plaintiff, nor any lack of skill or efficiency in the conduct of his trade or business or professional activity, if they hold him up to contempt, scorn or ridicule or tend to exclude him from society …

The case for Mr Berkoff is that the charge that he is 'hideously ugly' exposes him to ridicule, and/or alternatively, will cause him to be shunned or avoided … In the present case it would, in my view, be open to a jury to conclude that in the context the remarks about Mr Berkoff gave the impression that he was not merely physically unattractive in appearance but actually repulsive. It seems to me that to say this of someone in the public eye who makes his living, in part at least, as an actor is capable of lowering his standing in the estimation of the public and of making him an object of ridicule.

Millett LJ dissented from the opinion of his two fellow law lords (Neill LJ and Phillips LJ), when he stated that:

Many a true word is spoken in jest. Many a false one too. But chaff and banter are not defamatory and even serious imputations are not actionable if no one would take them to be meant seriously ... Mr Berkoff is a director, actor and writer. Physical beauty is not a qualification for a director or writer. Mr Berkoff does not plead that he plays romantic leads or that the words complained of impugn his professional ability. In any case, I do not think that it can be defamatory to say of an actor that he is suitable to play particular roles. How then can the words complained of injure Mr Berkoff's reputation? They are an attack on his appearance, not on his reputation. It is submitted on his behalf that they would cause people to 'shun and avoid him' and would bring him into 'ridicule' ... I have no doubt that the words complained of were intended to ridicule Mr Berkoff, but I do not think that they made him look 'ridiculous' or lowered his reputation in the eyes of ordinary people. Berkoff's appeal was dismissed.

What we can conclude from the Berkoff case is that a mere joke will not necessarily lower a person's reputation if it is not meant to be taken seriously. Let's have a look at the next case – *Charleston v. News Group Newspapers Ltd* [1995] – in which the HL was asked to consider a mock exposé in the *News of the World* that alerted the readership to new ways of making digital photographs and digital imaging.

Charleston v. News Group Newspapers Ltd [1995] 2 AC 65[14]

CASE STUDY

The defendants (MGN), as publishers of the *News of the World,* had published two photographs as a mock exposé on its front page in which the heads of the plaintiffs, the actors who played Harold and Madge Bishop in the Australian TV soap Neighbours, were superimposed on the bodies of two people engaged in sexual intercourse in sodomy and bondage gear. On the same page, there was a photograph in which the first plaintiff's head was superimposed on a woman dressed in a tight leather outfit with the headline, 'Strewth! What's Harold up to with our Madge?', and below this was a picture of a man and a woman nearly naked in a pornographic pose with the faces of the claimants and the subtext, 'Porn shocker for *Neighbours* stars'.

The caption under the photos and the text made it quite clear that the photos had been produced as part of a new computer game, but the plaintiff's faces had been used without their knowledge or consent and, thus, they could be described as 'victims'.

In their defence, the defendants argued that they were trying to show new ways of using digital imaging or computer-generated photography. The plaintiffs claimed that the photographs and headline were libellous in their ordinary and natural meaning and the readership might well think that the plaintiffs had posed for pornographic photos.

Lord Bridge noted that the two stars had been 'the unwitting stars of a sordid computer game' and his Lordship accepted that the publication had been 'deeply offensive and insulting' to the plaintiffs. However, he held that this was *not* defamatory, giving the following reasons (in summary):

- a prominent headline or photograph cannot be libellous in isolation from the related text of an accompanying article that was not in itself defamatory when considered as *a whole*
- if no legal innuendo was alleged, then the single natural and ordinary meaning to be ascribed to the words of an allegedly defamatory publication was the meaning that the words taken as a whole conveyed to the mind of an ordinary, reasonable, fair-minded reader
- the plaintiff cannot rely on an *isolated* defamatory passage in an article if other parts of the article negate the effect of the libel.

Accordingly, the plaintiff could not rely on a defamatory meaning conveyed only to a limited category of readers who only read headlines and so their appeal was dismissed.

The following case of *Lewis v. The Daily Telegraph* sets the precedent for true or 'legal' innuendo. There is true innuendo wherever the plaintiff argues that the facts or circumstances, which are not apparent from the words themselves ('extrinsic evidence'), give those words a meaning that they would not ordinarily have. As Lord Reid commented in this case:

What the ordinary man, not avid for scandal, would read into the words complained of must be a matter of impression. I can only say that I do not think that he would infer guilt or fraud merely because an inquiry is on foot. And, if that is so, then it is the duty of the trial judge to direct the jury that it is for them to determine the meaning of the paragraph but that they must not hold it to impute guilt or fraud because as a matter of law the paragraph is not capable of having that meaning.

CASE STUDY

Lewis v. The Daily Telegraph [1964] AC 234

Details of a criminal investigation into a large public company, Rubber Improvements Ltd, were leaked to *The Daily Telegraph*. The defendant newspaper printed a piece on its front page stating that the fraud squad was investigating the affairs of the company: 'Inquiry on firm by city police'. The paper named the chairman of the company, Mr John Lewis, stating:

Officers of the City of London Fraud Squad are inquiring into the affairs of Rubber Improvements Ltd and its subsidiary companies. The investigation was requested after criticisms of the chairman's statement and the accounts by a shareholder at the recent company meeting. The chairman of the company … is Mr John Lewis, former Socialist MP for Bolton.

Lewis sued in libel, arguing that readers might believe the words to be true, the sting of the libel being in, 'there was no smoke without fire'. He argued that the readership would infer that he must be guilty of something – fraud. The plaintiff claimed that the statement meant not only that the company was being investigated for fraud but also that he himself was guilty of fraud.

The HL held that the statement was *not* capable of bearing that alternative meaning. They argued that many people might draw an inference from the newspaper's comments, but that this was nonetheless a reasonable inference. Lewis was not allowed to treat the story as an allegation of fraud against him.

We have to see their Lordships' decision was governed by policy because to have ruled otherwise would have meant that crime investigations could never be reported.

Gillick v. BBC [1996] CA, *The Times*, 20 October 1995 EMLR 267[15]

Mrs Gillick, a prominent campaigner against contraceptive advice for young girls, was the participant in a live TV programme. The chat show presenter commented, 'there were at least two reported cases of suicide by girls who were pregnant'. Mrs Gillick claimed that these words accused her of being morally responsible for these deaths.[16]

The CA held that the words were capable of bearing that meaning in the eyes of the 'ordinary' viewer.

Donovan v. The Face [1992]

The magazine *The Face* purported to 'out' the actor and former *Neighbours* star, Jason Donovan. In 1992, *The Face* magazine wrote about a poster campaign starring the *Neighbours* actor with 'bleached-blond hair'; the magazine reproduced the poster. Jason sued for libel and won, possibly because his barrister argued that the innuendo 'bleached-blond hair' meant that it was a code for being 'gay'. Jason Donovan claimed the magazine implied that he was dishonest as he previously said he was straight. Donovan sued, saying that he had been accused not merely of being homosexual but also there was an underlying innuendo that he had concealed his supposed sexuality to preserve his stage image as a heterosexual.

A jury found the statement defamatory, awarding £292,000 in damages.

CASE STUDY

CASE STUDY

Malicious reporting

Though there is currently no 'legal aid' available in defamation cases, the law allows for financial legal services in cases where maliciousness (or 'injurious' or 'malicious falsehood') can be proved. 'Maliciousness' signifies an action that can be brought without the need for proof of loss of reputation. Most notably, legal aid (now called public funding)[17] is available for an action in malicious falsehood.

Generally, maliciousness is a false statement and will be actionable in defamation only where it leads to a lowering of the claimant in the estimation of right-thinking members of society and economic loss. In such cases, it may be possible for the claimant to bring an action in malicious (or injurious) falsehood. An example is to be found in the Stephane Grappelli case.

CASE STUDY

Grappelli and Another v. Derek Block (Holdings) Ltd and Another [1981] 2 All ER 272

The plaintiff, the famous jazz violinist, Stephane Grappelli, had employed the defendants as his managing tour agents. The defendants had arranged a number of concerts at various venues in England, but without the plaintiff's authority. Subsequently, the concerts had to be cancelled. As an 'excuse' to ticket holders, the defendants stated that the reason for the cancellation was that Mr Grappelli was 'seriously ill'. They also told concertgoers that it was doubtful if Grappelli would ever tour again. Though this statement was not in itself defamatory (as it is not damaging to someone's reputation to say that they are ill), this sort of announcement could clearly be damaging to Grappelli's career and future success.

Though the plaintiff's action in slander was dismissed, he was successful in his alternative plea of malicious falsehood.

Malicious falsehood is substantially concerned with protecting the plaintiff's economic interest rather than his or her reputation. It has to be pointed out that an action in maliciousness is more limited for a claimant (or plaintiff) than libel, as he or she is not entitled to a jury trial. Furthermore, he or she has to prove that the words were false, whereas in libel the burden of proving the words are true is on the defendant. He or she has to prove, further, that the words were published maliciously and that they were likely to cause him or her financial loss. Damages, however, if the plaintiff is successful, will amount to roughly the same as in a successful defamation action. There is nothing to stop a claimant bringing an action in both defamation and malicious falsehood (as was done in the Grappelli case).

Recent cases have expanded the scope of malicious falsehood. The principle of malicious (or injurous) falsehood was put to the *Kaye v. Robertson* test and further developed in *Reynolds v. Times Newspapers Ltd and Others* (see below and later in this chapter under 'Qualified privilege').

Kaye v. Robertson [1991] FSR 62

The claimant was a well-known actor and star of the TV series *Allo! Allo!*. He had been injured while driving in his car, when a piece of advertising hoarding, blown off by a gale, smashed through the windscreen. Gordon Kaye suffered serious injuries to his head and brain and was on a life-support machine in hospital. A *Sunday Sport* reporter gained access to Kaye's private hospital room, ignoring all the notices that indicated clearly that no one was allowed to be there, least of all conduct an interview with the actor. The journalist, accompanied by a photographer, attempted to conduct an interview with the actor and the photographer took pictures that showed substantial scarring to the actor's head.

Through his friend, who had seen a draft of the article, Kaye sought an interlocutory (interim) injunction to prevent publication of the piece. The article claimed, inter alia, that the actor had consented to the article, so the claimant alleged malicious falsehood. Kaye claimed that he had not agreed to the interview and had, in any event, not been in a fit state to consent. He also stated that, shortly after the interview, he had no recollection of the incident. This case also raised the question of the protection of privacy under present English law. Addressing both allegations of maliciousness and privacy, Glidewell LJ stated:

> It is well known that in English law there is no right to privacy, and accordingly there is no right of action for breach of a person's privacy. The facts of the present case are a graphic illustration of the desirability of Parliament considering whether and in what cir-cumstances statutory provision can be made to protect the privacy of individuals.

In the absence of any privacy legislation, the jury was then directed to consider the claim for an injunction on the following rights:

1 libel
2 malicious falsehood
3 trespass to a person
4 passing off.

In relation to the requirement that the words complained of be false, Lord Glidewell said:

> I have no doubt that any jury which did not find that the clear implication from the words contained in the defendants' draft article were false would be making a totally unreasonable finding. Thus the test is satisfied in relation to this cause of action.

In this course of action, 'malice' means to act without just cause or excuse and with some indirect, dishonest or improper motive. It is for the claimant to prove malice. The *Sunday Sport* reporter and photographer should have realised that Mr Kaye was in no fit state to be interviewed, but they went ahead with the interview anyway. Kaye's appeal was allowed and the injunction was granted (though varied). Therefore, the case set the requirements for 'malice' that are still applied today.

Note that any publication and subsequent republication would therefore also be regarded as malicious. The definition of 'maliciousness' was broadened in *Joyce v. Sengupta* (see below) when the plaintiff took out an action in both defamation and malicious falsehood.

CASE STUDY

Joyce v. Sengupta and Another [1993] CA, 1 All ER 897[18]

Today newspaper published an article on its front page headed, 'Royal maid stole letters' and 'Sacked as Anne names culprit'. The article, by Mr Kim Sengupta, the paper's crime correspondent, concerned love letters written to Princess Anne by Captain Lawrence. These had been stolen from the Princesss' private rooms at Buckingham Palace and had been delivered to the newspaper. The essence of the article read as follows:

> The thief who stole Princess Anne's intimate letters has been tracked down by police. She is a royal maid who has been interviewed by detectives four times. The Princess had told police that she believed the maid was the culprit and that she acted out of spite when she handed the four letters, written by the Queen's Equerry, to a national newspaper. After the theft, Anne immediately ordered that the maid should not go into rooms where there might be confidential papers. The servant, who is unmarried, will now be dismissed from royal service. As *Today* revealed two weeks ago, she will not be prosecuted. Buckingham Palace has told Scotland Yard that the Queen does not want the adverse publicity a court case will inevitably bring. But the maid will have to give a written guarantee that she will not discuss the sensitive letters from Tim Lawrence either in Britain or abroad. The woman, who has travelled abroad on royal tours, has repeatedly denied the allegation despite intense grilling by the Yard's Serious Crime Squad under Det. Chief Supt Roy Ramm. Her fingerprints were taken at Anne's home, Gatcombe Park in Gloucestershire, and will now be compared with forensic clues from the intimate notes. The results will be known within a week. Police have discovered that the maid had been on bad terms with the Princess for a long time. Anne had told her off several times. The maid has also complained to colleagues about poor pay and conditions. A senior detective said: 'This appears to be a classic case of a woman who feels she has been wronged. We have little doubt she is the guilty party and are now awaiting forensic confirmation. Even if we get the proof we cannot prosecute. The matter will be decided behind closed doors by the Palace.'

> Extract from the law report [1993] 1 All ER 897, p. 900.

The extract from the above law report states that the article in the *Today* newspaper clearly referred to the plaintiff and it had become quite clear (jigsaw identification) that the royal maid Linda Joyce was implicated – she had been working for Princess Anne since 1989. The CA, Civil Division, under Sir Donald Nicholls V-C, Elizabeth Butler-Sloss LJ and Sir Michael Kerr, regarded the article as grossly defamatory. Furthermore, the newspaper had not published any retraction or apology.

However, there was a difficulty confronting the plaintiff. She did not have the money needed to pursue libel proceedings at her own expense and legal aid was not available for defamation proceedings (*Legal Aid Act 1988*, sch. 2, pt II, para. 1). However, the plaintiff's legal advisers formulated a claim against Mr Sengupta and News (UK) Ltd, the publisher of the newspaper, for malicious falsehood. The law regards this claim in defamation as a serious action and legal aid claims can be made. Thus, a writ was issued on 31 August 1990 and the statement of claim was served on 21 September.

The defendants then applied to strike out the statement of claim as an abuse of the process of the court.

On 12 December 1990, Mr Gilbert Gray QC at the High Court in the Queen's Bench Division, acceded to that application. He decided that a case of defamation had been forced into the 'ill-fitting garb of an action for malicious falsehood'. From that decision, the plaintiff, Miss Joyce, appealed.

The CA held that a plaintiff could choose which course of action she wished to pursue when more than one cause of action was available to her. This meant that a person who was the subject of a defamatory article was entitled to bring an action for malicious falsehood with the assistance of legal aid. In order to succeed in a claim for malicious falsehood, the plaintiff had to establish that the defendant had maliciously made a false statement that had caused her damage or in respect of which she was relieved from proving damage by s. 3 of the *Defamation Act 1952* because the words complained of were calculated to cause the plaintiff pecuniary (financial) damage. As, in Miss Joyce's case, the plaintiff's statement of claim raised an arguable claim for malicious falsehood, she was entitled to pursue her claim, with legal aid being available to her. Her appeal was allowed.

Let us not forget, here, the impact of s.12 of the *Human Rights Act 1998* (HRA) is now capable of granting injunctions where malicious falsehood is concerned. However, the law also states that courts should not, on principle, be prepared to grant injunctions in malicious falsehood claims against publishers or editors who wish to defend the truth of their statement under Art. 10 ECHR ('freedom of expression') when the statement was made.

Malicious falsehood

In order to succeed in an action in malicious falsehood, the claimant must generally prove that the defendant:

- published or spoke words about the claimant that are false
- published or spoke words that are malicious
- there must also be proof of economic loss ('special pecuniary damage') on the claimant's part as a direct and natural result of the publication or slander.

Repetition and republication

Repetition and republication is particularly contentious and a major potential pitfall. This means that *every* repetition of a defamatory statement (or words) is a fresh publication and creates a fresh cause of action against each successive publisher, editor or author. The rule on republication is based on the 'multiple publication' precedent as set in the ancient nineteenth century case of *Duke of Brunswick v Harmer* [1849] QB 154. This means that each publication gives rise to a new cause of action, effectively circumventing the limitation period of one year for defamation. The Brunswick case involved a North German Duke (von Braunschweig), who saw himself being defamed by an article in the *Weekly Dispatch* of 19 September 1830. The offending article referred to an event seven days earlier, when the people of his dukedom rose up against the Duke's autocratic tendencies. The Duke had fled and lived for the next 43 years in exile in London, Paris and Geneva. In 1848, the Duke – then living in Paris – sent his manservant off to the British Museum to get hold of a copy of the offending article, published by the *Weekly Dispatch* 17 years earlier, which he believed had defamed him. Despite a limitation rule at the time of six years, the Queen's Bench Divisional Court decided that these reports constituted a new publication of libel and cause for action. He was awarded £500, a vast sum of money in those days.

The Brunswick case is best remembered for the three distinctive precedents:

1   each communication is a separate libel (known now as 'republication')

2   publication takes place where the words are heard or read

3   it is not necessary for the plaintiff to prove that publication of defamatory words caused him damage because damage is presumed.

The court also held that it does not matter if the publication is 'international', the English court can still be 'the most appropriate forum'. Transnational libels can be dealt with in the High Court of England to this very day and a number of overseas celebrities and business people have successfully sued in the High Court in London. All they have to show is that the story had more than a minimal circulation and that they had connections to the UK and a reputation to defend there.

How republication has seriously affected the Internet (particularly newspaper archives) was put to the test in *Loutchansky v. The Times Newspapers Limited* [2001] EWCA Civ 1805. In this case Mr Loutchansky, a Russian businessman, sued *The Times* in respect of articles published in the newspaper in September and October 1999, suggesting that he was part of the Russian mafia and was involved in money laundering. A year later, he commenced a separate action in respect of the same articles stored in *The Times'* online archive. *The Times* argued that this action was out of time as the limitation period should have run from the date the article was first published on the website, not from the time a visitor to the website happened to download it. They argued that the maintenance of online archives was a valuable public service and the multiple publication rule had the effect of meaning that online publishers were 'indefinitely vulnerable to claims for defamation for years, even decades after the initial hard copy and Internet publication took place'. They argued that this would place an excessive burden on online publishers and that this would have the effect of inhibiting freedom of expression.

The Court of Appeal, however, rejected these arguments, upholding the established common law position as identified in Brunswick. The CA also rejected *The Times'* qualified privilege defence to the publication. As each website publication is successive, they said it was necessary to look at the circumstances surrounding the online article at the time of publication when considering the defence of qualified privilege. In this case, *The Times* had not sought to justify the articles. The Court of Appeal found that this, together with their failure to draw to readers' attention the fact that the truth of the articles was 'hotly contested' until 10 months after the defence had been served, could not be described as responsible journalism. Although they did not have to remove the article, they should have placed a warning notice against it as soon as the claim was made.

How do the cases of Brunswick and Loutchansky affect editors and operators of online archives? They need to watch out for potentially defamatory or contentious articles, for each 'hit' on a website (say BBC Online or the *Guardian* archives) can be seen as a fresh publication, if the article is likely to be defamatory. This could mean re-defending the allegations years later. If a complaint is made, it is wise to either place a warning notice against the article or pull the article altogether. Though this does not protect the editor from a claim in defamation, it might give him the defence of qualified privilege. The Loutchansky decision places online publishers and those who maintain an archive in an impossible position. Recent editors of *The Times* and the *Guardian*, have respectively argued that the English courts should adopt the American 'single publication' rule. This states that publication takes place on the day the material is posted on the website. Thereafter, if it remains untouched by the hand of the publisher, there is no subsequent 'publication'. Thus the limitation period would run out a year after the date on which the material was first posted. We have to question whether the Duke of Brunswick case should still be relevant in today's fast-moving online age? Thus, a libel which is reprinted will bring new liability to the author, editor or publisher. For instance, a journalist who writes a newspaper article about a politician's speech may be sued regarding any defamatory matter contained in the speech. A newspaper editor (or subeditor), publisher, distributor or retail seller of the newspaper may also be sued for republication. The distributor and/or newsagent may, however, be able to avail themselves of the defence of innocent dissemination.

This is also becoming a problem for Internet service providers (ISPs), website operators and journalists who work for news websites, who can be, prima facie, liable for all defamatory material they pass on. The question of new website archives, in which defamatory articles may be stored, adds danger for editors, web hosts and journalists, though most responsible sites are now obliged to remove any such material if they become aware of it (*Godfrey v. Demon Internet* [2001] – see below). Newspapers, of course, also have archives, but it is likely that courts would take a more aggressive view of web archives as they are, by their nature, much easier to search.

CASE STUDY

Godfrey v. Demon Internet [2001] QB 201[19]

The defendants, who were in business as an ISP, received and stored on their news server an article that was defamatory about the plaintiff, Dr Laurence Godfrey. It had been posted by an unknown person using another ISP (from 17 January 1997). The plaintiff informed the defendants that the article was defamatory and asked them to remove it from their news server. The defendants failed to do so and it remained available on the server for some ten days until its automatic expiry.

The plaintiff brought proceedings for libel against the defendants, who relied in their defence on s. 1(1) *Defamation Act 1996*, contending that they were not the publisher of the statement complained of, that they had taken reasonable care in relation to its publication and they did not know and had no reason to believe that they had caused or contributed to the publication of a defamatory statement. The plaintiff applied to strike out that part of the defence as disclosing no reasonable or sustainable defence at law.

The CA granted the plaintiff's application. It ruled that an ISP *is* a 'publisher' (though the defendants were not deemed a publisher within the meaning of s. 1(2) and (3) of the 1996 Act). It stated that the defendants were not merely the passive owner of an electronic device through which postings were transmitted, but actively chose to receive and store the news group exchanges containing the posting that could be accessed by their subscribers. The defendants did fall under s. 1(1)(a) of that Act. Once they *knew* of the defamatory content of the posting and chose not to remove it from their news server, they could no longer satisfy the additional requirements of section 1(1)(b), that they took reasonable care in relation to the publication, or section 1(1)(c), that they did not know and had no reason to believe that what they did caused or contributed to the publication, and that, accordingly, the parts of their pleaded defence that relied on section 1(1) of the 1996 Act would be struck out.

Morland J concluded:

> In my judgment the defamatory posting was published by the defendants and, as from 17 January 1997 they knew of the defamatory content of the posting, they cannot avail themselves of the protection provided by section 1 of the Defamation Act 1996 and their defence under section 1 is, in law, hopeless. Therefore the plaintiff's summons to strike out succeeds. With regard to the defendants' application to amend the defence I make no definitive ruling but indicate that it is likely to succeed. It may also be helpful to suggest that on the basis of the proposed amended defence any award of damages to the plaintiff is likely to be very small.

Another important Internet case is that of *Totalise PLC v. Motley Fool Ltd and Another* [2001] EWCA Civ. 1897.[20] The case concerns anonymous (libellous) postings on Internet chatrooms. In this case, a fund manager posted libellous statements using a fictitious name – Zeddust – about a City firm on the UK Motley Fool financial website. The anonymous perpetrator used the anonymity of Motley Fool's bulletin board to spread what he now agrees was a 'grave slur' alleging serious criminal and dishonest wrongdoing.

Judge Owen in his judgment of 19 February 2001 stated:

> I have come to the conclusion that it was perfectly plain from the outset that the postings on both websites were highly defamatory and that, accordingly, the claimants were the victims of a sustained campaign amounting to an actionable tort. There was no other way in which the claimants could have proceeded, save by requiring identification of Zeddust from both defendants. I accept that the defendants had to carry out the balancing exercise, but in my judgment there was only one answer to that balancing exercise, namely that they should have complied with the requests made by the claimant. In those circumstances, I order the defendants to pay the claimant's costs of this application/action.

The judge then summarily assessed the costs to be paid by Interactive at £4817.

You might be concerned as journalists with spin-doctoring if you work in PR or corporate communications, so you will have to be careful of exaggeration, the spreading of rumours and the repetition of 'true facts'. Generally, the original spinner of the rumour remains liable for defamation when the repetition was authorised or intended or when repetition was reasonably foreseeable or the natural and probable consequence of the original publication. You will certainly be liable for a repetition of defamatory statements when you intend or authorise the repetition (*Parkes v. Prescott* [1869]),[21] unless a person to whom it was published was under a duty to repeat it (*Derry v. Handley* [1867]).[22]

Newspapers or broadcasting organisations will certainly be liable if the 'sting' of the libel is still present, as in *Slipper v. BBC* (see below). When the defamatory matter is contained in a book, journal or newspaper, there will be a series of publications – by the author, the publisher, the publisher jointly with the printer and so on, right to the distributor. Each repetition is fresh publication, creating a new cause of action (*Duke of Brunswick v. Harmer* [1849] 14 QBD 185). How the foreseeable repetition of a defamatory statement can lead to a further libel action can be seen in *Slipper v. BBC*.

CASE STUDY

Slipper v. British Broadcasting Corporation [1991] 1 QB 283, CA[23]

The plaintiff – a retired police officer – had been the subject of a TV programme about attempts to bring the escaped 'Great Train Robber' Ronnie Biggs back to Britain from Brazil. The plaintiff claimed that he had been portrayed as an 'incompetent buffoon'. The programme had been previewed by press and TV journalists, who subsequently wrote a number of reviews, which repeated the statement.

The plaintiff sued for libel regarding the film broadcast by the defendants – the BBC. The plaintiff claimed further that the 'sting' of the libel also lay in the republication of the defamatory statement when it was repeated in the press.

The defendants applied to have the claim based on the repetition of the libel struck out. The CA refused to strike out the defendant's argument that the repetition of a libel was only actionable in these limited circumstances.

The CA stated that the law on republication was said to be an aspect of *novus actus interveniens* (a new and intervening act). If the republication is unauthorised, then, prima facie, the chain of causation has been broken. It was said that, on the facts in this case, the defendants could arguably foresee that the libel would be repeated in their reviews.

The defendants (the BBC) wanted the claim, based on the repetition of the libel, struck out. They argued that defendants in a libel action are not liable for the repetition of such a libel by a third party who was not their agent, unless such a third party was authorised to do so. The CA held that *every* repetition of a defamatory statement is a new publication and creates a fresh cause of action against the person defamed. Then, the plaintiff may have an action not only against the person repeating the statement but also against the person originating the statements.

You should also look out for so-called 'linked publications', which raise the question of whether or not a plaintiff can put together a defamation action from two or more publications. This was brought to the attention of the courts in *Hayward v. Thomson* (see below).

Hayward v. Thompson [1982] QB 47[24]

During police investigations into Norman Scott's allegations that he had been the target of a conspiracy to murder in order to protect a former lover (the then Liberal Leader Jeremy Thorpe MP) and that Scott had been the target of a smear campaign by the *Daily Telegraph*, the newspaper had obtained a scoop from police sources about the allegations. The plaintiff, Mr Jack Hayward, was a wealthy man who had given large sums of money to the Liberal Party. Hayward claimed that what the article said meant that he was guilty of participating in or condoning a murder plot.

In the first article, the defendants stated that the police had the names of two more people associated with the Scott affair and one was a wealthy benefactor of the Liberal Party: 'Two more in Scott affair'.

> The names of two more people connected with the Norman Scott affair have been given to the police. One is a wealthy benefactor of the Liberal Party ... Both men, police have been told, arranged for a leading Liberal supporter to be 'reimbursed' £5000, the same amount Mr Andrew Newton alleges he was paid to murder Scott.

A second article, a week later, named the plaintiff and stated that the police wanted to interview him.

The CA relied on the Lewis[25] case and upheld the trial judge's ruling that the jury could look at the second article to see to whom the first article referred. The CA said, further, that the words would mean to the ordinary reader no more than that an inquiry was under way, hence the phrase that the suspect was 'assisting police with their inquiries'. The jury awarded the plaintiff £50,000 and the CA upheld the verdict because the article *was* capable of implying guilt.

Who is liable for publication?

!

A person will be liable for any publication:

- that is intended
- that he or she can reasonably anticipate
- when there is unintentional publication – it is published due to a want of care on his or her part.

Defences and remedies

Several general defences and remedies are available to journalists in defamation actions. These are generally:

- justification
- fair comment on a matter of public interest
- privilege – absolute and qualified
- an offer of amends as well as an apology are now available under the *Defamation Act 1996*
- innocent dissemination.

! General Defences

If you receive a libel claim you have several possible defences:

- justification – it's true and you can prove it
- fair comment – public interest; must be honestly held on basis of fact
- privilege (*Bill of Rights 1688*) –

    a) absolute privilege – freedom of MPs in House of Commons; fair, accurate and contemporaneous report in court

    b) qualified privilege – reports of speeches made by MPs in Parliament; news conferences (*Broadcasting Act 1990*).

Although an apology is not a true remedy, it can be used to reduce damages (s. 2 *Libel Act 1843*). In reality, no newspaper really publishes a prominent apology, other than some of the more serious papers. The *Guardian* or The *Independent*, for instance, publish apologies – usually on the 'letters to the editor' page. However, no apology will be given the same prominence as the original libel, except when ordered by the courts (as happened with Elton John's case).

One remedy that may be used in certain cases is that the High Court may grant an interim injunction (under s. 12 HRA), preventing allegedly defamatory material from being published. The plaintiff must act quickly to secure this remedy and prove that publication would amount to immediate and irreparable injury.

We said earlier that the tort of defamation does provide some protection of an individual's privacy, but only when the claimant has been portrayed in a 'false light', as was the case in *Tolley v. Fry* and *Kaye v. Robertson*, discussed earlier in this chapter. Glidewell LJ in *Kaye v. Robertson* [1991] addressed the notion of privacy in English law. As stated earlier, there is no right of action for breach of a person's privacy in English law. In the absence of such a right, the plaintiff's advisers sought to base their claim in malicious falsehood in the tort of defamation, as discussed above.

Justification

Under the tort of defamation, a defendant has a complete defence of justification if the words complained of prove to be substantially true. There is no need to demonstrate that their publication was in the public interest in this case. So, if the defamatory statement is true, the defendant has a defence, as long as this can be proved. It is not necessary to prove that every single detail of the statement is true (the sting of the libel), so long as the article taken as a whole is accurate.

Fair comment

Whereas justification provides a defence in questions of fact, fair comment defends opinions that, by their nature, cannot be true or false. Sometimes called the critic's defence, fair comment defends fair criticism. The comment must be on a matter of public interest (*London Artists Ltd v. Littler* [1969]).[26]

Telnikoff v. Matusevitch [1992] 2 AC 343

The plaintiff wrote an article in the *Daily Telegraph* criticising the BBC's Russian Service for overrecruiting from Soviet minority ethnic groups. The defendant published a reply in the same paper accusing the plaintiff of racism.

The HL considered whether or not a statement in the defendant's letter was fact or comment. It held that the letter must be considered without reference to the original article for context. It was likely that large numbers of people who read the letter would not have read the article.

Lord Ackner (dissenting) felt that the freedom to comment on matters of public interest was vital to the functioning of a democratic society and should be sufficient for the defendant to give an honest opinion and identify the publication on which he was commenting.

CASE STUDY

Thomas v. Bradbury, Agnew & Co. Ltd [1906] 2 KB 627

A book reviewer for *Punch* wrote a very critical review of the plaintiff's book. The defendant's malice was ascertained from the review itself and his conduct in the witness box.

The defence of fair comment failed because of the defendant's malice. Similar to 'justification', a journalist may have a defence if he or she can prove that the statement made was 'fair comment' on a matter of public interest. However, it was argued in *Tsikata v. Newspaper Publishing PLC* (see next) that there is no public interest defence for the media in English law.

CASE STUDY

Tsikata v. Newspaper Publishing PLC [1997] 1 All ER 655

The CA appeared to be prepared to accept the defendant's plea that qualified privilege at common law could apply to part of a statement that the plaintiff, a high-ranking Ghanaian government official, had masterminded the assassination of three judges in Ghana. The other part of the statement – a direct report of the Ghanaian judicial inquiry that followed the killings – was covered by statutory qualified privilege. The reciprocal public interest/public duty criteria were easily met in this case, as it was an inquiry into an abuse of human rights in a Commonwealth country. It was not a grand scheme for extending the defence to media defendants generally.

!

Fair comment

For this defence to succeed, the defendant must prove the following:

- the subject matter must be of public interest (the judge decides if it is), such as local or national government matters, people in public office and their remarks, trade unions, police, prison service and so on
- the words must be comments (not statements of fact)
- the comments (words) must be true (based on true facts)
- not all facts need to be true – only those facts on which the comments are based (s. 6 *Defamation Act 1952*)
- the comments must be honest and relevant
- the comments must be made without malice.

Privilege

In certain situations, the law will protect free speech over and above a person's reputation. We have a look at the two freedoms of absolute and qualified privilege below.

Absolute privilege   Absolute privilege gives the journalist (or author of a statement) utter freedom in the communication of views and information. This privilege of free speech is extended to all members of both Houses of Parliament, statements made during judicial or tribunal proceedings and by Ministers of State to each other – all under Art. 9 of the *Bill of Rights 1688*. This privilege is confined to Parliament and will not protect an MP outside the House (*Church of Scientology of California v. Johnson-Smith* [1972]).[27]

Absolute privilege

- any statement made in Parliament – in the 'lower' House of Commons or 'upper' House of Lords, (*Bill of Rights 1688*)
- any report published by either House, such as *Hansard* (s. 1 *Parliamentary Papers Act 1840*)
- any statement by an officer of the State to another, such as the Secretary of State or a minister in course of his or her duty
- any statement made by one spouse to another
- fair and accurate media reports of public judicial proceedings (s. 14 *Defamation Act 1996*)
- any statements by officials of the EU, the ECJ and the UN in exercising their functions (s. 14 *Defamation Act 1996*)
- statements made in judicial proceedings and tribunals, such as those by the judge, jury, witnesses, lawyers and so on
- an MP may waive privilege if he or she so desires (s. 13 *Defamation Act 1996*).

Qualified privilege   Qualified privilege arises when the need for such freedom is not quite so great but nevertheless warrants some protection from the threat of litigation (a defamatory action). This privilege goes back to the *Law of Libel (Amendment) Act 1888*. 'Qualified' means that it is not 'absolute' (as above) and there are certain conditions put on the author of the statement. There certainly must not be any evidence of malice as, if the plaintiff can prove that the defendant was actually 'malicious' or 'injurious' in his or her statement, then the qualified privilege defence will fail. A statement that is made in the performance of a duty will attract the defence of qualified privilege under common law, provided that the person making the statement has a legal, moral or social duty to make the statement and the person receiving it has an interest in him or her doing so.

Watts v. Times Newspapers [1997] QB 650[28]

The defendants published in their newspaper an item suggesting that the plaintiff author had plagiarised another author. By mistake, a photograph – intended to be of the author but, in fact, of a property developer of that name – was printed. The property developer demanded an apology and the defendants agreed, suggesting a neutral form of wording. However, at the insistence of the property developer's solicitors, a different wording was published, including a statement that the article and photograph suggested that the property developer had been a plagiarist. The plaintiff alleged that not only the original article but also the apology were defamatory to him. The defendants claimed that the apology was protected by qualified privilege.

The CA held that the general principle on which common law privilege was based was the public interest, and each party's claim to privilege should be looked at separately. When an apology tendered in mitigation of a libel was itself defamatory of a person other than the victim of the original libel, the question of whether or not the apology was protected by qualified privilege had to be considered separately, in relation to the person publishing the apology and the person at whose insistence it was published.

The defendants were not rebutting themselves – they could have published a simple retraction and made a statement in open court that would have been protected by absolute privilege. In these circumstances, the defendants could not claim any derivative privilege through the property developer and the publication of the apology with the defamatory words was not warranted, so the defendants had no privilege. The property developer (and his solicitors) were entitled to qualified privilege, as the property developer – as the victim of the attack – was entitled to a right of reply, as long as he did not overstep the bounds and include entirely irrelevant and extraneous material. The words used did not overstep these bounds and both the property developer and the solicitors were protected by qualified privilege.

The leading case for qualified privilege is now *Reynolds v. Times Newspapers* (see below). The case concerned allegedly defamatory statements published by the *Sunday Times* concerning a political crisis in Ireland leading to the resignation of the plaintiff, who was then Taoiseach (Prime Minister of Ireland).

The CA, stated that, inter alia, in the interests of maintaining a proper balance between the preservation of the right to free speech guaranteed by Art. 10 of the European Convention (now the *Human Rights Act 1998*) and the protection of a public figure's reputation, the defence of common law qualified privilege should be available to a newspaper regarding a defamatory and factually false publication that was honestly (not maliciously) made.

CASE STUDY

Reynolds v. Times Newspapers Ltd and Others [1999] UKHL 45, HL; [1998] 3 All ER 961, CA

The plaintiff was the former Taoiseach of Ireland, who sued over an article that he claimed falsely suggested that he had deliberately misled the Irish Cabinet. The newspaper (publishers, the editor and the author of the article) claimed qualified privilege as its defence.

The CA said that, when considering where qualified privilege can apply, it is necessary to remember that the rule is an aspect of public policy that is there because of the need to balance free speech on matters of public interest and the right to reputation of individuals, so any protection given by the rule has to be fair.

The court explained that, by 'status', it meant the extent to which the publication of the material would command respect. So, for example, cases involving publishing material derived from unverified and unidentified sources to large audiences would be unlikely to pass this test. In this case, the court said, the first two tests – duty to publish and duty to receive – were fairly easily satisfied as the fall from power of the plaintiff were very clearly of public interest in Britain. However, the third test was not satisfied, for several reasons. One concerned the way in which the story had been researched and presented, including the fact that one of the major sources of the claim that the plaintiff had lied was a colleague of his main political opponent (Dick Spring). Given the bitter atmosphere surrounding the resignation, he ought not to have been regarded as 'authoritative' for such a serious allegation and the paper had failed to ask the plaintiff for any comment on the allegations.

The claim of qualified privilege failed. The reasons for this were given in the HL on 28 October 1999 by Lord Nicholls of Birkenhead. He started by saying that freedom of speech under Art. 10 ECHR must be protected, but, equally, he maintained that the common law approach to misstatements of fact remains essentially sound and the common law should not develop 'political information' as a new 'subject matter' category of qualified privilege, whereby the publication of *all* such information would attract qualified privilege, whatever the circumstances. That would not provide adequate protection for reputations. Moreover, it would be unsound in principle to distinguish political discussion from discussion of other matters of serious public concern. The Lord stated:

> The elasticity of the common law principle enables interference with freedom of speech to be confined to what is necessary in the circumstances of the case. This elasticity enables the court to give appropriate weight, in today's conditions, to the importance of freedom of expression by the media on all matters of public concern.

The HL in the Reynolds case then established the ten-point list of criteria set out below.

The ten-point Reynolds test	!

1 *The seriousness of the allegation* The more serious the charge, the more the public is misinformed and the individual harmed if the allegation proves not to be true.
2 *The nature of the information* and the extent to which the subject matter is a matter of public concern.
3 *The source of the information* Some informants have no direct knowledge of the events, some have their own axes to grind or are being paid for their stories.

> **!**
>
> 4   *The steps taken to verify the information.*
> 5   *The status of the information*: does the publication command respect from the public at large?
> 6   *The urgency of the matter* News is often a perishable commodity.
> 7   *Whether or not comment was sought from the plaintiff* He or she may have information others do not possess or have not disclosed. An approach to the plaintiff is not always necessary, however.
> 8   Whether or not the article contained the *gist of the plaintiff's side of the story.*
> 9   *The tone of the article* A newspaper can raise queries or call for an investigation. It need not adopt allegations as statements of fact.
> 10   *The circumstances of the publication*, including the timing.

In the Reynolds case, the CA affirmed that the defence of qualified privilege would only be allowed in an individual case if a newspaper could satisfy a three-stage test. It would be worth your while to memorise these criteria, in addition to the ten-point test above.

1   **The duty test**: Was the publisher under a legal, social or moral duty to those for whom the material was published?

2   **The public interest test**: Did those for whom it was published have such an interest in receiving it?

3   **The circumstantial test**: Were the nature, status and source of the material and the circumstances of its publication such that, provided there was no proof of express malice, there was a public interest in protecting its publication?

The ten-point Reynolds test set out by Lord Nicholls is proving hard to meet in practice as the George Galloway case proved (see below). Even if something looks of benefit to the media, all ten points now have to be proved, if a defamatory statement, made by a newspaper (here the *Daily Telegraph*) is to be successfully defended.

The ten-point Reynold test was applied in the George Galloway case (*Galloway v. Telegraph Group Ltd* [2004],[29] in which the former Glasgow MP sued the publishers of the *Daily Telegraph* for libel – for publishing newspaper articles during April 2003 claiming that the claimant had 'received money from Saddam Hussein's regime, taking a slice of oil earnings worth £375,000 a year' and asked for 'a greater cut of Iraq's exports' and 'was profiting from food contracts'. A further article had stated that, according to the claimant's Iraqi intelligence profile, the claimant 'had a family history of loyalty to Saddam Hussein's Ba'ath Party', and referred to him as a 'sympathiser with Iraq'.

The defendant did not seek to plead justification, but raised the defences used in the Reynolds case of qualified privilege and, in relation to the two leader articles and two respective headlines, they also raised the defence of 'fair comment'. The High Court ruled that the defendants could not rely on the qualified privilege criteria given in the Reynolds case because not all of the criteria in the ten-point list were satisfied. Though, the court said, the subject matter was 'undoubtedly of public concern', the sources of information could not be regarded as 'inherently reliable' and the defendants had not taken 'steps to verify the information'. The court ruled in favour of Galloway (no jury was present) and awarded him £150,000 in damages as compensation.

In a damning judgment, which had repercussions for freedom of expression in the press, Mr Justice Eady criticised the newspaper for its 'dramatic and condemnatory' handling of the Galloway 'scoop'. He said the spin placed on a 'blizzard' of articles published in the *Daily Telegraph* on 22 and 23 April 2003, based on documents found in the bombed-out Iraqi foreign ministry in Baghdad after the fall of Saddam Hussein, amounted to 'serious defamation'. Crucially, he said, the defendants were not neutral and did not merely adopt the allegations but 'embraced them with relish and fervour', embellished them and then failed to put them to the former Glasgow MP.[30]

The result, he said, was that 'reasonable and fair-minded readers' would believe he was in the secret pay of Saddam to the tune of £375,000 a year, he had diverted money from the oil-for-food programme, he had probably used the Mariam Appeal (a fund aimed at raising the awareness of the plight of the Iraqi people under economic sanctions) for personal gain, and what he had done was tantamount to treason. Galloway also won costs against the *Telegraph*, a bill of more than £1.2m.

Mr Justice Eady denied the paper permission to appeal against the decision. However, the *Telegraph* was given leave from the Court of Appeal in mid-2005 to appeal over liability and the 'excessive' scale of the damages. The appeal was heard in November 2005, George Galloway took part in the popular Channel 4 series *Big Brother* in January 2006 when the *Telegraph* lost its legal appeal against the libel ruling on 25 January 2006. Galloway was evicted from the Big Brother house the next day. The paper's appeal was based on 'misunderstanding' by Mr Justice Eady in the High Court in 2004, that the judge had not sufficiently differentiated between fact and comment, and that the paper was unfairly punished for exposing the facts. This now means that the defences of 'quanlified priviledge' and 'fair comment' are now extremely narrow.

What can we learn from the three-part test in the CR and the ten-point list of HL criteria in Reynolds? With defamatory imputations of fact, the position is different and difficult. Those who read or hear such allegations are unlikely to have any means of knowing whether or not they are true. Regarding such imputations, a plaintiff's ability to obtain a remedy, if he or she can prove malice, is not normally a sufficient safeguard. Malice is notoriously difficult to prove. If a newspaper is understandably unwilling to disclose its sources, a plaintiff can be deprived of the material necessary to prove, or even allege, that the newspaper acted recklessly in publishing as it did so without further verification.

In the absence of any additional safeguard for reputation, a newspaper, anxious to be first with a scoop, would, in practice, be free to publish seriously defamatory misstatements of fact based on the slenderest of materials. Unless the paper chose later to withdraw the allegations, the politician thus defamed would have no means of clearing his or her name and the public would have no means of knowing where the truth lay. Some further protection for reputation is needed, if this can be achieved without a disproportionate incursion into freedom of expression. In the Galloway case, the *Daily Telegraph* had unsuccessfully relied on the Reynolds defence in December 2004, which originates from a case brought by Albert Reynolds, the former Irish Taoisseach, against the *Sunday Times* in 1999, and is meant to allow the publication of responsible journalism on matters of public interest. When this defence was first created, it was acclaimed as a charter for the media, who celebrated its recognition of the importance of freedom of expression. The HL set out a ten-point list of factors to take into account in assessing the responsibility of journalism, even recognising that news can be a perishable commodity.

It is only fair, then, that editors should be informed when claimants' solicitors seek either an injunction or legal regress in form of a libel action so that editors can exercise their possible right to freedom of expression (Art. 10 ECHR), asking the judges to apply s. 12(3) *Human Rights Act 1998* which grants provision for such relief if restraint of publication before a trial is sought by the individual. The courts then have to establish whether such restraint is likely or whether the publication should be allowed. This was known as the 'balance of convenience' test in old case law, before Reynolds came into force. Subsequently, Lord Nicholls made it clear in Reynolds that the effect of s. 12(3) is that the court is not to make an interim restraining order (injunction) unless satisfied that the applicant's prospects of success at the trial are sufficiently favourable to justify such an order being made in the particular circumstances of the case.

It now seems that the Reynolds defence (of qualified privilege) has been a disaster for the media. Too often, the responsible journalism test has turned proceedings into an excruciating trial for journalists who have written their stories without an eye to litigation. Galloway's success against the *Daily Telegraph* effectively means that breaking any one of the ten points listed in the Reynolds criteria means that the defence will be lost.

In reality, no journalist is that perfect, especially when dealing with news and current affairs. Does it now mean that a newspaper (editor, publisher, author or journalist) has to establish a legal, moral and social duty to the general public in order to publish the material in question (the duty test)? Does the paper also have to establish that the general public has a corresponding interest in receiving the information (the public interest test) and, finally, have to establish that the nature, status and source of the material and circumstances of its publication are such as to warrant the protection of privilege without malice (the circumstantial test)? It was the third test in the Reynolds case – the circumstantial test – that really caused the problem, as the source was not official. Moreover, the source material was obtained from the then Taoiseach's arch rival at the time (Reynolds' Deputy, Dick Spring), so it could be proven by the plaintiff that malice was involved (as the CA said, Mr Spring and the opposition party had 'an axe to grind').

The Reynolds judgment seemed so important at the time, potentially loosening up Britain's rigid libel laws. But it also put the emphasis on careful and balanced journalism. In his Galloway judgment the judge found the *Telegraph* wanting in just this, having failed either to put the charge properly to Mr Galloway ('seriousness of the allegation' and 'nature of the information') and seeking comment from the plaintiff (as per Reynolds' ten-point test). The outcome is a pity for the British media which could do with more case law in its favour, leaving the law on defamation seriously restrictive and continuing to protect the rich, famous and powerful from due scrutiny. In this case however, George Galloway deserved protection against some rather incriminating publications (allegations of corruption and treason). The message sent to newspapers by the judge is that they had the power to check these accusations, and they failed to do so.

While the CA in the Reynolds case suggested that the modern human rights context in the light of the *Human Rights Act 1998* meant that the first two criteria of the test would be more readily held to be satisfied than formerly, their Lordships in the HL ruling envisaged that consideration of those tests would be restricted to newspaper statements about public figures in their public life.

We can conclude from the ruling in the Galloway case, that a newspaper obtaining critical material on, say, a politician from one of his political opponents (or a dubious source), will not be able to rely on the qualified privilege defence, as the source of the material should be suspect and fail the Reynolds test. An analogous example here would be references given by past employers to a potential future employer. If the reference contains defamatory statements, the subject of the reference may have an action for negligence against the author. Only time will tell if Lord Nicholls' ten-point test in Reynolds is a positive result of the freedom of expression and the free press' defence of the public's right to know.

Defences

The allowable defences against libel are as follows:

- *justification*   The defendant proves that the statement is true. If the defence fails, a court may treat any material produced by the defence to substantiate it and any ensuing media coverage as factors aggravating the libel and increasing the damages
- *fair comment*   The defendant shows that the statement is a view that a reasonable person could hold, even if they are motivated by dislike or hatred of the plaintiff
- *absolute privilege*   The defendant's comments are made in Parliament or under oath in a court of law or are an accurate and neutral report of such comments
- *qualified privilege*   The defendant must not act out of malice, then he or she may claim 'privilege' for fair reporting of allegations that, if true, it is in the public interest to publish (*Reynolds v. Times Newspapers Ltd and Others* [1999] UKHL)
- *offer of amends*   Combinations of correction, apology and/or financial compensation are usually acceptable. This acts as a barrier to litigation in the courts.

Defamation Act 1996

In addition to qualified privilege in common law, journalists (editors, publishers and so on) now also have a defence under statute. The *Defamation Act 1996* was intended to provide for the defence of 'innocent dissemination' to cover publications in certain defined circumstances. Qualified privilege has therefore been enshrined in this 1996 Act in relation to the reporting, say, by newspapers or on the TV or radio news, or various matters of record. These include parliamentary and judicial proceedings, statements made on behalf of the government and the conduct of public meetings, tribunals or inquiries.

TASK

Please read the following passages from the *Defamation Act 1996* carefully as the defences are clearly set out. You never know when you might need them.

Section 1 is headed 'Responsibility for publication' (only the most relevant sections have been reproduced here).

It is important to note that, for the defence to succeed, s. 1(a), (b) and (c) have to be established by the defendant. 'Publisher' means a commercial publisher – that is, a person whose business is issuing material to the public or a section of the public and who issues material containing the statement in the course of that business.

Defamation Act 1996, s. 1

(1) In defamation proceedings a person has a defence if he shows that:

   (a) he was not the author, editor or publisher of the statement complained of

   (b) he took reasonable care in relation to its publication, and

   (c) he did not know, and had no reason to believe, that what he did caused or contributed to the publication of a defamatory statement.

(2) For this purpose ... 'publisher' [has] the following meanings, which are further explained in subsection (3).

(3) A person shall not be considered the author, editor or publisher of a statement if he is only involved –

   (a) in printing, producing, distributing or selling printed material containing the statement ...

   (c) in processing, making copies of, distributing or selling any electronic medium in or on which the statement is recorded, or in operating or providing any equipment, system or service by means of which the statement is retrieved, copied, distributed or made available in electronic form ...

   (c) as the operator of or provider of access to a communications system by means of which the statement is transmitted, or made available, by a person over whom he has no effective control. In a case not within paragraphs (a) to (e) the court may have regard to those provisions by way of analogy in deciding whether a person is to be considered the author, editor or publisher of a statement ...

(5) In determining for the purposes of this section whether a person took reasonable care, or had reason to believe that what he did caused or contributed to the publication of a defamatory statement, regard shall be had to:

   (a) the extent of his responsibility for the content of the statement or the decision to publish it

   (b) the nature or circumstances of the publication, and

   (c) the previous conduct or character of the author, editor or publisher.

The *Defamation Act 1996* (ss. 2–4) provides a procedure to enable cases to be resolved by means of an 'offer-to-make-amends' fast-track action. The offer of amends, as well as the usual apology, are now available with this procedure. Today, the commonest resolution is that the plea for an apology is also accompanied by payment of money into court by way of amends. The person who has published a statement alleged to be defamatory of another (the defendant) may offer to make amends by publishing a suitable correction or an apology to the defamed person (the plaintiff) and pay compensation and/or costs. Any offer of amends must be made before the serving of any defence and, if accepted, will end the defamation proceedings.

Human rights and defamation

We looked at English defamation legislation earlier in this chapter and it is clear that the present state of the law in this area pleases few. There is as yet no agreement on whether any problems are relatively minor, or whether they go to the roots of the present system. The defence of qualified privilege was widened as a result of the Reynolds case, but this has also narrowed the liability of secondary publications. Damages awarded by juries have been curtailed (in the most extreme form, to 1 Irish penny by the jury in the Reynolds case) and the judge can now advise a jury as to the amount of damages they might award in comparison to personal injury cases. The largest award made in a defamation case – £1.5m – was challenged before the ECHR, which ruled that the jury's award violated the defendant's right to free expression under Art. 10 ECHR (*Tolstoy Miloslavsky v. UK* (A/323) [1996]).[31]

At times, a court may also reduce the award of libel damages in appeals. This was the case when Jimmy Nail, the *Auf Wiedersehen Pet* star and singer/songwriter, lost his battle for an increase in the £37,500 damages awarded by a judge, which he claimed made libel 'cheap at the price' for newspapers. The 50-year-old actor was awarded the amount in the High Court in March 2004 by Mr Justice Eady, who said that he had cut the libel damages facing the *News of the World* and publishers HarperCollins by half because they had made immediate apologies and offers of amends (unders s. 2, 3(5) and 4 *Defamation Act 1996*). Nail sued in defamation against the former Editor of the paper, Rebekah Wade, regarding an which had commented on false allegations regarding the actor's sexual behaviour article on 19 May 2002, 'Auf Wiedersehen Jimmy's Secret Bondage Orgies', referring to a biography on Nail by Geraint Jones entitled *Nailed*, published in 1998.

The ruling in *Nail v. News Group Newspapers Ltd and Others* [2004],[32] left Nail with a legal costs bill of around £200,000 because he refused an offer totalling £37,000 to settle the case. In the CA, Lord Justices Auld, May and Gage said that the original Judge, Mr Justice Eady, had made no error of principle and had reached a balanced conclusion, so they dismissed Nail's appeal on 20 December 2004. The actor, who was not in court, was then faced with paying the costs of the appeal hearing, which was one of the first challenges to the 'offer of amends' procedure in libel cases.

As we have seen, the European Convention is not a free-standing law in the UK. Although it has been incorporated into UK legislation by means of the *Human Rights Act 1998*, the relevant articles for our purposes (Art. 8 ECHR 'right to privacy' and Art. 10 ECHR 'freedom of expression') are not absolute and independent rights in English legislation. In other words, Art. 10 will not provide an absolute defence to a journalist in defamation (and contempt) actions.

In *A. v. UK* [1997] (see below), the substantive question arose in the ECHR of reputation versus free speech and the role of the proportionality test, which is when courts decide whether or not interference with any particular right has been established. This case should also be seen in the light of the debate about the Reynolds case (see above) in that the Convention has been used as a basis on which to consolidate blanket-qualified privilege for political publications by the press.

A. v. United Kingdom [1997][33]

In *A. v. UK,* the Convention was applied (albeit unsuccessfully) to pick apart one of the oldest forms of privilege in the English common law – namely parliamentary and absolute privilege – and similar regimes in other EUMS. The ECHR pointed out that the immunity afforded to MPs in the UK was, in fact, rather narrower than that afforded to members of legislatures in certain other European states. The ECHR took as its example the fact that immunity in the UK only attaches to statements made in the course of parliamentary debates on the floor of the House of Commons or House of Lords, not to statements made outside Parliament, even if they amount to a repetition of statements made during the course of parliamentary debates on matters of public interest. Nor does any immunity attach to an MP's press statements published prior to parliamentary debates, even if their contents are repeated subsequently in the debate itself.

As a result, *A. v. UK* stated that Art. 6(1) ECHR did not guarantee a right to bring defamation proceedings regarding such statements and concluded that the applicant's complaint about his inability to do so was therefore incompatible with the Convention. At this point, the ECHR reinforced its attitude towards legal aid for defamation proceedings in the UK. However, this was overruled in the 2005 'McLibel' ruling (see below).

CASE STUDY

If we look at other countries, we note that in Austria, for instance, so-called 'professional immunity' applies, so a decision as to whether or not criminal or civil proceedings can be taken against an MP concerning words spoken in Parliament has to be run through a number of authorities who decide whether or not these statements are part of his or her professional function.

In Belgium, this immunity – even against acts infringing the rights of citizens – is regarded in domestic law and practised as an essential guarantee for the functioning of the legislature, and its absolute nature as essential to the efficacy of that guarantee. Private rights have to be regarded as ceding to the overriding public interest.

French MPs enjoy a near absolute immunity as in French law it covers all the acts they carry out in the exercise of their functions, and is permanent as it continues after expiry of their mandates. This immunity cannot even be waived by an individual member as it is not concerned with the private interests of the MP but with the function that he or she exercises. In Norway, this immunity extends even to speech where it is alleged that the member has intentionally expressed untruths or expressed himself or herself on a subject unconnected with the issue under debate.

The issue of 'free speech' (Art. 10 ECHR) and legal aid (in relation to Art. 6 ECHR) arose in the longest case in British legal history – the 'McLibel' case. Two London Greenpeace campaigners, Helen Steel and David Morris, were eventually successful in the ECHR in their challenging of Arts 6 and 10 ECHR.

CASE STUDY

Steel and Morris v. UK [2005] ECHR (appl. no. 68416/01) – the 'McLibel' case – judgment of 15 February 2005

The case concerned an application brought by two UK nationals, Helen Steel and David Morris. During the relevant period, Mr Morris was an unemployed postal worker and Ms Steel was either unemployed or of low wage (approximately £65 per week income as a gardener). Both were associated with London Greenpeace.

In the mid-1980s, London Greenpeace began an anti-McDonald's campaign. The pair were handing out leaflets outside McDonald's restaurants, which contained numerous allegations about McDonald's policies and restaurant practices. McDonald's sued them for libel. During the three years of court hearings, it became clear that neither Ms Steel nor Mr Morris had written the leaflets, but that they had became embroiled in the libel action launched by the Corporation in 1990, ending only in 1997 – the longest trial in English legal history, with 313 days spent in court between 28 June 1994 and 13 December 1996.

The applicants had been refused legal aid and had to represent themselves throughout the trial and appeal. In his judgment of 19 June 1997, the trial judge found that the applicants had published the factsheet, and awarded damages to US McDonald's and UK McDonald's. McDonald's had claimed damages of up to £100,000.

On appeal, the CA found that the defamatory allegations in the leaflets concerning pay and conditions (of McDonald's employees) were 'comment' and the allegation that people eating enough McDonald's food ran a very real risk of contracting heart disease was justified. The court reduced the damages payable to McDonald's, making Ms Steel liable for £36,000 and Mr Morris for £40,000.

The applicants' claim before the ECHR was lodged on 20 September 2000 and held in chambers on 7 September 2004. They complained under Art. 6(1) ECHR ('right to a fair hearing') that the proceedings were unfair, principally because they were denied legal aid in the English Courts. Furthermore, they said that they had been severely hampered by lack of resources – not just in the way of legal advice and representation, but also when it came to administration, photocopying, note-taking and the tracing, preparation and payment of costs and expenses for expert and factual witnesses.

The ECHR heard how, throughout the proceedings, McDonald's had been represented by leading and junior counsel, experienced in defamation law, and by one or two solicitors and other assistants. The couple also invoked Art. 10 ECHR ('right to freedom of expression') that the proceedings and their outcome constituted a disproportionate interference with their right to freedom of expression.

The ECHR found in favour of Steel and Morris on the basis of the failure of the UK government to provide legal aid for them in the action. It noted that Steel and Morris did not choose to commence defamation proceedings, 'but acted as Defendants to protect their right to freedom of expression, a right accorded considerable importance under the Convention'. Regarding the violation of Art. 6 (1), the court noted the massive length and complexity of the case against Steel and Morris and concluded, 'that the denial of legal aid to the Applicants deprived them of the opportunity to present their case effectively before the courts and contributed to an unacceptable inequality of arms with McDonald's'. Consequently, the first applicant was awarded €20,000 and the second €15,000 for non-pecuniary damages, as well as € 47,311.17 for legal costs and expenses.

The ECHR ruling in the Steel and Morris case is an important factor in determining future allocation of legal aid in defamation actions. It clearly points to the failure of the UK government to provide legal aid for such an action. As we saw above, the court noted, inter alia, that Steel and Morris had not chosen to commence defamation proceedings, 'but acted as Defendants to protect their right to freedom of expression, a right accorded considerable importance under the Convention'. The court also noted that the financial consequence of their failing to verify each defamatory statement was considerable. McDonald's had claimed damages of up to £100,000 and the court noted that 'the awards actually made, even after reduction by the Court of Appeal, were high when compared to the Applicants' low incomes'.

The result of the ECHR judgment in the 'McLibel' case is that the UK law of defamation, which had come under severe attack in the application, has still survived largely unscathed. However, although not everyone involved in a libel action will now obtain legal aid, the ECHR did note that the UK government will be obliged to rethink its refusal to provide legal aid in such cases in the future. Also, the courts will have to rethink what sums are appropriate for damages when large corporations sue irritant pressure groups in the tort of defamation.

With the global reach of the Internet is it now not time to see a reform of Britain's antiquated and rather eccentric libel laws? The Department of Constitutional Affairs is about to re-examine the judgment of the Duke of Brunswick case in 1849 by means of public consultation, in that the ruling currently states that each publication of a libel gives rise to a separate cause of action (multiple publication rule). This ruling has had chilling effects on the freedom of expression when it comes to republication on the Internet. Overseas individuals (for example, celebrities or business people) can still sue through the High Court in the Strand; all they have to show is that the story had more than a 'minimal circulation' and that they had connections to the UK and a reputation to defend there – leaving London still as the most famous libel capital of the world.

TASKS

Here are some cases that you might wish to study in addition to the ones mentioned in this chapter.

Regarding an untrue statement affecting the plaintiff's reputation

- *Byrne v. Dean* [1937] – raiding of a golf club for illegal gambling.

Regarding requirement that statements must refer to the plaintiff

- *J'Anson v. Stuart* [1787] – like a swindler, 'his diabolical character, like Polyphemus the man-eater, has but one eye, and is well known to all persons acquainted with the name of a certain noble circumnavigator'.
- *Knupffer v. London Express Newspapers Ltd* [1944] – an émigré Russian group that was a fascist organisation.
- *Newstead v. London Express Newspapers Ltd* [1940] – a 30-year-old Camberwell man who was a bigamist.

Regarding requirement that a statement must be published

- *Huth v. Huth* [1915] – a letter sent in an unsealed envelope was read by the butler.
- *Theaker v. Richardson* [1962] – third-party publication that could be foreseen: 'a lying low-down brothel-keeping whore and thief'.

QUESTIONS

How would you deal with the following short scenarios in your capacity as a journalist?

1 Carol writes an editorial in the *Middlesex Athletes' Gazette*, claiming that only those brought up in the UK are likely to show sufficient commitment when part of the national team. Corinne, a member of the UK national hurdles team, who is a French national, sues in libel. Will she succeed? Does it matter if her recent performance has been good or bad? Discuss.

2 A university lecturer sends a reference about a past student by fax to a recruitment agency, which has requested the reference. The lecturer is openly critical of the student's past performance in his studies. Would the student be able to take out an action against the lecturer? Explain your answer by using case law as well as statutory provision. Should the legal action go ahead?

3 Carol, an anti-fox-hunting protester, is carrying a defamatory placard about the Leader of the Conservative Party at a demonstration, which she knows is being televised. Would this make her liable for a lawsuit in defamation? If so, what would the plaintiff sue her for exactly?

4 Imagine it's a Saturday night and you are the Editor of BBC News Online, at home relaxing. Your subeditor is in charge. She reviews the Sunday papers for the news ticker around 2 a.m. Sunday morning. She notices a story that she found earlier in the *Mail on Sunday*: 'What the Nanny saw: revelations about Tony Blair's household'. The subeditor, Barbara, writes a review of this story online for the 2 a.m. newsticker.

At 5 a.m. you get a phone call from the AG's office telling you that the Prime Minister's wife brought a successful injunction against the newspaper at 10 p.m. the previous night and the *Mail on Sunday* Editor was told to 'pull' the story, which he did. What are the likely repercussions for you and your team, as well as for the BBC? Discuss with clear reference to case law and statutory legislation.

5 Gerald chairs an official inquiry into whether or not Heshmat, Hirut and George broke the law by authorising arms exports to warring states. In what circumstances will Gerald's report be privileged?

Here follow some questions for you to discuss in more detailed essay answers.

6 Discuss the dangers in the law of defamation when a broadcast mentions a complaint about a company but does not give the company's full title?

7 Every repetition of defamatory words is a fresh publication and so creates a fresh cause of action against each successive publisher. What does this mean for the author, printer, publisher or editor? Discuss with reference to case law.

8 Explain in detail (with relevant case references) the defence of 'fair comment'. What are the main criteria for this defence?

9 Comment on recent damages awarded by juries in libel actions. Why, in your opinion, have they been curtailed by judges and how should libel juries now be directed?

Now study the case of *Reynolds v. Times Newspapers Ltd and Others* [1999] (UKHL 45 and Court of Appeal [1998] 3 All ER 961) in detail and answer the following questions relating to the CA and HL judgments.

10 (a) There was no finite list of circumstances in which qualified privilege should apply, but what were the three questions that should now be answered in the High Court in a defamation action?
(b) The defence of qualified privilege has now been widened because of the Reynolds case, but what about secondary republications? Would they be allowed the same defence?
(c) Give the ten-point list of criteria that was established by the HL in the Reynolds case and should now be applied in the defence of qualified privilege. Would you be able to think of a recent example in which these have been applied by the courts?

Now read the case studies given at the end of this chapter and then answer the following questions:

11 In Case Study 1 ([*Michael*] *Marlow v. UK* [2000]) the ECHR in Strasbourg accepted that the right to silence may be restricted by the ability of the court to draw adverse inferences. How should a libel jury be directed if the claimant challenges this under Art. 6(2) and Art. 8 ECHR? How may defamation practitioners be interested in the court's reaction to the Art. 8 challenge?

12 Discuss parliamentary (absolute) privilege in the light of Case study 2 (*A. v. UK* [1997]). Would you say that Art. 6 ECHR conflicts with this doctrine?

13 The Internet has long protected anonymous complainants. In the light of Case Study 3 (*Totalise v. Motley Fool* [2001]), how can an individual be legally protected if he or she is being defamed on the Internet and what might be the consequences for webhosts? Discuss with reference to this and possibly other leading cases.

Selected case studies

Case Study 1: *Michael Marlow v. United Kingdom* [2000]

Decision by the ECHR: Admissibility Decision Application No. 42015/98. Third Section 5 December 2000.

Abstract

The criminalisation of incitement to cultivate drugs resulting in the prosecution of an author of a book about cannabis did not amount to a disproportionate interference with his freedom of expression.

Summary

The applicant, using a pseudonym, published a book about the cultivation and production of cannabis. The book was advertised for sale in three magazines. Some 500 copies were sold. The police obtained the names of various customers, established the identity of the applicant and arrested him.

The prosecution case was that the applicant's book amounted to an incitement of those who bought it to cultivate cannabis, contrary to the *Misuse of Drugs Act 1971*. The defence contended that the book was a genuine contribution to the debate about the legalisation of cannabis and it only contained general advice and information freely available elsewhere.

The judge, in his summing up, directed the jury that they could draw adverse inferences from the applicant's failure to give evidence at trial. There was, in fact, medical evidence that supported the applicant's inability to take to the witness box, but the judge did not mention this. The applicant was convicted and sentenced to a year's imprisonment.

The applicant complained that his contribution to the public debate about cannabis had been suppressed in violation of Art. 10. He contended that the interference was not 'prescribed by law' because the provision under which he was convicted did not mention cannabis in the offence of incitement. He also claimed that, because of the judge's direction to the jury, he had been deprived of the presumption of innocence, contrary to Art. 6(2). He also claimed that the judgment contained defamatory statements about his propensity to supply drugs and that this had an adverse effect on his family life under Art. 8.

Held

The complaint under Art. 10 was rejected. The court observed that cannabis production is clearly considered a crime under the 1971 Act and, despite the drafting error that led to the omission of the word 'cannabis' in the provision dealing with incitement, the court considered that the applicant should have been able to foresee, to a degree that was reasonable in the circumstances, a risk that publication of his book might fall foul of that section. As to whether or not the measure was a proportionate one in the prevention of crime, the court acknowledged that there was an increasingly vociferous lobby campaigning for the legalisation of cannabis. However, the lack of consensus on this issue across Europe meant that the continuing criminalisation of the drug fell within the UK's margin of appreciation. The court also ruled that the allegation that the trial was unfair was also manifestly ill founded and therefore inadmissible. The failure of the applicant's legal team to apprise the judge of the medical report explaining the applicant's inability to give evidence at trial did not engage the State's responsibility under Art. 6. As for the complaints about the adverse inferences generally, the court observed that the right to silence was not absolute. As far as this case was concerned, the court was of the opinion that it struck the right balance between the applicant's right to silence and the circumstances in which an adverse inference may be legitimately drawn from silence by the jury.

Finally, the complaint under Art. 8 was also considered manifestly ill-founded. What the applicant was complaining about, in essence, was the perceived affront to his dignity and reputation caused by statements made by the trial judge when handing down the sentence. This is not a matter that falls within the protection guaranteed by Art. 8 of the Convention.

CASE STUDY

Case Study 2: *A. v. UK* [1997][33]

Abstract

The doctrine of parliamentary privilege covering statements made in Parliament did not deny potential libel litigants their right of access to court under Art. 6.

Summary

The applicant CA was a United Kingdom national, born in 1971, who lives in Bristol. She is a young black woman with two children. She started receiving hate mail after a parliamentary debate on municipal housing policy during which the MP for her area named her, stated that her brother was in prison, gave her precise address and made derogatory remarks about the behaviour of both her and her children. He mentioned verbal abuse, truancy, vandalism and drug activity and called the family the 'neighbours from hell' – a phrase that was subsequently quoted in local and national newspapers.

The housing association responsible for her accommodation was advised that she and her children should be moved as a matter of urgency three weeks after the speech was given. They were eventually rehoused in October 1996 and the children were obliged to change schools. The MP's statement was protected by absolute parliamentary privilege under Art. 9 of the *Bill of Rights 1688*. The press reports – to the extent that they reported the parliamentary debate – were protected by qualified privilege. This privilege requires the reports to be fair and accurate and is only lost if they are published for improper motives or with 'reckless indifference' to the truth.

A. complained, under Art. 6 (1) of the Convention, that, given the absolute nature of parliamentary privilege, she was denied access to a court to defend her reputation and that legal aid was not available for defamation proceedings. She also relied on Arts 5, 8, 13 and 14 in that she was disadvantaged compared to a person about whom equivalent statements had been made in an unprivileged context.

Held

The court observed that the parliamentary immunity enjoyed by the MP in the present case pursued the legitimate aims of protecting free speech in Parliament and maintaining the separation of powers between the legislature and the judiciary.

The court maintained that a rule of parliamentary immunity, which was consistent with and reflected generally recognised rules within MS of the Council of Europe and the EU, could not, in principle, be regarded as imposing a disproportionate restriction on the right of access to court as embodied in Art. 6(1). Just as the right of access to court was an inherent part of the fair trial guarantee in that article, so some restrictions on access had likewise to be regarded as inherent.

In any event, victims of defamatory misstatement in Parliament were not entirely without means of redress. In particular, they could, where their own MP had made the offending remarks, petition the House through any other MP with a view to securing a retraction. In extreme cases, deliberately misleading statements might be punishable by Parliament as contempt. General control was exercised over debates by the Speaker of each House. The court considered all these factors to be of relevance to the question of proportionality of the immunity enjoyed by the MP in the present case.

It followed that the application of a rule of absolute parliamentary immunity could not be said to exceed the margin of appreciation allowed to states in limiting an individual's right of access to court. There had, accordingly, been no violation of Art. 6 (1) regarding the parliamentary immunity enjoyed by the MP.

As to the applicant's complaints about lack of funding for legal representation in defamation actions, she would still have been able to avail herself of the Green Form Scheme under which she could have made an informed decision as to whether or not to engage a solicitor under conditional fee arrangements. Thus, she was not prevented from having free access to court and, therefore, there had been no violation of Art. 6(1) under this heading either. No separate issue arose under Art. 8, Art. 14 was irrelevant and Art. 13 did not go so far as to guarantee a remedy allowing a contracting state's primary legislation to be challenged before a national authority on grounds that it was contrary to the Convention.

Case Study 3: *Totalise PLC v. Motley Fool Ltd and Another* [2001] EWCA, (Civil Division) 1897[34]

CASE STUDY

The claimant, Totalise PLC, is an ISP. Each of the defendants – Motley Fool Ltd and Interactive – operates a website containing web-based 'discussion boards' on which members of the public are able to post material. The defendants' website operator offered a series of boards relating to particular companies on which users could post information and opinions. Before making a posting, a user had to register and enter into a contract containing the operator's standard terms. Those terms obliged the operator to not reveal the identities of users.

On 31 January 2001, Interactive was sent a letter by solicitors acting on behalf of the claimants, Totalise PLC. The letter complained about the content of a number of postings on Interactive's website by a person using the nickname 'Zeddust'. The letter alleged that the postings contained defamatory statements and, both individually and when taken together, were maliciously designed to call into question the competency and integrity of Totalise's management team, the solvency of Totalise and generally to cause as much damage to Totalise's reputation as possible.

The letter went on to inform Interactive that the solicitors had written to the first defendant, Motley Fool Ltd, to complain about similar postings made by Zeddust – an anonymous contributor. Zeddust had made numerous postings about the claimant on the defendants' discussion boards. The claimant sought disclosure of the identity of Zeddust or of any material in the possession of or accessible to the defendants that could lead to the identification of Zeddust.

After the defendants informed the claimant that it was unable to provide that information because of the provisions of the *Data Protection Act 1998* and its terms and conditions, the claimant brought proceedings against it for disclosure of Zeddust's details.

At the initial court hearing, the operator's attitude was purely neutral. Judge Owen granted the relief sought by the claimant and ordered the operator to pay the claimant's costs, stating that those who operated websites did so at their own risk and, if it transpired that they were used for defamatory purposes by anonymous individuals, a claimant seeking to establish those individuals' identities was entitled to its costs. The operator appealed against the costs order, contending that the judge had exercised his on the wrong principles. Owen J stated in the original hearing:

> I have come to the conclusion that it was perfectly plain from the outset that the postings on both websites were highly defamatory and that, accordingly, the claimants were the victims of a sustained campaign amounting to an actionable tort. There was no other way in which the claimants could have proceeded, save by requiring identification of Zeddust from both defendants. I accept that the defendants had to carry out the balancing exercise, but in my judgment there was only one answer to that balancing exercise, namely that they

should have complied with the requests made by the claimant. In those circumstances, I order the defendants to pay the claimant's costs of this application/action.

The CA held

When a court has granted an application requiring an innocent third party to disclose the identity of an alleged wrongdoer, it should, in the normal case, order the applicant to pay the costs of the disclosing party, including the costs of making the disclosure. Aldous LJ ordered the defendants to pay costs of £4817 (23 February 2001) and summarised:

If it transpires that those boards are used for defamatory purposes by individuals hiding behind the cloak of anonymity, then in justice a claimant seeking to establish the identity of the individuals making such defamatory contents ought to be entitled to their costs.

FURTHER READING

Cooke, J. (2005) *Law of Tort*, 7th edn. Harlow: Pearson Education. Chapter 20, 'Defamation'.

Elliott, C., and Quinn, C. (2005) *Tort Law*, 5th edn. Harlow: Pearson. Chapter 8, 'Defamation and privacy'.

Hauch, J. M. (1994) 'Protecting private facts in France: the Warren and Brandeis tort is alive and well and flourishing in Paris', *Tulane Law Review*, 68, p. 1219.

Lunney, M., and Oliphant, K. (2000) *Tort Law: Text and Materials*. Oxford: Oxford University Press. Chapter 13, 'Defamation and privacy'.

Notes

1 [1894] 1 QB 671, CA.
2 [1934] 50 TLR 581; 99 ALR 964, CA.
3 [1936] 52 TLR 669.
4 *Steel and Morris v. United Kingdom* [2005] ECHR. Application no. 68416/01. Judgment of 15.2.2005.
5 *David John Caldwell Irving v. Penguin Books Ltd and Deborah Lipstadt* [1996] QBD. Judgment of 11 April 2000.
6 In *Beta Construction Ltd v. Channel Four TV Co. Ltd* [1990] 2 All ER 1012, the defendants had admitted liability in a libel action and the only issue that remained to be tried was that relating to the quantification of the damages.
7 Please refer to the Naomi Campbell case in Chapter 3.
8 See also s. 166(1) of the *Broadcasting Act 1990*.
9 For full coverage of the case, see BBC News Online, March 2003: 'Beckham pays out in slander row. Pop star Victoria Beckham has agreed to pay £55,000 damages to settle a High Court slander action after she allegedly said a shop was selling fake autographs of her husband' at: http://news.bbc.co.uk/go/pr/fr/-/1/hi/uk/2839319.stm

10 Also [1993] 3 WLR 953; [1993] 4 All ER 975; *The Times*, 6 April 1993; the *Independent*, 1 April 1993.

11 [1991] 1 QB 153.

12 See also [1996] 2 All ER 35; [1996] 3 WLR 593; *The Times*, 14 December 1995.

13 It was recommended by the Faulks Committee on Defamation in 1975 that juries should be abolished in defamation cases. However, juries still remain the selected mode of trial in the vast majority of cases.

14 See also [1995] 2 ALL ER 313; [1995] 2 WLR 450; *The Times*, 31 March 1995.

15 See also the *Independent*, 31 October 1995.

16 This followed the HL ruling in *Gillick v. Department of Health and Social Security* [1986] AC 112, when the HL considered the capacity of teenage girls to consent to contraceptive treatment by Family Planning Clinics. Lord Scarman said that the child's understanding would have to go further than a simple appreciation of the doctor's reasons for touching the child and the purpose behind the touching – the child would have to have an understanding of the wider social and moral implications of the contraceptive treatment (the Pill). Lord Donaldson MR held in *Gillick* that the notion of the 'competent child' would mean that she could give an effective consent to medical treatment, but that if treatment was refused, consent could be given by anyone exercising parental rights.

17 Legal aid was introduced after World War II to enable people who could not otherwise afford the services of lawyers to be provided with those services by the State. The system underwent various reviews and cutbacks during the late 1990s (White Paper, 'Striking the balance: the future of legal aid in England and Wales', 1996). The Department of Constitutional Affairs announced dramatic changes in February 2004 in its 'Recovery of defence cost orders with a view to reducing the (criminal) courts' discretion over legal aid disposition'. Now, as with Civil Legal Aid, the applicant in a criminal action has to pass a merits and means test (*Access to Justice Act 1999*). From 1 April 2000, the Legal Services Commission replaced the Legal Aid Board and it manages the Community Legal Service fund, assessing claimants as to their financial eligibility using a complicated 'merit' test.

18 See also [1993] 1 WLR 337; *The Independent*, 11 August 1992; *The Guardian*, 12 August 1992.

19 See also [1999] 4 All ER 342; [1999] EMLR 542.

20 See also [2003] 2 All ER 872; [2001] 1 WLR 1233.

21 [1869] LR4 EX 169.

22 [1867] 16 LT 263.

23 See also [1990] 1 All ER 165; [1990] 3 WLR 967.

24 See also [1981] 3 WLR 470; [1981] 3 All ER 450, CA.

25 *Lewis v. The Daily Telegraph* [1964] AC 234.

26 [1969] 2 All ER 193

27 [1972] 1 QB 522.

28 See also [1996] 1 ALL ER 152.

29 *Galloway v. Telegraph Group Ltd* [2004] EWHC 2786 (QB); [2004] All ER (D) 33 (2 December 2004).

30 During the spring of 2005, George Galloway, who had resigned his Glasgow seat, had formed a new political party, the Respect Party. On 6 May 2005, at the General Election, he took the Labour safe seat of Bethnal Green and Bow in East London, deposing the existing MP, Oona King. Mr Galloway gained a 26.2% lead in his favour, following a bitterly fought campaign. In his acceptance speech, George Galloway attacked Prime Minister Tony Blair. Galloway had fought on an anti-Iraq war manifesto that appealed to the large local Muslim population.

31 [1996] EMLR 152; *The Times*, 19 July 1995; the *Independent*, 22 September 1995.

32 [2004] EWCA Civ 1708; [2004] All ER (D) 326 (20 December 2004).

33 Application No. 35373/97, Grand Chamber, 17 December 2002, ECHR.

34 [2003] 2 All ER 872; [2001] I WLR 1233.

CHAPTER SEVEN

INTELLECTUAL PROPERTY

Key aim of this chapter:

> To enable you to understand the main principles of IP legislation.

Learning objectives

By the end of the chapter you should be able to:

- demonstrate a sound knowledge of IP legislation
- identify and appreciate copyright principles in your journalism and writing (authoring) practice
- identify moral rights inherent in and related to IP legislation
- be aware of and apply UK and international legislation related to IP
- identify relevant terminology associated with assigning and licensing rights in practical and contractual situations
- recognise the main principles in case studies and problem-solving exercises
- carry out IP research, including online.

Chapter contents

Introduction

Journalistic writing is a specialised and complicated craft and, at times, it needs protecting. This chapter introduces some of the complexities of intellectual property (IP) legislation – specifically, copyright law. We therefore go further than journalistic expertise and look at writing generally, authors' works and the creation of other works that may attract (immediate) copyright, such as original literary, dramatic, musical or artistic works, sound recordings, films or broadcasts. Though this book has not focused on contract law, this chapter finishes with a look at basic contractual terms (such as those licence agreements) that any author or photographer ought to be aware of when entering into, for instance, a publishing agreement.

This chapter is intended to raise your awareness of some of the fundamentals in this area of law in order to dispel a few common misconceptions and assist with more complicated issues when they arise, such as electronic rights or publication on the Internet or the creation of your own websites. Suffice to say, the original creator of a piece of 'work' is protected by copyright legislation, such as the *Copyright, Designs and Patents Act 1988*. This has been amended by some European legislation, such as the *Copyright Regulations Act 1995* and the *Copyright and Related Rights Regulations Act 1996*. These not only protect the rights of the originator, but also his or her heirs, who also have certain basic rights. For instance, they would continue to hold the exclusive right to use or authorise others to use the piece of work or photo on agreed (contractual) terms. The law is there to protect the creator of a work so that others are prevented from reproducing, copying or pirating that piece of original work, such as reprinting a publication or sound recording in their name.

We look, too, at related rights, such as those concerning public performances (such as for a play or musical work) and sound recordings (in the form of CDs, cassettes, videos and DVDs, for instance). Then there are copyright issues for broadcasts (such as on the radio or via cable or satellite) and separate rights that concern translations of works into other languages or adaptations of, say, a novel into a screenplay.

So, why should you protect your copyright? IP legislation is complicated and this chapter cannot cover all its multifaceted issues, but suffice it to say that copyright covers your original piece of work as a property right. Copyright and its related rights are essential to human creativity, giving creators incentives in the form of recognition and fair economic rewards in the form of royalties. IP legislation covers works as diverse as architecture, dress design, digital photography and computer software and includes trademarks. Under this system of IP rights, creators and authors can be assured that their works can be disseminated without fear of unauthorised copying or piracy. After all, your original piece of work helps increase the enjoyment of culture and entertainment and enhances knowledge all over the world. IP, then, is an inherent right to stop others copying your work without your permission.

Some fundamentals in copyright legislation

Copyright forms part of a bundle of rights known as 'intellectual property' (IP) rights. The practical overlaps between copyright, trademarks, passing off and the law of confidence is substantial. The law of contract also comes into play and is of particular importance when considering the terms and enforceability of any contract that deals with IP rights. Copyright protection also includes moral rights (see below), which involve the right to claim authorship of a work and the right to oppose changes to it that could harm the creator's reputation. If the creator (also known as the owner) of the copyright in a work feels that his or her work has been copied or pirated, he or she can enforce rights administratively and in the courts. The courts usually use equitable remedies for this, such as 'specific performance' in the form of an inspection of the 'copier's' premises for evidence of production or possession of illegally made or pirated goods related to your protected works, or in the form of an injunction to stop such activities. Then there are damages that the courts can order, which are for loss of financial rewards and recognition of your works.

IP is divided into two categories:

- industrial property
- copyright.

Industrial rights will usually have to be registered with, for example, the European Patent Office in Munich. The *European Patent Convention 2000* (EPC) covers this area of law as a treaty agreement. The World Trade Organization (WTO) in Geneva largely looks after legislation in this field, such as the Uruguay Round Agreement trademarks and their licensing.

The Uruguay Round (1996–2005) covers WTO trade agreements between 123 countries, from toothbrushes to pleasure boats, from banking to telecommunications, from the genes of wild rice to AIDS treatments. It has been the largest trade negotiation in modern history. Today, the WTO agreements cover goods, services and intellectual property. They spell out the principles of liberalisation, and the permitted exceptions. They include individual countries' commitments to lower customs tariffs and other trade barriers, and to open and keep open services markets. They set procedures for settling disputes. They prescribe special treatment for developing countries. They require governments to make their trade policies transparent by notifying the WTO about laws in force and measures adopted, and through regular reports by the secretariat on countries' trade policies (see: www.wto.org).

!	**Industrial property**
	• inventions (patents) • trademarks • industrial designs • geographic indications of source.

Copyright

What is the difference between copyright and patent? Both 'laws' provide different types of protection. Copyright protection extends only to expressions, not to ideas, procedures, methods of operation or mathematical concepts as such, whereas a patent is an exclusive right granted for an invention, which is a product or a process that provides a new way of doing something or offers a new technical solution to a problem.

Copyright is a property right with economic value. It is capable of being transferred to a third party, such as your spouse, your heirs and so on. The main legislation in the UK that covers copyright law is set out in the *Copyright, Designs and Patents Act 1988* (CDPA), which has been revised by implementation of EU Copyright Directives (for more, see below).

Copyright automatically arises when an original literary, dramatic, musical or artistic work is created, provided it is written down or otherwise recorded in some material form. This includes a digital medium, such as storage on the hard disk of your PC.

Ownership of copyright is quite distinct from ownership of the material that records that copyright work. Although a consumer buys a book, for example, the rights in the actual copyright work are those granted by the author and publisher over the work. The ownership of the copyright is quite distinct from the ownership of the book itself.

Copyright	!
It exists automatically in: • literary works – novels, poems and plays, films, musical works and so on • artistic works – drawings, paintings, photographs, sculptures and architectural designs, for example.	

Literary, dramatic, musical and artistic works have long been subject to exploitation and copying in the publishing, music or film business. For copyright to exist in these they must be recorded in writing (s. 3(2) CDPA). Writing is defined as any form of notation or code (s. 178 CDPA). It does not matter if the work is recorded by or with the permission of the author (s. 3(3) CDPA). Copyright subsists (is created) immediately. A prudent author dates and names a work and keeps it somewhere safe. A good idea is to put a hard copy and/or floppy disc of the work in a sealed envelope, post it to yourself and then not open the envelope on arrival. The postmark then acts as a copyright 'registration'.

How long is the duration of copyright? Usually the works are protected during the lifetime of the author plus 70 years. In the case of sound recordings, a term of 50 years runs from the end of the calendar year in which the work was released. Copyright in films expires at the end of the calendar year 70 years after the last of those in the following list dies: the principal director, the author of the screenplay, the author of the dialogue, the composer of music specially created for and used in the film.

Sources of IP legislation

The *Copyright Designs and Patents Act 1988* (CDPA 1988) is the principal statute governing UK copyright law. This statute has been amended by EU *Copyright and Related Rights Regulations 1996*. This legislation applies to UK and EU citizens and other countries by virtue of reciprocal agreements granted in various international conventions.

What, then, is the principal subject matter of copyright? As a starting point, s. 1(1) of the CDPA 1988 provides that copyright may subsist in:

- original literary, dramatic, musical or artistic works
- sound recordings, films, broadcasts or cable programmes
- the typographical arrangement of published editions.

The CDPA 1988 is also applied to authors from foreign countries by secondary legislation or so-called statutory instrument (SI), which states that the CDPA 1988 generally applies only to countries that give reciprocal protection to UK works. The countries specified in the statutory instrument are all members of one or other or both of the international copyright conventions, such as the Berne Convention.

Two international copyright conventions lay down minimum standards of protection for copyright owners between those countries that ratified the conventions. These are the Berne Convention and the Universal Copyright Convention (UCC). Both have many members and some countries, such as the UK, have ratified both treaties. While both conventions lay down general rules for copyright protection, there are some important differences for the formalities of protection. Under the UCC, the copyright work must contain the copyright symbol – © – along with the name of the copyright proprietor and the year of first publication. There is no requirement for such a mark under UK law, although it is essential for wide international protection.

We sometimes also hear 'related rights' to copyright. What are these? Related rights have developed alongside copyright over the past 50 years or so. Rights related to copyright include those of performing artists in their performances, producers of phonograms in their recordings and those of broadcasters in their radio and television programmes. Related rights have grown up around copyrighted works and provide similar protection although often more limited and of shorter duration.

!	**Related rights**
	These concern: • performing artists in their performances, such as actors and musicians • producers of sound recordings in their recordings, such as tape recordings, CDs, DVDs and so on • broadcasting organisations in their radio and television programmes.

Do you need to register to be protected?

Copyright protection is formality-free in countries party to the *Berne Convention for the Protection of Literary and Artistic Works* (the Berne Convention), which means that protection does not depend on compliance with any formalities, such as registration or deposit of copies. A patent is generally granted after completing an examination procedure by a government agency. Copyright itself does not depend on official procedures. A created work is considered protected by copyright as soon as it exists.

Is a name, title, slogan or logo protected by copyright? Copyright may or may not be available for titles, slogans or logos depending on whether or not they contain sufficient authorship. In most circumstances, copyright does not protect names.

According to the Berne Convention, literary and artistic works are protected without any formalities in the countries party to that Convention. However, many countries have a national copyright office and some national laws allow for registration of works for the purposes of, for example, identifying and distinguishing titles of works. In certain countries, registration can also serve as prima facie evidence in a court of law with reference to disputes relating to copyright.

Some extracts from the Berne Convention[1]

Art. 2(1) The expression 'literary and artistic works' shall include every production in the literary, scientific and artistic domain, whatever may be the mode or form of its expression, such as books, pamphlets and other writings; lectures, addresses, sermons and other works of the same nature; dramatic or dramatico-musical works; choreographic works and entertainments in dumb show; musical compositions with or without words; cinematographic works to which are assimilated works expressed by a process analogous to cinematography; works of drawing, painting, architecture, sculpture, engraving and lithography; photographic works to which are assimilated works expressed by a process analogous to photography; works of applied art; illustrations, maps, plans, sketches and three-dimensional works relative to geography, topography, architecture or science.

(2) It shall, however, be a matter for legislation in the countries of the Union to prescribe that works in general or any specified categories of works shall not be protected unless they have been fixed in some material form.

Art. 3(1) The protection of this Convention shall apply to:
(a) authors who are nationals of one of the countries of the Union, for their works, whether published or not;
(b) authors who are not nationals of one of the countries of the Union, for their works first published in one of those countries, or simultaneously in a country outside the Union and in a country of the Union.

(2) Authors who are not nationals of one of the countries of the Union but who have their habitual residence in one of them shall, for the purposes of this Convention, be assimilated to nationals of that country.

Art. 6(1) Independently of the author's economic rights, and even after the transfer of the said rights, the author shall have the right to claim authorship of the work and to object to any distortion, mutilation or other modification of, or other derogatory action in relation to, the said work, which would be prejudicial to his honour or reputation.

Art. 7(1) The term of protection granted by this Convention shall be the life of the author and fifty years after his death.
(2) However, in the case of cinematographic works, the countries of the Union may provide that the term of protection shall expire fifty years after the work has been made available to the public with the consent of the author, or, failing such an event within fifty years from the making of such a work, fifty years after the making.
(3) In the case of anonymous or pseudonymous works, the term of protection granted by this Convention shall expire fifty years after the work has been lawfully made available to the public.

Moral rights

The CDPA 1988 enables authors of copyright literary, dramatic, artistic and musical works and directors of copyright films to enjoy personal as well as proprietory rights in their works. These rights are known as moral rights, the principal ones being the rights of paternity and integrity. The right of paternity ('paternity rights') is the right to be credited as the author of the work. The right of integrity is the author's right to object to a derogatory treatment of the work.

It is a legal requirement that the author of a copyright work must assert authorship in writing – that is, claim the right to be identified as the author in order to exercise the right of paternity. This should be done at contractual level and it is usual, in the case of published works, for the formal assertion to appear at the front of the work or as part of the credits in a film or television programme.

Proprietory rights include the author's right to integrity and provide the author with the right to object to derogatory treatment of a work. This includes modification of a copyright work that distorts the work or affects the honour or reputation of the author. The right of integrity arises automatically at law, but does not apply to works included in periodicals or newspapers. Unlike the position in other European countries, in the UK moral rights can be waived. This means that the author can forgo the rights of paternity and integrity. A number of exceptions and limitations also exist in UK copyright legislation on the exercise of moral rights. Because moral rights are personal in nature, they are inalienable – that is, they cannot be transferred, except after the author's death.

Contractual agreements

Many creative works protected by copyright require mass distribution, communication and financial investment for their dissemination, such as publications, sound recordings and films. For this reason, creators often sell the rights to their works to individuals or companies best able to market the works in return for payment. These payments are often made dependent on the actual use of the work and are then referred to as royalties. These economic rights have a time limit, according to the relevant treaties (such as the Berne Convention) of 50 years after the creator's death, but the national laws of different countries may establish longer and different time limits. You need to familiarise yourself with this if you are going to use materials from other countries. These time limits enable both creators and their heirs to benefit financially for a reasonable period of time (royalties).

Nowadays, it might be wise for you to enter into some form of contractual agreement when you wish to transfer certain rights to, say, a publisher or broadcasting company. Remember, contracts are not set in stone – you can vary them! Often, you do not need a lawyer to do this for you.

With a contract, you can assign or licence certain transferred rights to the other party partially, exclusively or wholly. In this form, you permit them to 'exploit' your (the writer's or author's) work to the mutual benefit of you both. There will normally be clauses in the contract that include terms such as 'assignment' or 'licence'.

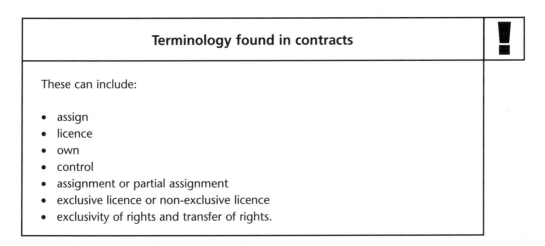

Terminology found in contracts	

These can include:

- assign
- licence
- own
- control
- assignment or partial assignment
- exclusive licence or non-exclusive licence
- exclusivity of rights and transfer of rights.

Writers are expected to sign contracts that contain terms such as those listed above and to fully comprehend the distinctions between them. You may wish to seek legal advice prior to your signing a contract if you feel that you do not like small print or it makes you feel safer to do so. Some publishers may shroud their expectations in a veil of jargon. Remember, they will draw up (publishing or broadcasting) agreements that are in their own best interests, but you can alter or amend clauses in the contract.

How do you assign copyright?

As we have seen, copyright is a property right. Therefore, if you wish to transfer all (or part of) the copyright in your work, you can do so. The transfer must be in writing (by means of a contract) and in return for money or money's worth (£1, for example), an advance against royalties or future royalties on book sales. Such a transfer is known as an assignment.

What, then, is a partial assignment? If you are the original copyright owner, you are entitled to restrict the use of your work – known as 'restricted acts' (RA). RA are mentioned in the CDPA 1988. However, when you make a contract, you may wish to bundle RAs separately and/or for different periods of time in different territories to different assignees. A partial assignment is less common in the publishing world because split rights may make it difficult for the publisher to exploit the work to your mutual advantage or, in some cases, at all.

If you have assigned all your rights in the work to a third party, you cannot, without their consent, read or perform it in public, photocopy it or do anything other than keep it. However, you can transfer all the rights in the work but keep the original – the original manuscript, disk or electronic file – as a memento to give to your grandchildren. Such is the unusual nature of copyright. All written agreements must be accompanied by a 'consideration', such as money.

A typical contractual form of wording for assigning copyright might be:

> The Author hereby assigns to the Publisher the copyright of the Work throughout the world for the term of copyright therein and shall, as appropriate, procure the assignment to the Publisher of the copyright in all material in the Work, which is not the property of the Author to the intent that the entire copyright in the Work shall vest in and become the property of the Publisher.

What is a licence?

A licence (also known as a licence agreement) grants certain rights in the copyright work to a third party, permitting the licensee to do certain things with the work. Again, this is achieved by means of a contract and must be done in writing.

A licence may be exclusive or non-exclusive. An exclusive licence looks and feels much the same as an assignment because the writer cannot offer the use of the work to anyone else during the currency of the agreement. An exclusive licence, however, may confer greater certainty as to scope of use and may be more easily enforced in infringement actions. However, a writer may favour the use of a non-exclusive licence to offer the work directly to different publishers in different territories.

A typical example of the wording in an exclusive licence might be:

> During the legal term of copyright and any extensions and renewals thereof the Author grants to the Publisher the sole and exclusive licence throughout the world to produce, publish and sell and to license production, publication and sale of the Work and all parts, adaptations and abridgements thereof in all forms and media in existence during the term of this Agreement in all languages.

A well-drafted agreement (contract) in which a work is licensed on an exclusive basis can overcome most of the obstacles mounted by publishers who hitherto have favoured an assignment. Publishers or recording labels are increasingly adopting licensing agreements in place of assignments and this practice should be encouraged.

For both parties to be adequately protected, they must ensure that their contracts specifically distinguish between the transfer of rights in the physical and electronic media. In order to do so, they require the flexibility of an exclusive licence within which rights can be subdivided.

Assignment or licence?

!

What is the difference?

From the publisher's point of view

- assignments provide greater flexibility when dealing with new media opportunities than licences, as the assignee (the person granted the assignment) knows that he or she is in control of all the rights and can use the work in whichever context is required
- alterations such as digitisation of the text and successive editions can be made by the assignee without recourse to the assignor (the writer)
- the assignee can seize on new opportunities and create new markets for the material.

> **!**
>
> - assignments create legal certainty as to ownership
> - assignments can be transferred at will to a third party, such as another publisher or recording labels
> - assignments are easy to enforce because rights do not have to be traced back to the original copyright owner.
>
> **From the writer's point of view**
>
> - an exclusive licence is preferable because the original copyright owner retains an element of control over the work
> - in the event of a dispute, the courts may be more willing to construe the terms of the licence more narrowly than they would those of an assignment. For example, they might insert into the terms of the contract a term restricting the right to make alterations to the work
> - moral rights arise automatically in a copyright work (unless they have been waived, consent has been granted not to exercise them or certain exceptions apply) and the right to make alterations is subject to the right of integrity, which an assignment cannot override
> - in enforcement actions against an infringement of copyright, the exclusive licensor (as the copyright owner) has concurrent rights of action with the licensee and, in certain circumstances, an action cannot be brought without leave of the court if both parties are not joined.

Licensing electronic rights

The fundamental issues that concern writers in the 'analogue world' are fundamentally the same as those in the digital 'new media' environment – access, control and authenticity. The degree of control over access and use is crucial to protection of a work. What type of legal framework exists to protect your (digital) work on the Internet?

Electronic rights were established by virtue of s. 17(2) of the CDPA 1988. Under the Act, storage in any electronic medium without the consent of the author or the relevant rights holder constitutes an infringement of the primary right of copying. Therefore, electronic storage – including temporary storage and caching on a hard disk – is a form of copying. It is not sufficient to consider electronic rights as one of the many subsidiary rights that appear (or not) in a publishing contract, nor should they be transferred wholesale with an exclusive licence.

In the digital environment, the way forward appears to be access via licence rather than ownership by means of purchasing. It therefore falls on communities of interests – both writers and publishers – to ensure that terms are understood and agreed prior to licensing the work with an end-user.

The difficulty lies in interpreting the terminology of contracts. Words and phrases that are adequate and precise when applied to the analogue world may become ambiguous or misleading when applied to the digital environment. Terms may take on a potentially wider meaning and effect when applied to electronic use. Furthermore, when rights in a work have not been distinguished or specified, problems of interpretation may arise that do not operate in either of the contracting party's interests. For example, the right of first publication may include electronic publication as well as the traditional print form. Additionally, authors who sign a 'non-exclusive licence' with a website owner to upload their works on to the pages of a website may find that, in reality, they have transferred all rights and interests in their work and to the world at large.

For both parties to be adequately protected, they must ensure that their contracts specifically distinguish between the transfer of rights in the physical and electronic media. In order to do so, they require the flexibility of an exclusive licence within which rights can be subdivided.

Electronic rights	!
Electronic rights can be split into: • offline types • online types.	

Some examples are:

- *Offline uses*   CD-ROM and multimedia products, such as videos, DVDs, filmstrips
- *Online uses*   CD-I, laser, record, copy, display and retrieve, perform, publish in online media, modify, edit, adapt the digital version, print off single copies of the whole or part of the material (reads as digital, optical or magnetic storage, retrieval and distribution).

Domain names (with the prefix http://www. plus the name) are registered on a first come, first served, non-territorial basis. In the UK, the non-profit-making Nominet is the national registry for domain names ending in .co.uk, .org.uk and .net.uk. The largest commercial registry is Network Solutions Inc., which provides worldwide registrations for all .com, .org and .net domain names.

For less than £50 a year, anyone can register a domain name with an Internet registry. However, this practice has been open to abuse by so-called 'cybersquatters'. These pirates have been quick to seize the opportunity to register well-known trademarks and names as their own and then frequently demand extortionate amounts of money from the relevant interested party to transfer ownership.

The international legal framework for protection of electronic rights already exists under the Copyright Treaty 1996. The EU *Directive on Copyright and Related Rights in the Information Society* enables European MS to provide greater protection for authors and their works in the digital environment.

Does this protect computer software? Today (after long EU discussions), there exists the generally accepted principle that computer programs should be protected by *copyright*, whereas apparatus using computer software or software-related inventions should be protected by *patent*.

Copyright protection of computer software has been established in most countries and harmonised by international treaties to that effect under the Berne Convention. The law relating to the patentability of software has still not been harmonised internationally, but some countries have embraced the patentability of computer software and others have adopted approaches that recognise inventions assisted by computer software. In view of the complexity of these matters, it is recommended that you contact a practising lawyer who specialises in IP – particularly if you are working in other countries.

Is a television format protected by copyright?

Broadcasting organisations are protected as holders of related rights under the *International Convention for the Protection of Performers, Producers of Phonograms and Broadcasting Organisations* (Rome Convention). Broadcast content as such – as opposed to broadcast signals – can also be protected by copyright and related rights, depending on national legislation.

Remedies

Each type of IP-infringement requires a slightly different approach to enforcement. If a patent or design is infringed the only option available is civil litigation. When a trademark or copyright is infringed you can pursue either civil or criminal action. Copyright is a private right and it can be difficult to enforce legally. Before becoming embroiled in an expensive court case, try to negotiate with the other party and come to some sort of agreement. However, if you decide to take legal action you will have to prove your case in civil court. In all cases, the courts consider such requests very carefully. They then weigh up proportionately the seriousness of the infringement and the remedies requested, as well as the interests of third parties. With regard to counterfeit trademark goods, for example, illegal copying of films or DVDs, this will be handled by the criminal courts. Generally, there are four options available to you under civil litigation: injunctions, damages, an account of profits or criminal litigation.

Injunctions

Injunctions are High Court orders that might tell a person that they are not allowed to do a certain act (other areas in which injunctions are applied are in harassment, threatening or assaulting behaviour towards others such as 'Domestic Violence Injunctions'). An *interlocutory injunction* prevents the infringer from exploiting the disputed IP while you and your representatives gather evidence for trial. This means that the judicial authority (usually the High Court) orders the party who has infringed your IP right to desist from the infringement by means of an injunction. However, the courts are reluctant to grant this option unless it is an open-and-shut case. If you lose and you have taken out an injunction against your opponent you may be liable for their loss of earnings.

You can get an injunction to stop your material from being misused; the damages (see below) you may receive could be considerable should you win your case. So, if you apply for an injunction you need to be absolutely sure that you will win your court case. You are required to set money aside while awaiting trial, in the event of your having to compensate an opponent should you lose. Therefore, it is important that the case comes to trial quickly.

Damages

The infringer will be ordered by the (High) court to pay the right-holder damages (in form of money), adequate by means of compensation, for the injury the right-holder has suffered because of the infringement of that person's IP right by the infringer who, knowingly, or with reasonable grounds to know, engaged in the infringing activity. Should you be successful, you will be paid an amount equivalent to what the court agrees is equal to your losses during the period of infringement.

An account of profits

If your sales have not been affected, but the infringing party has made money from your IP, you may be eligible to receive a proportion of its profits. This will be calculated by the court, and you will have to provide detailed accounts of profits and possible profits made by the infringing party.

Criminal Litigation

Where criminal offences concerning your copyright or registered trademark have been committed (e.g. counterfeiting) you can pursue the matter as a private criminal prosecution. A successful criminal prosecution can result in either fines or imprisonment for the offender/s. Fines might be more or less than damages pursued under civil litigation, but you would receive no compensation under criminal litigation because all fines are confiscated by the state.

Or, you could report the matter to the police or nearest Trading Standards office. At the same time you might enlist the help of HM Customs and Excise to seize the illegal goods. However, if your trademark has not been registered you can only pursue civil litigation (*Trade Marks Act 1994*). It is always advisable to register your trademark for about £200 for ten years.

Case studies

CASE STUDY

Case Study 1: *SABAM v. Tiscali* [2004][2]

On 1 December 2004, SABAM (Belgian Society of Authors, Composers and Publishers) won a significant victory in its anti-piracy case against the ISP Tiscali. This was probably the first such action against an ISP.

Brussels' Court of First Instance upheld SABAM's claim that Tiscali must block access to all 'peer-to-peer' (P2P) file-exchange systems and prevent the illegal exchange of copyrighted works.

In June 2004, in its ongoing efforts to combat music piracy online, SABAM called for a prohibitory injunction against the ISP for allowing its users to freely access P2P software. Rather than take action against individual Internet users, SABAM set a legal precedent by targeting ISPs directly and put an end to the P2P phenomenon in Belgium once and for all.

On 1 December 2004, the Court of First Instance in Brussels accepted SABAM's claim in principle and cited the EU Directive 'Information Society' as the basis for its judgment. The court agreed that some Tiscali customers were violating copyright and Tiscali, as an ISP, was ordered to block such actions. However, the court expressed realistic concern regarding the technical feasibility of imposing such a block and called on the opinion of an expert to investigate the matter further.

This concludes that even though as ISP can be ordered to cease a copyright infringement committed by a third party user, it remains to be seen whether in the expert's view, and taking into account existing technologies, an ISP is reasonably able to apply technical measures to block or filter illegal file exchanges without incurring disproportionate costs.

Case Study 2: *STIM v. TV 3 (Sweden) and Royalties* [2004] (unreported)

STIM (Swedish Performing Rights Society) reached an out-of-court settlement with the Swedish television channel TV3, bringing an end to their long-standing dispute over compensation to the creators of music. With the help of mediators, STIM and TV3 agreed to terms concerning back payments to its creators of music covering a period from July 1993 to 2004, and agreed to new terms.

For almost 14 years, STIM and TV3 disagreed over the amount and method of compensation to composers and songwriters for music played on TV3. STIM won the first round of a very extensive and prolonged court battle in the Stockholm District Court in December 2003, against which TV3 later appealed. In the summer of 2004, STIM agreed to mediation with Sweden's commercial TV companies.

As a result of these negotiations, TV3 agreed to compensate STIM for the period up to 13 December 2003 in the amount of 100m kronor. Payment for 2004 has also been settled and was based on agreements already in place between STIM and other Swedish television channels. Further, STIM and TV3 entered into a new agreement for 2005–2007, that established compensation by a royalty scale based on the amount of music the channel plays. As part of the deal, TV3 agreed to withdraw its appeal against the judgment of the District Court. As a result of this reconciliation, following years of uncertainty, STIM is now able to properly compensate its artists working in the commercial television sector.

QUESTIONS

1 State the remedies available for intellectual copyright infringement and explain briefly how these may be enforced by the right holder.

2 Name four remedies for breach of copyright available to the right holder under the relevant legislation.

FURTHER READING

Colston, C., and Middleton, K. (2005) *Modern Intellectual Property Law*. London: Cavendish.

Davis, J. (2003) *Intellectual Property Law*, Core Text Series, 2nd edn. London: Butterworths.

Smartt, U. (2004) 'Stay out of jail: performance, multimedia and copyright laws', in Leslie Hill and Helen Paris, *Guerrilla Performance and Multimedia*, 2nd edn. London/New York: Continuum.

Note

1 Of 9 September 1886, completed in Paris on 4 May 1896, revised in Berlin on 13 November 1908, completed in Berne on 20 March 1914, revised in Rome on 12 June 1928, Brussels on 26 June 1948, Stockholm on 14 July 1967 and Paris on 24 July 1971, and amended on 28 September 1979.

2 Court of First Instance in Brussels (criminal division), 28 April 2003 and 25 October 2005, published on http://www.droit–technologie.org/jurisprudences

CHAPTER EIGHT

SCOTTISH LEGISLATION

Key aim of this chapter:

To enable you to understand the main principles of the Scottish legal system and the framework of Scottish institutions.

Learning objectives

By the end of the chapter you should be able to:

- demonstrate a sound knowledge and appreciation of the Scottish legal system and its main institutions
- appreciate the separate functions of Scots law and its Parliament in relation to journalistic practices
- identify the terminology and court structure essential to the study of media and journalism law within the Scottish legal framework
- identify civil versus criminal law procedures and terminology
- recognise major Scottish, English and EU sources of law relevant to your course of study

Chapter contents

Introduction

In recent years, the arrival of dedicated Scottish editions of England-based popular tabloids has increased concerns among Scottish journalists. The establishment of the Scottish *Sun* in Glasgow in the early 1980s was followed in the 1990s by the 'tartan' version of the *Daily Mirror*, the *Daily Star*, the *Daily Mail* and *Daily Express* – all of which compete against Scotland's biggest-selling tabloid, the *Daily Record*, and the other indigenous morning titles.

Although the *Daily Record* is Scotland's main national newspaper (in terms of overall sales), it is also part of the Mirror Group. When Englishman Peter Cox (an ex *Sun* executive) took over the editorship of the *Daily Record* in 1998, he set about challenging those restrictive aspects of Scots law that did not apply to the press 'south of the border'. This was particularly true of reporting on children, contempt of court and defamation actions. His stance was supported by the Scottish editors of the national titles who had dared to publish (often against local legal advice) in areas where more established Scottish papers (such as Glasgow's *Herald* and *Evening Times*) dared not venture.

This included the publication of pictures of children involved in court cases or children's hearings. The law is strictly, and literally, applied in Scotland – 'no picture' means 'no picture', even if the child cannot be identified in the image concerned, such as in a pixelated photo or where the child's face cannot be seen. Increasingly, however, papers such as the *Daily Record*, the *Sun* or other English titles in Scotland show children's faces blanked out (pixelated) or publish, for example, back views of children involved in legal proceedings. Editors of indigenous Scottish papers, such as the Aberdeen-based *Press and Journal*, have felt increasingly hard done by, as it appears that the Crown is often not reacting to the English press by pursuing these titles for contempt. While Scottish newspaper editors still adhere to Scots law, in the strictest legal sense, editors of English papers published north of the border appear to challenge Scots law and get away with it. Indeed, some media lawyers who act for both the Scottish and England-based titles often find that their recommendations go unheeded by the papers based in the South, which prefer to apply the English interpretation of the law. This means that in areas of contempt, defamation or child news coverage, for example, these titles sometimes simply ignore Scots law. The *Contempt of Court Act 1981* covers both legislations for contempt.

How the *Human Rights Act 1998* (which came into Scots law a year earlier than it did in English law – in 1999) and the law of contempt have impacted on Scottish journalism can be seen from the following case. During the Luke Mitchell trial (2004/05 – see Case Study 1 below), the company that owns the Aberdeen-based newspaper *Press and Journal* was charged with a so-called 's. 47' offence for breaching the *Criminal Procedure (Scotland) Act 1995*, which bans the publication of details that would lead to the identification of anyone under 16 involved in criminal proceedings before a court. The newspaper had reported that Jodi Jones' boyfriend, Luke Mitchell (then 15), had been charged with her murder. *The Press and Journal* faced contempt charges concerning its story 'Boyfriend is charged with murdering schoolgirl Jodi' (April 2004). Those under 16 appearing in court are not allowed to be named in Scots law. The appeal judges ruled that the story should be cleared because it was not a report of court proceedings.

The Press and Journal contempt case was heard at the Aberdeen Sheriff Court in February 2005. Eventually, the paper was found not guilty of being in breach of the s.47 offence.

The Scottish legal system

As in English law, EU law is supreme in Scots law. All Community treaties (such as the *Treaty of Rome*, the *Single European Act*, the *Treaty on the European Union* and so on) apply, as do the regulations, directives and decisions of the Council of Ministers, the Commission and the ECJ. However, Scots law is distinctly different from English law in a number of areas, such as the 'not proven' verdict and the 110-day rule (the time period within which an accused person in custody must be brought to trial). Though it is fair to say that English statutes cover many of the same areas as Scots law, the major areas of difference between Scots and English law, as mentioned above, are those concerning reporting on children and young people, contempt of court and defamation actions. The *Human Rights Act 1998* has impacted greatly on a number of administrative and journalistic practices (such as Art. 10 ECHR 'freedom of expression') and is taken very seriously by editors and broadcast journalists. Accused people can bring actions to the Scottish Lord Advocate if they feel that their human rights have been breached.

As mentioned at the beginning of Chapter 2, Scotland's approach to privacy is somewhat different from the English system, though, as we have seen, there is no privacy in English law. There is some dispute in Scotland about whether or not certain aspects of privacy can still be protected by the remedy based on *convicium*, the essence of which is the holding of an individual up to public ridicule or contempt – the principle of *actio injuriarum* still providing a remedy for injuries to honour.[1]

In Scotland, defamation is a civil wrong and damages can be claimed (whereas in English law, strictly speaking, defamation is a criminal offence). As in English law, only the person defamed can sue and no claim can be made for defaming a dead person. While in England a written defamation is libel and the spoken word is slander, in Scots law there is no distinction and all cases are referred to as slander. As a rule, *any* statement which implies something socially or morally discreditable is actionable. This usually includes allegations of sexual immorality, drunkenness, dishonesty; and imputations against character or reputation, including business and financial reputation have all, in the past, been held as defamatory. Statements which are actionable must be false, and truth or *veritas* is a complete defence, but the defender must prove the allegations are true. The 'English' defence of 'fair comment' equally exists, as do absolute (i.e. statements in Parliament or in court) and qualified privilege. These reports have to be made without malice.

Now for a brief word on the Scottish Parliament. The *Act of Union 1707* abolished both the Scottish and English Parliaments and brought about the United Kingdom (UK) Parliament, based in London. However, in 1999, some powers previously residing in the UK Parliament were devolved and elections took place for the first Scottish Parliament. There are now some 129 Members of the Scottish Parliament (MSPs) who deal with the devolved Scottish legislation, including criminal law, criminal justice and prosecution, civil and criminal courts procedure, legal aid,[2] prisons and probation, most judicial appointments, health, education, social work, housing, use of land and so on.

MSPs are elected by an 'additional member system', unlike the traditional 'first past the post' system generally applicable in England. The Scottish Parliament sits for a fixed term of four years, though, under certain circumstances, elections can be called sooner, for example if there was a vote of no confidence.

Sources of Scots law

As we saw in Chapter 1 on English and European law, there are various sources of law and this is so for Scottish legislation, too.

First, there is legislation – that is, enacted law, which includes acts of Parliament and subordinate legislation conferred by Parliament. Apart from legislation passed by the Parliament in Westminster, London, there is now also

Scotland-specific legislation, passed by the Scottish Parliament. Statutes of the Scottish Parliament under the *Scotland Act 1998* now have the force of law.

In addition to primary legislation, there is also subordinate legislation, which is usually in the form of Orders in Council, made by the Queen in Council. These are regulations made by the government, or court procedural rules, ministerial rules, instruments and local authority by-laws. 'Acts of Sederunt' and 'Acts of Adjournal' regulate court procedures and, similarly, are a source of law. The Court of Session regulates procedure in civil cases – Acts of Sederunt. The High Court of Justiciary regulates procedure in criminal cases – Acts of Adjournal.

Second, there are 'precedents', which are similar to common law or 'judge-made law'. These exist in the form of case law and are set in the same way that they are in the English courts – by decisions and judicial judgments in courts of law made by judges in important cases. As with the English law reports – such as the *All England Law Reports* or *Weekly Law Reports* – Scottish law reports record case law and precedents, too. In the absence of relevant statutory provision, judicial precedent prevails as a source of law.

Precedents

The doctrine of precedent operates within the hierarchy of the courts and the following general principles apply:

- decisions by the House of Lords in Scottish appeals bind the House itself and all lower Scottish courts
- decisions by either division of the Inner House of the Court of Session bind each division and all lower courts
- the decisions of single judges, sheriffs principal and sheriffs are not binding.

Although the highest court of appeal is still the HL in criminal cases, it does not regard itself as absolute, being bound by its own previous decisions in civil cases, as the ECJ is supreme.

Furthermore, there are so-called 'writers' (or 'institutional texts') that count as the third source of Scots law. Certain highly respected 'institutional' authors of law texts – written principally in the seventeenth, eighteenth and nineteenth centuries – have been given a special place in Scots law (this is similar to Blackstone in English law). There is the seventeenth-century writer Stair, who wrote, inter alia, *The Institutions of the Law of Scotland* (1681), or the eighteenth-century writer Erskine, who is famous for his *The Institute of the Law of Scotland* (1773). Other such institutional writers are Craig, with his *Jus Feudale* (1655), Bell and his *Commentaries on the Law of Scotland* (1800) and *Principles of the Law of Scotland* (1829), Mackenzie for his *Laws and Customs of Scotland in Matters Criminal* (1678), Hume and his *Commentaries on the Law of Scotland Respecting Crimes* (1797) and Alison for his *Principles* (1832) and *Practice of the Criminal Law of Scotland* (1833).

Another source of law is 'custom'. This is where English and Scots law differ most notably. Scots law is largely based on Roman law – that is, it is similar to the Continental European jurisdiction. Therefore, when Scottish lawyers refer to 'civil law' they mean that they might actually have criminal law or 'wrongful acts' in mind, or ones that are harmful to society and punishable by the State. When Scottish lawyers refer to 'private law', they generally mean anything that refers back to the *Act of Union 1707*. As we saw with English law, private law regulates relationships between private subjects, while public law regulates relationships between the State and the individual.

'Equity' is the final source of law and incorporates the principles of natural justice and fairness. Unlike in England, equity is applied by the Scottish courts without being distinguished from the law as quoted above, thus avoiding the highly complicated juristic construct of equity as it is applied by the English courts (such as in the Chancery Division of the High Court).

!

Sources of Scots law

- EU law
- legislation (enacted law or statutes)
- precedents (case or 'common' law)
- writers
- custom
- equity.

The *Freedom of Information (Scotland) Act 2002* (FOI) came into full force on 1 January 2005. Similar to its English counterpart, the Act aims to increase openness and accountability in government and across the public sector by ensuring that people have the right to access information held by Scottish public authorities. People (such as journalists) are now able to access information about how such bodies function, how decisions are made and what information is held about them as individuals. The Act allows any person or organisation to ask for information held by a Scottish public authority, such as the Prison Service. It does not matter how old the information is or why it was created, if the authority holds the information, it will have to give you access to it, unless an exemption applies (ss. 18–20).

The Scottish Law Commission has created a publication scheme in consultation with the Law Commission for England and Wales and approved by the Scottish Information Commissioner Kevin Dunion in 2005. Its purpose is to set out the classes or types of information that the Commission proactively provides, so that members of the public can access it easily (including the Internet). In order to reduce the number of requests it has to deal with, the Scottish Information Commission has encouraged all Scottish public authorities to make available as much information as possible in terms of their publication schemes.

> *Example:* A journalist who wishes to obtain information relating to one of the Scottish Law Commission's law reform projects could start by looking at the Scottish Law Commission's publication scheme website (www.scotlawcom.gov.uk). You will find that some information is available on request only in the form of a hard copy. If the information sought is not available under the publication scheme, you can make a request for it in writing and the Commission must deal with your request, as laid down in the *2002 Act.*

Public authorities are encouraged to favour disclosure wherever possible. However, under s. 9 of the Act, a public authority may charge a fee.

As we saw with the English *Freedom of Information Act 2000* (FOI), this does not mean that you will have automatic access to all public information. The Act also provides for exemptions, so, under s. 18 of the Scottish FOI, there are 17 categories of exempt information, covering areas such as government interests and relations, public-sector administration, national security and defence, law enforcement and commercial interests. There are two types of exemption – 'absolute' and 'non-absolute'.

- *Absolute exemptions*: The public authority will not release the information if, for example, it concerns matters of national security or is confidential material.
- *Non-absolute exemptions*: The public interest test is applied by the public authority to decide whether or not the information should be released.

The court system

The Court of Session is Scotland's supreme civil court and sits in Parliament House in Edinburgh as the Court of First Instance and Court of Appeal. The personnel is similar to that of the English High Court. The court – the origins of which can be traced back to the early sixteenth century – is headed by the Lord President. Second in rank is the Lord Justice Clerk, followed by 30 other judges. These 32 judges are designated Senators of the College of Justice or Lords of

Council and Session. They are appointed to the Divisions by the Secretary of State after consultation with the Lord President and Lord Justice Clerk. When reporting on them, please bear in mind that each judge takes the courtesy title of 'Lord' or 'Lady', followed by his or her surname or a territorial title.

For the purposes of hearing cases, the Court of Session is divided into the Outer House and the Inner House. The Outer House consists of 19 Lords Ordinary, sitting alone or, in certain cases, with a civil jury. They hear cases at first instance on a wide range of civil matters, including cases based on delict (tort) and contract, commercial cases and judicial review. These judges cover a wide spectrum of work, but designated judges deal with intellectual property disputes. Special arrangements are made to deal with commercial cases.

The Inner House is, in essence, the Appeal Court, though it also has a small range of first instance business.

The Inner House is divided into the First and Second Divisions. Despite their names, they are of equal authority and presided over by the Lord President and the Lord Justice Clerk, respectively. Each Division is made up of four judges, but the quorum is three. Due to pressure of business, frequently an 'extra Division' of three judges sits.

The Divisions hear cases on appeal from the Outer House, sheriff courts and certain tribunals and other bodies. On occasion, if a case is particularly important or difficult, or if it is necessary to overrule a previous binding authority, a larger court of five or more judges may be convened.

In terms of law reporting and where to find reported cases and decisions, you need to look at the law reports.

Law Reports
• *Justiciary Cases* cited as, for example, 2005 JC 100. These are the decisions of the High Court.
• *Session Cases* cited as, for example, 2005 SC 100. These are the decisions of the Court of Session.
• *Scottish Civil Law Reports* cited as 2005 SCLR 100, for instance.
• *Scots Law Times* cited as 2005 SLT 100 and so on.

The High Court of Justiciary (known as the High Court) is Scotland's supreme criminal court. As such, it sits in cities and larger towns throughout Scotland. When exercising appellate jurisdiction, it sits only in Parliament House in Edinburgh.

The court consists of the Lord Justice General, the Lord Justice Clerk and 25 additional judges of the Court of Session who, when sitting in the High Court, are known as Lords Commissioners of Justiciary. It has jurisdiction over the whole of Scotland and over all crimes, unless its jurisdiction is excluded by statute. In practice the High Court deals with serious crimes such as murder, culpable homicide, armed robbery, drug trafficking and sexual offences involving children.

The main difference between Scottish and English criminal courts is that criminal cases are tried by a judge and a jury of 15 men and women in Scotland, 12 jurors in an English Crown Court.

When hearing appeals against convictions, the High Court consists of at least three judges. There are two when hearing sentence appeals. Appeals are heard from the High Court, sheriff courts and district courts. The Lord Advocate may refer a point of law that arose in the course of a case to the High Court for its opinion. This allows the High Court to give an opinion setting out the law for future similar cases, but does not affect the outcome of the case itself.

Scottish criminal courts

- *High Court*: normally 1 judge
- *Sheriff court*: normally 1 sheriff
- *Stipendiary magistrate's court*: normally 1 magistrate
- *District court*: normally 1 Justice of the Peace (JP), though there can be more
- *Judge, sheriff, magistrate or JP* sits at the head of the courtroom on a raised platform (the bench).

Scottish legal vocabulary

- pursuer *not* plaintiff
- defender *not* defendant
- fire-raising *not* arson
- advocates *not* barristers (members of the Society of Advocates in Aberdeen are Solicitors)
- culpable homicide *not* manslaughter
- housebreaking *not* burglary.

Please Note: in Scots Law there are no inquests, coroners' courts, juvenile courts, crown courts, prosecutions by the police, opening speeches to the jury, committal proceedings, *Habeas corpus* or injunctions. These are all peculiar to England.

The court structure

Criminal courts

High Court of Justiciary

|

Judge

|

Murder, rape, serious drug offences

|

No appeal to other courts

Sheriff Court

Sheriff

|

Criminal cases either with/without a jury, depending on the
seriousness of the case

District court

Justice of the Peace/Magistrate

|

Minor criminal cases

Civil courts

Court of Session

|

The supreme civil court in Scotland

Only in Edinburgh

Judge

Hears cases at first instance and
cases appealed from Sheriff Court

|

Appeals can be made from the Court of Session to the House of Lords

Sheriff court

Sheriff

|

Family cases, smaller money claims, etc.

Scottish Land Court

For determination of agricultural land disputes

Land Valuations Appeal Court

For rating questions

Court of the Lord Lyon

For matters of heraldry

Source: Law Society of Scotland (visit: www.lawscot.org.uk)

Court personnel

Scottish judges serve in a dual capacity, dealing with both criminal and civil cases. When reporting on them, make sure that you designate them appropriately as High Court or Court of Session judges. The High Court in Scotland is the supreme criminal court (whereas the High Court in England is largely a civil court, except for the Court of Appeal in criminal cases). Significant High Court reforms were introduced in April 2005, following Lord Bonomy's comprehensive review. These introduced new preliminary hearings in criminal proceedings similar to English plea and directions hearings, and the extensive care of victims and their support. Scotland's highest judge has two titles – Lord President of the Court of Session when sitting as a civil judge, and Lord Justice General when sitting in his criminal capacity. Lord Justice Clerk, the second highest post, remains the same in any court. The Principal Law Officer of the Crown in Scotland is the Lord Advocate, who is *not* a Law Lord. He is responsible for all prosecutions and directs a national system of public prosecutors called Procurators Fiscal. They are full-time civil servants and prosecute in the inferior courts. In the High Court, prosecutions are conducted by the Lord Advocates' deputies known as Advocates Depute or Crown Counsel. The Lord Advocate's deputy is the Solicitor-General for Scotland.

Other courts and bodies are:

- **The Lands Tribunal for Scotland** – hears disputes over feudal land obligations, allocation of feu duty and compensation in compulsory purchase orders.
- **Land Valuations Appeal Court** – hears appeals by ratepayers over the valuation of property.
- **Scottish Land Court** – comprises a judge ranking with a Court of Session judge and four laymen who specialise in agriculture. They deal with agricultural tenancies and crofting tenancies.
- **Courts Martial** – the law affecting all three (Army, Navy and Air) Services at courts martial based on English law.

The Scottish legal profession is divided into advocates – similar to English barristers – and solicitors. Advocates are members of the Faculty of Advocates and are referred to as 'counsel'. Such Queen's Counsel, 'learned in the law', have existed in Scotland since 1892. Until recently, advocates had an exclusive right of audience with the House of Lords, the Judicial Committee of the Privy Council, the Court of Session and the High Court of Justiciary, but, since 1990, they share that right with solicitor-advocates.

Solicitors constitute the larger of the two groups. Solicitors deal with all manner of legal affairs, including litigation, conveyancing, executry and trust work and general advising to, say, the media. They are regulated by statute – the *Solicitors (Scotland) Act 1980* – and are governed by the Council of the Law Society of Scotland, which deals with the admission, professional regulation and discipline of solicitors.

Solicitor-advocates – members of the Law Society of Scotland – are experienced solicitors and obtain an extension of their rights of audience by undergoing additional training in evidence and the procedures of the Court of Session. In addition, a practitioner from another MS of the EU may appear for a client in the circumstances prescribed by the *European Communities (Services of Lawyers) Order 1978*. An individual may conduct his or her own case in court, but a firm or a company must always be represented by counsel or a solicitor-advocate.

All criminal cases in the High Court are nominally brought 'in the public interest' by the Lord Advocate. Then, in court, they are prosecuted by advocates or solicitor-advocates (known as 'advocate deputes') chosen to represent the Lord Advocate. As in English courts, it is possible, although rare, for a private prosecution to be brought. An advocate or solicitor-advocate will usually conduct the defence.

! Courts and court personnel

- *High Court*: has 15-member jury and hears the most serious criminal cases
- *sheriff, magistrate, justice of the peace* (JP): hears less serious cases and sits alone (without jury) to decide whether or not the accused is guilty
- once guilt has been established, the judge, sheriff, magistrate or JP decides on the penalty.

Several tables follow listing how Scottish justices and members of the Bar should be addressed, both orally in court and in correspondence and, therefore, when you report on them.

Scottish judges and the Bar

Senior judges   The Lord President of the Court of Session and Lord Justice General are privy counsellors and should be addressed as follows.

Division	Address (in correspondence)	Dear ...
Civil	The Right Honourable Lord Doe Lord President of the Court of Session	Lord President
Criminal	The Right Honourable Lord Doe Lord Justice General	Lord Justice General

Judges   Judges of the Court of Session are all Senators of the College of Justice in Scotland and have the courtesy style and title of 'Lord' or 'Lady'. They should be addressed as follows.

	Address (in correspondence)	Dear ...
Male Not a privy counsellor Privy counsellor Retired Wife of retired judge	The Honourable Lord Doe The Right Honourable Lord Doe The Honourable Lord Doe Lady Doe	Lord Doe Lord Doe Lord Doe Lady Doe
Female Not a privy counsellor Privy counsellor Retired Husband of retired judge	The Honourable Lady Doe The Right Honourable Lady Doe The Right Honourable Lady Doe No title	Lady Doe Lady Doe Lady Doe

The Bar – use of QC   The description of Scottish advocates is exactly the same as for the English barristers.

Address (in correspondence)	Dear ...
Members of the Bar – no special form of address	Their usual titles in their private capacities
Queen's counsel or, when the sovereign is a king	John Doe Esq. QC John Doe Esq. KC
QC/KC appointed as a Judge of the Court of Session	Never use QC/KC

Criminal procedure

The Crown Office and the Procurator Fiscal Office are responsible for all criminal prosecutions, investigation into sudden and suspicious deaths, as well as all complaints against the police. As there are no committal proceedings in Scotland, an accused appears in private before a sheriff on petition for judicial examination. If he is remanded in custody for further investigation and is not allowed bail, then he cannot be detained longer than 110 days, by which time his trial must begin. If he is on bail, the trial must begin within 12 months. The Crown must prove a case 'beyond reasonable doubt' and an accused is 'innocent until proved guilty'. An accused need not give evidence, and at the end of the Crown case the defender can plead 'no case to answer'. There are 15 people on a jury (12 in England).

!

The Scottish criminal courts are

- High Court of Justiciary
- Sheriff Court
- District Court (Justice of the Peace/magistrate).

There are two types of criminal justice procedures – solemn and summary. Summary covers less serious offences involving a trial by sheriff or magistrate (some qualified as lawyers and a few who are lay people, as in England), who sit alone on the Bench.

Solemn (similar to English 'indictable') offences cover the most serious cases, involving trial on indictment before a judge or sheriff sitting with a 15-member jury. Jurors are selected at random from the electoral roll.

In the High Court, all trials are heard by a jury, as are the more serious cases in a sheriff court. The 15-member jury thus facilitates a simple majority verdict to establish guilt or innocence (such as 8:7). This differs substantially from England, where unanimous verdicts are generally preferred by judges with a 12-member jury.

Criminal court personnel

- the Lord Advocate (or one Advocate Depute) presents the case in High Court against the person charged with the crime
- the Procurator Fiscal (or one Advocate Depute) presents the case in a sheriff court, stipendiary magistrate's court, or district court
- the accused's solicitor conducts the case on behalf of the accused and provides the court with background information on the accused.

There are three types of verdict available to a Scottish jury – guilty, not guilty, or not proven. A 'not proven' verdict means an acquittal of the accused, but, as the words suggest, it does not mean that the members of the jury found the defendant 'not guilty', just that they could not agree on the simple majority verdict and, thus, are 'undecided'.

Which case in which court?

- *High Court*: Hears the most serious (solemn) cases (including murder and rape). The prosecutor decides in which court the case should be heard.
- *High Court*: Can impose a prison sentence or fine (there is no upper limit on either).
- *Sheriff court*: Hears summary and (some) solemn cases.
- *Stipendiary magistrate's court*: May impose a maximum of 3 months in prison, 6 months for a second or subsequent conviction, and a fine up to £5000.
- *District Court*: Hears minor cases, can give a maximum prison sentence of up to 60 days and fines of up to £2500.
- *Solemn cases* (*serious crimes*): A sheriff court can impose a prison sentence of up to three years or a fine (of any amount).
- *Summary cases* (*less serious crimes*): A sheriff court can impose a maximum prison sentence of 3 months, 6 months for a second or subsequent conviction, or fines up to £5000.

As in English law, when the person charged with a criminal offence pleads not guilty to a crime (that is, denies his or her involvement in the crime), a trial is held, at which evidence is presented to determine whether or not he or she is guilty.

There are a number of factors that determine which court will hear which type of case. First, this depends on the severity of the crime as well as the likely severity of the sentence to be imposed. Second, it depends where the crime was committed. Cases that are to be heard in a district court, stipendiary magistrate's court or sheriff court will normally be heard in the court closest to where the crime occurred. Cases in the High Court may be heard in the High Court buildings in Edinburgh or Glasgow, or in a sheriff courthouse in a town or city near where the crime was committed.

! Criminal procedure in a nutshell

- High Court of Justiciary ('the High Court') – supreme criminal court
- Lord Advocate brings a criminal prosecution
- jury of 15 people come to a majority verdict
- solemn offences are the most serious
- summary offences are less serious – such a trial is conducted by a sheriff, magistrate or JP
- there are three types of verdict: guilty, not guilty or not proven.

Sentencing is a matter for only the judge, sheriff, magistrate or JP (currently a layperson) to administer. If the accused admits his or her guilt, the prosecutor will provide the court with a brief account of the circumstances surrounding the crime. If the accused is then found guilty after a trial, the court will already have this information. Before sentencing, the prosecutor will also provide the court with details of any previous record that the accused may have.

Range of sentences available to the courts

- *Absolute discharge*: Given when it is considered inappropriate to punish the accused – perhaps because of the circumstances of the crime – or the character of the accused.

- *Admonition*: A warning given to the person found guilty of the crime.
- *Caution*: Requires the accused to lodge a sum of money with the court as security for his or her good behaviour for a certain period – up to six months for a district court or one year for a sheriff court. At the end of this period, if the accused has exhibited good behaviour, he or she can apply to the court to have the money reimbursed.
- *Fine:* What fine is given depends on the court the accused appears in. Fines can be paid in a lump sum or instalments. Fine defaulting requires the accused to appear at a fines inquiry court, where he or she may be given further time to pay or sentenced to a period of imprisonment as an alternative to paying the fine.
- *Supervised Attendance Order:* Instead of imprisonment or failing to pay a fine, the court may impose a Supervised Attendance Order, which requires the accused to carry out constructive activities, such as unpaid work, for 10 to 100 hours.
- *Compensation:* In addition to, or instead of, a fine or most other sentences, the court may order the accused to pay compensation to the victims for loss or injury resulting from the crime. The court will consider the accused's financial circumstances. Monies are paid to the court, then forwarded to the victims.
- *Probation Order:* This requires the accused to be under the supervision of a local authority officer for six months to three years.
- *Community Service Order:* This is a direct alternative to imprisonment and requires the accused to undertake between 80 and 300 hours of unpaid work in the community under the supervision of a social worker.
- *Imprisonment:* What sentence is given depends on the type of court the accused appears in. For example, a youth aged between 16 and 21 would be a sentenced to young offenders institution.

There are several other penalties that can be imposed, such as endorsement of an accused's driving licence, disqualification from driving, forfeiture or destruction of property (for example, of weapons or tools used during a crime, or drugs), forfeiture of money or goods acquired as a result of a crime, restriction of liberty (tagging) orders, drug treatment and testing orders, non-harassment orders and deportation. Many of these are similar to sentences given in magistrates' courts in England and Wales.

Stages of Procedure in the Scottish Criminal Justice System

First calling	In *serious* cases that will be heard by a jury, this stage may involve one or two procedural hearings, which are held in private, i.e. no public access. The accused may be held in custody, or released on bail. In *less serious* cases, there may also be one or two procedural hearings, held in public. At these hearings the accused will indicate whether or not (s)he admits that (s)he committed the crimes. The accused may be ordered to be held in custody, or released, possibly on bail.
Not guilty	If the accused denies committing the crimes, a date will be fixed for hearing evidence in the case, i.e. a trial. This date is likely to be several months ahead.
Intermediate or First Diet	If for any reason the trial cannot go ahead on the planned date, a new date will be fixed.
Guilty	The accused can decide to admit that (s)he committed the crimes at any stage in the proceedings. This can be done on a date already fixed for hearing the case, or the accused can ask for the case to be advanced for this purpose. Once the accused has admitted to the court that (s)he committed the crimes, the case will proceed to Sentence.
Trial	At the trial, the Prosecutor will call witnesses. Note: the case may not go ahead on the arranged day. This can happen for a number of reasons, for example the accused or an important witness may not appear, or some other evidence may not be available.
Verdict	After all the evidence has been presented, a decision will be taken about whether or not the accused is guilty. In the most serious cases this decision will be taken by the jury. In other cases the decision will be taken by the Sheriff/ Stipendiary Magistrate/JP.
Sentence	If the accused admits (s)he is guilty, or is found guilty after a trial, the Judge/Sheriff/Stipendiary Magistrate/JP will impose a sentence. This may be done on the same day, or the case may be continued for a few weeks, to obtain background or medical reports on the accused.
Appeal	If the accused feels that some element of his/her trial was unfair, or that the sentence was unduly harsh, (s)he can appeal to the *High Court of Justiciary*. The prosecutor can also appeal if (s)he believes that the sentence was too lenient. An appeal can take several months, and the accused may be released pending the appeal.

Court reporting and contempt of court

As in England, Scottish court reporting is, first and foremost, covered by the *Contempt of Court Act 1981* (CCA; see also Chapter 4). Here, the same principle applies, in that justice must be seen to be fair and a trial should not be prejudiced by adverse media coverage. Thus, a jury should 'arrive in the jury box without knowledge or impression of facts, or alleged facts, relating to the crime charged on the indictment' (The Lord Justice General, Lord Emslie, in *R. v. Sindicic* [1988]).[3]

The CCA 1981 also covers civil proceedings at the point where 'the record is closed' (similar to the English courts when 'arrangements for a hearing are made') or from the time the hearing begins. As discussed in Chapter 4, journalists are strongly advised to adhere to the strict liability rule under the 1981 Act, which applies to the Court of Session and civil cases in the sheriff courts. Therefore, particular care needs to be taken in defamation actions or family proceedings. This is because civil proceedings remain active until they are disposed of, discontinued or withdrawn. The same applies to inquiries or tribunals where the Lord Advocate may issue newspaper editors with anonymity warnings. This happened in the Dunblane Primary School shooting inquiry in March 1996 when Lord Mackay warned of the dangers of contempt.

In fatal accident Inquiries (such as the Lockerbie aeroplane bombing disaster in 1990), usually presided over by one Sheriff with no jury present, anonymity is a vital issue. In relation to the Lockerbie Inquiry in 1991, there were contempt hearings at Dunoon Sheriff Court against the *Glasgow Evening Times* and the *Glasgow Herald* concerning a Glasgow lawyer who had lost her life whilst hillwalking when the Pan Am Flight 103 crashed on her on 21 December 1988. The *Glasgow Evening Times* had mentioned in its coverage that the woman had been an experienced hillwalker and that she had died in 'fair weather conditions'. It was argued that this and a similar article in the *Glasgow Herald* would seriously impede future evidence in criminal proceedings and that any future witnesses (including those giving evidence at the inquiry) would be influenced by what they had read in the papers.

Scottish courts are very strict on the application of contempt, as exemplified when the *Glasgow Evening Times* reported on the actor Ian McColl, who played alongside the famous Scottish TV character Rab C. Nesbitt, a drunken down-and-out. McColl had appeared at the Glasgow Sheriff Court on a charge of threatening sheriff officers with an axe when they arrived at his home to execute a warrant over unpaid debts. The *Glasgow Evening Times* published a detailed account of how McColl had spent a night in the cells after this alleged incident. The Crown subsequently argued that the article had created a substantial risk that the course of justice would be seriously impeded under the CCA. At appeal, Lord Rodger pointed to Art. 10 ECHR, stating that:

In assessing the risk we have to take account of the time which would elapse between publication and the likely date of the trial. ... Here, in a case where Mr McColl was released on bail, trial would be likely to take place within 12 months but, realistically, would not be likely to take place within the first three months. In fact we know that it is unlikely to take place until around nine months after publication. ... We must also assume that a jury will hear and pay attention to the evidence led in the case, that they will be addressed by the Procurator Fiscal Depute and by the agent for Mr McColl and that they will then be given the standard directions by the trial Sheriff, including the direction that they are to consider only the evidence which has been laid before them in court. ... We then have to ask ourselves whether we are satisfied beyond a reasonable doubt that, when published, the article created a substantial risk that the deliberations of the jury would be so affected as to give rise to serious prejudice to the course of justice. ... We consider it rather unlikely indeed that anyone cited to serve as a juror would even recall the article.

The newspaper was found not guilty of contempt, in spite of the fact that the story had involved a famous TV personality.

There are no known cases in recent times of a Scottish editor being imprisoned for contempt, though s. 15 CCA allows for a fixed-term prison sentence of up to two years, imposed by the High Court or a sheriff court in indictable cases. Fines have been more common – the maximum fixed penalty fine currently being £2000 in summary cases or unlimited in indictable cases.

There is no law that 'gags' newspapers from drafting a carefully constructed background article to particular issues involved in a case. However, such a 'backgrounder' must not be published until after the case has finished – that is, when the case is inactive.

!	Contempt of court

- *Active*: a person has been charged with a criminal offence, a warrant for their arrest has been issued, an indictment has been served or the record is closed in civil proceedings.
- *Inactive*: the accused has pleaded guilty or been acquitted or been sentenced or the charges have been dropped and the proceedings have been discontinued.
- *Appeals*: watch out for 'substantial risk' of prejudice around these.
- *Backgrounder*: must be published *after* case has finished and is inactive.
- There is conflict between Art. 10 ECHR and the *Contempt of Court Act 1981*.

Children and young people in the criminal justice system

While in England the age of criminal responsibility begins when a child reaches the age of 10,[4] in Scotland it is 8, as set down in s. 41 of the *Criminal Procedure (Scotland) Act 1995*:

> It shall be conclusively presumed that no child under the age of 8 years can be guilty of any offence.

This makes Scotland one of the most punitive countries in Europe with regard to children's criminal responsibility, as most other countries set the age at around 14. That said, children in Scotland between the ages of 8 and 15 who commit a criminal offence are seldom subjected to the adult system of prosecution and punishment, as 41(1) of the 1995 Act provides that:

> No child under the age of 16 years shall be prosecuted for any offence except on the instructions of the Lord Advocate, or at his instance; and no court other than the High Court and the sheriff court shall have jurisdiction over a child under the age of 16 for an offence.

The Lord Advocate has issued administrative directions to procurators fiscal on the prosecution of children. In effect, this means that the Lord Advocate does not have to give express authority in each case. If a child is found guilty or pleads guilty to an offence that, if committed by someone aged over 21, could lead to imprisonment, a sheriff sitting summarily can sentence the child to a period of detention in local authority residential accommodation for up to one year. In practice, nearly all child offenders below the age of 16 are dealt with by the children's hearing system (discussed below) and only around 0.5 per cent of them are prosecuted in the criminal courts. Of the few who are prosecuted and found guilty, nearly one third are remitted to a children's hearing for subsequent action.

The *Social Work (Scotland) Act 1968* effectively abolished youth courts. Until then, children over the age of 8 who committed a criminal offence in Scotland were dealt with by ordinary criminal courts. Concerned about this, the then Secretary of State for Scotland appointed a committee chaired by Lord Kilbrandon in 1961, to 'consider the provisions of the law of Scotland relating to the treatment of juvenile delinquents and juveniles in need of care or protection or beyond parental control'.[5]

The ethos of the Kilbrandon Committee was that children who appeared before the courts because they had committed an offence or who had simply come to the attention of local authorities (for example, as a result of truanting at school) with deviant behaviour, needed protection rather than State punishment.

General principles set out by the Kilbrandon Committee are known as 'common needs' and include:

- a separation between the establishment of issues of disputed fact and decisions about the treatment of the child
- the use of lay panels to reach decisions about treatment
- the recognition of a child's needs as the primary consideration
- the vital role of the family in tackling children's problems
- the adoption of a preventative and educational approach to these problems.

What followed was the setting up of the children's hearing system – much admired inside and outside the United Kingdom (see the next section, below)

When a person under 17 years old is in custody, generally speaking there should be no press reporting (s. 46 *Children and Young Persons (Scotland) Act 1937*). This can be overruled by s. 47 of the *Criminal Procedure (Scotland) Act 1995* if a judge, confirmed by the First Minister, believes that naming the young person would be of public interest.

The *Fatal Accidents and Sudden Deaths Inquiry (Scotland) Act 1976* (c.14) states that no one under the age of 17 must be named in fatal accident inquiries. In an inquiry into the death of a six-week-old boy in 1984, Sheriff Principal Philip Caplan, QC, ordered that no one, especially the parents, should be named for fear of jigsaw identification. The main reason for doing this was to protect the 3-year-old sister of the dead boy. You will recall that jigsaw identification means disclosing information (other than directly naming the child) that could lead to that young person's identification.

In addition to the *Children and Young Persons Act 1933* s. 39 (no reporting on juveniles in active court proceedings), Scots law provides different protection for children. While in England the media cannot report or name a juvenile under the age of 18, Scots law is different. The most important legislation is found in s. 47 of the *Criminal Procedure (Scotland) Act 1995*, which provides complete anonymity for children under the age of 16 in civil and criminal legal (court) proceedings, children's hearings and fatal accident inquiries. These young people must not be identified in any way whatsoever – including in photographs or TV images. This ban applies to the name, address, school and any other information, such as naming a parent, because of jigsaw identification, and covers the media per se in civil and criminal actions once these proceedings are active. For example, a newspaper can be prevented from naming a jailed mother for fear that her children will then be identifiable in this way. In December 2004, a headline in Glasgow's *Evening Times* read, 'Jail for mum who abandoned kids', with the first paragraph stating, 'A 34-year-old woman has been jailed for six months after leaving her two young children "home alone" while she went on holiday with her boyfriend' (18 December 2004).

In another case, a headline in Glasgow's *Evening Times* read, 'Boy, 11, on charge as baby hurt', with the first paragraph stating, 'An 11-year-old boy has been charged with attempted murder after a nine-month old baby was seriously injured' (18 December 2004). This shows that, where children are involved, newspaper editors tend to be very careful not to identify them at all through jigsaw identification, for instance by naming either their parent, school or neighbourhood.

Jigsaw identification

This happens by disclosing information that could lead to a young person (or young witness, or rape or sexual assault victim) being identified. To avoid this happening, do not mention the names of the young person's:

- village or small community
- school or youth club
- teacher
- parent(s).

To additionally protect a young person, a 's. 47' order can be made under the provision of the *Criminal Procedure (Scotland) Act 1995* (this is similar to a s. 39 order in English law under the *Children and Young Persons Act 1933*). The s. 47 order prohibits the press from, for instance, naming a parent or teacher of a particular child involved in court proceedings. Strictly speaking in reporting terms no child under the age of 16, once charged with a criminal offence, can be identified and reported on. However, under s. 43 of the *Youth Justice and Criminal Evidence Act 1999* (backed up by the *Criminal Procedure (Scotland) Act 1995*), a Scottish High Court judge may lift reporting restrictions on a youth (under the age of 15), if it is felt that the matter or identification is in the public interest. However, permission to do so would have to be sought from Scotland's First Minister. To date, no such order has been granted, though it is worth noting that the Aberdeen-based *Press and Journal* was acquitted in February 2005 for reporting on 15-year-old Luke Mitchell who had been charged with the murder of his 14-year-old girlfriend Jodi Jones in April 2004 (see case studies below).

The children's hearing system

The children's hearing system, set up, as we saw earlier, under the *Social Work (Scotland) Act 1968*, began operating in 1971. The 1968 Act laid down that a child could only be prosecuted for an offence on the instruction of the Lord Advocate and that no court other than the High Court of Justiciary and a sheriff court had jurisdiction over a child for an offence.

The *Children (Scotland) Act 1995* represented the first major reform of Scottish childcare law, but largely preserved the children's hearing system of the 1968 Act. The 1995 Act made some procedural alterations and specified the grounds of referral for a child to a hearing via a local authority children's panel.[6] Today, each local authority area has a children's panel, made up of volunteers appointed by the First Minister on the advice of the area's Children's Panel Advisory Committee. The First Minister appoints a chair on each authority's panel, who then chooses the three members who attend a hearing.

!

The children's hearing system

- it provides separate adjudication for young offenders and delinquents
- the cases are heard by a children's hearing panel – a lay tribunal
- the emphasis is on family participation
- they are informal hearings.

The *Children (Scotland) Act 1995* also specifies the grounds for referral to a reporter.[7] Reporters in this case are nothing to do with newspapers but independent officials who act as 'gatekeepers' to the children's hearing system. Anyone – including parents, teachers and social workers – can refer a child to a reporter if they think that the child may be in need of compulsory measures of care. However, referrals for an alleged offence must come from law enforcement agencies (the police or a procurator fiscal). Most referrals are for criminal offences.[8]

!

What a children's reporter does

When a reporter receives a referral, he or she can decide to:

- inform the child's parents or guardian and give them a warning
- take no further action
- make a referral to the local authority for informal advice and guidance from the social work department
- refer the child to a children's hearing panel, stating the grounds for the referral
- make a care order, if the reporter thinks that the child may need compulsory measures of care.

A hearing cannot continue unless grounds for it have been established or there is a court ruling to that effect. Then, those at the hearing, including the child and any relevant person, discuss the grounds and any reports. The hearing must by law obtain the child's views.

The aim is to reach consensus about what should happen as a result of the hearing. When the child and any relevant person have agreed to a 'voluntary disposal' (that is, the child and parents or guardian agree to a specific order), the hearing may decide that no compulsory measures of care are required, or may place the child on supervision and issue a non-residential or residential supervision order. There is the right to appeal against the hearing's decision to a sheriff within 21 days. This will be granted if the hearing's decision was 'not justified in all the circumstances of the case'.

If a young person is involved in an incest or sexual offence case, probably involving one or more adults, the media must follow the same rules that apply for children under the age of 16 where their identification is concerned, and s. 47 of the *Criminal Procedure (Scotland) Act 1995* applies here once again. Also, editors and journalists must be careful to avoid jigsaw identification, particularly where two or more reports are published as each must try to protect the anonymity of the child particularly when they are read together or over time. Today, it is common practice for Scottish newspapers to simply report that 'a serious offence against a child' has been committed, rather than mentioning incest.

Identifying children and young people

- s. 47 *Criminal Procedure (Scotland) Act 1995* bans identification of those under the age of 16, whether they are the accused, victims or witnesses in court at civil and criminal proceedings
- no naming of children is allowed in incest or sexual offence cases
- no naming of children under the age of 18 taking part in children's hearings is allowed (s. 58 *Social Work (Scotland) Act 1968* and *Children (Scotland) Act 1995*)
- there can be no naming of young people in custody who are under 17 years of age (s. 46 *Children and Young Persons (Scotland) Act 1937*)
- no identification of children or young people under the age of 17 is allowed in fatal accident inquiries (*Fatal Accidents and Sudden Deaths Inquiry (Scotland) Act 1976*).

Case studies and opinions of court

Reporting on children

Case Study 1: Luke Mitchell murder trial (2004–2005)

There can be certain lacuna (legal loopholes) in Scottish reporting, whereby the media can be seen to get away with reporting on juveniles under the age of 16, unlike in England, where reporting restrictions are very strong concerning young people up to the age of 18, particularly when they are involved in criminal or family court proceedings. A good example of this happening is the case of 16-year-old Luke Mitchell, who stood trial at the High Court in Edinburgh for the alleged murder of his girlfriend Jodi Jones. At the time of Mitchell's arrest, in April 2004, he was 15.

Mitchell's girlfriend, Jodi Jones, 14, had gone missing on 30 June 2003 after going to meet him. When found, later that day, Jones had been stripped, tied up and savagely stabbed to death in woods near her home in Dalkeith, Midlothian.

Mitchell's murder trial began on 18 November 2004 and ran for 42 days – said to be the longest trial of a single accused in recent Scottish legal history. The jury at the High Court in Edinburgh decided by majority verdict to convict Mitchell of the killing. Presiding Judge Lord Nimmo Smith told the teenager that he was 'truly wicked' for committing this murder.

During the trial, the court heard how Mitchell's mother, Corinne Mitchell, had done everything possible to shield her son from justice in order to cover up his savage crime. Corinne Mitchell, a 45-year-old caravan dealer, had been charged in April 2004 with attempting to pervert the course of justice, but later the charge against her was dropped.

She was by Mitchell's side during Jones' funeral and by his side when he defiantly gave an interview from their home to Sky TV denying murdering the 14-year-old. Asked by reporter James Matthews if he had killed Jodi, Mitchell replied, 'No. I never, I wouldn't. In all the time we were going out, we never had one argument at all, never fell out or anything.'

At the trial, as Mitchell's mother was in the witness box, it was alleged by the prosecution that she had lied on her son's behalf and destroyed crucial evidence in a log burner in their garden. The jury was told how Mrs Mitchell had completely lost control of her son and could see no wrong in anything he did. Facing Jones' mother, Judith Jones, across the courtroom, Mrs Mitchell had insisted, 'My son did not kill Jodi Jones.' The judge even said, after Mitchell was found guilty, that she had adopted the role of accomplice.

Luke Mitchell's conviction for the murder of Jodi Jones was reported extensively in the British (and some European) papers. Mitchell was found guilty of murder by a majority verdict on 21 January 2005 (and also, by majority verdict, of supplying cannabis). Presiding Judge Lord Nimmo Smith told Mitchell: 'It lies beyond any skill of mind to look into the black depths of your mind … You have been convicted of a truly evil murder – one of the most appalling crimes that any of us can remember – and you will rightly be regarded as wicked ... I have no idea what led you to do what you did. Maybe it was a desire for notoriety, to achieve something grotesque. I leave it to others to fathom' (21 January 2005, the *Press and Journal* online). The judge reserved sentencing.

On 11 February 2005, at the High Court in Edinburgh, Luke Mitchell was sentenced to a minimum of 20 years in prison. Setting out the minimum punishment period of 20 years, which 'the killer must serve before being considered for parole', Lord Nimmo Smith told the court that this was 'one of the worst cases of murder of a single victim to have come before the court in many years'. The judge continued, 'it is very rare for a person so young to be convicted of such a serious murder. Looking back over the evidence I still cannot fathom what led you to do what you did.' The judge said that he would have handed down an even longer sentence if Mitchell had not been so young. He added, 'It is nevertheless a lengthy one and one during which I hope that you will benefit from your time in custody and gain some insight into those aspects of your character which led you to commit this dreadful crime.'[9]

On 14 April 2004, at the time of his arrest, the Crown Office had issued guidance to newspaper editors confirming that Mitchell had been charged with Jodi Jones' murder and was to appear in court the next day. The majority of the Scottish press reported that 'a boy' had been arrested as a suspect in relation to Jones' murder, but the *Press and Journal* fully named the then 15-year-old boy. The headline (*Press and Journal*, 15 April 2004) was: 'Boyfriend is charged with murdering schoolgirl Jodi' with the first paragraph naming him fully:

> 'The boyfriend of teenager Jodi Jones was yesterday arrested and charged with her murder. Fifteen-year-old Luke Mitchell's mother was also arrested by police investigating the death of the 14-year-old schoolgirl last June.

Subsequently, the company (not the editor of the newspaper), Aberdeen Journals, was charged with a so-called s. 47 offence for breaching the *Criminal Procedure (Scotland) Act 1995*, which bans the publication of details that would lead to the identification of anyone under the age of 16 involved in criminal proceedings before a court. The Crown alleged that the article of 15 April 2004 had included details 'calculated to lead to the identification of Mitchell as a person under the age of 16'.

The case was heard at the Aberdeen Sheriff Court on 18 February 2005. Fiscal Depute Caroline Mackay argued at the hearing that proceedings were active when the offending article appeared. She also stated that a petition warrant had been granted for Mitchell's arrest at Edinburgh Sheriff Court on 7 April and so he should not have been named. People under 16 involved in court proceedings were protected by the court, she said.

Paul Cullen QC, for Aberdeen Journals, argued that Mitchell had not appeared in court when the article was published and it had not mentioned the warrant. Mr Cullen argued that by naming Mitchell, the *Press and Journal* had not broken the law, as it was not a report of proceedings in court. Section 47, which prevents newspapers from naming people under the age of 16, begins with the words, 'No newspaper report of any *proceedings in a court* shall reveal ... ', and Mr Cullen argued that, therefore, the *Press and Journal* report did not breach the s. 47 order.

Sheriff Graham Buchanan said that it had been known for a very long time that, when there was some doubt about the proper interpretation of the law, the accused would be given the benefit of the doubt. 'What appeared in the newspaper on the 15th of April was simply not a report of any proceedings in a court,' said Sheriff Buchanan. 'Although it might be thought that what did appear might be regarded as an attempt to circumvent the provisions of s. 47, I believe that the correct approach to the matter was to strictly construe this section and when I do that I simply have no difficulty in concluding that what appeared in the newspaper on the day in question did not amount to a breach of s. 47.'

The headline in the *Press and Journal* on 19 February 2005 read:

The *Press and Journal* (P&J) was cleared of breaking the law of contempt by naming the 15-year-old Luke Mitchell at the point of his arrest.

Speaking after the court case, the Editor of the *Press and Journal*, Derek Tucker, said, 'Not only do we not breach the law, but we do not breach the spirit of the law. The wording of this particular section is so precise that we thought it inconceivable that it was considered to have broken the law. Mr Cullen was of the opinion that the Fiscal had confused the provisions of the Contempt of Court Act with the Criminal Procedure (Scotland) Act.' The *Press and Journal* was cleared of breaking the law by naming a 15-year-old boy accused of murder on 18 February 2004.[10]

Case Study 2: Naming of the Home Secretary's son – 'Home Secretary's son in cannabis honey trap' (1997)

On 13 December 1997, sections of the media discovered that the then 17-year-old son of the then British Home Secretary Jack Straw had sold some marijuana to a *Daily Mirror* newspaper reporter, Dawn Alford. The *Daily Mirror* had set up an in-depth investigation alongside a campaign by the *Independent on Sunday* to 'legalise it' (cannabis). Both the *Daily Mirror* and the *Sun* were subsequently gagged by the High Court, which issued an injunction to not name either the Home Secretary or his son. Though Jack Straw had agreed to be named in the scandal, the High Court injunction was meant to cover the Home Secretary's anonymity because of possible jigsaw identification of the boy. The High Court felt that the *Daily Mirror*'s trawl through the minister's son's private life had been in particularly bad taste and, furthermore, there was a need to protect the juvenile's anonymity with reference to s. 39 of the *Children and Young Persons Act 1933*.

Rumours regarding the identity of the minister intensified during the Christmas period. It is fair to say that the media establishment was in the know by Christmas Eve 1997. The story was, of course, of particular interest and importance to the media as the Home Secretary was responsible for the nation's law and order policies, and the amiable MP for Blackburn had dedicated his entire political life to the fight against crime and drugs.

The story was that the minister's son had supplied a small amount of cannabis (1.97 grams) to an undercover 'investigative journalist' employed by the *Daily Mirror* newspaper. It was alleged that the attractive blonde reporter had 'set up' the young A-level student, by encouraging him to consume large quantities of alcohol with her. She had then 'invited' the teenager to supply her with drugs.

On 20 December, Straw senior was confronted by the reporter, as well as by the *Daily Mirror*'s Editor, who informed him that the paper was about to publish the story.

Two days later, Jack Straw took his son to Blackburn police station, where he asked the police to charge the 17-year-old with possession of cannabis. William Straw was arrested and released on bail.

Two days later, the *Daily Mirror* ran the story, but was legally barred from identifying the accused or his father. Meanwhile, the *Daily Mirror*'s reporter, Dawn Alford, had also been arrested for possession of marijuana and had then been freed on bail. The headline in The *Independent* read, 'Journalist arrested over drugs bought in "sting"' (30 December 1997, story by John Penman). It was reported that Scotland Yard took no further action against Alford.

On 12 January 1998, William Straw was cautioned by the police for the incident. For several days, many people had speculated as to which senior British Cabinet member had a son who allegedly sold drugs.

However, the Home Secretary had overlooked applying to the High Court for an *interdict* to cover Scotland at the same time as the injunction had been granted to cover the anonymity of the Home Secretary and his son in England. Therefore, there was nothing to stop the Scottish press from printing stories giving both identities. English law – in the form of the injunction and s. 39 of the *Children and Young Persons Act 1933* – prohibits English papers from publishing the names of those under the age of 18 involved in criminal proceedings. However, in the absence of an *interdict* from the High Court, the Scottish papers can happily roll off the press, as they can publish and name any juvenile involved in criminal proceedings from the age of 16. Three Scottish newspapers named both the Cabinet Minister and his son William Straw in the drug case. The *Scotsman* wrote, 'Straw's son cautioned in drug case' (13 January 1998). It was revealed that Internet newsgroups, such as alt.britain. politics, had also revealed the identity of the Minister. William's identity had been published extensively online and in newspapers in France.

Following the developments in Scotland and France, the *Sun* appealed against the (gagging) injunction. On 2 January 1998, the AG in the High Court lifted the injunction in Straw's son's case, saying that the restriction was 'no longer realistic'. The AG ruled that newspapers were now allowed to publish both names involved in the 'honey-trap' case. The *Sun* had won its right to publish the name of the Cabinet Minister Jack Straw.[11]

Only a few days later, on 5 January, Jack Straw was talking publicly about marijuana in the context of medical prescriptions. His view was that medical marijuana could be prescribed by doctors only after researchers proved that it had beneficial medical uses: 'The law does not say that, because a drug is classed as illegal, it therefore should not be available on prescription. What it does say, however, is that before drugs are available on prescription they've got to be properly tested and researched. ... So far the medical researchers have not been able to prove, indeed very few have tried, that there are real beneficial medicinal effects from cannabis' ('Straw rejects cannabis as a cure', the *Scotsman,* 5 January 1998).[12]

Case Study 3: The Orkney child abuse cases (1989–1993)[13]

Children's hearings are heard in private (in camera) and are presided over by three members of a children's panel. Such hearings usually minimise the number of people attending the hearing in order to safeguard and not intimidate the child. The media can be present, though, in reality, their attendance is rare – unless there is a high-profile case. Such was the situation regarding the Orkney hearings – well-publicised child abuse cases.

In the Orkney hearings it was alleged that nine children from three separate but closely related families had been abused while in social care. Specific allegations were made by the *ninth youngest* (E) about one of her older brothers sexually abusing her. On 22 June 1989, the youngest eight children were taken into care (under s. 37(2) of the *Social Work (Scotland) Act 1968*) on the basis of allegations of sexual abuse by siblings. Two (Q and S) were placed on Orkney and the other six in the Highland region. E was taken into care at the request of her mother. She remained there for six weeks before returning home.[14] The children in the Highland region were made the subject of Place on Safety Orders in that region on 26 June 1989.

On 11 July 1989, the grounds for referral to the children's hearing on Orkney related to those children whom the reporter had referred, were established in Kirkwall Sheriff Court. On the same day, two of the children in care in the Highland region – the two youngest boys, L and B – made formal statements to the police alleging that they had suffered sexual abuse by their eldest brother, who was then aged 21.

On 13 July 1989, a children's hearing decided that the children should return home under supervision, with a condition that they should not have contact with their older brothers. These older brothers, of whom there were four, ranging in ages from 17 to 21, left home to facilitate this. E, L and B all subsequently retracted their allegations.

All seven girls were taken into care and removed to mainland Scotland. Of these girls, four were medically examined on 12 November 1990 by a consultant paediatrician. All showed signs consistent with chronic penetrative vaginal abuse. It was believed that two girls were subjected to repeated sexual abuse while residing with W and other children of the family, following P's imprisonment. W always denied his guilt, which was never proved. At a children's hearing in Kirkwall on 12 November 1990, W denied that the alleged abuse had occurred as stated in the grounds of referral. An application was therefore made to have the grounds of referral established and, after the hearing in Kirkwall Sheriff Court on 12, 13 and 14 December 1990, they were established.[15]

Subsequently, the parents of the children (the petitioners) did not accept the grounds of referral. The petitioners took out an application of objection against the reporter to the children's panel for the Strathclyde region via the sheriff in June 1990 (under s. 42(2) of the *Social Work (Scotland) Act 1968*).[16]

What makes this case particularly interesting are the reporting orders and restrictions. Up until that time, the Scottish media had interpreted provisions under the *Social Work (Scotland) Act 1968* rather liberally when it came to showing photographs or TV images of children. At the start of the Orkney hearings in 1990, they would frequently show pictures of a child taken from behind or blank out (pixelate) their faces on TV. Although a sheriff has the discretion to exclude the press, this was never strictly exercised. However, as the Orkney hearings progressed, the presiding sheriff proceeded to order extremely strict reporting bans that were extended to protect the children under the age of 18, including all those children who had a Supervision Order in force. An additional order stated that there must be no newspaper, radio or television coverage of *any* of these Orkney hearings, any hearings before a sheriff or appeal hearings before the Court of Session. There followed a complete life-long ban on naming any of the children in the Orkney cases, revealing their addresses or schools, or any particulars calculated to lead to the identification of any child concerned by means of jigsaw identification, such as naming a parent or carer in a particular child's case.

The initial pictures taken of the children were not challenged in the courts until February 1993 in the case of Bette McArdle (Elizabeth Jean Stewart Anderson or McArdle), the Editor of the *Highland News*, which had shown pixelated and blanked-out photos of the children and mother. The Editor was charged with breaching ss. 42 and 58 of the *Social Work (Scotland) Act 1968* in relation to reports on the proceedings before the sheriff and a picture of a child concerned in these proceedings. The charge read:

> You, being the editor of the *Highland News* newspaper, did on 17th August 1991 at the premises occupied by the said *Highland News* newspaper at Henderson Road, Inverness, publish an edition of the said newspaper and the said edition contained a report of proceedings before the Sheriff under section 42 of the aftermentioned Act and a picture of a child concerned in the said proceedings: contrary to the *Social Work (Scotland) Act 1968*, section 58(1) and (2).

At the trial at Inverness Sheriff Court on 10 April 1992, Bette McArdle was found guilty and fined £250. She appealed to the High Court of Justiciary, but the AC dismissed her appeal. The court took the view that, as the sheriff had ordered that *all* pictures of children under the age of 18 involved in children's hearings were prohibited (under s. 58 of the *Social Work (Scotland) Act 1968,)*[17] – this was to be interpreted strictly: 'no reporting' and 'no pictures' meant no reporting and no pictures.[18]

Lessons to be learnt from the Orkney case are that children involved in children's hearings, as well as any appeal hearings, who are under the age of 18 cannot be reported on. In such proceedings, there is to be *no* reporting concerning the children, vulnerable people or witnesses under the age of 18. No photos must be shown, not even blanked-out or pixelated ones. Even if children are now over the age of 18 are involved, a sheriff has to determine if any present or future reporting on the child or young adult be permitted. It is common that the children are not named or given pseudonyms (see *O. v. Rae* [1992] (SCLR 318) (unreported) regarding the Orkney children's hearing and inquiry).

CASE STUDY

Case Study 4: Human rights issues – freedom of expression versus the right to privacy – Cox and Griffiths – the *Daily Record* case (1998)[20]

As indicated in the introduction to this chapter, a major challenge presented itself with the arrival of Peter Cox as Deputy Editor at the Glasgow-based *Daily Record* in 1998. In this case we are going to look at the *Daily Record's* challenging the law of contempt in relation to Art. 10 ECHR ('freedom of expression').

On 10 April 1998, Stuart Griffiths, a reporter, had written a story with the headline 'Armed convoy', and the subheading, 'gun cops on guard as prisoners switch jails'. The story was about a dozen high-risk prisoners who were transported 'under massive armed police guard' from Glasgow's Barlinnie Prison along the M8 motorway to Saughton Prison, near Edinburgh. The prisoners were to stand trial on heavy drugs and fraud charges at the High Court in Edinburgh on 14 April 1998. Griffiths further reported that the prisoners were described by prison and police sources as 'heavy-duty guys' and the police were working on the premise that 'someone might try to bust them'. He quoted a police insider: 'We are taking no chances on this lot. It was an impressive sight and part of an intricate plan to ensure these "heavy-duty guys" got to their destination. They are facing a lot of heavy charges.'

At the start of the trial, counsel for one of the accused asked the judge to adjourn proceedings until 17 April. He drew the judge's attention to the *Daily Record* article and submitted that it constituted a contempt of court in that the article had caused 'substantial risk of prejudice' and would seriously impede the forthcoming trial of the accused. Cox and Griffiths were charged under s. 1(1) *Contempt of Court Act 1981* under the 'strict liability rule' – that the article would seriously impede legal proceedings and the course of justice in relation to the impending trial. The petitioners Cox and Griffiths appeared before the trial judge and it was submitted on their behalf that the article did not constitute a contempt of court. The judge held the petitioners to be in contempt. A fine of £1500 was imposed on the Deputy Editor Peter Cox and the same on the author of the article, Stuart Griffiths. They appealed under *nobile officium* – that is, against the fine and the finding of contempt. Their appeal was based on the claim that the journalists' right to freedom of expression under Art. 10 ECHR had been infringed and relied on the fact that the *Human Rights Act 1998* had just been brought into Scottish legislation.

The appeal was dismissed on the grounds that the article appeared in a paper with a wide circulation in the Glasgow and Edinburgh areas within a week before the trial was to be held. It would therefore be highly likely that some of the jurors in the forthcoming proceedings would have read the article. In the appeal, the Lord Justice General, Lord Rodger, agreed with the original trial judge, stating that, 'in my view a juror might well make the connection' and using terms such as 'high-risk prisoners' and 'heavy-duty guys' may well have amounted to contempt.

Counsel for the appellants argued that readers of tabloids did not really believe everything they read in the popular press and stories were only written to entertain the masses rather than inform. They relied on *AG v. ITN* (see Chapter 4) in which the judge had said, 'that the odds against the potential juror reading any of the publications is multiplied by the long odds against a reader remembering it, [and] the risk of prejudice is, in my judgment, remote.[20]

Lord Rodger continued:

> Juries will often see that some accused are on bail, while others are held in custody, while still others are taken to and from court under conditions of particular security. There is nothing to suggest that jurors' awareness of these particular facts affects their ability to return a proper verdict based on the evidence which they have heard in court. ... There is similarly no reason to suppose that an article in a newspaper referring to security precautions will interfere with a juror's ability to judge the case properly.

However, in the end, Lord Rodger took a different view from the original trial judge in this case, who had attached particular importance to the words 'this lot' and 'these heavy-duty guys'. Eventually, Lord Rodger decided that the article did *not* amount to contempt:

> It seems to me that an attentive reader of the article would be likely to carry away an abiding impression that the prisoners concerned, as a group, were facing very serious charges and were people who, for that reason and perhaps for other reasons, the police considered had to be kept under tight security conditions in case someone engineered their escape.

He also examined the *Contempt of Court Act 1981* in the light of the new *Human Rights Act 1998*, with the 'freedom of expression', enshrined in the European Convention:

> It is important, however, to recall that the due course of justice is only one of the values with which the *Contempt of Court Act 1981* was concerned. The other value was freedom of expression. Parliament passed the 1981 Act in order to change the law of the United Kingdom and so to bring it into conformity with the interpretation of Art. 10 of the European Convention on Human Rights ... the Act was designed to regulate the boundary which had always, of course, existed between freedom of expression and the requirements of the due course of justice. ... That boundary may have been displaced from the familiar place where once it ran. ... Parliament may have redrawn the boundary at a point which would not have been chosen by people looking at the matter primarily from the administration of justice. ... But these factors simply make it all the more important that the course faithfully observe the boundary which Parliament has settled in order to meet the international obligations to the United Kingdom.

He felt that a juror who might have read the article and, after hearing the submissions of the Crown and the defence for the prisoners, was properly directed by the trial judge, would have been able to make up his or her own mind without being seriously impeded or prejudiced by the article. Lord Prosser agreed, stating that the 1981 Act was not only concerned with the due course of justice, but also the freedom of expression. He stated:

I think it worth emphasising that, quite apart from the 1981 Act and quite apart from the European Convention on Human Rights, there was in my opinion never any excuse for the courts extending the boundary, and diminishing freedom of speech, on the basis that some wider boundary is more convenient, or simpler, or provides a useful *cordon sanitaire* or the like. ... Just as Parliament, in defending the boundary, denies freedom of speech only where necessary, so the courts in applying the limitation on freedom need have no qualms about going to the boundary. ... On the outer side of the boundary, and right up to it, it seems to me that the press and public are entitled to express themselves as they wish, and I would regret it if they felt that the courts were discontented or critical, or felt entitled to tell them to keep further away.

Lord Prosser referred to the Kray twins case of 1969, quoting Lawton J:

I have enough confidence in my fellow countrymen to think that they have got newspapers sized up ... and they are capable in normal circumstances of looking at a matter fairly and without prejudice even though they have to disregard what they may have read in newspapers.[21]

Lord Prosser then turned to the present – Cox and Griffiths – appeal and said:

Anyone reading this particular article can see an element of drama, or indeed melodrama, in the way the whole events are described. One might add that it would be extremely boring if this were not so. ... At all events, it is not merely the language but the essence of the report that is telling the reader not merely that there is to be a serious trial, or that there are perhaps security problems, but that there are 'goings on' surrounding the trial which are of popular interest in a very familiar way. ... The atmosphere created, or re-created by the article seems to me to be fairly typically (and acceptably) 'tabloid' – but it is an atmosphere very familiar from television and indeed an atmosphere created in the first place (deliberately or otherwise) by the way in which 'high-risk' prisoners are normally conveyed to court by the police.

Finally, Lord Coulsfield agreed with his fellow lords to grant the appeal ('petition granted') and the finding of contempt was quashed.

The ruling in this case appears extremely liberal and shows a change in attitude on the part of the court in the light of the impending *Human Rights Act 1998*. The Scottish Appeal Court (Court of Sessions) put greater emphasis on a journalist's freedom of expression (Art. 10 ECHR) than on contempt and took a robust attitude to juries. However, there may be cases where newspapers will be dealt with for contempt in spite of the ruling in this case. Lord Prosser's distinction between broadsheets and tabloids also poses interesting questions and creates certain difficulties. Does this mean that the tabloid reader is to be taken less seriously than, for example the reader of the *Scotsman*? Their Lordships' approach in the Cox and Griffiths case has led to certain misunderstandings and paradoxical situations regarding tabloids and more serious Scottish papers, and the ruling is by no means clear.

Case Study 5: The supremacy of Parliament and Scots law – *MacCormick v. Lord Advocate* [1953] SC 396

Summary

In *MacCormick v. Lord Advocate* – an action regarding the legitimacy of the title 'Queen Elizabeth II' – Lord President Cooper hypothesised that, because the fundamental law of Scotland merged with that of England into the law of Great Britain at the time of the Treaty of Union in 1707, the supremacy of Parliament was extinguished. He also raised the question of whether or not such fundamental laws could be judged by an English or Scottish court in the same manner as other countries consider constitutional cases.

MacCormick, a prominent Scottish Nationalist raised an action against the government to prevent Her Majesty's ministers from causing her to be described as 'Elizabeth II'. The action took place just at the time of Queen Elizabeth's (II) Coronation. Scottish Nationalists such as MacCormick had long felt that England and English (legal) history dominated Scotland. The underlying question in this case was one of constitutional legitimacy.

MacCormick argued that Parliament had enacted a law purporting to confer the title of 'Elizabeth II' on the Queen, which was, in fact, a breach of the *Treaty of Union 1707* between Scotland and England. Among other things, the Treaty had guaranteed the continuing sovereignty of Scotland for all time. MacCormick further argued that the misdesignation of the Queen (as a monarch who reigns over Scotland and Great Britain, as well as England) was in breach of that guarantee, which meant that the Act was incompetent. He asked the court to strike out the 1707 Act.

The Court of Session found against MacCormick on the narrow grounds that, as a private person, he had no title to sue and the Queen's title was a matter of her own choice within the Royal Prerogative, untouchable by law.

During his judgment, Lord President Cooper called into question the hitherto judicially unchallenged doctrine of parliamentary sovereignty – the idea that Parliament has the power to make and unmake laws. He described this as a purely English concept with no counterpart in Scottish constitutional law and said:

> Considering that the Union legislation extinguished the parliaments of Scotland and England and replaced them by a new Parliament, I have difficulty in seeing why the new Parliament of Great Britain must inherit all the peculiar characteristics of the English Parliament but none of the Scottish. ... I have not found in the Union legislation any provision that the Parliament of Great Britain should be absolutely sovereign in the sense that Parliament should be free to alter the Treaty at will. ... Accepting for the moment that there are provisions in the Treaty which are 'fundamental law' and accepting for the moment that something has been done in breach of that fundamental law, the question remains whether such a question is determinable as a justiciable issue in the courts of

either Scotland or England in the same fashion as an instance of constitutional vires would be cognisable by the Supreme Courts of the United States or of South Africa or Australia. I reserve my opinion.

This celebrated case, with Lord President Cooper's famous reservations, leaves open the question whether Scottish courts can strike out an (English) Act of Parliament, as it is believed that Scots law is based on the *Treaty of Union*. In MacCormick, Lord Cooper in support of its claims to sovereign rule over Scotland, states on page 413 of Scottish Law Report: 'This is at least plain, that there is neither precedent nor authority of any kind for the view that the domestic Courts of either Scotland or England have jurisdiction to determine whether a Governmental act of the type in controversy is or is not conform to the provisions of a Treaty....'. MacCormick remains a symbolic case, affirming the distinctiveness and separation from the Scottish Constitution with the framework of the United Kingdom. This case became relevant once again during the conception of separate Scottish Parliament in 1999.

QUESTIONS

1 Explain the term 'legislation' in Scots law.

2 Name the sources of Scots law.

3 Explain the difference in court personnel between Scottish and English courts in criminal actions.

4 What is the main difference between the Scottish and English jury system in criminal procedure?

5 Describe the role of the sheriff in criminal proceedings.

6 What length of prison sentence may a sheriff impose in less serious (summary) cases?

7 Describe the role of the Lord Advocate.

8 Are you free to report on a 15-year-old boy who has been charged at a Glasgow police station with the murder of his 14-year-old girlfriend? Cite relevant statutory provisions and case law to back up your answers.

9 In the light of the Cox and Griffiths case, what is the impact of the *Human Rights Act 1998* on contempt of court?

Key thinkers

At the end of this chapter you may wish to study Scots law further or familiarise yourself with some of Scotland's prominent lawyers. Here are some suggestions.

John Knox (1514–72)

Knox was a notary in Haddington from 1540 to 1543. His greatest claim to fame was as one of the great leaders of the Reformation movement, which swept Europe during the sixteenth century. In the early days of the Reformation, he was imprisoned and sentenced to be a galley slave. He was a powerful preacher, and his most famous book was *The First Blast of the Trumpet against the Monstrous Regiment of Women* (1558, republished 1995, Edinburgh Akros).

James Boswell (1740–95)

Boswell was admitted as an advocate, but did not practise much during his lifetime. His fame comes from his close friendship with Dr Samuel Johnson, with whom he toured the Highlands and islands of Scotland. His most famous literary work is a biography – *The Life of Johnson* (1791, republished 1986, Harmondsworth: Penguin).

Sir Walter Scott (1771–1832)

Scott practised as an advocate in Edinburgh and the Borders for most of his working life. He was called to the Bar in 1792 and became Clerk of Session in Edinburgh in 1806. His first visit to the Highlands was on legal business, supervising an eviction. He is certainly better known as a great novelist of the nineteenth century – his work including *Rob Roy* (1817) and *Ivanhoe* (1819). He was a contemporary of Donizetti, Rossini, Bizet and Boïeldieu, who all wrote successful operas based on his novels. Sadly, though, he died in relative poverty.

Thomas Muir (1765–98)

As an advocate, Thomas Muir was one of the first fighters for human rights and civil liberties – he was known to take on the 'hopeless' cases. However, he is best known as one of the Scottish 'martyrs', fighting for Scottish independence and parliamentary reform in Scotland. In 1792, a 'Society for the Friends of the People' was formed to promote parliamentary reform. The government reacted strongly and Thomas Muir, a member of the Society, was convicted of treason. A group of radical reformers, including Muir, calling themselves the 'United Scotsmen' continued to meet in secret, but, after further trials, the movement broke up. Muir was arrested after supporting the French Revolution at a public meeting in Glasgow. He fled to France, but, after his return in 1793, he was arrested again and sentenced to 14 years transportation, being exiled to the prison colonies of Australia. George Washington personally ordered a warship to rescue him and bring him to America. Unfortunately, the ship, after picking up Muir, was shipwrecked in South America. After many adventures, Muir found his way to France and was made an honorary 'Citizen of the Republic'. He died in 1798 at the age of 33.

Donald Dewar (1937–2000)

A former Glasgow solicitor, Donald Dewar is best known for his political career and achievements with the Labour Party. When Labour won the 1997 General Election, Dewar, by then the longest-serving member of the Shadow Cabinet, was the obvious choice for Scottish Secretary, with responsibility for honouring Labour's commitment to a Scottish Parliament. He became First Minister of the Scottish Executive on 1 July 1999. Dewar's sponsorship of the complicated devolution legislation through Westminster and his leadership of the government campaign for a 'Yes' vote in the devolution referendum helped bring about home rule for Scotland.

Professor J. Ross Harper CBE (born 1935)

As a Glasgow solicitor, Ross Harper co-founded the firm of Ross Harper & Murphy in 1961 as well as Harper Macleod, engaging in corporate and commercial law in 1989, which is enjoying great success and Professor Harper remains Consultant with the firm. Ross Harper & Murphy is one of the largest law firms in Scotland. Now Professor Emeritus, he was appointed as Professor of Law at Strathclyde University in 1986, and was awarded an Honorary Doctorate for Services to Law at Glasgow University in 2002. He has a distinguished political career and has been active in many charitable activities, such as the Ross Harper Foundation. He was awarded a CBE for public and political services in 1986. He was President of the International Bar Association (1994–1996) and, prior to this, President of the Law Society of Scotland from 1988–1989. He has written a number of books on criminal law, including a book on the infamous 'Glasgow Rape Case' with Arnot McWhinnie (1983, Hutchinson).

Winnie Ewing (born 1929)

While a young mother, Mrs Ewing trained as a solicitor in Glasgow. In the 1967 Hamilton by-election, she took on the Labour establishment and won, in one of the first and most famous victories for the Scottish National Party. Mrs Ewing represented the Highlands and Islands constituency in the European Parliament for 24 years (from 1975 onwards) and became known as Madame Ecosse. On 12 May 1999, Dr Ewing took the chair at the first session of the new Scottish Parliament. At the age of 69 and the oldest Member of the Scottish Parliament (MSP for Highlands and Islands), the Scottish National Party's Winnie Ewing was first to take the oath on the stroke of 09.30 in the temporary Parliament building on the Mound in Edinburgh: 'The Scottish Parliament adjourned on the 25th day of March 1707 is hereby reconvened'. She repeated the words in Gaelic.

Lord Mackay of Clashfern (born 1927)

James Peter Hymers Mackay, born in Edinburgh on 2 July 1927, he came from a humble family (his father was a Highlands railway worker) and is known as one of the intellectually most brilliant Scotsmen – first in mathematics, then as a lawyer. In 1979, the then Prime Minister Margaret Thatcher invited Lord Mackay to become Lord Advocate. In the same year, he became a life peer. In 1984, he was appointed a Senator of the College of Justice in Scotland (a member of the Court of Session). In 1985, he became a Lord of Appeal in Ordinary – one of the two Scottish members of the Appellate Committee in the HL, the highest court in the UK. He was appointed Lord Chancellor on 27 October 1987. This unprecedented appointment of a 'foreign' lawyer as head of the English judiciary and legal system was a singular honour for Lord Mackay, and a mark of the respect in which he was held – by both the judiciary and his political colleagues. His ten years as Lord Chancellor (1987–97) were controversial as he pushed through some fundamental reforms (such as abolition of barristers' monopoly rights to plead in the higher courts). Now retired from politics and from the law lords, Lord Mackay occasionally sits as an honorary sheriff in the Highland town of Dingwall.

Ian Hamilton (born 1925)

Ian Hamilton QC, known for his busy life as an advocate, sheriff, university rector and amateur pilot, made legal history earlier on in his life. On Christmas Day 1950, Hamilton and three young Scottish Nationalists went to London with treason on their minds. They broke into Westminster Abbey and made off with the Stone of Destiny (the symbol of Scottish nationalism), which had been carried 'south of the border' by the victorious Edward I of England in 1307. What followed over the next few months was high farce as the stone – by now in pieces – was ferried around England and Scotland from one hiding place to another. Hamilton eventually surrendered the stone and it once again took its place under the coronation chair at Westminster Abbey. Ironically, 45 years later, the stone was returned to Scotland on the orders of the then fiercely unionist British government, anxious to show its support for Scotland. Three years later, Hamilton sued the government in the celebrated case of *MacCormick and Another v. Lord Advocate* [1953] (see above). The case was lost, but not without an important principle on Scotland's status under the *Treaty of Union 1707*.

FURTHER READING

Bonnington, A., McInnes, R., and McKain, B. (2000) *Scots Law for Journalists*, 7th edn. Edinburgh: W. Green/Sweet & Maxwell.

Walker, D. M. (1981) *Delict*, 2nd edn. Edinburgh: W. Green.

Notes

1 See D. M. Walker (1981) *Delict,* 2nd edn. Edinburgh: W. Green, p. 736.

2 The Scottish Legal Aid Scheme also known as the 'Assistance by Way of Representation (ABWOR) was introduced with the *Legal Aid (Scotland) Act 1986*. Criminal legal aid by means of ABWOR was brought into effect by the Scottish Legal Aid Board. The *Criminal Legal Aid (Scotland) (Fees) Amendment (No. 2) Regulations 2005* set out the fees and changes for ABWOR.

3 The case concerned a long-standing international police search for the Croatian (ex-Yugoslav) Secret Service – UDBA – Agent Vinko Sindicic. In 1988 he attempted to murder a Croat dissident, Nikola Stedul, in Kirkcaldy, Scotland. The attempt failed. Yugoslav diplomats put up an alibi for Sindicic, claiming that he had attended a Yugoslavia v. Scotland Football match. This attempt failed, as forensic evidence showed residue from firearms discharge in his skin. The case received press attention in the UK. The *Daily Mirror* ran the memorable headline 'Pet dog foils Red hitman's gun bid'. The High Court in Dunfermline – under a major security screen – sentenced him to 15 years' imprisonment for attempted murder after an 11-day trial. In 1998, Sindicic was extradited to Croatia, though he was wanted for a number of murders in the UK and elsewhere before and afterwards. One of these was Jill Dando's, the TV presenter, murdered on 26 April 1999; though in July 2001 Barry George was convicted of her murder. In March 2000, charges against Sindicic in relation to the murder of Croatian dissident Bruno Busic in Paris were thrown out for lack of evidence.

4 This is the age below which a child is considered to lack the mental capacity to commit a crime – also known as the doctrine of *doli incapax*.

5 Lord Kilbrandon (1964) 'Report of the Committee on Children and Young Persons, Scotland', known as the Kilbrandon Report, Cmnd 2306, HMSO

6 Section 44(1) of the *Criminal Procedure (Scotland) Act 1995* states that if a child who is under the supervision of the Children's Hearing System is found guilty of, or pleads guilty to, an offence in the High Court, then the court has the option of asking for a hearing to advise them as to disposal (the children and parents or guardian agree to a specific order). If this occurs in a sheriff court, then a hearing must advise on disposal.

7 Section 52(2) (a) (i) concerns a child who 'has committed an offence', while (j) and (k) are concerned with children involved in alcohol, drugs or substance misuse.

8 In 1998/99 some 42,457 referrals were made in relation to offences out of an overall total of 72,457 referrals.

9 Full story by Hillary Duncason and Russell Fallis, 'Jodi's teenage killer to spend 20 years behind bars' in the *Press and Journal*, 12 February 2005.

10 For further details, see Angela Taylor, 'P & J cleared of breaking law by naming Luke Mitchell', 19 February 2005 – visit: www.thisisnorthscotland.co.uk

11 John Burgess, 'British judge says press can publish name of Home Secretary's accused son', *Washington Post*, 5 January 1998, p. A15; Alexander MacLeod, 'Drug-fighter turns in his child, wins praise', *Christian Science Monitor*, 5 January 1998, p. 6; Ray Mosely, 'Son's drug case tests British aide's get-tough view', *Chicago Tribune*, 4 January 1997; Susan Taylor Martin, 'British marijuana law comes under attack', *St Petersburg Times*, 3 January 1998, p. A2.

12 See also Ian Brodie and Roger Boyes, 'Straw warns of perils of legalising cannabis', *The Times*, 5 January 1998. This was followed by the declassification of cannabis in English law (see David Wastell, 'MPs to press for inquiry into cannabis', the *Daily Telegraph*, 4 January 1998).

13 *F. v. Kennedy* (No. 1) (IH) [1992] SCLR 139: *F. v. Kennedy* (No. 2) (IH) [1992] SCLR 75: *H. v. Reporter for Strathclyde Region*, Court of Session, 6 December 1989 (unreported).

14 E (a minor) (Child Abuse: Evidence) [1991] 1 FLR 420.

15 See para. 2.36 of 'The Report of the Inquiry into the Removal of Children from Orkney in February 1991' (the Clyde Report), number 35/2 of process.

16 *L. and Others v. Kennedy* (Reporter to Children's Panel Strathelyde Region) [1993] SLT 1310.

17 Now also covered by s. 47 *Criminal Procedure (Scotland) Act 1995*.

18 *McArdle v. Orr* (Procurator Fiscal, Inverness) [1994] SLT 463; [1993] SCCR 437.

19 *Re. Cox and Another* [1998] (sub nom. Cox and Griffiths) SCCR 561.

20 [1995] 2 All ER 370.

21 Lawton J in *R. v. Kray* [1969] 53 Cr. App. R., at p. 414.

APPENDIX 1: GLOSSARY OF BRITISH PARLIAMENTARY AND LEGAL JARGON

A

Accused

The person charged. The person who has allegedly committed the offence.

Acquittal

Discharge of defendant following verdict or direction of not guilty.

Act of Parliament

Primary legislation; statute. Usually the House of Commons and the House of Lords both debate proposals for new laws and at this stage they are called bills.

Actual bodily harm (ABH)

It is an offence contrary to s. 47 of the *Offences Against the Person Act 1861* (OAPA) to commit an assault occasioning actual bodily harm. The *actus reus* (see also *actus reus*) of the offence consists of the actus reus for an assault or a battery plus a requirement that actual bodily harm is caused. The expression 'actual bodily harm' includes 'any harm … which interferes with the health or comfort of the victim'. See also grievous bodily harm.

Actus reus

Guilty act. The actions in the offence of which the defendant is accused: '*Actus non facit reum, nisi mens sit rea*' (an act does not make a person legally guilty unless the mind is legally blameworthy). It is a general principle of English criminal law that liability depends on proof of conduct (*actus reus*) and a guilty mind (*mens rea*). The proscribed behaviour, conduct or act contained within the definition of the offence. The *actus reus* of murder, for example, is the killing of a human being in the Queen's (or King's) peace.

Adjudication Judgment or decision of a court or tribunal.

Adversarial Refers to the common law justice system with a 'party prosecution' of a dispute. Parties (the Crown prosecutor and defence lawyer) present the facts to the court and have the primary responsibility for defining the issues in a legal dispute and for investigating and advancing the dispute – not the judge, as in France or Germany. See also inquisitorial.

Advocate A barrister or solicitor representing a party in a hearing before a court.

Affidavit A written statement of evidence confirmed on oath or by affirmation to be true and taken before someone who has authority to administer it.

Affirmation Declaration by a witness who has no religious belief, or has religious beliefs that prevent him or her taking the oath, that the evidence he or she is giving is the truth.

Alternative dispute resolution (ADR) An alternative method by means of which parties can resolve their dispute – this could be arbitration.

Annul To declare no longer valid.

Antecedents Information about an offender's background received in court as part of the sentencing process.

Appeal Application to a higher court or authority for review of a decision of a lower court or authority.

Appellant Person who appeals.

Applicant Person making the request or demand – a person who issues an application.

Application The act of applying to a court.

Arson See **criminal damage**.

ASBO Anti-social behaviour order. This is a civil order, but criminal standards apply. *Crime and Disorder Act 1998.*

Assault Actual physical (or verbal, psychological) injury to a person. The defendant can be charged with either grievous bodily harm (GBH) or assault occasioning actual bodily harm (ABH) under the *Offences Against the Person Act 1861*. ABH is a relatively minor assault and GBH is a more serious injury (both triable either-way) Bruising or scratching is regarded as 'common assault' (Summary offence).

Attorney General (AG)	Government's principal legal adviser. Usually an MP, he or she provides advice on a range of legal matters, including prepared legislation. The AG has the final responsibility for criminal law. His deputy is the Solicitor General.

B

Backbencher	MP or peer (in the House of Lords) who holds no official position in government or in his or her party. Backbenchers sit on the back benches (seats) in the House of Commons or House of Lords on either side of the chamber that are not occupied by government or opposition spokespeople.
Bail	Release of a defendant from custody until his or her next appearance in court, subject sometimes to security being given and/or compliance with certain conditions.
Bailiff	Officer of a county court empowered to serve court documents and execute warrants.
Bankrupt	Insolvent – unable to pay creditors and having all goods/effects administered by a liquidator or trustee and sold for the benefit of creditors as a result of an order under the *Insolvency Act 1986*.
Bar	The collective term for barristers.
Barrister	See also **silk**. A member of the Bar – the branch of the legal profession that has rights of audience before all courts.
Basic intent crimes	An offence in which recklessness will suffice. Offences of basic intent include:

- involuntary manslaughter – *Lipman* [1970]
- rape, sexual offences (*Sexual Offences Act 1956*, s.1)
- malicious wounding, GBH (OAPA 1861, s. 20) – *Majewski* [1987] HL
- criminal damage (*Criminal Damage Act 1971*, s.1(1)) *R. v. G. and another* [2003] UKHL 50.
- ABH (OAPA 1861, s. 47)
- common assault and battery (CJA 1988, s. 39).

Battery	A person is guilty of battery if he or she intentionally or recklessly applies unlawful force to the body of another person (CJA 1988, s. 39) – see *Fagan v. Metropolitan Police Commissioner* [1969] 1 QB 439.
Bench warrant	A warrant issued by a judge for an absent defendant to be arrested and brought before a court by the police.

Bill	Proposal for a new law, which is debated by Parliament. A Bill becomes an Act when it has received Royal assent. A Bill may be introduced into either House, with the exception of money Bills, which the Lords cannot initiate or amend. See also **Act of Parliament**.
Bill of indictment	A written statement of the charges against a defendant sent for trial to the Crown Court and signed by an officer of the court.
Bind over	Form of sentence of unspecified date in a magistrates' (rarely in the Crown) court, signed by an officer of the court. Failure to observe this order may result in a forfeit or penalty being enforced.
Brief	Written instructions to counsel to appear at a hearing on behalf of a party, prepared by the solicitor and setting out the facts of the case and any case law that will be relied on.
Burden of proof	In general, the prosecution must prove the defendant's guilt beyond any reasonable doubt (see *Woolmington v. DPP* [1935] HL). See also **insanity** and **diminished responsibility**.
Burglary	Trespassing upon another's property and stealing or attempting to steal.
C	
Case	Lawsuit. Comprehensive term for any proceeding in a court whereby an individual seeks a legal remedy (such as against a landlord in civil law or the Crown against a defendant in criminal law).
Case law	Also known as common law or judge-made law. Refers to judges' decisions when they try a case. Decisions are known as 'judgments'.
Case name	Each legal case in court is given a name – usually based on the family name of the parties involved such *R. v. Smith* (R. = Rex/Regina) – the Crown's case against (versus) Smith.
Case number	A unique reference number allocated to each case by the issuing court.
Case to answer	The prosecution evidence must always be sufficient in itself to support a conviction or the charge must be dismissed on the ground that there is 'no case to answer'.
Caution	Warning given by a police officer to a person charged with an offence or warning given by a police officer instead of a charge.

CCRC	Criminal Cases Review Commission.
CDH	Criminal Directions Hearing. Hearing by a bench, single magistrate or justices' clerk (or legal adviser) to deal with issues of case management.
Chambers	Private room or court from which the public is excluded in which a district judge (DJ) or judge may conduct certain sorts of hearings. Also, offices used by a barrister.
Charge	A formal accusation against a person that a criminal offence has been committed.
CICA	Criminal Injuries Compensation Authority.
Circuit judge	A judge who sits in a county court and/or Crown Court.
Civil	Matters concerning private rights, not offences against the State.
Civil justice reforms	The result of the 'Access to Justice' report by Lord Woolf (1999). The aim was to provide more effective access to justice via quicker, cheaper and more proportionate justice for defended cases. It introduced a unified set of Rules and Practice Directions for the county and High Courts and judicial case management.
CJA	*Criminal Justice Act*, such as CJA 2003.
Claimant	The person issuing the claim. Also known as the plaintiff.
Committal	'Committal for trial' – following examination by magistrates of a case involving an indictable or either-way offence, the procedure of directing the case to the Crown Court to be dealt with there because of the seriousness of the offence. 'Committal for sentence' – when the magistrates consider that the offence justifies a sentence more severe than they are empowered to impose, they may commit the defendant to a Crown Court for the sentence to be passed by a judge. 'Committal Order' – an order of the court committing someone to prison.
Common law	The law established, by precedent, from judicial decisions and established within a community. See also **case law**.
Community sentence	Single 'community punishment' order under CJA 2003 with a number of options attached (such as unpaid

work in the community) available to justices instead of a prison sentence.

Compensation order	Sum of money demanded to make up for or make amends for loss, breakage, hardship, inconvenience or personal injury caused by another (*Crime and Disorder Act 1998*).
Concurrent sentence	A direction by a court that a number of sentences of imprisonment should run at the same time.
Conditional discharge (CD)	A form of sentence. The convicted defendant is discharged on condition that he does not reoffend within a specified period of time.
Consecutive sentence	An order for a subsequent sentence of imprisonment to commence as soon as a previous sentence expires, so it applies to two or more sentences.
Contempt of court	Disobedience or wilful disregard for the judicial process (*Contempt of Court Act 1981*).
Counsel	A barrister.
Count	An individual offence set out in an indictment.
Court of Appeal (CA)	Divided into:

- Civil Division
- Criminal Division. Hears appeals:
  - from decisions in the High Court and county courts
  - against convictions or sentences passed by the Crown Court.

Court room	The room in which cases are heard.
CPS	Crown Prosecution Service.
Crime	An activity that is classified as such within the criminal laws of a country. Specific form of deviance; breaking of legal State norms (rules). See also deviance.
Criminal	Person who has been found guilty of a criminal offence.
Criminal damage	Section 1(3) of the *Criminal Damage Act 1971* provides that a person who, without lawful excuse, destroys or damages any property belonging to another, intending to destroy or damage such property, or being reckless as to whether or not any such property would be destroyed or damaged, is guilty of an offence punishable on conviction on indictment with imprisonment for a maximum of ten years.

Section 1(2) provides that a person who, without lawful excuse, destroys or damages any property whether belonging to him- or herself or another (a) intending to destroy or damage any property or being reckless as to whether or not any property would be destroyed or damaged, and (b) intending by the destruction or damage to endanger the life of another or being reckless as to whether or not the life of another would be thereby endangered is guilty of an offence.

If the damage or destruction is caused by fire, the offence is charged as arson and is punishable with a maximum of imprisonment for life (s. 1(3)).

The Crown Court deals with all crime committed for trial by magistrates' courts. Cases for trial are heard before a judge and jury. The Crown Court also acts as an appeal court for cases heard and dealt with by the magistrates.

Crown Court

The Crown Court is divided into tiers, depending on the type of work dealt with.

The first tier deals with:

- defended High Court civil work
- all classes of offence in criminal proceedings
- committals for sentencing from magistrates' courts
- appeals against convictions and sentences imposed at magistrates' courts.

The second tier deals with:

- all classes of offences in criminal proceedings
- committals for sentencing from magistrates' courts.
- appeals against convictions and sentences imposed at magistrates' courts.

The third tier deals with:

- class 4 offences only in criminal proceedings
- committals for sentencing from magistrates' courts
- appeals against convictions and sentences.

D

Damages

An amount of money claimed as compensation for physical or material loss, such as personal injury or breach of contract (ordered in a civil court).

DCA

Department of Constitutional Affairs (replaced the Lord Chancellor's Department).

Defendant	Person standing trial in a criminal court – the accused.
Devolution	Decentralisation of government's power, such as setting up the Scottish Parliament, National Assembly for Wales and Northern Ireland Assembly.
Diminished responsibility	The *Homicide Act 1957* s.2 (1) provides that, 'Where a person kills or is a party to the killing of another, he shall not be convicted of murder if he was suffering from such abnormality of mind (whether arising from a condition of arrested or retarded development of mind or any inherent causes or induced by disease or injury) as substantially impaired his mental responsibility for his acts and omissions in doing or being a party to the killing.' A successful plea of diminished responsibility reduces liability from murder to manslaughter (s. 2(3)).
Disclosure	Inspection of legal documents and evidential material. The mutual exchange of evidence by prosecution and defence of all relevant information held by each party relating to the case.
Discontinuance	Notice given by the court, on instruction from the CPS, that it no longer wishes to proceed with the case. The CPS may reopen the case at any time.
Dismissal	Notice given to a court by the CPS that the case is dismissed.
District judge	A judicial officer of the court whose duties involve hearing applications made within proceedings and final hearings subject to any limit of jurisdiction (previously known as a stipendiary magistrate).
Divisional Court	As well as having an original jurisdiction of their own, all three divisions of the High Court have appellate jurisdiction to hear appeals from lower courts and tribunals. The Divisional Court of the Chancery Division deals with appeals in bankruptcy matters from county courts. The Divisional Court of the Queen's Bench Division deals largely with certain appeals on points of law from many courts. The Divisional Court of the Family Division deals largely with appeals from magistrates' courts in matrimonial matters.
Dock	Enclosure in a criminal courtroom for the defendant to sit or stand in during the trial.

DTTO	Drug Treatment and Testing Order – part of a community sentence.
E	
ECHR	European Convention on Human Rights and Fundamental Freedoms (the Convention). Also stands for the European Court of Human Rights in Strasburg.
Either-way offence	An offence for which the accused may elect that the case be dealt with either summarily by magistrates or by committal to a Crown Court to be tried by jury.
Estate	Rights and assets of a person regarding property.
European Parliament	Directly elected democratic Parliament of Europe. All 25 MS that belong to the EU are entitled to send representatives to the Parliament in Brussels.
Execution	Seizing of debtors' goods following non-payment of a court order.
Executor(s)	A person or people specified to carry out the provisions of a will.
Exempt	Free from liability.
Exhibit	Item or document referred to and used as evidence during a court trial.
Ex parte	In the absence of a party to the proceedings. Usually means a one-sided application under judicial review. Now termed 'on the application of'.
Expert witness	A qualified person giving evidence on a subject in which they have expertise in a trial, such as a medical practitioner, forensic examiner or computer specialist. Experts can give evidence of opinion and be given permission by the court to sit in court to hear other witnesses before they give evidence.
F	
Fee	Monies payable on issue of a claim or subsequent process, such as a statutory declaration made in a magistrates' court.
Fraud	Obtaining property by deception.
G	
GBH	Grievous bodily harm, defined in *DPP v. Smith* as meaning 'really serious harm'. GBH also includes psychological harm (see *Burstow* [1998] HL).

Going equipped	To carry out a theft or burglary or cheat (contrary to the *Theft Act 1968*).
Guardian	A person appointed by the court to safeguard, protect or manage the interests of a child or person with a mental disability.

H

Handling	Stolen property.
Hansard	Official report of the proceedings of Parliament, published daily when Parliament is sitting. Records everything that is said and done in both the House of Commons and House of Lords.
Hate crime	Group harms that are aimed at specific minority groups, such as homosexuals. Hate crimes involve racial intimidation, ethnicity, religion or other attacks on minority groups, including assaults, graffiti and property attacks.
HDC	Home Detention Curfew. Also known as electronic tagging.
Hereditary peers	In the HL, peers inherit their titles, which have five ranks – duke, marquess, earl, viscount and baron. Peerages may become extinct or fall into abeyance, but, so long as there is an heir, the title will continue.
High Court	A civil court that consists of three divisions: • Queen's Bench Division (can be known as King's Bench Division if a king is on the throne) – deals with civil disputes for recovery of money, including breach of contract, personal injuries, libel/slander • Family – concerned with matrimonial matters and proceedings relating to children, such as wardship • Chancery – deals with property matters, including fraud and bankruptcy.
Homicide	There are a number of offences involving homicide. The two most important are murder and manslaughter. They share a common *actus reus* – the killing of a human being. Involuntary manslaughter differs from murder in terms of the *mens rea* required, whereas it is the availability of one of a number of specific defences that distinguishes voluntary manslaughter form murder. See: **provocation**, **diminished responsibility** and **intention**.
Hostile witness	A witness seemingly biased against the person calling them as a witness and evading what they had said in a previous, out-of-court, statement. If the court agrees, they can be cross-examined by the person calling them.

Glossary

House of Commons	Lower chamber of the UK Parliament where elected MPs sit in debates.
House of Lords (HL)	Upper chamber of the UK Parliament, made up of appointed and hereditary peers. HL – law lords – acts as the final court on points of law for the UK in civil cases, and for England, Wales and Northern Ireland in criminal cases. Its decisions bind all courts below it.
HRA	*Human Rights Act 1998*
In camera	In private. Exceptionally, the public – but not necessarily the media – can be excluded from court proceedings. Magistrates or judges sit in private. Usually used for youth or family courts.
Indictable offence	A criminal offence triable only by the Crown Court. The different types of offence are classified as 1, 2, 3 or 4. Murder is a Class 1 offence.
Injunction	An order by a court either restraining a person or persons from carrying out a course of action or directing a course of action to be complied with. Failure to carry out the terms of the order may be punishable by imprisonment.
Inquisitorial	Refers to civil code justice systems (such as those in Germany, France, Spain and Greece) in which the 'inquisitorial' judge has primary responsibility for investigating a case.
Insanity	As the defence of insanity concerns the effect of psychological conditions on responsibility, the question as to whether or not a defendant can take advantage of this defence is a legal one and is not resolved simply by reference to the medical evidence. The legal definition of insanity is contained in the M'Naghten Rules (1843):

1 Everyone is presumed sane until the contrary is proved.
2 It is a defence for the defendant to prove that he was labouring under a defect of reason, due to disease of the mind, such that he either did not know the nature and quality of his act or, if he did know that, he did not know that what he was doing was wrong.

Intention (*mens rea*)	The *mens rea* for a number of offences is defined in terms of 'intention' or 'with intent to ... ', or 'intentionally', indicating that recklessness will not suffice. Where it is not the defendant's aim or purpose, but he or she foresaw that it was a virtually certain result of his actions,

then the jury may infer that he intended it (see *Moloney* [1985] HL; *Hancock and Shankland* [1986] HL; *Nedrick* [1986] CA; *Savage and Parmenter* [1991] HL).

Intoxication	Although a lack of *mens rea* caused by voluntary intoxication will 'excuse' a crime of 'specific intent', the defendant may be convicted of an offence of 'basic intent' despite his lack of *mens rea* (see *Majewski* [1987] HL; *Lipman* [1970]).

J

J.	Chief Justice (sometimes followed by K.B. or Q.B. for King's or Queen's Bench)
J.O.	Judge Ordinary (Divorce Court).
John Doe Order	Injunction that binds the world at large to not disclosing the contents or material of a book or article to any unnamed and presently unknown people who wrongfully come into possession of the original piece of work and who seek to disclose its contents to the public at large.
Judge	An officer appointed to administer the law and who has the authority to hear and try cases in a court of law.
Judgment	The final decision of a court.
Judicial/Judiciary	Relating to the administration of justice or to the judgment of a Court. Also, a judge or other officer empowered to act as a judge.
Jurisdiction	The area and matters over which a court has legal authority.
Juror	A person who has been summoned by a court to be a member of the jury. See also **jury**.
Jury	Body of jurors sworn to reach a verdict according to the evidence in a Crown Court (or the High Court in defamation – for example, libel – actions; also in an inquest).
Justice of the peace (JP)	A lay magistrate. A member of the public who has been appointed to administer judicial business in a magistrates' court. It is an unpaid role and a JP is usually not a lawyer. Also sits in a Crown Court with a judge or recorder to hear appeals and committals for sentence.
Juvenile	Person under 18 years of age.

L

Law	The system made up of rules established by an act of Parliament, custom or practice enjoining or prohibiting certain actions. See also **common law**.

Law lords	Also called Lords of Appeal in Ordinary. They are senior judges (or holders of high judicial offices) who are given life peerages in order to carry out the judicial work of the House of Lords (HL). See also **House of Lords**.
Law reports	Record of 'test' cases that lay down important legal principles. Over 2000 law reports are published each year. An example is the *All England Law Reports* – known in short as All ER. Each case is given a reference to explain where exactly it can be found – that is, the year, volume, such as the criminal appeal reports – Cr. App. R. – or Queen's Bench Division – QBD – and page number.
Limited right	Right by virtue of the HRA so that, within the scope of the limitation, the infringement of a guaranteed right may not contravene the Convention. See **HRA**.
Litigation	Legal proceedings.
Lord Chancellor (L.C.) (Lord Smith of London, L.C.)	Cabinet minister who acts as Speaker of the House of Lords and oversees the hearings of the Law Lords. Responsibilities include supervising the procedures of courts other than magistrates' or coroners' courts and the selection of judges, magistrates, Queen's Counsel and members of tribunals. See also **DCA**.
Lord Chief Justice	Senior judge of the Court of Appeal (Criminal Division) who also heads the Queen's Bench Division of the High Court.
Lord Justice of Appeal	Title given to certain judges sitting in the Court of Appeal (CA).
M	
Magistrate	Another name for justice of the peace (JP). Carries out legal duties in the local criminal court (see also magistrates' court). JPs are unpaid lay persons who are not legally qualified. They deal with most criminal cases involving the less serious offences (summary and triable either-way, such as minor theft, criminal damage, public disorder and motoring offences). When sitting in a family court, they deal with a range of issues affecting families and children and, on special committees, they deal with gaming and betting-shop applications.
Magistrates' court	A court where criminal proceedings are commenced before justices of the peace (JPs) who examine the evidence and/or statements and either deal with the case themselves or commit it to a Crown Court for trial or

sentence. Also has jurisdiction in a range of civil matters, such as a family court.

Malice aforethought

A misleading term, signifying the *mens rea* for murder – that is, an intention to kill or cause grievous bodily harm (GBH).

Malicious wounding

Inflicting grievous bodily harm (see **GBH**). This is an offence under s. 20 OAPA 1861, punishable by a term of imprisonment not exceeding five years. GBH can include very serious psychological harm as well as physical injury (see *Ireland and Burstow* [1998] HL).

Manslaughter

There are several modes of committing manslaughter:

1. *Constructive manslaughter* Also known as 'killing by an unlawful act', this offence is committed where the defendant *intentionally* commits an unlawful and dangerous act resulting in death.
2. *'Reckless' manslaughter* requires Caldwell-type recklessness (see **recklessness**) in terms of some injury.
3. *Provocation – manslaughter* A person (the defendant), who killed with malice aforethought will, nevertheless, be acquitted of murder and convicted of manslaughter if, at the time of the killing, he or she, as a result of *provocation*, suffered a sudden and temporary loss of self-control and the jury is satisfied that any reasonable person would, in the circumstances, have done as the defendant did.
4. *Diminished responsibility – manslaughter* If the defendant killed with malice aforethought but was, at the relevant time, suffering from diminished responsibility then he or she will be convicted of manslaughter (see *Ahluwalia* [1993]).

Master of the Rolls (MR)

Senior judge of the Court of Appeal (Civil Division).

MCA

Magistrates Courts Act 1980.

McKenzie friend

Unqualified person who can be allowed by the court to assist a defendant informally. The name 'McKenzie friend' technically disappeared after a Leicester community charge case, although it is often still used. The defendant has a right to such assistance, unless there are compelling reasons to disallow it.

Member of Parliament (MP)

Elected by a particular area or constituency in Britain to represent its people in the House of Commons. An MP represents all people in his or her constituency and can ask government ministers questions, speak about issues

	in the House of Commons and consider and propose new laws.
Mens rea	The term refers to the state of mind expressly or impliedly required by the definition of the offence charged. Most serious (and certain lesser) crimes require the prosecutor to establish some mental element, such as an intention to or recklessness concerning an assault or criminal damage (see also *actus reus*). In the case of murder, the prosecution must prove that the defendant intended to kill or cause some serious harm to the person.
Ministers	Make up a government (members of the House of Commons or the HL). There are three main types of minister: departmental ministers, ministers of state and junior ministers.
Minor	Someone below 18 years of age and unable to sue or be sued without representation, other than for wages. A minor sues by a next friend and defends by a guardian. See also **guardian** and **next friend**.
Mitigation	Reasons submitted on behalf of a guilty party in order to excuse or partly excuse the offence committed, in an attempt to minimise the sentence.
Murder	Murder is committed when the defendant, *intending* to kill or cause grievous bodily harm (GBH), caused the death of a human being. The offence carries a mandatory penalty of imprisonment for life (life imprisonment, life sentence).

N

Newton hearing	A 'trial within a trial' to determine the facts in the event of dispute following a 'guilty' plea, such as the amount stolen or whether injuries were caused by fists or feet.
Next friend	A person representing a minor or mental patient who is involved in legal proceedings. See also **guardian** and **minor**.
Non-molestation	An order within an injunction to prevent one person from physically attacking another.
NPS	National Probation Service.

O

Oath	A verbal promise by a person with religious beliefs to tell the truth.

Official solicitor	A solicitor or barrister appointed by the Lord Chancellor and working in the Lord Chancellor's Department (now Department of Constitutional Affairs – DCA). The duties include representing, in legal proceedings, people who are incapable of looking after their own affairs – that is, children or those suffering from mental illness.
Ombudsman	Alternatively, Parliamentary Commissioner for Administration – the Parliamentary Ombudsman. Investigates complaints from members of the public about government departments, has wide powers to obtain evidence and makes recommendations about cases he or she hears. All cases heard must be referred to the Ombudsman by an MP.
Omission	Apart from those offences defined specifically in terms of an 'omission to act', English law imposes liability for omissions only where it can be said that the defendant was under a duty to act. There is no general obligation to act for the benefit of others. The duty to act to save or preserve the life of another arises only in a number of stereotyped situations, such as parental duty or a doctor's duty. See *Airdale NHS Trust v. Bland* [1993] HL.
Open justice principle	The public (and media) have the statutory right to attend most court proceedings, unless they are held in camera. See **in camera**.
Oral examination	A method of questioning a person under oath before an officer of the court to obtain details of their financial affairs.
Order	A direction by a court.
Original offence	When an offender breaches certain court orders (such as a community sentence), he or she can be dealt with for the original offence as well as for any new offence.

P

Parliament	The British Parliament is made up of three parts: the Crown, House of Lords and House of Commons. Parliament is where new laws are debated and agreed.
Party	Any one of the participants in a court action or proceedings.
Penal notice	Directions attached to an order of a court stating that the penalty for disobedience may result in imprisonment.

Personal application	Application made to the court without legal representation.
Plea	A defendant's reply to a charge put to him or her by a court – that is, guilty or not guilty.
Power of arrest	An order attached to some injunctions to allow the police to arrest a person who has broken the terms of the order.
Precedent	The decision of a case that established principles of law that act as an authority for future cases of a similar nature.
Pre-trial review (PTR)	A preliminary appointment at which magistrates or a district judge consider the issues before the court and fix the timetable for the trial; now also: case management hearing.
Prosecution	The institution or conduct of criminal proceedings against a person. See also **CPS**.
Prosecutor	Person who prosecutes. See also **prosecution** and **CPS**.
Provocation	A common law defence, amended by s. 3 of the *Homicide Act 1957*. It is a defence to murder only and applies where the defendent. killed the victim with *malice aforethought* but acted under a sudden and temporary loss of self-control (see **malice aforethought**).
PSR	Pre-sentence Report, produced by the National Probation Service (NPS).

Q

Qualified right	Right by virtue of the *Human Rights Act 1998* (HRA) that, in certain circumstances and under certain conditions, can be interfered with.
Quash	To annul – that is, declare a sentence no longer valid.
Queen's Bench Division	See **High Court**.
Queen's Counsel (QC)	Barristers of at least ten years' standing may apply to become Queen's Counsel. QCs undertake work of an important nature and are referred to as 'silks', derived from the court gown that is worn. Will be known as King's Counsel if a king assumes the throne.

R

Race	Process of social construction and social role model that occurs via the various means of socialisation, such as family, school, peers and so on. Racial

classifications, a product of labelling over time outside of the family.

Recklessness

For most offences, recklessness as to whether or not a particular consequence will result from the defendant's actions, or as to whether or not a particular circumstance exists, will suffice for liability. For certain crimes, recklessness bears a broader meaning. This used to be determined by the Caldwell-type (objective) recklessness, but has now been superseded by the ruling in *R. v. G* [2003] HL. Therefore, the 'reasonable person test' will now no longer apply. Now for criminal damage (including arson) Cunningham-type (subjective) recklessness applies, which imposes on the prosecution the burden of proving that the defendant him- or herself was aware of the particular risk of the consequence occurring or the circumstance existing (see *Caldwell* [1982] HL; *Cunningham* [1957]).

Recorder

Member of the legal profession (a barrister or solicitor) who is appointed to act in a judicial capacity.

Registrar

Registrars and deputy registrars were renamed district judges and deputy district judges respectively in the *Courts and Legal Services Act 1990*. See also **district judge**.

Remand

To order an accused person to be kept in custody or placed on bail pending further court appearances.

Reparation order

An object of sentencing (and a form of sentence operating only in the youth court) – that is, reparation to a victim. The term is also used more generally to mean 'making good' by a defendant and may feature in mitigation. It is also a statutory basis for deferment of sentence under the *Crime and Disorder Act 1998*.

Reprimand

Whereas an adult may be cautioned, a juvenile who admits an offence may be reprimanded or warned by the police under a statutory scheme, instead of being prosecuted.

Restorative justice

A form of criminal justice that seeks to 'repair' harm, as between offenders and victims (*Crime and Disorder Act 1998*).

Right of audience

The entitlement to appear before a court in a legal capacity and conduct proceedings on behalf of a party to the proceedings such as a solicitor.

Robbery

Theft, or threat of theft, by force or intimidation of another.

Royal asssent (RA)	The monarch's agreement to make a Bill into an Act of Parliament. The monarch has the right to refuse RA, but this really does not happen.
S	
Security	Deposit (see **surety**) or other item of value left with the court on grant of bail.
Sex offender register	Local record maintained by the police for which certain sex offenders are obliged to provide information about themselves and their whereabouts.
SI	See **statutory instrument**.
Silk	See **Queen's Counsel**. A senior barrister, sometimes referred to as a leader or leading counsel.
Slander	Spoken words that have a damaging effect on a person's reputation.
Solicitor	Member of the legal profession chiefly concerned with advising clients and preparing their cases and representing them in some courts. May also act as an advocate before certain courts or tribunals, but not generally in Crown Courts.
Specific intent crimes	An offence of specific intent is one for which the prosecution must prove intention in relation to one or more of the elements in the *actus reus*. Recklessness will not suffice (see **basic intent crimes**). The significance of the distinction between offences of specific intent and basic intent is that whereas a lack of *mens rea* resulting from voluntary intoxication will excuse in the case of an offence of specific intent, it will not excuse the defendant for crimes of basic intent. Specific intent crimes include:
	• murder (*Beard* [1920])
	• GBH with intent (s. 18 OAPA 1861; *Bratty* [1963])
	• theft (s. 1 *Theft Act 1968*; *Majewski* [1987];
	• burglary with intent to steal (s. 9 *Theft Act 1968*; *Durante* [1972]).
Statement	A written account by a witness of the facts or details of a matter.
Statutory instrument (SI)	Rules or regulations named within an Act of Parliament and made by a minister of state. SIs affect the practical workings of the original Act (such as the Prison Rules 1999 under the *Prison Act 1952*). Also called 'delegated legislation' or 'secondary legislation'.

Stay of execution	An order following which judgment cannot be enforced without leave of the court.
Strict liability	Not all offences require proof of *mens rea*. By a crime of strict liability is meant an offence of which a person may be convicted without proof of intention (*mens rea*), recklessness or even negligence. The prosecution is only obliged to prove the commission of the *actus reus* and the absence of any recognised defence (see *Adomako* [1998]).
Subpoena	A summons issued to a person directing their attendance in court to give evidence.
Summary offence	A minor criminal offence that is triable only in a magistrates' court. See also **indictable offence** and **either-way offence**.
Summing-up	A review of the evidence and directions as to the law by a judge immediately before a jury retires to consider its verdict.
Summons	Order to appear or to produce evidence to a court.
Summons (jury)	Court order to attend for jury service.
Summons (witness)	Court order to appear as a witness at a hearing.
Supreme Court of Judicature	Collective name for the High Court of Justice, Crown Courts and Court of Appeal.
Surety	A person 'stands surety' – that is, gives an undertaking to be liable for another's default or non-attendance at court.
Suspended sentence	A custodial sentence that will not take effect unless there is a subsequent offence within a specified period.
T	
Tagging	Electronic tagging or monitoring. Used with a home detention curfew order (HDC).
Theft	To dishonestly appropriate property belonging to another with the intention of permanently depriving them of it.
Tort	A civil wrong committed against a person for which compensation may be sought via a civil court, such as for personal injury, neighbourhood nuisance, libel and so on.
Tribunal	A group of people consisting of a chairman (sometimes a solicitor or barrister) and others who exercise a

judicial function to determine matters related to specific interests. An example would be an employment tribunal.

V

Verdict

The finding of guilty or not guilty by a jury.

Victim

The victim of an offence – sometimes called the aggrieved.

W

Ward of court

The title given to a minor who is the subject of a ward-ship order. The order ensures that custody of the minor is held by the court, with day-to-day care of the minor being carried out by an individual(s) or local authority. As long as the minor remains a ward of court, all decisions regarding the minor's upbringing must be approved by the court – transfer to a different school, or medical treatment, for example.

Wardship

High Court action making a minor a ward of court.

Warning

'Final warning' under the statutory scheme of reprimands and warnings, for juveniles only.

Warrant of delivery

Method of enforcing a judgment for the return of goods (or value of the goods) whereby a bailiff is authorised to recover the goods (or their value) from the debtor and return them to the creditor.

Warrant of execution

Method of enforcing a judgment for a sum of money whereby a bailiff is authorised, in lieu of payment, to seize and remove goods belonging to a defendant for sale at public auction.

Warrant of possession

Method of enforcing a judgment for possession of a property whereby a bailiff is authorised to evict people and secure it against their re-entry.

Warrant of restitution

A remedy available following illegal re-entry of premises by persons evicted under a warrant of possession. The bailiff is authorised to evict all occupants found on the premises and redeliver the premises to the plaintiff.

White paper

Document produced by government setting out details of future policy on a particular subject. A white paper is the basis for a Bill before Parliament. A white paper allows government an opportunity to gather feedback before it formally presents the policies as a Bill. See also **Bill**.

Witness	A person who gives evidence in court.
Wounding or malicious Wounding with intent	Wounding – causing grievous bodily harm *with intent* (*mens rea* – see *Belfon* [1976] CA; *Bryson* 1985 CA; *Purcell* 1986 CA). An offence under s. 18 OAPA 1861. The maximum penalty is a term of imprisonment for life (life sentence). To amount to a 'wound', the inner and outer skin must be broken, so a bruise is not a wound (it must be 'a break in the continuity of the whole of the skin' – a 'rupture of an internal blood vessel' – see *JCC (a minor) v Eisenhower* [1984] QB). Breaking a collarbone is not 'wounding' under s. 18, but amounts to GBH s. 20 OAPA 1861 (see *Wood* [1830]). See also **GBH**.
Y	
YOI	Young offender institution, which is a prison for young offenders (usually under 18, but at times up to 21).
Youth Justice Board	Government agency dealing with young and juvenile offenders.
YOT	Youth Offending Team. Inter-agency, dealing with reports on, and community sentences for, juveniles.

APPENDIX 2: THE PCC CODE OF PRACTICE (2005)

The Press Complaints Commission is charged with enforcing the following Code of Practice which was framed by the newspaper and periodical industry and was ratified by the PCC on 13 June 2005.

THE CODE

All members of the press have a duty to maintain the highest professional standards. This Code sets the benchmark for those ethical standards, protecting both the rights of the individual and the public's right to know. It is the cornerstone of the system of self-regulation to which the industry has made a binding commitment.

It is essential that an agreed code be honoured not only to the letter but in the full spirit. It should not be interpreted so narrowly as to compromise its commitment to respect the rights of the individual, nor so broadly that it constitutes an unnecessary interference with freedom of expression or prevents publication in the public interest.

It is the responsibility of editors and publishers to implement the Code and they should take care to ensure it is observed rigorously by all editorial staff and external contributors, including non-journalists, in printed and online versions of publications. Editors should co-operate swiftly with the PCC in the resolution of complaints. Any publication judged to have breached the Code must print the adjudication in full and with due prominence, including headline reference to the PCC.

1 Accuracy

  i) The Press must take care not to publish inaccurate, misleading or distorted information, including pictures.

  ii) A significant inaccuracy, misleading statement or distortion once recognised must be corrected, promptly and with due prominence, and – where appropriate – an apology published.

iii) The Press, whilst free to be partisan, must distinguish clearly between comment, conjecture and fact.

iv) A publication must report fairly and accurately the outcome of an action for defamation to which it has been a party, unless an agreed settlement states otherwise, or an agreed statement is published.

2 Opportunity to reply

A fair opportunity for reply to inaccuracies must be given when reasonably called for.

3 *Privacy

i) Everyone is entitled to respect for his or her private and family life, home, health and correspondence, including digital communications. Editors will be expected to justify intrusions into any individual's private life without consent.

ii) It is unacceptable to photograph individuals in private places without their consent.

Note – Private places are public or private property where there is a reasonable expectation of privacy.

4 *Harassment

i) Journalists must not engage in intimidation, harassment or persistent pursuit.

ii) They must not persist in questioning, telephoning, pursuing or photographing individuals once asked to desist; nor remain on their property when asked to leave and must not follow them.

iii) Editors must ensure these principles are observed by those working for them and take care not to use non-compliant material from other sources.

5 Intrusion into grief or shock

In cases involving personal grief or shock, enquiries and approaches must be made with sympathy and discretion and publication handled sensitively. This should not restrict the right to report legal proceedings, such as inquests.

6 *Children

i) Young people should be free to complete their time at school without unnecessary intrusion.

ii) A child under 16 must not be interviewed or photographed on issues involving their own or another child's welfare unless a custodial parent or similarly responsible adult consents.

   iii) Pupils must not be approached or photographed at school without the permission of the school authorities.

   iv) Minors must not be paid for material involving children's welfare, nor parents or guardians for material about their children or wards, unless it is clearly in the child's interest.

   v) Editors must not use the fame, notoriety or position of a parent or guardian as sole justification for publishing details of a child's private life.

7 *Children in sex cases

1. The press must not, even if legally free to do so, identify children under 16 who are victims or witnesses in cases involving sex offences.
2. In any press report of a case involving a sexual offence against a child –
     i) The child must not be identified.
     ii) The adult may be identified.
     iii) The word "incest" must not be used where a child victim might be identified.
     iv) Care must be taken that nothing in the report implies the relationship between the accused and the child.

8 *Hospitals

   i) Journalists must identify themselves and obtain permission from a responsible executive before entering non-public areas of hospitals or similar institutions to pursue enquiries.

   ii) The restrictions on intruding into privacy are particularly relevant to enquiries about individuals in hospitals or similar institutions.

9 *Reporting of Crime

   (i) Relatives or friends of persons convicted or accused of crime should not generally be identified without their consent, unless they are genuinely relevant to the story.

   (ii) Particular regard should be paid to the potentially vulnerable position of children who witness, or are victims of, crime. This should not restrict the right to report legal proceedings.

10 *Clandestine devices and subterfuge

   i) The press must not seek to obtain or publish material acquired by using hidden cameras or clandestine listening devices; or by intercepting private or mobile telephone calls, messages or emails; or by the unauthorised removal of documents or photographs.

   ii) Engaging in misrepresentation or subterfuge, can generally be justified only in the public interest and then only when the material cannot be obtained by other means.

11 Victims of sexual assault

The press must not identify victims of sexual assault or publish material likely to contribute to such identification unless there is adequate justification and they are legally free to do so.

12 Discrimination

i) The press must avoid prejudicial or pejorative reference to an individual's race, colour, religion, gender, sexual orientation or to any physical or mental illness or disability.

ii) Details of an individual's race, colour, religion, sexual orientation, physical or mental illness or disability must be avoided unless genuinely relevant to the story.

13 Financial journalism

i) Even where the law does not prohibit it, journalists must not use for their own profit financial information they receive in advance of its general publication, nor should they pass such information to others.

ii) They must not write about shares or securities in whose performance they know that they or their close families have a significant financial interest without disclosing the interest to the editor or financial editor.

iii) They must not buy or sell, either directly or through nominees or agents, shares or securities about which they have written recently or about which they intend to write in the near future.

14 Confidential sources

Journalists have a moral obligation to protect confidential sources of information.

15 Witness payments in criminal trials

i) No payment or offer of payment to a witness – or any person who may reasonably be expected to be called as a witness – should be made in any case once proceedings are active as defined by the Contempt of Court Act 1981.

This prohibition lasts until the suspect has been freed unconditionally by police without charge or bail or the proceedings are otherwise discontinued; or has entered a guilty plea to the court; or, in the event of a not guilty plea, the court has announced its verdict.

*ii) Where proceedings are not yet active but are likely and foreseeable, editors must not make or offer payment to any person who may reasonably be expected to be called as a witness, unless the information concerned ought demonstrably to be published in the public interest and there is an over-riding need to make or promise payment for this to be done; and all reasonable steps have been taken to ensure no financial dealings influence the evidence those witnesses give. In no circumstances should such payment be conditional on the outcome of a trial.

*iii) Any payment or offer of payment made to a person later cited to give evidence in proceedings must be disclosed to the prosecution and defence. The witness must be advised of this requirement.

16 *Payment to criminals

i) Payment or offers of payment for stories, pictures or information, which seek to exploit a particular crime or to glorify or glamorise crime in general, must not be made directly or via agents to convicted or confessed criminals or to their associates – who may include family, friends and colleagues.

ii) Editors invoking the public interest to justify payment or offers would need to demonstrate that there was good reason to believe the public interest would be served. If, despite payment, no public interest emerged, then the material should not be published.

The public interest

There may be exceptions to the clauses marked * where they can be demonstrated to be in the public interest.

1. The public interest includes, but is not confined to:

    i) Detecting or exposing crime or serious impropriety.
    ii) Protecting public health and safety.
    iii) Preventing the public from being misled by an action or statement of an individual or organisation.

2. There is a public interest in freedom of expression itself.
3. Whenever the public interest is invoked, the PCC will require editors to demonstrate fully how the public interest was served.
4. The PCC will consider the extent to which material is already in the public domain, or will become so.
5. In cases involving children under 16, editors must demonstrate an exceptional public interest to over-ride the normally paramount interest of the child.

APPENDIX 3: *DEFAMATION ACT 1996* (c. 31)

An Act to amend the law of defamation and to amend the law of limitation with respect to actions for defamation or malicious falsehood (4 July 1996).

BE IT ENACTED by the Queen's most Excellent Majesty, by and with the advice and consent of the Lords Spiritual and Temporal, and Commons, in this present Parliament assembled, and by the authority of the same, as follows:

Responsibility for publication

Responsibility for publication

1(1) In defamation proceedings a person has a defence if he shows that:

   (a) he was not the author, editor or publisher of the statement complained of;

   (b) he took reasonable care in relation to its publication; and

   (c) he did not know, and had no reason to believe, that what he did caused or contributed to the publication of a defamatory statement.

(2) For this purpose 'author', 'editor' and 'publisher' have the following meanings, which are further explained in subsection (3):

   'author' means the originator of the statement, but does not include a person who did not intend that his statement be published at all;

   'editor' means a person having editorial or equivalent responsibility for the content of the statement or the decision to publish it; and

   'publisher' means a commercial publisher, that is, a person whose business is issuing material to the public, or a section of the public, who issues material containing the statement in the course of that business.

(3) A person shall not be considered the author, editor or publisher of a statement if he is only involved:

(a) in printing, producing, distributing or selling printed material containing the statement;

(b) in processing, making copies of, distributing, exhibiting or selling a film or sound recording (as defined in Part I of the Copyright, Designs and Patents Act 1988) containing the statement;

(c) in processing, making copies of, distributing or selling any electronic medium in or on which the statement is recorded, or in operating or providing any equipment, system or service by means of which the statement is retrieved, copied, distributed or made available in electronic form;

(d) as the broadcaster of a live programme containing the statement in circumstances in which he has no effective control over the maker of the statement;

(e) as the operator of or provider of access to a communications system by means of which the statement is transmitted, or made available, by a person over whom he has no effective control.

In a case not within paragraphs (a) to (e) the court may have regard to those provisions by way of analogy in deciding whether a person is to be considered the author, editor or publisher of a statement.

(4) Employees or agents of an author, editor or publisher are in the same position as their employer or principal to the extent that they are responsible for the content of the statement or the decision to publish it.

(5) In determining for the purposes of this section whether a person took reasonable care, or had reason to believe that what he did caused or contributed to the publication of a defamatory statement, regard shall be had to:

(a) the extent of his responsibility for the content of the statement or the decision to publish it;

(b) the nature or circumstances of the publication; and

(c) the previous conduct or character of the author, editor or publisher.

(6) This section does not apply to any cause of action which arose before the section came into force.

Offer to make amends

Offer to make amends

2(1) A person who has published a statement alleged to be defamatory of another may offer to make amends under this section.

(2) The offer may be in relation to the statement generally or in relation to a specific defamatory meaning which the

person making the offer accepts that the statement conveys ('a qualified offer').

(3)   An offer to make amends:

(a)   must be in writing;

(b)   must be expressed to be an offer to make amends under section 2 of the Defamation Act 1996; and

(c)   must state whether it is a qualified offer and, if so, set out the defamatory meaning in relation to which it is made.

(4)   An offer to make amends under this section is an offer:

(a)   to make a suitable correction of the statement complained of and a sufficient apology to the aggrieved party;

(b)   to publish the correction and apology in a manner that is reasonable and practicable in the circumstances; and

(c)   to pay to the aggrieved party such compensation (if any), and such costs, as may be agreed or determined to be payable.

The fact that the offer is accompanied by an offer to take specific steps does not affect the fact that an offer to make amends under this section is an offer to do all the things mentioned in paragraphs (a) to (c).

(5)   An offer to make amends under this section may not be made by a person after serving a defence in defamation proceedings brought against him by the aggrieved party in respect of the publication in question.

(6)   An offer to make amends under this section may be withdrawn before it is accepted; and a renewal of an offer which has been withdrawn shall be treated as a new offer.

Accepting an offer to make amends   3(1)   If an offer to make amends under section 2 is accepted by the aggrieved party, the following provisions apply.

(2)   The party accepting the offer may not bring or continue defamation proceedings in respect of the publication concerned against the person making the offer, but he is entitled to enforce the offer to make amends, as follows.

(3)   If the parties agree on the steps to be taken in fulfilment of the offer, the aggrieved party may apply to the court for an order that the other party fulfil his offer by taking the steps agreed.

(4)   If the parties do not agree on the steps to be taken by way of correction, apology and publication, the party who

made the offer may take such steps as he thinks appropriate, and may in particular:

(a) make the correction and apology by a statement in open court in terms approved by the court; and

(b) give an undertaking to the court as to the manner of their publication.

(5) If the parties do not agree on the amount to be paid by way of compensation, it shall be determined by the court on the same principles as damages in defamation proceedings.

The court shall take account of any steps taken in fulfilment of the offer and (so far as not agreed between the parties) of the suitability of the correction, the sufficiency of the apology and whether the manner of their publication was reasonable in the circumstances, and may reduce or increase the amount of compensation accordingly.

(6) If the parties do not agree on the amount to be paid by way of costs, it shall be determined by the court on the same principles as costs awarded in court proceedings.

(7) The acceptance of an offer by one person to make amends does not affect any cause of action against another person in respect of the same publication, subject as follows.

(8) In England and Wales or Northern Ireland, for the purposes of the Civil Liability (Contribution) Act 1978:

(a) the amount of compensation paid under the offer shall be treated as paid in bona fide settlement or compromise of the claim; and

(b) where another person is liable in respect of the same damage (whether jointly or otherwise), the person whose offer to make amends was accepted is not required to pay by virtue of any contribution under section 1 of that Act a greater amount than the amount of the compensation payable in pursuance of the offer.

(9) In Scotland:

(a) subsection (2) of section 3 of the Law Reform (Miscellaneous Provisions) (Scotland) Act 1940 (right of one joint wrongdoer as respects another to recover contribution towards damages) applies in relation to compensation paid under an offer to make amends as it applies in relation to damages in an action to which that section applies; and

(b) where another person is liable in respect of the same damage (whether jointly or otherwise), the person whose offer to make amends was accepted is not required to pay by virtue of any contribution under section 3(2) of that Act a greater amount than the amount of compensation payable in pursuance of the offer.

(10) Proceedings under this section shall be heard and determined without a jury.

Failure to accept offer to make amends

4(1) If an offer to make amends under section 2, duly made and not withdrawn, is not accepted by the aggrieved party, the following provisions apply.

(2) The fact that the offer was made is a defence (subject to subsection (3)) to defamation proceedings in respect of the publication in question by that party against the person making the offer.

A qualified offer is only a defence in respect of the meaning to which the offer related.

(3) There is no such defence if the person by whom the offer was made knew or had reason to believe that the statement complained of:

(a) referred to the aggrieved party or was likely to be understood as referring to him; and

(b) was both false and defamatory of that party, but it shall be presumed until the contrary is shown that he did not know and had no reason to believe that was the case.

(4) The person who made the offer need not rely on it by way of defence, but if he does he may not rely on any other defence.

If the offer was a qualified offer, this applies only in respect of the meaning to which the offer related.

(5) The offer may be relied on in mitigation of damages whether or not it was relied on as a defence.

BIBLIOGRAPHY

Barendt, E. (1989) 'Spycatcher and freedom of speech', *Public Law*, 204.

Bindman, G. (1989) 'Spycatcher: judging the judges', *New Law Journal*, 139, 94.

Bonnington, A., McInnes, R., and McKain, B. (2000) *Scots Law for Journalists*, 7th edn. Edinburgh: W. Green/Sweet & Maxwell.

Bryan, M. W. (1976) 'The Crossman diaries: developments in the law of breach of confidence', *The Law Quarterly Review*, 92, 180.

Carey, P. and Sanders, J. (2004) *Media Law*, 3rd edn. London: Sweet & Maxwell.

Clutterbuck, R. (1981) *The Media and Political Violence*. London: Macmillan.

Colston, C., and Middleton, K. (2005) *Modern Intellectual Property Law*. London: Cavendish.

Cooke, J. (2005) *Law of Tort*, 7th edn. Harlow: Pearson Education.

Davis, J. (2003) *Intellectual Property Law* (Core Text Series), 2nd edn. London: Butterworths.

Deards, E., and Hargreaves, S. (2004) *European Union Law: Textbook*. Oxford: Oxford University Press.

Elliott, C., and Quinn, C. (2005) *Tort Law*, 5th edn. Harlow: Pearson.

Elliott, C., and Quinn, F. (2005) *English Legal System*, 6th edn. Harlow: Pearson.

Gibson, B. (2004) *Criminal Justice Act 2003: A guide to the new procedures and sentencing*. Winchester: Waterside Press.

Hauch, J. M. (1994) 'Protecting private facts in France: the Warren and Brandeis tort is alive and well and flourishing in Paris', *Tulane Law Review*, 1219, p. 68.

Howard, A. (ed.) (1979) *Diaries of a Cabinet Minister: Richard Howard Stafford Crossman, 1964–'70*. London: Hamish Hamilton.

Lee, S. (1987) 'Spycatcher', *Law Quarterly Review*, 103, 506.

Leigh, I. (1992) 'Spycatcher in Strasbourg', *Public Law*, 200.

Lowe, N. V., and Willmore, C. J. (1985) 'Secrets, media and the law', *Modern Law Review*, 48, 592.

Lunney, M., and Oliphant, K. (2000) *Tort Law: Text and Materials*. Oxford: Oxford University Press.

Markesinis, B. (1999) 'Privacy, freedom of expression, and the horizontal effect of the Human Rights Bill: lessons from Germany', *The Law Quarterly Review*, 115.

Moreham, N. '*Douglas and Others v. Hello! Ltd* – the protection of privacy in English private law', *Modern Law Review*, 64, 767.

Muncie, J. (2004) *Youth and Crime*, 2nd edn. London: Sage.

Nicol, A., Millar, G., and Sharland, A. (2001) *Media Law and Human Rights*. London: Blackstone.

Robertson, G., and Nicol, A. (2002) *Media Law*, 4th edn. London: Penguin.

Rowling, J. K. (2005) *Harry Potter and the Half-Blood Prince*. London: Bloomsbury.

Sereny, G. (1998) *Cries Unheard: The Story of Mary Bell*. London: Macmillan.

Shannon, R. (2001) *A Press Free and Responsible: Self-regulation and the Press Complaints Commission, 1991–2001*. London: John Murray.

Sheridan Burns, L. (2003) *Understanding Journalism*. London: Sage.

Slapper, G., and Kelly, D. (2004) *The English Legal System*, 7th edn. London: Cavendish.

Smartt, U. (2004) 'Stay out of jail: performance, multimedia and copyright laws', in Leslie Hill and Helen Paris, *Guerrilla Performance and Multimedia*, 2nd edn. London/New York. Continuum.

Turnbull, M. (1989) 'Spycatcher', *Law Quarterly Review*, 105, 382.

Wadham, J., and Mountfield, H. (2003) *Blackstone's Guide to the Human Rights Act 1998*, 2nd edn. London: Blackstones.

Welsh, T., and Greenwood, W. (2005) *McNae's Essential Law for Journalists*, 18th edn. London: Butterworths.

Walker, D. M. (1981) *Delict*, 2nd edn. Edinburgh: W. Green.

Weatherill, S. (2004) *EU Law: Cases and materials*, 6th edn. Oxford: Oxford University Press.

Williams, D. G. T. (1976) 'The Crossman diaries', *Cambridge Law Journal*, 1.

Wilson, W. (1990) 'Privacy, confidence and press freedom: a study in judicial activism', *Modern Law Review*, 53, 43.

Wright, P. (1987) *Spycatcher: The candid autobiography of a secret intelligence officer*. Australia: William Heinemann and Viking Press.

TABLE OF CASES

TABLE OF STATUTES

English legislation

Unless otherwise stated, the following statutes cover the jurisdiction of Great Britain. Please note that certain enactments may not extend to Scotland, Northern Ireland and the Channel Islands, where different legislation may apply.

1997   *Protection from Harassment Act 1997* (c. 40)
        Crime (Sentences) Act 1997 (c. 43)
1998   *Human Rights Act 1998* (c. 42)
        Data Protection Act 1998 (c. 29)
        Crime and Disorder Act 1998 (c. 37)
        Public Interest Disclosure Act 1998
1999   *Youth Justice and Criminal Evidence Act 1999* (c. 23)
        House of Lords Act 1999
2000   *Freedom of Information Act 2000* (c. 36)
        Political Parties, Elections and Referendum Act 2000
        Terrorism Act UK 2000
2001   *Anti-terrorism, Crime and Security Act 2001* (c. 24)
2003   *Communications Act 2003* (re. Ofcom) (c. 21)
        Antisocial Behaviour Act 2003 (c. 38)
        Criminal Justice Act 2003 (c. 44)
        Courts Act 2003 (re. lay Justices of the Peace) (c. 39)
        Sexual Offences Act 2003 (c. 42)
2005   *Constitutional Reform Act 2005* (c. 4)

Scottish legislation

1707   *Act of Union 1707* (c. 7)
1815   *Jury Trials (Scotland) Act 1815* (55 and 56 George. 3, c. 42)
1933   *Administration of Justice (Scotland) Act 1933* (23 and 24 George 5, c. 41)
1937   *Children and Young Persons (Scotland) Act 1937* (1 Edward and 1 George 6, c. 37)
1968   *Social Work (Scotland) Act 1968*
1971   *Sheriff Courts (Scotland) Act 1971* (c. 58)
1973   *Local Government (Scotland) Act 1973* (c. 65)
1974   *Criminal Procedure (Scotland) Act 1974* (c. 21)
1976   *Fatal Accidents and Sudden Deaths Inquiry (Scotland) Act 1976* (c. 14)
1977   *Presumption of Death (Scotland) Act 1977* (c. 27)
1978   *Adoption (Scotland) Act 1978* (c. 28)
1980   *Bail (Scotland) Act 1980* (c. 4)
        Law Reform (Miscellaneous Provisions) (Scotland) Act 1980 (c. 55)
        Criminal Justice (Scotland) Act 1980 (c. 62)
1982   *Civic Government (Scotland) Act 1982* (c. 45)
1984   *Mental Health (Scotland) Act 1984* (c. 36)
1986   *Legal Aid (Scotland) Act 1986* (c. 47)
1993   *Damages (Scotland) Act 1993* (c. 5)
1995   *Children (Scotland) Act 1995* (s. 36)

Criminal Procedure (Scotland) Act 1995 (c. 46)
Criminal Procedure (Consequential Provisions) (Scotland) Act 1995 (c. 40)
1997   *Crime and Punishment (Scotland) Act 1997* (c. 48)
1998   *Human Rights Act 1998 (Scotland)* (c. 46)
       Scotland Act 1998
2000   *Judicial Appointments (Scotland) Act 2000* (asp. 9)
       Regulation of Investigatory Powers (Scotland) Act 2000 (asp. 11)
2002   *Freedom of Information (Scotland) Act 2002* (asp. 13)
2003   *Criminal Justice (Scotland) Act 2003* (asp. 7)
2004   *Vulnerable Witnesses (Scotland) Act 2004* (asp. 3)
       Criminal Procedure (Amendment) (Scotland) Act 2004 (asp. 5)
2005   *Protection of Children and Prevention of Sexual Offences (Scotland) Act 2005*
       (asp. 9)
2005   *Criminal Legal Aid (Scotland) (Fees) 2005 Amendment (No. 2) Regulations* (SI
       2005, No. 584)

Statutory Instruments (SI)

1978   *European Communities (Services of Lawyers) Order 1978*
1982   *Crown Court Rules* (SI 1982/1109)
1991   *Family Proceedings Courts (Children Act 1989) Rules* (r.16)
1996   *Copyright and Related Rights Regulations* (SI 1996/2967)
1997   *Copyright and Rights in Databases Regulations* (SI 1997/3032)
1998   *Civil Procedures Rules* (SI 1998/3132)
2000   *Data Protection Act 1998* (commencement) Order 2000 (SII 2000/183)
2002   *Electronic Commerce (EC Directive) Regulations* (SI 2002/2013)
2003   *Privacy and Electronic Communications Regulations* (SI 2003/2426)
       Copyright and Related Rights Regulations (SI 2003/2498)

European legislation

1950   *European Convention for the Protection of Human Rights and Fundamental*
       Freedoms (the Convention)
1957   *Treaty of Rome*
1986   *Single European Act*
1992   *Treaty on European Union (Maastricht Treaty)* (c. 191)
1997   *Treaty of Amsterdam* (amending the *Treaty on European Union*, the
       Treaties establishing the European Communities and certain related acts)
       (c. 340/03)

2001   *Treaty of Nice* (amending the *Treaty on European Union*, the Treaties establishing the European Communities and certain related acts) (c. 80)
2002   *Treaty Establishing the European Community* (c. 325/33)
2004   *Treaty Establishing a Constitution for Europe, Rome* (c. 310)

EC/EU regulations

1997   *Copyright and Rights in Databases Regulations 1997* (SI 1997/3032)
2003   *Copyright and Related Rights Regulations 2003* (implemented EC Directive 2001/29/EC)

EC/EU directives

1989   *Directive on Transfrontier Television* (89/552/EEC)
1995   *Directive on the Protection of Individuals with Regards to the Processing of Personal Data and on the Free Movement of Such Data* (95/46/EC), which gave effect to the *Data Protection Act 1998*
2001   *Directive on Copyright and Related Rights* (2001/29/EC)
2002   *Directive on Electronic Commerce* (SI 2002/2013)
2003   Directive on Privacy and Electronic Communications (SI 2003/2426)

INTERNET SOURCES AND USEFUL WEBSITES

Acts of the UK Parliament:
www.opsi.gov.uk/acts.htmwww.hmso.gov.uk/acts.htm
Advertising Standards Authority (ASA): www.asa.org.uk/asa
Agence France (French News Agency): www.afp.com/english/home
Aljazeera European Service: http://english.aljazeera.net/HomePage
All African News Agency: www.afrol.com
ANSA (Italian News Agency): www.ansa.it
Arab Times (online English): www.arabtimesonline.com/arabtimes
Associated Press (AP) (Global News Network): www.ap.org
Association of Journalism Education (AJE): www.ajeuk.org
Australian Associated Press (AAP): http://aap.com.au
Authors' Licensing and Collecting Society Limited (ALCS): www.alcs.co.uk
BBC News Online: http://news.bbc.co.uk
BBC Northern Ireland Service online: www.bbc.co.uk/northernireland
BBC Radio websites: www.bbc.co.uk/radio
BBC World Service: www.bbc.co.uk/worldservice
Bloomberg (World Market News): www.bloomberg.com.
Canadian Press (Association): www.cp.org
Chartered Institute of Journalists: www.ioj.co.uk
China View (Chinese News Agency): www.xinhuanet.com/english/index.htm
CNN International: http://edition.cnn.com
Commission for Racial Equality: www.cre.gov.uk
Corbis (Images and Photos): http://pro.corbis.com/splash.aspx
Council of Europe: www.coe.int
Criminal Justice System of England and Wales: www.cjsonline.gov.uk
Crown Prosecution Service (CPS): www.cps.gov.uk
Daily Express: www.express.co.uk
Daily Mail: www.dailymail.co.uk
Daily Record (Scotland): www.dailyrecord.co.uk

Daily Star: www.dailystar.co.uk
Daily Telegraph: www.telegraph.co.uk
Department for Constitutional Affairs (DCA): www.dca.gov.uk
Deutsche Presseagentur (German News Agency): www.dpa.de/en/unternehmenswelt/index.html
Economist, The: www.economist.com/index.html
Europa Press (Spanish News Agency): www.europapress.es
European Commission: http://europa.eu.int/comm/index_en.htm
European Court of Human Rights (ECHR): www.echr.coe.int/echr
European Court of Justice (ECJ): www.curia.eu.int
European Parliament: www.europarl.eu.int
European Patent Office, Munich: www.european-patent-office.org
Evening Standard: www.thisislondon.co.uk/news
Financial Times (online): http://news.ft.com/home/uk
Freedom of Information Act 2002 (FOI): www.foi.gov.uk
Guardian (unlimited online): www.guardian.co.uk
Hansard: www.parliament.the-stationery-office.co.uk/pa/cm/cmhansrd.htm
Hello! Magazine: www.hellomagazine.com
Her Majesty's Court Service: www.hmcourts-service.gov.uk
Herald, Glasgow: www.theherald.co.uk
HM Prison Service: www.hmprisonservice.gov.uk
Home Office: www.homeoffice.gov.uk
House of Lords: www.parliament.uk/about_lords/about_lords.cfm
Human Rights Legislation (Crown Office): www.humanrights.org.uk
Independent: www.independent.co.uk
International Confederation of Societies of Authors and Composers (Confédération Internationale des Sociétés d'Auteurs et Compositeurs): www.cisac.org
International Press Institute (IPI): www.freemedia.at
Irish Times: www.ireland.com
Itar-TASS (Russian News Agency): www.itar-tass.com/eng
ITV News (Independent Television): www.itv.com/news
Law Society of Scotland: www.lawscot.org.uk
Legal Services Commission (CLS) (formerly 'legal aid'): www.legalservices.gov.uk
Magistrates' Association: www.magistrates-association.org.uk
Metropolitan Police: www.met.police.uk
Ministry of Defence (MoD): www.mod.uk/mdp
Mirror: www.mirror.co.uk
Morning Star: www.morningstaronline.co.uk
National Archives: www.nationalarchives.gov.uk
National Association of Youth Justice: www.nayj.org.uk
National Council for the Training of Journalists (NCTJ): www.nctj.com

National Probation Service: www.homeoffice.gov.uk/justice/probation
National Union of Journalists (NUJ): www.nuj.org.uk
NUJ Training: www.nujtraining.org.uk
News International: www.newsint.co.uk
News of the World: www.newsoftheworld.co.uk
Observer: http://observer.guardian.co.uk
Ofcom (Office of Communications): www.ofcom.org.uk
Office of National Statistics: www.statistics.gov.uk/glance
OK! Magazine: www.ok-magazine.com
Parliament, UK: www.parliament.uk
People: www.people.co.uk
Police Information Technology Organisation (PITO): www.pito.org.uk
Polska Agencja Prasowa (PAP) (Polish News Agency): www.pap.com.pl
Press Association Group: www.thepagroup.com
Press and Journal (P&J) (Aberdeen, Scotland): www.thisisnorthscotland.co.uk
Press Complaints Commission (PCC): www.pcc.org.uk
Press Trust of India (India's News Agency): www.ptinews.com/pti/ptisite.nsf
Reuters: http://about.reuters.com/home
Reuters News Online: http://today.reuters.co.uk/news/default.aspx
Saudi Press Agency: www.spa.gov.sa/newsen.htm
Scottish Court Service: www.scotcourts.gov.uk
Scots Law & Legal Directory: www.scottishlaw.org.uk
Scottish Law Commission: www.scotlawcom.gov.uk
Scottish Prison Service: www.sps.gov.uk
Scotsman: www.thescotsman.scotsman.com
Sky News Online: www.sky.com/skynews/home
Society of Authors: www.societyofauthors.net/index.php4
Society of Editors: www.societyofeditors.co.uk
South African News Agency: www.sapa.org.za
South China Morning Post: www.asia-pacific.com/southchina.htm
Sun: www.thesun.co.uk
Times, The (online): www.timesonline.co.uk
Times of India, The: http://timesofindia.indiatimes.com
UK Parliament: www.parliament.uk
United Nations: www.un.org/english
United Press International (UPI)(US Global News Network): www.upi.com
Voice of America (US World Radio News Network): www.voanews.com/english/portal.cfm
Voices of Iraq (pooled international news agency): www.aswataliraq.info/?newlang=eng
World Wide News in English (online): www.thebigproject.co.uk/news
Youth Justice Board: www.youth-justice-board.gov.uk/youthJusticeboard

INDEX

LIBRARY, UNIVERSITY OF CHESTER